Rereading Huizinga

Portrait of Huizinga, drawing in pencil by Harm H. Kamerlingh Onnes

Signed in the upper right corner: J. HUIZINGA AET. 64

Academic Historical Museum, Leiden

Rereading Huizinga

Autumn of the Middle Ages, a Century Later

Edited by
Peter Arnade, Martha Howell, and Anton van der Lem

Routledge
Taylor & Francis Group
LONDON AND NEW YORK

First published in 2019 by Amsterdam University Press Ltd.

Published 2025 by Routledge
4 Park Square, Milton Park, Abingdon, Oxon OX14 4RN
605 Third Avenue, New York, NY 10158

Routledge is an imprint of the Taylor & Francis Group, an informa business

ISBN: 9789462983724 (hbk)
ISBN: 9781041185383 (pbk)
ISBN: 9781003702870 (ebk)
NUR 684

Cover illustration: Jan van Eyck, *The Arnolfini Portrait*, detail
Source: London, National Gallery

Cover design: Coördesign, Leiden

DOI 10.5117/9789462983724

Table of Contents

List of Illustrations

Acknowledgements

This collection of essays, timed to coincide with the centennial anniversary of Huizinga's 1919 *Herfsttij der Middeleeuwen*, began as a lively conference held at Flanders House in New York City in 2016. Organized by Columbia University's Studies of the Dutch-Speaking World program and its European Institute, and cosponsored by Columbia's Deparment of History, the General Delegation of the Government of Flanders to the USA and the Consulate General of The Netherlands in New York, the conference assembled historians, art historians, and literary scholars from across the globe to consider the intellectual culture in which Huizinga wrote and to examine his book's legacy in the century since its publication. We are grateful to Matthew Jones of Columbia University's Department of History, whose original and expert comments on the day's proceedings and on Huizinga's *Autumn* more generally provided a perfect coda to the workshop. The formal papers delivered at the conference are included in this volume, along with another by Willem Otterspeer, who graciously added an epilogue to the collection.

Amsterdam University Press invited us to publish this book and provided crucial support and help in the process. We thank Inge van der Bijl for her early encouragement, and Julie Benschop-Plokker for her steady editorial hand and guidance. Deborah Shulevitz provided crucial help with editing as we readied the essays for this volume. Anton van der Lem is one of this volume's contributors, but his role went much further. As a leading Huizinga expert, he offered his unparalleled knowledge and assistance to the entire project. He also very generously helped to prepare the final manuscript, pulled together a single bibliography from our essays' separate ones, and prepared the index as well. His role was therefore fundamental and his aid extraordinarily generous.

Introduction

Peter Arnade and Martha Howell

In 2016 in an interview for the *New York Times*, the American science writer Mary Roach recalled that Johan Huizinga's *Waning of the Middle Ages* was the most challenging book she had read as a college student in the 1970s:

> I was memorably tormented by *The Waning of the Middle Ages* by Johan Huizinga. But wait! I just did an Amazon 'Look Inside' to reacquaint myself. It's good! He opens describing the sights and sounds of village life:
>
>> The modern town hardly knows silence or darkness in their purity, nor the effect of a solitary light or a single distant cry. Here he is on the tolling of church bells, which were known by their names: big Jacqueline, or the bell Roland. Everyone knew the difference in meaning of the various ways of ringing. [...] What intoxication the pealing of the bells of all the churches, and of all the monasteries of Paris, must have produced [...] when a peace was concluded or a pope elected.
>
> I was an idiot.[1]

Herfsttij der Middeleeuwen, published in 1919, and translated into English both as *The Waning of the Middle Ages* (1924) and *Autumn of the Middle Ages* (1996), is a century old. It remains one of the most enduring books of medieval European history and with recent editions in Korean, Mandarin and Japanese, it now is a truly global phenomenon, not just a 'must read' on syllabuses in the United States and Europe. Huizinga himself was one of the Netherlands' most famous academics – nominated repeatedly in his lifetime for a Nobel Prize. He was also a gifted writer; the eleventh edition of the standard Dutch dictionary Van Dale contained a remarkable 282 attributions to Huizinga, most of them from *Autumn*. When he died

1 Roach, 'By the Book'.

Arnade, Peter, Martha Howell, and Anton van der Lem (eds), *Rereading Huizinga: Autumn of the Middle Ages, a Century Later*. Taylor & Francis Group, 2019
DOI: 10.5117/9789462983724_INTRO

three months before the liberation of the Netherlands in 1945, Huizinga had become a renowned essayist concerned with the shattered world of mid-twentieth-century Europe. He had also written *Homo ludens* (1938), his wholly original study of play motifs in human history and societies, which became a foundational text in game theory.

The reputation and readership of *Autumn* grew by leaps and bounds in the decades after his death. It was translated first into German and English (1924), Swedish (1927), then into Spanish (1930), and finally into French (1932), by which time the book's reputation began to take off. By the 1970s, thanks in part to new editions of the various translations, to the abridged 1924 translation into English by Frits Hopman (with Huizinga's cooperation), and the issuance of a cheap paperback edition the book gained a popular readership. The 1924 Hopman English translation and the 1932 French translation also substituted 'Waning' and 'Decline' for 'Autumn', even though the latter more accurately reflected the Dutch neologism Huizinga had employed in 1919: *Herfsttij*, or Autumn-tide. Huizinga himself approved of the revised usage in the two translations because he had come by that time to regret his original title and believed designations such as decline and waning better captured his thesis about the dusk of the middle ages. Despite Huizinga's mixed feelings about the book's original title, *Herfsttij*'s reprint in France (1975) and a new translation in the United States (1996) both restored 'Autumn' to the title.

Notwithstanding its fame, a century after its publication *Autumn* remains more read by those outside the academic field of the Burgundian Low Countries and northern France than those in it. Indeed, as Mary Roach's comment reveals – and as similar remarks by countless students and scholars over the past century have echoed – the book is in some ways hard going. The problem is not, however, its readability. It is a pleasure to accompany Huizinga as he recreates the sights and sounds of the medieval town, as in the passage quoted by Mary Roach, or as he selects passages from chronicles, poetry, and other literary texts to display the joys, anxieties, and dreams of the Burgundian elites who are his principal subjects, or as he stands, awestruck, before the meticulously rendered portraits drawn by the Van Eycks and other so-called Flemish Primitives (*Primitifs flamands*). The problem is that the text ignores practically all the rules of scholarship in any of the fields through which he seems so randomly to roam – history, sociology, anthropology, art history. The book seems to fit nowhere, to tell a story that explores no aspect of the place and age systematically enough for other scholars to build upon, and to leave out so much that the whole he provides seems to distort rather than illuminate the age.

This volume, which follows from a workshop that featured early versions of the articles included here, guides the twenty-first-century reader through this extraordinary text. After reviewing the reasons for the book's decidedly mixed reception by scholars then and even now, we place the book in Huizinga's time and place and analyze Huizinga's methodology, relating it to his purposes in writing the book. In a final section we discuss the ways that Huizinga not only anticipated disciplinary changes that have occurred during the last century but also helped generate those changes, and we close by arguing that the book has important lessons for scholars and students today. In sum, this volume does not seek to restore a reputation, for *Autumn*'s fame has not diminished over the last century. Rather, its goal is to explain why, despite all the book's flaws, all its omissions and unevenness, *Autumn* is considered one of the masterpieces of Western historical scholarship.

1

It is easy to identify *Autumn*'s weaknesses and to agree with those scholars and students who have been mystified by its style, uncertain about its bold claims, and frustrated by its disregard for scholarly protocols. Despite his claim that Flemish painting was the book's inspiration, Huizinga relied almost entirely on published French-language literary and narrative sources for his evidence – this in a region that was multilingual and where archival material would have yielded a much wider variety of sources, much of them in Middle Dutch, Latin, or even German and many of them penned or read by people his sources never touched. His references to late medieval art were idiosyncratic and highly selective. He paid little attention to civic life in what was one of Europe's most densely urbanized regions, concentrating almost exclusively on the court of the Burgundian dukes and the elites who populated it. He almost completely ignored commerce – an astonishing omission given that this was the home of some of the period's most powerful commercial cities, whose riches directly fed the court on which he concentrated. He seemed to dismiss the religious fervor of the day as a calcified expression of decayed spirituality rather than an early sign of the Reformation(s) to come. He cited only a few secondary historical studies and directly referenced little of the important work in sociology or anthropology that was then revolutionizing (if not giving birth to) these social sciences. Last, even though he had training in philology and was no stranger to the rules of *Quellenforschung* then ascendant in historical scholarship (as demonstrated in his earlier work on medieval charters in Haarlem), his *Autumn* overlooks any such principles.

No wonder then that Dutch medievalists paid little attention to the book. As Peter Arnade, Marc Boone, Walter Simons, and Myriam Greilsammer point out in this volume, Dutch medieval studies were still in their infancy and struggling to become 'more scientific' in the Von Rankean mode, and the book's disregard of those protocols gave it no entry, not even in Huizinga's own country. Attitudes in Belgium, Simons further explains, were predictably divided along confessional lines: historians at the Catholic University of Louvain took no interest in a book that displayed the brittleness of medieval Catholic piety, whereas at the University of Ghent, traditionally rather anticlerical, the 'Pirenne school of Medieval History' was embarking on its grand projects in the history of economic and social life, politics and legal institutions, subjects left aside in *Herfsttij*. The founders of the French Annales school, although in many ways more sympathetic to Huizinga's book (which they had to read in German, the French not being made available until 1932) also had reservations because, as Myriam Greilsammer details, Huizinga gave socioeconomic matters so little attention and because he seemed only to describe emotions rather than explain them with the help of cultural psychology or sociological theory. In fact, although at first both Marc Bloch and Lucien Febvre, the founders of the Annales school and the journal that bears its name, thought Huizinga might be closer to their research interests than he in fact was, as the correspondence among them that Greilsammer examined reveals. Invitations for Huizinga to contribute to the *Annales* journal never materialized into an actual submission, though Huizinga offered several possible subjects for a potential essay, including one on the play element, clearly adumbrating *Homo ludens*. It was only later, in the 1970s, as we will discuss, that Huizinga's book was embraced by a newer generation of *Annalistes*.

Art historians were even more indifferent. As Diane Wolfthal observes, initially they were slow to give the book serious attention, in large measure because Huizinga himself did not immerse himself in the literature of the field as he prepared his study. Instead, he worked impressionistically, using different artworks to support his central point that the art of the era was an idealistic flight from reality, even if its exact renderings of daily life were things of great achievement. No surprise then that leading scholars of the era like Aby Warburg did not engage the book's arguments about Flemish art, even if he did acknowledge the volume.

Yet, although *Autumn of the Middle Ages* found no comfortable home among the scholars of his day, the book is in some ways very much of its time, both of the age and of a moment in Huizinga's own intellectual trajectory. Although *Autumn* drew more heavily on late medieval literature than it did on art, it was in fact late medieval art, and painting in particular, that inspired Huizinga to prepare his study. Carol Symes, Birger Vanwesenbeeck and Diane Wolfthal, among others, all make clear the effect the famous 1902 exhibit of Flemish Primitives in Bruges had upon Huizinga. The exhibit had been an effort of the still young Belgian state to stake out a national cultural past and identity by claiming the glories of medieval Flemish painting as its ancestry – in direct competition with Flemish nationalists and Pan-Germanic ethnonationalists who regarded these artworks as their own heritage. Huizinga, however, intended to free art of such political or social purposes, keeping it out of the story of nationalism and nineteenth- and early-twentieth-century politics, and locate it in what he referred to as the 'century of the Van Eycks' (his shorthand for southern Low Country painting, manuscript illumination and sculpture) and its significance for Burgundian history. Carol Symes's essay in this volume pursues this argument, explaining that Huizinga abhorred the corrosive nationalism of his era and made it plain as early as *Autumn*, long before his later, well-known role as a social critic of the mid-twentieth century and the destructive effects of European nationalism. His book of 1919 ignored borders and moved across regions; written by a Dutchman and focused on Francophone sources, it flatly refused to place medieval history in the service of nationalism.

Huizinga's close contemporary, Henri Pirenne in Ghent, was no ardent nationalist either, but his multivolume history of Belgium did, as Symes notes, provide the Belgian state with a cohesive narrative of its Middle Ages. Marc Boone explores the intricate professional and personal relationship between Pirenne and Huizinga through their body of work and personal correspondence. Very different historians with distinct interests and temperaments, they viewed the Valois dukes of Burgundy differently, as both openly acknowledged. For Pirenne, the fifteenth-century dukes created the administrative and political infrastructure for the vibrant commercial society that sowed the seeds of the two nineteenth-century nation-states of Belgium and the Netherlands. Huizinga also acknowledged the fundamental contribution of the dukes of Burgundy, but saw their success more in galvanizing a sense of Burgundian identity distinct from the late medieval French monarchy and not so much in political or institutional terms. For Huizinga, Burgundy did not adumbrate Belgium and certainly not the Netherlands, even if both countries and their histories were shaped by the legacy of the late fourteenth and fifteenth centuries. As Boone rightly points out, neither Pirenne nor Huizinga was a specialist of the Burgundian period, but they managed to bequeath to subsequent scholars two of the most important visions of what the Valois dukes achieved, thereby setting the terms of all subsequent scholarship on the history and nature of this region and its links to the modern age.

Although Huizinga's book is clearly situated – and indirectly situates itself – in the charged politics of early-twentieth-century nationalisms and competing claims to the medieval past, *Autumn* also reflects other aspects of Huizinga's intellectual milieu. As both Carol Symes and Birger Vanwesenbeeck discuss, Huizinga's attraction to the late-nineteenth-century Symbolist movement might well have influenced his thinking about the late medieval Burgundian era as a close to an era. Both rightly point to George Rodenbach's 1892 novella *Bruges-la-morte*. Serialized in the French newspaper *Le figaro*, it featured a widower protagonist who mourns his late wife by withdrawing to Bruges and cherishing the city's late medieval timbre of melancholy and nostalgia in its old canals and buildings. Bruges was also, not coincidentally, the site of the 1902 Flemish Primitives exhibit. Vanwesenbeeck's essay allows us not only to see these intellectual connections but also to better read Huizinga, to understand his fascination with late periods, his immersion in the style of the time he wrote about, and his effort to make time stand still as a way of dealing with ends and beginnings.

Élodie Lecuppre-Desjardin and Jan Dumolyn, along with Symes, Vanwesenbeeck and Simons, point to another connection between Huizinga and the intellectual culture of his day: late-nineteenth and early-twentieth-century German historiography, in particular the hermeneutics of scholars like Wilhelm Dilthey. *Autumn* registers this influence in its focus on aesthetics and sensation or what Huizinga called the 'forms' of thought through which the Burgundians expressed their understanding of their world. Lecuppre-Desjardin and Dumolyn connect this approach even to Huizinga's treatment of urban society; although they acknowledge that he read urbanity through the disparaging comments made by elites of the day, exiled it to the north and the Dutch state that would emerge more than a century later, or even completely ignored it, Huizinga did, however, provide a connection between the courtly world he studied and cities like Bruges. Urban elites, he argued, had absorbed and put to their own uses the 'forms' of chivalric society, thus borrowing from the court its aesthetics and rituals for their own purposes.

Huizinga's treatment of religion even more clearly reflects his own history. Huizinga had much to say about late medieval religion, especially the excesses he perceived in actual practice, with mind-numbing numbers of rites and rituals in the devotional calendar, with raw displays of emotion, and with the wide gulf between formal theology and worship itself. As both Walter Simons and Andrew Brown observe, in part Huizinga's attitudes about late medieval religion had something to do with his Mennonite upbringing; his critical position toward Catholic religious practice reflects a typical Protestant stance. But as Simons explores further, it had also to do with his personal conviction that religion should posit a moral order of piety and transcendence, and that the routine and overexcited performances of faith described in *Autumn* betrayed that essence. As Simons also points out, even in Huizinga's early work on Buddhism, he attended to the gulf between its foundational beliefs and original cosmology and its evolution in practice over time, where ceremonialism and ritual orders similarly evolved, where holy men and women and others turned the religion in new directions, away from its spiritual core and toward material enactments of its forms.

Given Huizinga's debts to hermeneutical approaches, if not to related philosophical studies themselves, and his resultant emphasis on aesthetics and sensations, given his own studies and experience of religion, and given his love of art and literature, it is perhaps no wonder that his book focused on what he called the 'forms' of thought that governed the experience of late medieval Burgundian elites. No wonder too, given that the cultural forms he studied were, he thought, corrosive of medieval courtly society, that he emphasized the decay and attrition of these forms, the bizarre, almost frenzied, play of opposites. Huizinga interpreted the patterns as symptoms of a large dynamic at play in the Burgundian territories: the gulf between the reality of a late medieval world grim with conflict and violence and the desire in art, literature and ritual for a world without either, a world of beauty and perfection. This fundamental contrast animates the structure of *Autumn* as a book, as it does much of Huizinga's work, which, as Willem Otterspeer so rightly observes, is built upon the play of contrasts.[2] It is not, and Huizinga did not intend it to be, a portrait of Burgundian society writ large. Political events, economic structure and patterns, institutional histories, wars and treaties, ecclesiastical matters – all the usual stuff of history books – were not on his agenda. Rather, he sought to describe and to understand the meaning of texts, whether literary, visual or even aural, and their impact on cultural behavior in the Burgundian court where a heightened, if overwrought, formalism took root.

Thus Huizinga relied so heavily on chronicles and verse; in these writings he could apprehend most tangibly attitude and mood that reflected subjective voice. As Graeme Small makes clear, most of Huizinga's sources were necessarily Francophone because Huizinga wanted to apprehend the sensibility of the Burgundian court itself, where the language was almost

2 Otterspeer, *Reading Huizinga*.

exclusively French. Small's essay carefully enumerates these sources, revealing how selectively Huizinga chose, turning especially to Chastelain, La Marche, Monstrelet and other court chroniclers and poets, always in search of the language that expressed what he considered the best examples of the anguish and the aspirations of this rarefied society. It naturally followed that Huizinga ignored Middle Dutch sources though he knew very well that there existed a substantial body of such literature, and knew, too, that the chambers of rhetoric, to take one example, had produced a significant body of written work. But urban Dutch sources to Huizinga were *burgerlijk*, the seeds of early modern Dutch history, and not essential to the Burgundian realm, even if they were part of it. His working methods mirror his concerns. As Anton van der Lem details, in the Huizinga archive in the Leiden University Library, there are 330 envelopes of Huizinga's notes for *Autumn*, filled with strips (*snippers*) of horizontally cut paper upon which Huizinga wrote quotes and made notes, which he assembled according to subject and theme. The hundreds of envelopes and strips within them reveal a scholar moving freely and widely across a body of printed sources that were produced and circulated within one slice of a complex society, organizing them in a systematic but kaleidoscope fashion.

2

Huizinga's text, as rooted as it is in the period in which he lived, also provides a more specific set of arguments about the fifteenth-century North and the Burgundian world he studied that have endured long beyond his day, and in fact have yielded fruit in many branches of historical scholarship. One of Huizinga's shrewdest points was the power of chivalry and its ethos. As Andrew Brown points out, while scholars no longer read the Burgundian attachment to chivalry as a retreat into an archaic medieval ideal, they do now, as they once did not, take seriously the rituals and literature of chivalry the Burgundian dukes, aristocrats and even urban merchants championed, just as Lecuppre-Desjardin and Dumolyn noted. As Brown also shows, Huizinga's careful consideration of Burgundian chivalry, and court ritual more generally, laid the groundwork for his later work on the 'play element' in history, but more generally, for historians to take up the study of ritual as a political and cultural form.

Huizinga's vision of the Burgundian court as a power center of an elaborately constructed world of high ceremony and literary and artistic production has also inspired a large body of scholarship on the late medieval court as a vehicle of political and cultural patronage and identity making. Larry Silver's contribution in this volume explores the affinities between Emperor Maximilian's German court at the beginning of the sixteenth century and the Burgundian court on whose model he – and other princes to come – would draw. Silver traces the connections between Franco-Burgundian and German court traditions from the early fifteenth century to the sixteenth, when they culminated in Maximilian's perfection of the theater state model. What is more, Maximilian became the vehicle for Habsburg dynasty's wholesale incorporation of the Burgundian chivalric heritage, including the Order of the Golden Fleece, and its court ceremonial in their early modern territories.

These moves, as Peter Arnade demonstrates, identify Huizinga as an anthropologist avant la lettre, even a scholar who anticipates symbolic anthropology, especially the work of Clifford Geertz. In this sense, Huizinga's *Autumn of the Middle Ages*, and his landmark *Homo ludens*, have a more contemporary aspect to them, even if their language and intellectual shape are of Huizinga's era. Geertz strove to move anthropology past the obligations of social scientific categories. Instead of the enumeration of the organizing principles of a society, Geertz foregrounded how language and cultural practices spin 'webs of signification' by which meaning is produced in human societies. Although Huizinga hardly operated with a mature theory of signification as did Geertz, some historians have explicitly noted the Geertzian element in Huizinga's *Autumn*. In 1985, Wim Blockmans and Walter Prevenier, for example, drew on one of Geertz's most celebrated books to describe late medieval Burgundy as a 'theater state'.[3] Although the court Geertz described was quite unlike the Burgundian, Huizinga did introduce to medieval history the idea that the court was a performative act, the charismatic center that modeled power and comportment to its clients and subjects. As Arnade more fully adumbrates in his article, Huizinga's freshness as an early theorist of court ceremony is remarkable.

Huizinga's attention to devotional practices and ritual was never systematic, but these themes were clearly enough explored in *Autumn* to also anticipate, even help to inspire, the large body of scholarship that developed in the 1970s onward on late medieval religion most clearly associated with practitioners of the Annales school's cultural turn in Europe and North America. Simons in particular rightly notes that the whole field of the history of emotions, both in the study of religion and elsewhere, owes much to *Autumn*. Another of Huizinga's most important contributions is his use of literary and artistic sources in *Autumn*, exemplifying an interdisciplinary

3 Blockmans and Prevenier, *Burgundian Netherlands*.

spirit in 1919 that would become much more standard practice in medieval history and other fields after the cultural turn of the 1970s. As is well known, Huizinga had deep artistic interests through his life, was a patron of music, literature and art, and in his youth was an eager advocate of the so-called 1880 Movement, an 'arts for art's sake' celebration of aesthetics.

Huizinga's book had a much more direct effect on the scholars associated with the Annales school, as both Simons and Greilsammer explain, but not until the 1970s when French historians like Jacques Le Goff and his colleagues revived interest in Huizinga. It is ironic that it was the successive generations of the Annales school that has since kept *Autumn* on the intellectual front burner, but considerably more so in France, England and the United States than in Belgium and the Netherlands. It is only in recent years, and more in the Netherlands, where Huizinga is now celebrated as one of the twentieth century's leading intellectuals, than in Belgium, where Pirenne holds pride of place, that scholars treat this book as more than an aberrant, if brilliant, piece of historical writing.

Huizinga not only launched a series of arguments or suggested methodological routes that have informed scholarship since his time, he also left us with tools for rethinking Burgundian society and its period. Andrew Brown's essay, for example, invites us to think about ritual as a form of play. While Huizinga may have in this respect been anticipating his later *Homo ludens*, scholars today can reread medieval ritual through the analytical lens provided by that study, thereby deepening our understanding of how and why ritual forms work. Jun Cho suggests another way to reread Huizinga. He shows how Huizinga's attention to the cultural tropes of the late medieval Burgundian court could be pushed further to penetrate the commercial themes embedded within them. Cho specifically tackles the relationship between commerce and the Burgundian court (a subject Huizinga ignored) by describing what writers then and since have understood as *magnificence*: the prince's obligation and ability to 'perform great deeds' and to appear as capable of such deeds, which included, of course, military prowess but also displays of grandeur befitting (and constitutive of) a prince able to provide for the common good. By returning us to the concept of the performative court described by Huizinga and analyzed by scholars such as Blockmans and Prevenier, Cho, like Brown in his essay, proves the value of Huizinga's attention to courtly discourse and ritual but reverses their understanding of them. For Cho, the 'forms' that in *Autumn* appear so superannuated were in fact enactments not just of the artifice affecting courtly culture but also displays, even perhaps self-conscious displays, of the commercial wealth on which the court depended.

Huizinga also provides us sharper perspective on the Italian Renaissance, at least as described in Burckhardt's famous *The Civilization of the Renaissance in Italy* (*Die Kultur der Renaissance in Italien*) of 1860, a book to which *Autumn* was in many ways a response. The Dutchman holds up a Burgundian mirror to the Italian Renaissance and invites us to see how little the latter's likeness is altered when we do so. Burgundy, Huizinga confidently asserts, did not so much presage the Renaissance as mark the end of the prior era. It was, in Small's words, 'the supernova of the Middle Ages, increasingly incapable of bearing the crushing weight of its own gravity, brilliantly foreshadowing the black hole into which all that was medieval eventually disappeared'.

Historians today, just as those of Huizinga's own time, are not convinced by this, the book's main claim; the portrait he paints is, they know, incomplete, his sources too homogeneous and his literary style too elusive. But they now rightly consider the book an enthralling study of a cultural moment so far from our own sensibilities that it can seem otherworldly. The book is also now recognized as a methodological wonder – not in some linear way a precursor of contemporary cultural studies, it is a completely original attempt to treat cultural forms and the materials that express them as reliable, if inherently imbalanced, historical evidence. It is also a cautionary tale about the politics of history-writing and a constructive reminder that the sources left by an age are all we have to make sense of it. A hundred years after *Autumn*'s publication, readers still have much to learn from the book, and many reasons to keep rereading it.

About the Authors

Peter Arnade is Professor of History and Dean of the College of Arts and Humanities at the University of Hawai'i. His most recent book is *Honor, Vengeance and Social Trouble: Pardon Letters in the Burgundian Low Countries* (Cornell University Press, 2015), co-authored with Walter Prevenier.
parnade@hawaii.edu

Martha Howell is Miriam Champion Professor of History at Columbia University in New York City. A specialist in social, economic, cultural, and gender history, she concentrates on the greater Low Countries during the Burgundian period. Her most recent book is *Commerce before Capitalism* (Cambridge University Press, 2010). congletonhowell@gmail.com

is performed before Duke Philip the Good as well as the chivalric Feast of the Pheasant; living emotions are 'ossified'; the 'edifice of the God-willed' becomes a 'necropolis'; mortuary practices oscillate between splendor and austerity.[1] Huizinga even helps us toward this summary in his original preface: 'The luxuriant growth of old compelling forms over the living core of thought, the drying and rigidifying of a rich culture: this is the main content of the following pages. In writing this book, my eye was trained as though on the depths of the evening sky – but a sky filled blood red, heavy and desolate with threatening leaden clouds, filled with the false sheen of copper'.[2]

The trophonian gloom induced by entering Huizinga's vision seems a good reason not to read *Autumn* any longer, except as a historical curiosity. For modern tastes, it appears too rooted in nineteenth-century concerns, whether Hegel's holistic zeitgeist, Dilthey's *Erlebnis*, or Schiller's aesthetics; too locked in debate with Burckhardt's Renaissance; too ready to jettison economic data.[3] Any number of critics have questioned Huizinga's 'cultural forms' as artificially freestanding: surely chivalric games or religious rituals served social functions[4]; surely elitist court life cannot be detached from its urban context,[5] or theologians from their social networks?[6] Others attribute Huizinga's apparent distaste for elaborate Catholic practices to his links with the Protestant Mennonite sect[7]; while historians have used his negative comments on decaying religious thought as a foil for revisionist interpretation of the late medieval Church.[8] His description of medieval emotional displays as 'childlike' forms a point of departure for historiography

1 Huizinga, *Herfsttij* (6th ed.), esp. pp. 55, 65-66, 126-128, 203, 210, 249, 251, 297, 306, 307, 367. For an English translation (1996): Huizinga, *Autumn*, pp. 45, 53-54, 101-104, 165, 172, 203, 205, 240, 248, 249, 300. There are criticisms of this translation (cf. Peters and Simons, 'The New Huizinga', pp. 591-597); and the earlier English translation by F. Hopman (*Waning*, 1924) is still worth reading for the grace and power of its prose. Yet it is an abridgement (though approved by Huizinga); and the newer translation includes the Dutch text's nuances of argument (cf. Huizinga, *Autumn*, pp. xiii-xvii). In addition, with the Hopman version, the legacy to the Anglophone world was a rather darker version of Huizinga's original vision (see further below).

2 Huizinga, *Herfsttij*, p. v.

3 For fuller discussion of the cultural influences on Huizinga, see in particular: Van der Lem, *Johan Huizinga*, pp. 28-43; Krul, 'In the Mirror'; Peters and Simons, 'The New Huizinga', pp. 596-604; Senger, 'Eine Schwalbe', pp. 17-24; Otterspeer, *Reading Huizinga*.

4 For instance: Keen, 'Huizinga, Kilgour', pp. 1-20; Vale, *War and Chivalry*, pp. 1-12.

5 Lecuppre-Desjardin, *La ville des cérémonies*; Brown and Small, *Court and Civic Society*.

6 Courtenay, 'Huizinga's Heirs', p. 31.

7 Colie, 'Johan Huizinga', pp. 619-620; Burke, 'Huizinga', p. 26.

8 Duffy, *The Stripping of the Altars*, pp. 4-5, 301. On Huizinga and religion, see Walter Simons's contribution in this volume (chapter 2).

on emotions, only to be summarily dismissed.[9] Huizinga's work, we might say, is simply too presentist. The image of a declining Burgundian court reflects Huizinga's value-laden reaction to a perceived cultural decadence in his own society; while his divorce of the medieval world from the modern is now at odds with the postmodernist embrace of medieval culture.[10]

Some aspects of Huizinga's approach, though, are not so outmoded. The 'cultural turn' since the 1970s, and attempts to build integrated narratives of cultural manifestations and to understand societies from a multiplicity of viewpoints, have given *Autumn* renewed currency.[11] But in reassessing the legacy of Huizinga's work, more attention should also be paid to the nuances of his thesis. He did wonder whether he had overdone the gloom[12]; and he did not present quite such a monolithic vision of late medieval culture as familiar summaries of *Autumn* would suggest. He was well aware of the social and political dimensions of cultural forms, and in ways that anticipate the focuses of later studies: the 'commercial power of the bourgeoisie' (which, he notes, contemporaries like Chastellain chose to ignore)[13]; the 'monetary power of princes' and the rise of the 'Burgundian state'[14]; the social aspirations of burghers[15]; and even the political agendas behind princely claims to rule for the 'public good'.[16] The dukes' funerals

9 Rosenwein, 'Worrying about Emotions', pp. 823, 826; Rosenwein, 'Thinking Historically', pp. 828-829.

10 See, for instance: Nichols, 'The New Medievalism', pp. 8-9; Aurell, 'Introduction', pp. 9-23.

11 See, for example, Hunt, *The New Cultural History*; Burke, 'Historians, Anthropologists', esp. pp. 272-273.

12 Note his equivocal comment in the Dutch preface to his work (cited above) – which does not appear in the preface of the Hopman translation (*Waning*, pp. 7-8). There are a number of places in which the emphasis of the latter is gloomier. Compare the darker: 'No other epoch has laid so much stress as the expiring Middle Ages on the thought of death' (*Waning*, p. 134), with the subtly less comprehensive (and closer to the Dutch – Huizinga, *Herfsttij*, p. 192): 'No other age has so forcefully and continually impressed the idea of death on the whole population as did the fifteenth century' (p. 156). The sentence in the book's final paragraph: 'A profound pessimism spread general gloom over life' (*Waning*, p. 318), does not appear in the Dutch; nor does the bleak conclusion to the chapter on 'Forms of Thought' ('the dark system of delusion and cruelty' [*Waning*, p. 231]).

13 Huizinga, *Herfsttij*, p. 74 (*Autumn*, p. 61). This reference is omitted in *Waning*.

14 Huizinga, *Herfsttij*, pp. 45, 74 (*Autumn*, pp. 37, 61). Huizinga disagreed later with Pirenne over the existence of a Burgundian state; see Small, *George Chastelain*, pp. 1-6. On the differences between Huizinga and Pirenne, see Tollebeek, '"Au point sensible"', pp. 403-443; but for similarities of outlook between them, particularly with reference to urbanity, see Boone, '"L'automne du Moyen Age"'.

15 Huizinga, *Herfsttij*, p. 131 (*Autumn*, p. 105).

16 Huizinga, *Herfsttij*, p. 141 (*Autumn*, p. 113). This reference is omitted in *Waning*.

and commemorative masses are not without political consequences.[17] Medieval emotions are not simply 'childlike' and may indeed reflect their social context: 'the higher the rank', Huizinga writes, 'the more heroic the display of pain'.[18] His description of Catholic practices was not necessarily colored by denominational bias: he wanted to avoid too 'Protestant' a view; the Reformation did not change certain forms of thought.[19] Some of his passages on late medieval religion, particularly on 'credulity and doubt' and 'superstition', sit quite comfortably with more recent historiography on the vulnerability of pre-Reformation piety or on the 'complex' growth of superstitions.[20] After all, the criticisms he levies against superstitions, mechanical piety or devotional excess, are the criticisms made by contemporaries such as Jean Gerson.[21]

There is in fact a fractured complexity in Huizinga's aesthetic response to medieval religious forms. At times this appears almost contradictory. There are extremes of behavior (revivalist fervor in French cities and *Devotio* calm in Holland) but also a spectrum of religious thought (since the 'spirit of the *Devotio*' could be found in Franco-Burgundian regions).[22] But what Huizinga particularly points to are the paradoxes and tensions within medieval religious attitudes and practices: popular views on superstition, witchcraft and magic are 'vacillatory and fluid'[23]; while an 'element of religious tension' exists 'in the highest realm of politics'.[24] Exactly the same ambivalence and tension appear in all Huizinga's cultural forms. There is autumnal decay but also 'exuberance' in the medieval mind. The 'symbolizing mode of thought was almost spent' yet it retains a 'lively emotional value'; and mourning

17 See further below.

18 Huizinga, *Herfsttij*, p. 66 (*Autumn*, p. 54).

19 Huizinga, *Herfsttij*, p. 213 (*Autumn*, p. 174) – noted also in Peters and Simons, 'The New Huizinga', p. 617, n. 101. The comment is omitted from *Waning*. See also Huizinga's comments on the continuity of ideas of holiness beyond the Reformation (Huizinga, *Herfsttij*, p. 258; *Autumn*, p. 21).

20 See, for instance, Bernard, *Late Medieval English Church*; Cameron, *Enchanted Europe*, esp. pp. 15-18, 135-139 (on Jean Gerson), and p. 75 (for the increasingly 'complex and many-branched' growth of folkloric piety). On superstition, Huizinga also implies a cultural milieu that crosses social divides, which fits with recent discussion of acculturation between elites and lower social groups (e.g., Arnold, *Belief and Unbelief*, pp. 27-68).

21 Huizinga, *Herfsttij*, esp. p. 247 (*Autumn*, esp. p. 201). This forms a counterpart to contemporary criticisms Huizinga cites of court life (*Herfsttij*, pp. 183-184; *Autumn*, p. 124). Admittedly, Huizinga ignores the wider ecclesiastical context and pastoral agenda of Gerson's writings.

22 Huizinga, *Herfsttij*, pp. 248, 272, 275 (*Autumn*, pp. 203, 221, 223).

23 Huizinga, *Herfsttij*, p. 351 (*Autumn*, p. 287). In the Hopman translation this fluidity is transformed into a 'want of balance' in the late medieval mind (*Waning*, p. 228).

24 Huizinga, *Herfsttij*, pp. 14, 254 (*Autumn*, pp. 12, 207).

customs too retain 'living cultural drama'.[25] There is a 'wild growth' of chivalric games as well as of religious ideas, and a 'luxuriant' growth in the cults of saints; games may be 'empty' but they can be 'beautiful and uplifting'.[26]

Huizinga's perspective on chivalric games in particular tends to be negative, for they amount generally to a retreat into a dream world of illusion. But there is a tension even here: dreams also 'aim at ennobling life itself with beauty and fill communal life with play and forms'.[27] This paradox, as well as the tensions in other cultural forms, are worth exploring further, particularly with reference to 'play' as Huizinga later came to define it. For this, we must turn to *Homo ludens*; but as we shall see later, although the concept is not fully developed within *Autumn*, play as it appears in this work can itself generate fruitful lines of inquiry.

1 *Homo ludens*

'It was in trying to describe the purpose of all this [sumptuous apparatus of medieval chivalry] in my earlier book', wrote Huizinga, 'that the intimate connexion between culture and play first dawned on me'.[28] And in describing medieval play in *Homo ludens* (1938), Huizinga lifted some of the morbidity that had shrouded late medieval culture in *Autumn*. Competitive events where play was evident – whether in tournaments, law courts or even cathedral building – were potentially powerful and creative forces. Few cultural forms had 'real culture-creating function' except the ideal of courtly love, yet the 'play-spirit' was exuberant and positive.[29] In *Homo ludens* it is now Baroque society of the eighteenth century that tended to 'overdo' things; while the modern routine-driven world, and its lack of the play-element, compares more unfavorably with the medieval.[30] The influence of the 'play-spirit' in the Middle Ages, writes Huizinga, was 'extraordinarily great'.[31]

25 Huizinga, *Herfsttij*, pp. 239, 299, 67-69 (*Autumn*, pp. 56-58, 193, 242).

26 Huizinga, *Herfsttij*, pp. 51-53, 55, 216, 248 (*Autumn*, pp. 42-43, 45, 176, 202).

27 Huizinga, *Herfsttij*, pp. 47-48 (*Autumn*, pp. 38-39).

28 Huizinga, *Homo ludens* (1970), p. 126. But note too that his interest in certain forms of play preceded *Autumn*: as a Sanskrit philologist, he had written on the figure of the jester in ancient Indian drama (e.g., Otterspeer, *Reading Huizinga*, pp. 43, 87, 102).

29 Huizinga, *Homo ludens*, pp. 98-99, 110-111, 114, 205.

30 Huizinga, *Homo ludens*, pp. 208, 221-240. For Huizinga's experiences in America as part cause of his views on modern play, see Anchor, 'History and Play', pp. 72-73; Van der Lem, *Johan Huizinga*, pp. 213-219.

31 Huizinga, *Homo ludens*, p. 205.

Modern theorists in 'play studies' pay greater homage to *Homo ludens* than medievalists do to *Autumn*.[32] Few accept the historical trajectory Huizinga traced from 'primitive' to modern cultures, or privilege competitive games above other kinds.[33] But certain key – and paradoxical – aspects of Huizinga's definitions of play have proved particularly productive. The first is his emphasis on play as a distinct category or activity, outside ordinary social events yet at the same time part of society; 'a well-defined quality of actions which is different from ordinary life', when 'ordinary life' is at a 'standstill' but can interrupt play.[34] The second is his emphasis on play not just as an activity, but as a 'spirit' or disposition: the 'play element' is a mode of cultural experience that can operate in all areas of life, not just within games.[35] These emphases have spurred on theorists ever since to reevaluate the boundaries between play and other apparently oppositional categories, such as 'real life' or 'work'.[36] Of equal interest has been the paradoxical relationship between play and social life that *Homo ludens* also highlighted: play can be serious, and the serious playful. Play events are contests for 'something' and a representation of 'something'[37]; they can therefore articulate the values of society and even relations of power, but they are not straightforwardly functional.

Huizinga took the implications of play's paradoxes a little further. The porous boundaries between play and real life allow the one to affect the other: ordinary life can interrupt play, but play has the potential to transform ordinary life. It can promote the formation of social groupings, but also allow reflection on social status. Games open up possibilities: they can become arenas where received ideas are rearranged. 'Stepping out of common reality into a higher order' means that 'symbolic events' can be

32 See, for instance, Henricks, *Play Reconsidered* (in which Huizinga's work forms the starting point and recurrent theme); and frequent references to Huizinga in recent overviews: Johnson et al., *The Handbook of the Study of Play*, pp. 4, 41, 46, 54, 102, 126, 142-143, 181-184. There were precedents for Huizinga's thinking, of course, notably in Schiller's ideas: Henricks, 'Classical Theories of Play', pp. 164-169.

33 Henricks, *Play Reconsidered*, pp. 20-22. For further expansion of the definition of 'games', beyond the agonistic, a starting point is: Caillois, *Man, Play, and Games*, pp. 14-26. But note some acceptance of the idea of 'play' (or at least 'sport') becoming more 'instrumental' in modern, routinized society; and some overlap of Huizinga's views on historical changes in play with Elias's influential 'civilizing process': Dunning, 'Sociological Reflections'; Henricks, *Play Reconsidered*, pp. 101-105.

34 Huizinga, *Homo ludens*, p. 32.

35 Huizinga, *Homo ludens*, pp. 26, 32.

36 Henricks, *Play Reconsidered*, esp. pp. 192-207.

37 Huizinga, *Homo ludens*, pp. 28-32.

played out 'to change cosmic order' as well as social order: within games social status may be reflected on but also 'renegotiated'.[38] Certainly as theorists since Huizinga have argued, even the most fluid of play events can be controlling and conformative, serving the interests of those in power.[39] But the dynamic potential of play to effect social change has not been discounted. Anthropologists like Victor Turner have interpreted play events as liminal situations in which received ideas are rearranged.[40] Sociologists (Pierre Bourdieu, for example) note how recreation helps people sustain a public identity, while emphasizing the improvisational and open-ended quality of social processes.[41] A further paradox of Huizinga's 'play' has also stimulated reflection, that is, the interplay it sets up between order and disorder. Play 'creates order, *is* order', but it is tension laden[42]: the outcomes of games are inherently indeterminate, within themselves and in their effects beyond. The uncertainty or ambiguity of the 'ludic', within a game and as a disposition in social life, points to its transformative but also its transgressive potential: play's contingency and connection with disorder open up interpretative divergences, possibilities of resistance, and alternative viewpoints on social order.[43]

38 Huizinga, *Homo ludens*, p. 32.

39 For the 'rhetoric' of play as power and domination, see Sutton-Smith, *The Ambiguity of Play*, pp. 74-90. For a schematic view of an ambivalent Western philosophical 'discourse' on play and its relation to power, see Spariosu, *Dionysius Reborn*, esp. pp. 5-27.

40 For the influence of Huizinga and others (Caillois and Csikszentmihalyi) on Turner's ideas on play as a liminal experience, see Turner, *From Ritual to Theater*, pp. 56-59, 84-86.

41 Bourdieu (who does not quote *Homo ludens*, however) emphasizes the dynamic 'opposition' in sporting games between 'respect for forms' and 'symbolic subversion of the rituals of bourgeois order', which contribute to the expression of a distinctive social 'habitus' (Bourdieu, *Distinction*, pp. 209-255). Note also his comments on 'tak[ing] part in the game and be[ing] taken in by it' as part of a disguised struggle to appropriate cultural capital (ibid., pp. 250-251).

42 *Homo ludens*, p. 29.

43 Roger Caillois picked up Huizinga's point about the uncertainty of games (*Man, Play, and Games*, pp. 7-9). On the variability and indeterminacy of play, and the ambiguities of rhetorics of play, see especially Sutton-Smith, *The Ambiguity of Play*, pp. 214, 216, 221-222 (and reference to Huizinga, in discussion of the subversion of power through play, ibid., pp. 76-80). Spariosu argues for a 'prerational notion of play as chance-necessity' resurfacing throughout the history of Western thought (Spariosu, *Dionysius Reborn*, esp. pp. 14-15). See also Malaby's emphasis, referring to Huizinga's 'play-element', on play as a disposition 'intimately connected with a disordered world [...] that always carries within it the possibility of change' (Malaby, 'Anthropology and Play', p. 210). Also: Bateman, 'Implicit Game Aesthetics', pp. 15-16. For discussion of play as 'resistance', see Henricks, *Play and the Human Condition*, pp. 195-206. The interpretive possibilities and deconstruction of play is very much a postmodern emphasis: Henricks, 'Sociological Perspectives', pp. 114-115.

These insights will be worth bearing in mind when we revisit *Autumn*; and especially in combination with another aspect of play encountered in *Homo ludens*. Huizinga posed questions about the boundaries between play and ordinary life or work, but also between play and ritual. Huizinga's play, at least in 'primitive' and medieval societies, is intimately linked to ritual activity'.[44] The emphasis in *Autumn* with respect to medieval ritual is often on its empty formalism. Not so in *Homo ludens*: 'The influence of the play-spirit was extraordinarily great in the Middle Ages, not on the inward structure of its institutions, but on the ceremonial with which that structure was expressed and embellished'.[45] And play is also linked to the sacred: it is itself part of a broader 'play-festival-rite'. 'Ritual, magic, liturgy, sacrament, and mystery' can 'all fall within the play concept'. The playground to a degree resembles the 'hallowed spot' so crucial to rituals.[46] 'The ritual act', Huizinga asserts, 'has all the formal and essential characteristics of play [...] particularly in so far as it transports the participants to another world'.[47] Not all theorists since Huizinga have agreed on this intimacy between sacred ritual and play[48]; the ludic has seemed present in the ceremonies of some societies more than in those of others.[49] Some social anthropologists distinguish ritual as more instrumental, predictable and conformative than play.[50] Even so, others entertain the notion of ritual as a playful activity[51]; and rituals, it seems, can communicate subversion and deconstructions of social order, their performance bringing latent social conflict to the surface.[52] Adopting a ritual mode may even have disruptive potential: rituals have

44 Huizinga, *Homo ludens*, pp. 34-46. On Huizinga and ritual, see Peter Arnade's contribution in this volume (chapter 12).

45 Huizinga, *Homo ludens*, p. 205.

46 Ibid., pp. 32, 37-39, 187, 192, 195, 197.

47 Ibid., p. 37.

48 Caillois rejected the link Huizinga made between the sacred and play (*Man, Play, and Games*, p. 4); see Henricks, 'Modern Theorists of Play', pp. 184-185.

49 For the ludic as part of ritual traditions in Japanese society: Raveri, 'Introduction', p. 6. See also Van Bremen, 'Japan in the World of Johan Huizinga', pp. 214-227.

50 For Henricks's distinction between ritual and play, though they both occupy a spectrum of social activity, see Henricks, *Play Reconsidered*, pp. 201-208; and comment on ritual/play combinations: Henricks, *Play and the Human Condition*, pp. 64-65.

51 Droogers, 'Enjoying an Emerging Alternative World', pp. 138-154 (in which ritual can contain the ludic, and *homo ludens* manages ritual repertoires).

52 For one example among many, see Handelman, *Models and Mirrors*, pp. 63-81; and see various interpretations of ritual failure in Hüsken, *When Rituals Go Wrong*. For 'deep play' as 'risk-taking': Geertz, 'Deep Play', pp. 1-37. A further dimension of the 'ludic' as ritual inversion, of course, underlies Mikhail Bakhtin's oft-quoted work on carnival.

been defined as fluid processes,[53] or 'displacements of intentional meaning',[54] thus like the ludic, creating space for divergent interpretations.

Homo ludens has therefore been an important stimulus for reflection on the connections between play and ritual, play events and ordinary social life; and on the paradoxical tensions set up by play-events between power and its subversion. These themes may also be applied to Huizinga's vision of Franco-Burgundian culture. But before returning to *Autumn*, a final point from *Homo ludens* may be noted. Play – as 'play-festival-rite' – occurs in a great variety of rituals, including the most seriously sacred. The game of reciprocal gift-giving can be found in any important ceremony, whether birth, marriage or death.[55] As Victor Turner commented, Huizinga's ludic is full of rituals, even funeral rituals.[56] The uncertainties of play might therefore be found in mortuary rites, too. Funeral ceremonies are often highly traditional, even rigid, in form; they may serve as mechanisms for reproducing existing norms; but they can also become occasions for social negotiation.[57] So while death broods over Huizinga's Franco-Burgundian culture, its effects on social activity are perhaps not entirely ossifying.

2 The Ludic in *The Autumn of the Middle Ages*

Peering once more through the gloom in *Autumn*, we may discern a great deal of 'play' in the forms later described in *Homo ludens* – as activities separated from ordinary life and as experiences within it. The first chapters, notwithstanding the emotive words of some of their titles (e.g., 'intensity (*felheid*)', 'desire or craving (*zucht*)', 'dream'), are also about bodily performances, rituals and social play. Life and play are interweaved; 'communal

53 For ritual as a process of 'ritualization': Bell, *Ritual*. Emphasis on ritual as a social process as well as a mode of expression also points toward its dynamic potential (e.g., Turner, *From Ritual to Theater*, p. 85). For the creative potentiality of ritual itself, see Handelman, 'Epilogue', p. 217.

54 Humphrey and Laidlaw, *Archetypal Actions*, esp. p. 260.

55 Huizinga, *Homo ludens*, pp. 78-90.

56 Turner, *From Ritual to Theater*, p. 85. See also Driver, *The Magic of Ritual*, pp. 156-165; and comments in Otterspeer, *Reading Huizinga*, pp. 121-125.

57 Kawano, 'Mortuary Rituals', pp. 52-68. For the role of play in the sacred, see Raj and Dempsey, *Sacred Play*; and with particular reference within to Huizinga: Raj, 'Serious Levity', pp. 21-36; Harman, 'Laughing Till It Hurts', pp. 119-120, 151; Schmalz, 'A Catholic Charismatic Healer at Play', pp. 187-192, and 202 (where even a deathbed scene could be a form of play). On social conflict released from performance specifically of funeral rituals: Geertz, 'Ritual and Social Change', pp. 32-54.

life' is filled with 'play and forms'.[58] Returning to these links in Chapter 17, Huizinga refers to the appearance of play and mockery in war, heraldry, and etiquette: the 'blending of seriousness and play is characteristic of several areas [of life]'.[59] These references foreshadow Huizinga's later definition of the ludic; we do not need to retrofit *Homo ludens* onto *Autumn* to see that play has creative potential even in the earlier work.

The emphasis in *Autumn* is certainly that all cultural activity is 'overdone' and that its formalism takes on a 'hollow and superficial character'.[60] Yet this does not preclude either playfulness or practical effects. Social aspirations can be communicated and developed in playlike forms or situations. Symbolism, including heraldic emblems, runs to seed, but 'lions, lilies and crosses become symbols in which an entire complex of pride and aspiration, fidelity and a sense of community are expressed'.[61] Power can be communicated through play. The ducal residence at Hesdin and its mechanical amusements, revamped by Duke Philip the Good, blended the needs of entertainment with those of propaganda. Huizinga comments how some contraptions produced meteorological special effects to imitate the 'magic tricks' of Medea, alluding to the story of Jason and the Golden Fleece[62] – and thus to a myth which the duke had appropriated for dynastic purposes. Recreation at the court of Duke Charles the Bold could also slip from levity into serious statements of magnificence and sacred authority. As Huizinga notes (from Chastellain), Charles's formal enthronements, when the duke hectored his nobles to mend their ways, were preceded or interspersed with 'games and laughter'.[63] Table etiquette at Charles's court (described by Olivier de La Marche) becomes almost play-festival-rite, with services regulated with 'nearly liturgical dignity'. Court etiquette is linked with faith, the 'ennobling

58 Huizinga, *Herfsttij*, pp. 46-47 (*Autumn*, pp. 38-39).

59 Huizinga, *Herfsttij*, pp. 337-338, 349-350 (*Autumn*, pp. 276-277, 285: Chapter 11 in this translation). In *Waning*, the first of these references is omitted (p. 223); the second, to 'playfulness', is mentioned but as a form of insincerity (ibid., p. 228) rather than, in effect, as an immersion in the ludic. See also Huizinga's comment that the 'sacredness of ritual' and the 'exuberance of the joy of life' could still be conjoined in medieval culture despite the influence of Christianity (Huizinga, *Herfsttij*, pp. 154-155; *Autumn*, p. 130).

60 Huizinga, *Herfsttij*, pp. 345-346 (*Autumn*, pp. 281, 283).

61 Huizinga, *Herfsttij*, pp. 337-338 (*Autumn*, p. 276).

62 Huizinga, *Herfsttij*, p. 380 (*Autumn*, pp. 310-311) – from Chastellain, *Oeuvres*, V, p. 26. For Huizinga, these artistic devices were part of a courtly 'tastelessness' – but also a need to 'display splendor'. The '*danses et festes*' at Hesdin also served as backdrop to the diplomatic entertainment of the queen of France in 1464 (Chastellain, *Oeuvres*, V, pp. 26-33). On Hesdin, see, for instance, Van Buren, 'Reality and Literary Romance', pp. 117-134; Farmer, 'Aristocratic Power', pp. 644-680 (though the discussion here is on 'artifice' rather than 'play').

63 Huizinga, *Herfsttij*, pp. 52-53 (*Autumn*, p. 43); Chastellain, *Oeuvres*, V, p. 368.

forms of life' with a liturgical element that 'raises the observance of these forms almost to a religious realm'.[64] The slippages Huizinga refers to here between play and sacred ritual suggest how recreation might combine the serious and nonserious, and how it might facilitate the communication of power and authority.

At the same time, however, *Homo ludens* reminds us to consider tensions and even subversion within play events: they could usefully serve power but were they inherently stable? The 'games and laughter' that attended a ducal harangue perhaps opened spaces for reciprocal complaint: Charles the Bold's formal sittings in state apparently provided occasions for courtiers to bring the duke's own faults to his attention.[65] In *Autumn*, Huizinga also refers to criticism emerging from recreational contexts. The pleasures of Hesdin served as backdrop for displaying power, but also for delivering censorious remonstration: at the castle, the bishop of Chalon presented a 'serious warning over political activities' to Philip the Good, on St. Andrew's Day in 1437, in the form of an allegory.[66] Playfulness as power and power's disruption both operate in *Autumn*.

The implications of Huizinga's views on play are most obviously explored in the context of chivalric games. In *Autumn*, the Feast of the Pheasant in 1454 and the vows taken to go on crusade are framed largely as examples of Burgundian decadence.[67] It does seem that Huizinga's question about the feast – 'How serious is this all?' – is meant to be answered 'well, not very'.[68] From *Homo ludens*, though, the answer to the same question would emphatically be the opposite. There, the feast and the vows are recast as examples of the 'potlatch' spirit, and of the potential of competitive gift-giving and vows to consider and renegotiate social status. Yet even in *Autumn*, Huizinga does not actually dismiss the serious potential of the feast.[69] His commentary on the event is ambiguous: the vows, he says, remain based on strong emotion;

64 Huizinga, *Herfsttij*, pp. 53-54 (*Autumn*, pp. 43-44).

65 Vaughan, *Charles the Bold*, pp. 171-173.

66 Huizinga, *Herfsttij*, pp. 301-302 (*Autumn*, p. 244) – commenting also on the 'vital function' that allegory might have to 'make an impression'.

67 For the following, see Huizinga, *Herfsttij*, pp. 126-128, 372-373 (*Autumn*, pp. 101-104, 304-305); Huizinga, *Homo ludens*, pp. 79-82 (and for the potlatch spirit evident also in heraldic games). Huizinga quotes Marcel Mauss *Essai sur le don*. The potlatch (for instance as 'wasteful' play performed in deadly earnest) has been the focus of many studies since.

68 Historians have labored to show how politically serious the feast in fact was, sometimes in direct response to Huizinga's question. For instance: Caron, *Les voeux du faisan*, esp. pp. 69-72; and recently (though Huizinga is not mentioned): Strøm-Olsen, 'Political Narrative'.

69 Huizinga in *Waning* apparently does, however. There, the feast is more negatively a reflection of a dying culture; and the 'actors' in it 'pretend' to take it seriously (*Waning*, p. 90).

they are still regarded as 'serious and dangerous'; there is 'competition' in their performance; and the knightly ideal on which they are based, even if 'artificial and worn out', continues 'to exert a powerful influence on the purely political history of the late Middle Ages'. His reference to the courtier knights at the feast 'mocking' or 'laughing at' their own ideals invites us to ponder the more social and subversive potential of 'beautiful games'.[70]

Play also applies to the solemn rituals of death. There is more to death in *Autumn* than paralyzing decay. On the one hand, for all their traditional formality, funerals are used to promote or reassert political authority. Burgundian funerary sculpture was much concerned with 'glorifying princely grandeur'.[71] The elaborate arrangements and processions for John the Fearless's funeral were intended in part to have a 'political effect'.[72] Huizinga notes the endowment of masses for the dead and the extreme penances inflicted on townsmen as punishment, to atone for victims of their rebellions.[73] Yet, on the other hand, he also refers to transgressive and playlike moments in funerals that occur even when time-honored procedures are followed. 'Massive disputes' arose at Charles VI's burial in 1422, repeated in 1461 at Charles VII's, over the traditional rights two parties claimed over the funeral clothing, which ended (in 1461) with the royal corpse being unceremoniously dumped in the middle of the road.[74] Also noted is the palpable shock caused by failure to follow expected ceremony, and when the marks of honor were not observed or even reversed.[75] While Huizinga emphasizes the dour formalism of funeral rituals, he nonetheless points us to their ludic and unsettling potential.

Huizinga has perhaps too little to say about the politics of Valois Burgundian funerals; how the death of rulers created political hiatuses while

70 See also his comment that the chivalric stylizing of love was 'more than a vain game': Huizinga, *Herfsttij*, p. 153 (*Autumn*, p. 128).

71 Huizinga, *Herfsttij*, p. 364 (*Autumn*, p. 307). For Huizinga's recognition (albeit combined with aesthetic distaste) that works of art, including funerary sculptures, promoted princely magnificence, see the approving comments in Van der Velden, *The Donor's Image*, pp. 3-6. See further Diane Wolfthal's contribution in this volume (chapter 6).

72 Huizinga, *Herfsttij*, p. 66 (*Autumn*, p. 54). Huizinga notes the appearance of the duke of Lorraine at Charles the Bold's funeral dressed in mourning '*à l'antique*', to celebrate his own triumph (*Herfsttij*, p. 465; *Autumn*, p. 387). Huizinga might have noted that one of Charles the Bold's 'Seven Magnificences', according to Chastellain, was the duke's splendid reburial of his father, Philip the Good, in 1473 ('dont il s'acquit los et gloire'): Chastellain, *Oeuvres*, V, pp. 504-505.

73 Huizinga, *Herfsttij*, p. 345 (*Autumn*, p. 281). On the symbolic punishment of cities, with the imposition of commemorative masses, see Boone, 'Destroying and Reconstructing', pp. 21-22.

74 Huizinga, *Herfsttij*, pp. 62-63 (*Autumn*, p. 51).

75 Huizinga, *Herfsttij*, pp. 70, 257 (*Autumn*, pp. 57, 209).

succession was confirmed; and how these created tensions and opportunities for subjects to renegotiate their relationship with a new ruler.[76] He also has less to say about opposition to Burgundian power beyond the court – in which play in the form of drama, song, and even laughter, could also form a context for political and social complaint, and indeed rebellion.[77] Yet Huizinga is not unaware of wider complaint, and he does prompt us to consider the possible role of play in events following rulers' deaths, in which the serious and play-elements comingle to produce political effects. For instance, the succession of Charles the Bold in 1467 to the county of Flanders was assured, but he was required ceremonially to swear and receive oaths in Ghent as part of his inauguration as count. His entry into the city almost cost him his life. The details of the event have been well studied,[78] but attention can be drawn to the presence of play within it. While the procedures of rebel protest often followed a repertoire of well-established rituals,[79] they could also be accompanied by play as Huizinga defined it. The duke's entry was unfortunately timed with the rowdy return from Houtem of pilgrims carrying the shrine of St. Lieven. As Huizinga notes, Chastellain bewails their drunken 'howling, singing and dancing, mocking everything in sight'.[80] This behavior was a prelude to 'rabid bestial fury'; but within his derogatory description, Chastellain reveals something about rebel use of the playful. He notes how a great number of revelers wore toy hauberks as brooches, in mock defiance of the humiliating Peace of Gavere (1453) imposed on them by the Philip the Good, which had prohibited processors from carrying real weapons. Some rabble-rouser apparently declared that these toy hauberks would soon be made of 'lead, iron and steel'.[81]

76 For instance, the Ghenters adopted ritual funeral and anniversary forms for their own purposes in 1483 after the death of Margaret of Burgundy: Haemers, 'L'anniversaire gantois', pp. 341-365.

77 For song in rebel action: Dumolyn and Haemers, 'A Bad Chicken', pp. 60-63.

78 See particularly Arnade, 'Secular Charisma', pp. 69-94; Lecuppre-Desjardin, *La ville des cérémonies*, pp. 296-300.

79 Arnade, 'Crowds, Banners and the Market Place', pp. 471-97; Boone, *'Armes, coursses, assemblees'*, pp. 7-33; Dumolyn, 'The Vengeance of the Commune', pp. 251-289.

80 Huizinga, *Herfsttij*, p. 226 (*Autumn*, p. 184).

81 Chastellain says that 'lead objects' typically sold at the fair associated with the saint's day, were for the amusement of children and professes himself ignorant of the reason ('ne sçay si c'estoit d'aventure ou de fait avisé) why so many of these objects, on this occasion, were made in the form of hauberks (Chastellain, *Oeuvres*, V, pp. 259-260; translation in Brown and Small, *Court and Civic Society*, p. 191) – though earlier he notes that the rebels wore these to feign obedience to the Peace of Gavere and to be seen as playing a game ('faignans vouloir obeir [...] pensans que cela seroit tourné a jeu et agas' [ibid., p. 253]).

Play could have a role in political processes, and in this case it was used to present more serious political agendas as though in jest. But it had other effects, too. Entering the city corn market, Chastellain writes, the rebels were 'chanting and yelling, singing songs and fooling about'; and a different source informs us that the rebels also used another rallying cry: 'God and the good city of Ghent, kill all those in government'.[82] The 'rhythmic structure of the Middle Dutch text shows that it was meant to be chanted or sung', and was doubtless intended to have an 'intimidating' effect.[83] Huizinga does not refer to this text; but his definition of play as potentially secular and sacred encourages further interpretations of such events. Slipping from song to ritualistic chanting may also have helped the Ghenters to elevate their complaint, already addressed to God, to a quasi-liturgical level. There were other occasions when rebels, in asserting the righteousness of their cause, adopted forms that borrowed from ecclesiastical traditions. In March 1488, when the hated *schout* (sheriff) Pieter Lanchals was finally unearthed from hiding by the people of Bruges, to be executed shortly after, he was led through the streets amid popular joy and 'festive noise'. According to a later version of the chronicle of Flanders, a 'procession of children and young men' also accompanied him to prison 'singing' that they had the 'liver-eater' in their hands.[84] There is a seamless movement implied in this account from festive noise and song to liturgical ritual: processions, adapted from hallowed tradition, that included children or young men (as a designated group) thanking or asking for God's grace, were familiar in fifteenth-century Bruges and elsewhere.[85] The use of play-ritual forms could do more than simply disguise other agendas: they allowed those agendas to be expressed within the public domain, and simultaneously legitimated them in a realm beyond the mundane.

82 From a fragment of Middle Dutch poetry: 'God ende die goede stede van Ghent, slaet al doot dat heeft regiment', quoted in Arnade, 'Secular Charisma', p. 69.
83 Dumolyn and Haemers, 'A Bad Chicken', pp. 76-77.
84 Despars, *Cronycke*, IV, p. 382. However, a more contemporary version of the chronicle of Flanders has the children 'shouting' (*Dits die excellente cronike*, fol. 236r). On Lanchals's imprisonment and funeral, see Boone, 'Un grand commis', pp. 63-88. Note comment on the 'quasi-liturgical' parades of craft guilds during the Bruges revolt of 1488: Haemers and Lecuppre-Desjardin, 'Conquérir et reconquérir', pp. 119-143.
85 Brown, *Civic Ceremony*, p. 90.

Conclusion

Medieval games have become the subject of serious study among literary scholars,[86] but 'play' in general also deserves more attention from historians of late medieval society. Huizinga's ideas, particularly on the 'play-element', are prompts to look for the possible connections between play and sacred rituals, and the potential effects of the ludic on ceremonial performances and on social practices. *Homo ludens* is an important point of reference, but so too is *The Autumn of the Middle Ages*. A holistic vision, overshadowed by morbidity and death, does dominate Huizinga's approach to Franco-Burgundian cultural forms; but *Autumn* is not merely about a dying culture. Play has creative properties even within this earlier work. Within its pages, there are contradictions and tensions that fragment cultural forms, and play elements that break up their apparent rigidity. Even in death and in mortuary rites, playful uncertainty appears, in which power is advanced but also subverted. These are themes still worth exploring. *Autumn* may reflect legacies from the nineteenth century, but it continues to have the capacity to stimulate fresh research in the twenty-first.

About the Author

Andrew Brown is Associate Professor at the School of Humanities, Massey University, New Zealand. Among his publications is *Civic Ceremony and Religion in Medieval Bruges, c. 1300-1520* (Cambridge University Press, 2011).
A.D.Brown@massey.ac.nz

86 Cf. Kendrick, 'Games Medievalists Play', esp. pp. 43-45; Hardwick, *The Playful Middle Ages* (for playfulness in art and literature); Patterson, *Games and Gaming*. In the latter, several contributors take issue with Huizinga's idea of games defined as taking place within a closed 'magic circle' (pp. 9-10, 127-129, 147, 194-198), but his concept of the ludic, fluidly crossing boundaries of games and social life (see above) also needs to be considered further. For a more historical perspective on games, see Mehl, *Des jeux*.

2 Wrestling with the Angel

Huizinga, *Herfsttij*, and Religion

Walter Simons

Abstract

Herfsttij made an undeniable impact on mainstream historiography of religious life in late medieval Europe, not in the least because of the book's powerful image of an atrophied culture in its waning days. Although Huizinga frequently claimed that the autumnal metaphor was purely representational, it permeated the book's central argument and seemed to confirm older, mainly confessional treatments of the period as a time of religious crisis. Several key themes of *Herfsttij*, like the *danse macabre*, the obsession with death, and the multiplication of funeral services, found their way into the new approaches to religious history developed from the 1960s onward by historians associated with the French Annales school, charmed by Huizinga's inroads into historical psychology. By around 1980, the new religious history thus created largely left those themes behind to explore such areas ignored by *Herfsttij* as heresy, gender, or interfaith relations. However, more recent trends in the history of emotions, of the senses, and of religious art may revive interest in *Herfsttij*. This chapter suggests ways in which current research has altered our views on religion in the Low Countries and northern France during the fourteenth and fifteenth centuries, particularly by expanding the social horizon and including urban life. In the final section, I return to Huizinga's personal views on religion, colored, as is well known, by his family's Mennonite background, but even more, I argue, by his training in the study of Buddhism and the influence of the German-British scholar F. Max Müller, one of the founders of the study of comparative religion. These influences shaped Huizinga's conviction that the essence of religion is purely transcendental, and that any worship extending beyond the recognition of God's majesty is a diversion; hence the many personal value judgments scattered throughout the discussion

Arnade, Peter, Martha Howell, and Anton van der Lem (eds), *Rereading Huizinga: Autumn of the Middle Ages, a Century Later.* Taylor & Francis Group, 2019
DOI: 10.5117/9789462983724_CH02

of religious practice in *Herfsttij*, which should not distract from the book's enduring allure.

Keywords: religious history, Annales school, Mennonites, Oswald Spengler, F. Max Müller

Decline, decay, death: no image conjured by Johan Huizinga's *Herfsttij*[1] has proved to be as enduring as that of a withering medieval civilization, wasting away in the late fourteenth and fifteenth centuries, in no small part because of the titles by which the book was known in its first English and French translations: *The Waning of the Middle Ages* (1924) and *Le déclin du Moyen Age* (1932). Applied to the religious sphere, the vision of an atrophied culture merged almost seamlessly with older views of the age embedded in confessional historiography, which portrayed the period as an age of religious crisis, resulting in Reformation and Counter-Reformation. Calling *Herfsttij*, 'the most powerful book ever written about the period', Howard Kaminsky singled it out as the primary basis for 'the waning-model' of late medieval history, an essentially organic model that, substituting periodization for argumentation, lets the Middle Ages recede through processes of decay that are rarely defined or properly investigated.[2] Given the popularity of the book in American undergraduate education until recently, it is not surprising that textbooks in European history covering late medieval religion still give pride of place to stories of late medieval 'superstition', mysticism, and the *danse macabre* that could have been plucked from *Herfsttij*'s pages.

To be sure, academic historians specializing in religious history now usually treat the 'waning-model' with circumspection. Apart from the model's potential affinity with conventional Protestant narratives, many historians of religion have reservations about its explanatory power or doubt that it is helpful to understand the undeniable challenges experienced in the religious realm[3]; still

1 I would like to thank my Dartmouth colleagues M. Cecilia Gaposchkin (History) and Gil Raz (Religion) for their advise in thinking about Huizinga and his classic book.
Despite the diversity of editions and translations by which the work is known, I will refer to it as *Herfsttij*, reflecting its original Dutch title. Quotations and page references will be to the 1997 edition of the final Dutch version, Huizinga, *Herfsttij*, as well as to the more commonly available edition in Huizinga, *Verzamelde werken* (hereafter *VW*), III, pp. 1-435, and the English translation, *Autumn*, despite its shortcomings (see Simons, '[Review of] Johan Huizinga').

2 Kaminsky, 'Lateness', p. 86.

3 For a brief discussion of such critiques, see Van Engen, 'The Church in the Fifteenth Century'; D'Avray, 'Symbolism'; Courtenay, 'Huizinga's Heirs'; Bailey, 'Late-Medieval Crisis'. Steel, 'From

others reject it out of hand, arguing, for instance, that theology and mysticism enjoyed an extraordinary period of fertility, which Heiko Oberman superbly examined in a book whose title, *The Harvest of Medieval Theology*, deliberately rephrased Huizinga's autumnal metaphor to underline such productivity.[4] Yet, while the latter view may be in the ascendant among scholars of late medieval religion today, the waning-model and the images of 'senescence, decadence, and termination' it has strewn still exert a powerful presence, 'surviv[ing] nevertheless to haunt the thinking even of those who reject them', as Kaminsky put it.[5] Such themes from *Herfsttij* as the preoccupation with death, the formalization and ritualization of worship, the externalization of abstract concepts in visual images, or the religious pessimism and disarray, have accordingly hardened to become fixtures in the religious landscape of the era.

In this essay, I will examine how certain features of *Herfsttij* gained prominence in historical work on religion shortly after the mid-twentieth century, tracing their influence to the appreciative but critical reception by historians of the Annales school, who, I shall argue, prepared their absorption into the received narrative of religious life in the late Middle Ages and early modern period. I will then discuss the revival of interest in *Herfsttij* in more recent decades and suggest ways in which the book could be exploited – and expanded – by specialists of late medieval religion in the Low Countries and northern France. In the final pages, the essay will return to the figure of Huizinga himself and to his personal religious beliefs, which historians should keep firmly in mind when reading and rereading this complex work.

Before addressing the book's reception, however, we should pause to consider the relationship of the autumnal metaphor to the central argument on culture and religion in *Herfsttij*, because it has been contested since the book's publication, first of all by its own author.

1 *Herfsttij*: Metaphor, Image, and Content

Some otherwise perceptive readers of *Herfsttij* have attributed the book's pervasive mood of dejection to the influence of Oswald Spengler's *The Decline*

Siger of Brabant to Erasmus', examines Huizinga's portrayal of philosophy in the Burgundian Netherlands in particular.

4 Oberman, *Harvest*. Bernard McGinn adopted the metaphor for the fourth volume of his massive history of mysticism in the West (see especially McGinn, *Harvest*, pp. 1-4). A similar point of view dominates *Christianity in Western Europe*.

5 Kaminsky, 'Lateness', p. 86.

ference with the organic metaphors underlying Spengler's vision went to the heart of Huizinga's concept of 'historical sensation' in which poetry and prose, the senses and the rational mind, cooperated in a complex dynamic. The historian should render an account of the past through the invocation of sensory images, necessarily subjective and emotionally charged, but based on wide and profound familiarity with primary sources, visual, textual, material as well as sonic. These sources and the fundamental forms of thought they displayed generated an empathic connection with the past which must be kept in check by aiming for the highest possible objective truth. The procedure contained an aesthetic element (the representation in the form of images) and mobilized the powers of literary metaphor but was neither artistic nor literary. In no way did it confuse subjective perception and objective reality, and, of course, it never assigned any organic or biological existence to the historical culture such imagery sought to evoke.[16]

Huizinga was certainly right to call out Spengler's historical determinism and to dissociate himself from it. Yet the inherent limitations and contradictions of his own method were many, and its execution in *Herfsttij* was far from perfect or even consistent. However often Huizinga attempted to clarify *Herfsttij*'s aims in later years, there was no denying that the book's natural metaphors had far outgrown (pun intended) the level of mere representation and instead formed an integral part of the argument itself. As late as 1935, he insisted that he 'had never renounced *Herfsttij*, only regretted sometimes its title'.[17] But the famous preface, already cited, forever contradicted those claims, for it linked the autumnal imagery very explicitly to 'the last stage in life of medieval civilisation' described in the book,

> as a tree with overripe fruit, completely unfolded and ripened. The overgrowth of old, unbending forms of thought over the living nub of an idea, the withering and stiffening of a rich civilization – that is the main content of these pages.

16 Among the many studies devoted to this aspect of Huizinga's work, see Tollebeek, *De toga van Fruin*, pp. 210-234, and Tollebeek, 'De middeleeuwen dromen'. On the relationship of Huizinga's method with literary analysis, see Otterspeer, *Reading Huizinga*, especially pp. 169-185. According to his own testimony (Huizinga, *De wetenschap der geschiedenis*, p. 166), the term '[historical] sensation' was born from his exposure to the literary 'Movement of the 1880s' (*Beweging van Tachtig* or the *Tachtigers*), notably his reading of Lodewijk van Deyssel's essay on Herman Gorter of 1891 (published in Van Deyssel, *Prozastukken*, pp. 61-72); see also Kamerbeek, 'Huizinga', especially p. 151; Peters and Simons, 'The New Huizinga', pp. 607-608.

17 'Ten onrechte meent Dr. T.B. [Menno ter Braak], dat ik *Herfsttij der Middeleeuwen* verloochend zou hebben. Alleen den titel heb ik wel eens berouwd.' Huizinga, *De wetenschap der geschiedenis*, p. 172, n. 1.

He admitted that,

> now that I have given the image line and color, it may have become more somber and less serene than I thought to perceive it at the beginning of my labor. It can easily happen that when one's attention is fixated on decline, expiration, and wilting, too much of the shadow of death is cast over the work.[18]

But that *is* the work he wrote, and changing its title would hardly have altered that fact.

Despite those avowals and obfuscations, the preface could not be clearer: imagery and argumentation were inextricably tied.[19] We thus find the same metaphors not only in the title but throughout the book supporting the thrust of the argument: in this age of brutal extremes, *Herfsttij* proclaims, the human mind and body sought recourse in flight, found either in dreaming of a virtuous life or in preparation of death and the afterlife, that is, in religious thought. All of these endeavors required careful calibration of passions according to prescribed norms. The ensuing formalization and ritualization of life and thought necessarily resulted in ossification. Indeed, since readers of *Herfsttij* were invited to join that process in the late fourteenth century, when its last stage had been reached already, the book is essentially an analysis of the multiple ways in which thought and action crystallized into empty formalism:

> The final Middle Ages display this entire world of thought at the extreme end of its flowering. The world lay spread out in that all-encompassing symbolism, whose symbols became like petrified flowers. [...] Symbolism latches on to thought as a parasite and degenerates into mere habit, a reflexive virus. [...] The symbolic form of thought was virtually worn out.

18 *Herfsttij*, p. 10; *VW*, III, p. 3; compare Huizinga, *Autumn*, pp. xix-xx. Although 'the shadow of death' mentioned here primarily alludes to the theme of death in *Herfsttij*, the phrase may also have contained a veiled allusion to the tragedies of World War I, just concluded, and to his own family circumstances: his beloved first wife, Mary, had died in 1914. Several historians have explained *Herfsttij*'s dark mood by pointing to contemporary events – or more broadly, to the influence of the fin de siècle. See Kennedy, 'Autumns'; Kaminsky, 'Lateness', pp. 86-89 (with further references).

19 Hanssen, *Huizinga*, pp. 246-247, comes for different reasons to a similar conclusion. Romein, 'Huizinga', p. 287, noted that for Huizinga, 'the "aesthetic component" did not remain limited to the representation of what the historian discovered, but gave impetus and direction to research itself' ('Bij hem [is] het "esthetische bestanddeel" niet beperkt gebleven tot het uitbeelden van het gevondene, maar [gaf] reeds stuwing en richting aan het onderzoek zelf').

> [...] As soon as symbolism slips away from the expression of the purely religious to the solely moral, one recognizes it as hopeless degeneration.[20]

Or, on the imagery of death:

> Church doctrine of the late Middle Ages knows only two extremes: the lament over transience, over the end of power, honor, and pleasure, over the demise of beauty, and the joy over the soul, saved and blessed. Everything in between remains unspoken. In the unrelenting representation of the dance of death and in the icy skeleton, vital feeling is petrified.[21]

Numerous other examples could be found throughout the volume: this is an age of religious atrophy, spent, dried up, and yes, lifeless. It is difficult not to call the process 'decline'.

During the 1920s Huizinga seriously contemplated giving the title metaphor of *Herfsttij* a firmer basis by writing a 'prequel' devoted to the twelfth century, a time of 'Spring'. He completed three essays on Alain de Lille, John of Salisbury, and Peter Abelard in which he tentatively sketched a 'ripening' of European civilization. All three religious philosophers, concerned with moral, ethical, and political challenges, exemplified the vitality of Christianity in this age, combining serious topics with a playful poetics, which Huizinga associated with a 'primitive' energy. As Lodi Nauta has pointed out, the materials reveal Huizinga's first sustained bid to explore the creative element of play in human culture, treated more fully, of course, in *Homo ludens* of 1938.[22] Perhaps for that reason he put the project on the twelfth century aside; perhaps he also doubted that the 'forms of thought' he perceived in these figures could be replicated elsewhere in a full-blown treatment of the age; perhaps he realized, I should suggest, that the 'spring' or 'ripening' metaphor once again threatened to infiltrate the argument to an extent that was difficult to control. In any case, nothing further came of the book.

20 *Herfsttij*, pp. 215, 216; *VW*, III, pp. 252, 253; compare Huizinga, *Autumn*, pp. 240, 242.

21 *Herfsttij*, p. 157; *VW*, III, p. 179; compare Huizinga, *Autumn*, p. 172.

22 Huizinga used these materials for a series of lectures in Paris in 1930, but they were not published until 1932-1935: *VW*, IV, pp. 3-122. Two of them, 'John of Salisbury: A Pre-Gothic Mind' and 'Abelard', were translated and published in English in Huizinga, *Men and Ideas*. See Nauta, 'Huizinga's Lente'; Krul, *Historicus*, pp. 234-238; Peters and Simons, 'The New Huizinga', pp. 595-596, 604; and the important sources on the project discussed in Van der Lem, *Johan Huizinga*, pp. 219-222. Gombrich, 'Huizinga's *Homo ludens*', pp. 136-138, places the seeds of the book on play as early as 1897, when Huizinga completed his dissertation on the *vidusaka* in Sanskrit drama.

Instead, Huizinga made one more attempt to suggest his vision of the late Middle Ages was not as bleak as people made it out to be: reviewing, in 1932, Henri Pirenne's *La fin du Moyen Age*, published the year before, Huizinga objected to the volume's tone and title. After conceding that 'Nobody will suspect me of a tendency to regard the Late Middle Ages too much as a time of ascent', he found fault with Pirenne's emphasis on decline and disaster,

> not only in the titles but throughout the whole work. [...] This creates in my view a completely false impression since [...] what of the powers and forces of the medieval West (because that's what it's all about) had truly gone to ruin?[23]

Few readers will have believed him by now.

2 Reception and Responses

Herfsttij was an immediate commercial success in the Netherlands, soon reprinted and by 1924 also translated into German, but, as is well known, academic historians in his home country and Belgium, normally the primary audience for a book on Burgundian culture, reacted with indifference. The book seemed to have little to offer to Dutch medieval studies, still in their infancy and struggling to become 'more scientific' (that is, based on archival charters, critically examined). Attitudes in Belgium were predictably divided along confessional lines: historians at the Catholic University of Louvain took no interest in the product of a Protestant scholar mercilessly analyzing the failings of medieval Catholic piety, whereas at the University of Ghent, traditionally (somewhat) anticlerical, the 'Pirenne school of Medieval History' was about to embark on its grand projects in the history of economic and social life, politics and legal institutions, subjects left aside in *Herfsttij*. Thus, in both Louvain and Ghent, but for different reasons, medieval historians ignored the book, and it was not reviewed in Belgian historical journals. As late as 1947, when Frits Hugenholtz (one of Huizinga's last students) arrived for a year's study of medieval history at the University of Ghent, he discovered that no one knew the book; a puzzled Hugenholtz was told that professors did not believe it mattered.[24]

23 Huizinga, '[Review of] *La fin du Moyen Age*', pp. 564-565.
24 Hugenholtz, 'The Fame', p. 98. See also Prevenier, 'Johan Huizinga'; Simons, 'The *Annales* and Medieval Studies in the Low Countries'.

Reception of the book in Germany was similarly muted. Norbert Elias certainly welcomed its ideas, absorbing them into his *The Civilizing Process*, the roots of which date to the early 1930s, but he may have read *Herfsttij* only after his emigration to England in 1933 (an English translation had appeared in 1924 but was barely acknowledged).[25] We can only wonder how it affected Ernst Kantorowicz, completing *Laudes Regiae*, his great study of religious royal ideology and the liturgy, in the 1930s, and then beginning a project on Charles the Bold and Burgundian culture, for which he conducted research in Brussels in 1936-1937. When Kantorowicz fled Germany after Kristallnacht, a year later, he abandoned the project, and relatively little about it is known.[26]

Herfsttij's impact on religious history was surely the greatest in France, where scholars picked up several of its themes after World War II. Philippe Ariès's influential studies on death and the macabre owe much to Huizinga's earlier fascination with the subject. A historical demographer by training and a self-described 'amateur historian', Ariès first came to the attention of academic historians with a study of childhood and the family in the Ancien Régime, originally published in French in 1960, followed by a more widely read English translation in 1962.[27] His famous thesis (now largely debunked) positing an absence of the concept of childhood before the eighteenth century seems inspired by a stray sentence in *Herfsttij*: 'Neither ecclesiastical nor secular literature [of the Middle Ages] really knows the child.'[28] Ariès acknowledged *Herfsttij* as a model for his own subsequent work on death in premodern Europe at the 1972 Groningen conference on the centenary of Huizinga's birth and in his three classic volumes on the subject published between 1975 and 1983.[29] They initiated a host of French studies on the religious and social aspects of death, afterlife, confession, and wills in late medieval and early modern Europe, followed by similar projects in other countries of Europe in the 1970s through 1990s.[30] In a sign of

25 Van Krieken, *Norbert Elias*, pp. 24-25; Peters and Simons, 'The New Huizinga', p. 613.

26 As explained in Peters and Simons, 'The New Huizinga', pp. 612-614, Kantorowicz may have become aware of Huizinga's work through the Dutch poet Albert Verwey, a friend of both Huizinga and Stefan George, to whose 'Kreiss' Kantorowicz belonged during the 1920s and 1930s. The wonderful new biography by Lerner, *Kantorowicz*, did not bring to light new information on Kantorowicz's reading of Huizinga.

27 Ariès, *L'enfant*.

28 Huizinga, *Herfsttij*, p. 157; *VW*, III, p. 178; Huizinga, *Autumn*, p. 171. As far as I can tell, Ariès never discussed in print Huizinga's statement on childhood in medieval culture.

29 Ariès, 'Huizinga et les thèmes macabres'. See Ariès, *Essais*; Ariès, *L'homme*; Ariès, *Images*.

30 For example: Braet and Verbeke, *Death in the Middle Ages*; Lemaître, *L'église et la mémoire des morts dans la France médiévale*; Schmid and Wollasch, *Memoria*; Vovelle, *La mort*; Lorcin, *Vivre et mourir*.

enduring resonance of Huizinga's pages on death, French research endowed the book with new interpretations or built on features of late medieval devotion that Huizinga had explored only in passing. Jean Delumeau, for instance, utilized Huizinga's characterization of the medieval mind as childlike to frame guilt, fear of damnation, and confession as an elementary fright-and-reassurance system that governed the Church's penitential practices until the end of the Ancien Régime. Jacques Chiffoleau developed the concept of a late medieval 'salvational calculus' ('mathématique du salut') leading to obsessional multiplication of funerary services – a process that Huizinga analyzed briefly in *Herfsttij* with reference to fifteenth-century critics, well aware of the trend.[31] Huizinga would probably also have agreed with Chiffoleau's portrayal of the era as traumatized and its faith as 'flamboyant religion'.[32]

But there were also important departures. The lines of intellectual genealogy did not run directly from Huizinga to the French historians mentioned above but rather via Lucien Febvre, cofounder of *Annales*, and the *histoire des mentalités* associated with the journal. That 'history of mentalities' was in no small part shaped by Febvre's followers, Jacques Le Goff and Robert Mandrou, a medievalist and an early modernist, who were sympathetic to Huizinga's subject matter but critical of his methodology and more open to the newest developments in the social sciences, especially (religious) sociology and anthropology. The religious history of the Middle Ages that emerged from the *Annales* was diachronic where Huizinga was synchronic, and preferred the *longue durée* (the long Middle Ages defined by Le Goff as the period from c. 1100 to the end of the Ancien Régime) rather than the 150 years to which Huizinga had confined himself. It discerned multiple tensions between learned faith and practices that deviated from it, whereas Huizinga wrote of a largely homogenous religious culture, internally conflicted. It cast its eyes widely and voraciously on the history of marginal movements, heresy, and witchcraft; to dreams, ghosts, and the murky world of Purgatory; to visual images as instruments of worship. It was highly successful (though not uncontested), entering the mainstream of medieval studies in Europe and in the United States in the 1980s.[33]

31 Delumeau, *La peur*; Delumeau, *Le péché*; Delumeau, *Rassurer et protégér*; Chiffoleau, *La comptabilité*. See Huizinga, *Herfsttij*, pp. 160-161; *VW*, III, pp. 181-184.

32 Chiffoleau, 'La religion flamboyante'. As one (of many) examples of Chiffoleau's influence, see Deregnaucourt, 'Autour de la mort à Douai'.

33 Witness the surveys by Clark, 'French Historians' (note that the same issue of *Past & Present* also contained Bossy's famous article 'The Mass as a Social Institution 1200-1700' while Jacques Le Goff made a guest appearance commenting on *Past & Present*'s coverage of history from 1959

This 'new religious history' found willing interlocutors among historians of Germany, Italy, France, Britain, and the Low Countries who had independently expanded conventional horizons to explore the faith of the laity in the late Middle Ages. Some, like Herbert Grundmann,[34] Marie-Dominique Chenu,[35] Raoul Manselli, and Cinzio Violante,[36] were motivated by a confessional though unorthodox background (Protestant for the former, Catholic for the latter three) advocating ecclesiastical, social, and political reform; others came from the erudite circuits of the history of philosophy, theology, and the liturgy; still others regarded religion as an essential component of social history.[37]

It is fair to say that their projects invariably gave and still give an appreciative nod of recognition to Huizinga's *Herfsttij* whenever they cross paths with it, but the book rarely, if ever, seems to have played a significant role in them. A case in point is provided by the fascinating debate set off by John Van Engen's 1986 article, 'The Christian Middle Ages as an Historiographical Problem', calling for a greater emphasis on the study of faith in everyday life within the traditional framework of the parish – a call that some interpreted as a manifesto against 'the new religious history' and its apparent preoccupation with the extraordinary and outlandish. It is telling, however, that neither Van Engen's essay nor the two responses by Michel Lauwers and Jean-Claude Schmitt published in its immediate wake – each covering broad swaths of scholarship on medieval religion – as much as mentions Huizinga or *Herfsttij*.[38] Nor will we find his name in any of the debates central to the history of gender and religion or of interfaith relations

to 1982: Le Goff, 'Later History'; Peters, 'Religion'. See also Little and Rosenwein, 'Religion and Society'.

34 Fundamental is his *Religiöse Bewegungen*, whose influence came slowly.

35 Though covering the 'high' rather than the 'late' Middle Ages, the essays collected in his *La théologie au douzième siècle* exerted a major influence on a generation of medieval historians of religion.

36 Manselli, *La religion populaire*; Violante, *Studi sulla cristianità medioevale*.

37 A small selection out of many, necessarily biased by my own interests: Vauchez, *La sainteté*; Angenendt, *Geschichte der Religiosität*; Milis, *De heidense Middeleeuwen* and *Religion, Culture, and Mentalities*; Bossy, *Christianity*; Moore, *Formation*; Rubin, *Corpus Christi*; Rubin, *Mother of God*. An example of Huizinga's early influence on the study of witchcraft is the remarkable book by Bonomo, *Caccia alle streghe*; see p. 483, n. 38.

38 Van Engen, 'The Christian Middle Ages'; Lauwers, '"Religion populaire"'; Schmitt, 'Introduzione'. See also Bredero, *Ontkerstening*, pp. 422-437. More specifically on French historiography of religion, see Vauchez, 'Orientations'. It may be noted that Lauwers, *La mémoire des ancêtres* (with a preface by Jacques Le Goff), examining the period before 1300, accepts Chiffoleau's conclusions for the late medieval era, implicitly invoking Huizinga's *Herfsttij* as well (pp. 54-55). The most successful implementation of Van Engen's program (even though written with a different agenda)

(between Christians, Jews, and Muslims), two other important subfields of religious history that have animated the community of medievalists and early modernists since 1986.

Has *Herfsttij* thus become irrelevant for historians of medieval religion? Not at all, I should argue. New perspectives have come from several subfields of history that touch on *Herfsttij* and may help us to reinterpret – and reread – the book. The burgeoning histories of emotions and of sensations (the two are related but should be separated) form a natural context to reexamine *Herfsttij*. Like all new fields of scholarship, they struggle to define their agenda and method, nor is there agreement on how they may inform the study of religion. All parties involved, however, recognize Huizinga as a pioneer. The volley of sensory images opening *Herfsttij* not only alerted the reader to a different world of physical and psychological extremes, it also signaled the importance of the senses in late medieval culture, to be tamed and redirected toward the divine, to be sure, but understood as primary instruments of knowledge, material as well as spiritual. Huizinga was quite right to underscore the ease with which his subjects mixed the profane with the sublime, how colors 'worked' on both a symbolic and sensory level, or how visual and aural stimuli 'spoke' to metaphysics as well as bodily needs. Scholars of the medieval liturgy have recently recast their findings to capture those aspects of late medieval worship, while historians of late medieval music now include the physical environment when considering religious and intellectual context.[39] In a new book on the Burgundian Low Countries that draws explicit parallels to Huizinga's sensory world, Matthew S. Champion even investigates that most abstract of concepts, time (secular as well as religious), from the perspective of its physical experience.[40]

It is, of course, one thing to hail Huizinga as a forerunner of the history of emotions and another to exploit his insights responsibly. After all, the emotions on display in *Herfsttij* were said to be 'extreme', 'extravagant', 'bizarre', 'fierce', 'overly sensitive', in short, 'naïve' and 'childlike', that is, primitive and uncontrolled.[41] Norbert Elias relegated them to the same crude, undisciplined status in his canonical *The Civilizing Process*, in part on the basis of Huizinga, which in turn motivated Peter and Carol Stearns

may be Duffy, *The Stripping of the Altars*, with a discussion of *Herfsttij* on pp. 301-309, rejecting Huizinga's view that the late medieval cult of 'last things' expressed religious pessimism.

39 Pycke, *Sons, couleurs, odeurs*; Caseau, 'The Senses in Religion'. The 'townscape as soundscape' concept was already present in Strohm, *Music*.

40 Champion, *Fullness of Time*.

41 Quotations selected, among many others, from *Herfsttij*, pp. 13-33, 183-198; *VW*, III, pp. 5-33, 211-232; Huizinga, *Autumn*, pp. 1-29, 203-222.

in their authoritative work on 'emotionology' to declare the premodern era largely devoid of internalized emotional control.[42] Barbara Rosenwein, the most vocal critic of this paradigm, and other medievalists have moved beyond the facile contrast between modern perceptions of primitive and modern, 'civilized' emotional behaviors.[43] With the added benefit of the history of gender, historians are now better equipped than ever to probe, for instance, concepts and practices of empathy and compassion that underlie the imitation of Christ, surely the most compelling religious model of the late Middle Ages, or the mechanisms by which the Modern Devout conditioned daily behavior in monastic communities for women.[44]

Great strides have also been made in the history of religious art (and objects). Long gone are the days when such objects were seen as mere illustrations of concepts, thoughts, and symbols whose significance in devotion should be studied primarily on the basis of texts or worse, as the locus of superstitious beliefs hovering above the level of animism. Historians are increasingly aware of a more complex relationship in medieval Christianity between objects and the growing desire, in the later Middle Ages, to reflect on the power of images, their materiality, and their meaning. Caroline Bynum, in particular, has demonstrated how devotional objects became the subject of sophisticated intellectual analyses that could be contradictory and certainly affected Reformation thought on matter, divine power, and human response to both. Scholars like Chiara Frugoni and Jeffrey Hamburger have investigated an important aspect of those changing attitudes, the relationship between vision, visionary experience (often of women), and visual representation, while Bret Rothstein has renewed the way we think of the art of Van Eyck (and his contemporaries) and their audiences, arguing that their work challenged viewers to reflect on their own position toward the illusionary world they conveyed.[45]

Time has come, then, to return to *Herfsttij* and reinvestigate its 'forms of life and thought' as they relate to belief and worship. It may be naïve to

42 Elias, *Civilizing Process*; Stearns, 'Emotionology', especially p. 826.

43 Rosenwein, *Emotional Communities*; Rosenwein, *Generations*; Plamper, *The History of Emotions*, especially pp. 48-49 (on Huizinga), 40-43 (on Lucien Febvre, here considered the founder of the subfield), and 49-51 (on Elias); Boquet and Nagy, *Sensible Moyen Âge*. For a fine repositioning of Huizinga's analysis of emotions vis-à-vis the later, more 'scientific' approaches, see Otterspeer, *Reading Huizinga*, pp. 220-233.

44 See, for instance, McNamer, *Affective Meditation*; Roodenburg, 'Empathy'; Hanselaer and Deploige, '"Van groeter bannicheit"'.

45 Bynum, *Christian Materiality*; Frugoni, 'Female Mystics'; Hamburger, *The Visual and the Visionary*; Rothstein, *Sight and Spirituality in Early Netherlandish Painting*. See also Camille, *Gothic Idol*; Belting, *Likeness and Presence*.

imagine a new *Herfsttij*, on late medieval religion, written today, and it certainly could be called blasphemous, but let me sketch out a few parameters of such a work – no doubt a collaborative effort – on the basis of preliminary studies already in place.[46]

The project would expand the territory and social groups under examination – to include the cities and countryside of the Burgundian Netherlands, naturally, but also the adjacent Rhineland, the origin of many new trends in religious thought and practice during the fourteenth and fifteenth century. Inclusion of urban communities so glaringly overlooked by Huizinga would add a wealth of data on religious practice gathered since the 1960s. These are the result of pragmatic research in the vast archives of Netherlandish and northern French cities, revealing a greater variety of religious organizations and practices than Huizinga knew, and a lay population more engaged and informed about matters of faith – the consequence, it has been argued, of high levels of literacy since the urban revolution of the central Middle Ages.[47] Lay people and clerics in this area generated an enormous devotional literature in the Dutch and French vernaculars that was little studied in Huizinga's day but now is the subject of several research programs by teams composed of historians and scholars of literature.[48] Lay religious movements like those of the Beguines (to a lesser extent also those of the male Begards), later followed by communities of the Common Life, sustained urban religious life in cities; much of it was in the hands of confraternities and parish institutions, all of which barely made an appearance in *Herfsttij*.[49]

Integration of those urban and rural social groups into the purview of study would do more than simply expand the research base: it would allow redefinition of the 'religious crisis' of the late Middle Ages, formerly attributed to weakened ecclesiastical authority or efficacy, today rather seen as a result of higher literacy and the multiplication of religious voices – women now prominently included.

The expanded social horizon would foreground another phenomenon absent from *Herfsttij*, the growth of 'civic religion', manifested, for instance,

46 For an example on the scale of a single city, see Brown and Callewier, 'Religious Practice'.

47 See the overview, for Flanders, in Simons, '"Dieu"'. Important new work for other regions can be found in Bogaers, *Aards, betrokken, en zelfbewust*; Tabbagh, 'La pratique sacramentelle'; Verhoeven, *Devotie en negotie*; De Boer and Jongen, *In het water gevonden*.

48 For a fine example of devotional literature examined within its social, urban context, see Warnar, *Ruusbroec*.

49 Fundamental is Van Engen, *Sisters and Brothers*; Trio, *Volksreligie*. See also Simons, *Cities of Ladies*.

as his grandfather recorded in his diary with a hint of sarcasm.[57] Throughout his life, Huizinga stayed clear of public identification with a particular branch of Protestantism. His children, never baptized, were taught to respect all faiths,[58] and as is well known, his second marriage late in life was to a Catholic woman.

A few Huizinga scholars have perceived in his stance an evolution toward a more pronounced Christianity as he grew older, with the 1920s forming a pivotal decade of crisis and introspection, and it is true that in his published cultural criticism of the 1930s he advocated a deeper engagement with Christian values, although he privately doubted that he could follow his own advice since he was, like Erasmus, a 'very weak Christian', he noted to himself in 1943.[59]

Of greater significance for his religious analysis, it seems to me, was his training in Sanskrit and his years as a scholar of Buddhism at the start of his academic career in Groningen. The eighteen-year old who composed a confession of faith armed with the tools of anthropology, to his grandfather's chagrin, read widely in the field of comparative religion as it was taking shape in the 1870s and the 1880s. Edward Tylor's *Primitive Culture* (1871) was an early companion which remained a reference throughout his scholarly life, and while it is not named in *Herfsttij*, it nonetheless broadly supported the book's preoccupation with cultural survival and corruption – the conversion of 'vital' cultural forms into irrational remnants.[60] Huizinga did cite William James's *Varieties of Religious Experience* (1903), possibly before any other historian did.[61] Direct comparisons between late medieval culture and Indian or Buddhist history abound in *Herfsttij*, even though Huizinga reduced them in later editions of his work. For instance, in the original edition of *Herfsttij*, he called Thomas à Kempis's *Navolging van Christus* 'the most Buddhist work of Christianity', and paired François Villon's 'belle heaulmière' with 'the old pious nun Ambapâlî, whose ancestry is similar, cited in one of the poetic books of southern Buddhism's holy scripture'. Both of these comparisons disappeared in the second printing of the Dutch work

57 Van der Lem, *Johan Huizinga*, p. 26 (extract from Jacob's diary); the confession of faith itself has not been preserved.

58 Huizinga, *Herinneringen*, pp. 155-156, 186.

59 Heering, *Johan Huizinga's religieuze gedachten*, pp. 48-49; MacKay, 'Johan Huizinga'; Wesseling, *Zoekt*, pp. 40-41; Van der Lem, *Johan Huizinga*, p. 237; Krul, *Historicus*, p. 24.

60 Krul, *Historicus*, pp. 224-225, shrewdly identified Tylor's influence as the one that added a much-needed diachronic dimension to *Herfsttij*.

61 Van der Lem, *Johan Huizinga*, p. 142; Peters and Simons, 'The New Huizinga', pp. 610-611.

and subsequent editions; they were also omitted in most translations.[62] Despite such later cuts, *Herfsttij*'s allusions to other religions and cultures undoubtedly enhanced its appeal to historians of medieval Christianity who read it from the 1960s onward.[63]

One towering figure seems of crucial importance to Huizinga's conception of religion as an object of scholarly analysis *and* in his personal faith as well: F. Max Müller (1823-1900), the British philologist (of German origin) famous for translating Vedic scriptures and his monumental edition of the *Sacred Books of the East*, which Huizinga perused for many years. Müller is also considered one of the founders of 'comparative religion' as an academic field. In 'My Path to History', Huizinga recalls that while he was still in high school, in 1888-1889, his father brought home from the University Library two treatises of Müller's, which Johan 'read and excerpted, and took for unmistakable wisdom'. His grandfather found him again buried in volumes by Müller during the summer of 1891, between high school and college.[64] Müller's deployment of philology and etymology to explain elementary cultural constructions fascinated Huizinga because of Müller's concomitant thesis that culture – and religion as a particular manifestation of culture – relied on concepts abstracted from primary, physical impressions (hence also Huizinga's interest in synesthesia).[65] Etymology as key to the origins of cultural forms makes an appearance in one of Huizinga's first publications, *Van den vogel Charadrius* (On the bird Charadrius, 1903), which also combined the study of ancient Indian culture with that of western European religious art, the latter based on Émile Mâle's *L'art religieux du XIIIe siècle en France* (of 1898), another long-time favorite.[66]

Müller's broader significance in the study of religion came from his conviction that 'there was truth in all religions, even in the lowest', and that even primitive forms of religion knew abstractions from sensory experiences and were thus conscious of the divine. Far from being the result of absurd illusion or fetishism – as enlightenment thinkers had argued – primitive

62 See Van der Lem, *Johan Huizinga*, p. 142; Krul, *Historicus*, p. 149. Strangely, the latter example did make it into the English translation by Payton and Mammitzsch, which is largely based on the German translation of 1924: Huizinga, *Autumn*, p. 163.
63 These comparisons had their limitations. Zen Buddhism, for instance, was poorly known in the West around 1900. More complete information on the topic would have allowed Huizinga to draw further parallels with certain forms of late medieval mysticism in Europe.
64 Huizinga, *Mijn weg*, p. 21; Krul, *Historicus*, p. 136.
65 Peters and Simons, 'The New Huizinga', p. 609; Otterspeer, *Reading Huizinga*, pp. 148-165.
66 Huizinga, *Van den vogel Charadrius*.

or 'natural' religion, Müller thought, was capable of attaining higher truths such as the infinite, albeit it in a 'childlike' manner:

> However childish a religion might be, it always places the human soul in the presence of god; and however imperfect or childish the conception of god may be, it always represents the highest ideal of perfection which the human soul can reach and grasp.

Fetishes and other material objects ('the worship of odds and ends of rubbish') used in religion were to be considered aberrations, the result of degeneration or corruption of more abstract religious thought.[67] That such a view of 'pure religion' corresponded to a great extent with Müller's own Protestant (and idealist) beliefs, and with Calvinist perceptions of the divine in the late-nineteenth-century West more generally, is, of course, not a coincidence. While Müller's theories were certainly not adopted wholesale by all academic scholars of religion of the era (Huizinga cites approvingly the critique of the folklorist Andrew Lang, whom he also read in those years),[68] the vision of religion at their core was shared by many, in particular by scholars of Buddhism, who tended to assign to that system an original purity (preserved in ancient texts), marred by externalization and the increasing reliance on visual objects in later stages of Buddhist history.[69]

That conception of religion also fitted with Huizinga's latent Mennonite faith – or rather, Huizinga hoped it would. Much like his father had rebelled against the faith through naturalist science, Huizinga reached for the 'scientific' study of religion to guide him forward at a very young age. Those studies confirmed to him that the divine is imponderable and infinite; worship should remain focused on the transcendental. Indeed, beyond recognition of the wide divide separating the divine and the world, there is not much in worship that is not secondary. Hence his reservations about personal testimony of faith or even discussion of divine things, and his sympathy for certain forms of mysticism (especially the more 'moderate' forms associated with the Modern Devout), so obvious in *Herfsttij* and expressed concisely in his 1931 essay on the Russian mystic Leo Sjestow, where God is said to be known only *per negationem*.[70] Hence also the starkness of the prayers

67 Morris, *Anthropological Studies*, pp. 91-94 (quotations from p. 93, taken from Müller's *Introduction to the Science of Religion*, originally published in 1873). I am grateful to Gil Raz, my colleague in Dartmouth College's Department of Religion, for directing my attention to Max Müller.
68 Huizinga, *Mijn weg*, p. 21.
69 Kieschnick, *Impact*, pp. 16-21.
70 Huizinga, 'De immoralist die God vond'; see also MacKay, 'Johan Huizinga', pp. 17-18.

he wrote shortly before his death, begging God to preserve the lives of his family, especially of his newborn daughter; they were kept private and have only recently been published.[71] To be sure, Christian doctrine exerted its own influence on his thought, but it did so, with few exceptions, as a set of moral and ethical principles rather than as a religious belief system. As he wrote in a personal letter to Menno ter Braak in 1938:

> You always want to conscript me to the land of ministers, to which you had to say goodbye yourself. I never needed to do so: my father had done it before me [...] and I never lived in it. When my ethical and worldviews were forming (not before my college years), I already lived on uniquely free soil. [...] From about 1900 onward and to an increasing extent, I knew, outside of any confessional bounds whatsoever, that the Christian moral law was the supreme guide to all human life; to that was added, many years later, the conviction that some of its doctrinal principles contain the most adequate expression of our existence. Never did any skeptical or other text make me doubt the stable truth, albeit unattainable for humans.[72]

Collective moral guidelines, he argued in *In the Shadow of Tomorrow* (1935), could be summarized by the triad of balance, moderation, and the longing for a higher ideal, themes he had treated 20 years earlier with regard to medieval culture in *Herfsttij*.[73] The many testimonies by his contemporaries about his proverbial self-control, tolerance, and spiritual idealism suggest he set similar principles for individuals, though he seems to have rarely expressed them in personal terms.[74]

The implications of Huizinga's understanding of religion are evident in a text usually not read in conjunction with *Herfsttij*, the 1903 lecture 'On the Study and Appreciation of Buddhism' with which he inaugurated his brief appointment as 'private professor in the antiquity and literature of India' at the University of Amsterdam (1903-1904). It starts with a warning: contemporary Buddhism has been

> infiltrated by a colorful pack of gods, ghosts and demons which should be thought away [to discover original Buddhism], and with them also the

71 Huizinga, *Mijn weg*, pp. 91-105.

72 Huizinga, *Briefwisseling*, III, pp. 269-270, no. 1374.

73 Huizinga, *Schaduwen*, see especially pp. 328-334.

74 Heering, *Johan Huizinga's religieuze gedachten*, pp. 56-59, reports private conversations between the author and Huizinga that seem to suggest additional principles, but they may derive largely from fundamental transcendentalism.

> shabby song and dance of relics, the hocus pocus of magic practice, the exorbitant belief in miracles, the accumulation of empty cosmological fantasies with which it is pervaded.

After discarding successfully all such paraphernalia to study Buddhism's ancient texts, we might indeed learn of certain values: self-control, compassion, and 'a melancholic humanity'. The study of Buddhism would therefore surely work to our benefit, we are told, were it not for the 'tone of dull despondency that saturates the entire Buddhist literature. [...] Buddhism recommends the flight from the world for a solely practical and selfish goal: because all passion will generate sorrow'. Huizinga then turns to the contrast between abstraction and materiality, arguing against Müller (not named) that in some cases primitive magic may become wrapped up in spiritual contemplation of a higher order rather than the reverse. Yet on the whole, he laments, one is repulsed by the 'monstrous outgrowths' of Buddhism's original thoughts 'in a morbid direction'. Attempting to express infinite space and the divine, it loses itself hopelessly in endless repetition of particulars, a tendency which Huizinga declares 'pathological'.[75]

Much of this prefigures Huizinga's verdict on late medieval Christianity in *Herfsttij*, written almost two decades later – so much of it, in fact, that it seems futile to deny that in both cases idealized visions of religion clouded his analysis of the evidence at hand, conveying the messy realities of religious thoughts and practices. 'On the Study and Appreciation of Buddhism' thus already presents us with the themes of superstition and materiality, excessive repetition of the particular at the expense of 'pure' transcendentalism, pathological imbalance, flight from the world (for the 'wrong' reasons), melancholy, and morbidity – all those qualifiers of decadence which *Herfsttij* attached to late medieval religion for generations to come. We even find here, sixteen years before *Herfsttij*, in another time, space, culture, and religion, the metaphor of 'outgrowth'.

In sum, Huizinga's religious outlook predisposed him to examine religious systems through a polarized lens, opposing the pure, spiritual pursuit of the divine at its origins and core, on the one hand, to material or 'superstitious' peripherals, the later 'outgrowths', at the other. This should not come as a surprise. Decades of scholarship on Huizinga has made evident that he was a man and a historian made up of contrasting and even conflicting passions – passions, it goes without saying, that were always carefully regulated. And so he was in his religious belief as well. For all his moderation and tolerance in

75 Huizinga, *Over studie en waardeering van het Boeddhisme*, quotations from pp. 70, 71, 87.

matters of faith, nothing was more abhorrent to him than the claim of being 'close' to God (to use an American phrase). Rather, human approximation of the divine centered on acknowledging its majestic otherness and one's own humility. All one could hope for was a 'spark of the soul', the *scintilla animae* of Thomas Aquinas or the *vonksken* of Thomas à Kempis.[76] What he wrote about Spengler's attempts to master the whole of history as if he were God, determining the plan of humankind,[77] applied to those aiming to know God as well: they were, like Spengler and Jacob, wrestling with the Angel and would inevitably suffer defeat.

Taken together, these observations may help us to read Huizinga's critique of late medieval religion in *Herfsttij* with fresh eyes. We must see its dark tonalities in perspective: not the temporal perspective of the fin de siècle, World War I, or the death of his wife, Mary, but the cosmological perspective in which Huizinga evaluated human worship: there was little there to praise, and much to deplore, or at best to ignore. This is not to say that he did not understand late medieval devotion; quite the opposite is true, since he thought deeply about it and addressed its central questions with a sincerity rarely found in contemporary scholarship. But precisely because he treated such questions seriously, he felt compelled to judge. In these judgments, we do not need to follow him. Suffice it to be inspired by his questions, and to answer them as best we can.

About the Author

Walter Simons earned his PhD in History from Ghent University, Belgium, in 1985. He is currently Professor of History at Dartmouth College in Hanover, New Hampshire, USA. His research deals with religious movements of the central Middle Ages, urban history, gender, and historical methodology.

76 See the final line of *Mijn weg tot de historie*: 'In the language of the congregation of Windesheim, I had received only a spark, which once in a while was willing to glow' ('Ik had, om in de taal van de Windesheimers te spreken, maar een vonkske ontvangen, dat af en toe wel gloeien wilde') (Huizinga, *Mijn weg*, p. 79). Huizinga wrote of the image earlier (1928) and extensively in a letter to the poet Martinus Nijhoff: Huizinga, *Briefwisseling*, II, pp. 189-191, no. 744. On the *scintilla animae* in medieval theology, see Grabmann, 'Lehre'. The image appears in Thomas à Kempis, *De imitatione Christi*, p. 27 (bk I, c. 15).

77 'Spengler failed because he attempted to bridge two worlds of thought between which there is no bridge other than a rainbow. [...] But let us give him that much: he wrestled with the Angel' ('Spengler heeft gefaald, omdat hij twee werelden van gedachte heeft willen verbinden, waartusschen geen andere brug is dan de regenboog. [...] Doch laat hem de eer blijven, dat hij met den Engel geworsteld heeft') (Huizinga, 'Twee worstelaars', pp. 486-487).

house, where they were told of the duke's illness. They immediately began to cry and pray and lit great fires while the bells pealed the entire night. 'Can one imagine a livelier picture of the childish impulsiveness of a medieval city's population?' Huizinga succinctly and rhetorically asked.[1]

Neither Huizinga's main biographers nor his principal commentators have ever explicitly confronted the problem of the city or urban culture in his writings.[2] This question never piqued interest precisely because it did not seem of importance to Huizinga himself. Yet the 'century of Burgundy' was obviously not one of courtly splendor alone; it was a period of a flourishing civic culture in the metropolitan centers of the northern dominions of the Valois dukes. Huizinga's 'silence' regarding urban culture in *Herfsttij der Middeleeuwen*[3] is conspicuous, and calls for an explanation.[4]

Between 1905 and 1909, when he was first a schoolteacher in Haarlem and then a young professor in Groningen, Huizinga published a number of works on the history of both cities, demonstrating his ability to study urban life. However, as Kossmann-Putto has observed, this early work was certainly not *cultural* history.[5] An article on the Groningen patricians is rather brief and lacks depth. While Huizinga's work on medieval Haarlem is solid, it exemplifies the genre of institutional and legal history of towns that was typical of the period. *De opkomst van Haarlem* (*The Rise of Haarlem*) is a reliable work on the city's topographic, economic, political, institutional, and legal development; it engages the work of Karl Hegel, Denis Jean Achille Luchaire, Wilhelm Eduard Wilda, Karl Lamprecht, Karl Bücher and other prominent researchers of the time, as well as the more innovative socioeconomic work of Henri Pirenne – albeit briefly.[6] Meanwhile, Huizinga's publication of the urban bylaws of Haarlem is both erudite and technically perfect, but he never intended to use these sources for social or cultural history, despite

1 Reprinted in Huizinga, *De Nederlandse natie*, p. 11 (quotation from Chastellain, *Oeuvres*, IV, p. 201).

2 For instance, Tollebeek, *De ijkmeesters*; Van der Lem, *Het Eeuwige*; Van der Lem, *Johan Huizinga*.

3 All page numbers cited directly in the text refer to the 1975 edition of *Herfsttij*. Most other texts, smaller contributions, book reviews, or letters by Huizinga are mostly quoted from his collected works (Huizinga, *Verzamelde werken*, hereafter *VW*), unless explicitly otherwise stated in the notes.

4 This absence has also only rarely been explicitly discussed by Huizinga's biographers, for instance, Krul, 'In the Mirror', p. 372.

5 Kossmann-Putto, 'Huizinga als mediëvist', p. 98; Huizinga, 'Over de oudste geschiedenis van Haarlem'; 'Het oudste patriciaat en de immigratie in de stad Groningen tot omstreeks 1430' (*VW*, I, pp. 427-439).

6 *VW*, I, pp. 203-364.

such material's potential for providing valuable insights into the life and world of late medieval city dwellers.[7]

Of course, few of Huizinga's contemporaries would have thought to do so either. The roots of urban history in the Netherlands are found in the work of Robert Fruin and his student Pieter Johannes Blok, starting in the 1870s.[8] Yet until the middle of the twentieth century Dutch medieval urban history was a small field with lackluster practitioners – certainly in comparison to that of its neighbor Belgium and the flourishing Pirenne School. The most important work on cultural history in Huizinga's time was still Jacob Burckhardt's *The Civilization of the Renaissance in Italy*. Although a distinct critic of Burckhardt's interpretation of the Renaissance, Huizinga was in many ways nevertheless a follower of the great Swiss historian's method.[9] Like his predecessor who had revolutionized cultural history, Huizinga was very attentive to basic cultural forms such as violence, shame, humor, family life, or ridicule. These interests, however, only became clear in *Herfsttij* and not in his early work.[10]

Even as Huizinga was engaging in traditional forms of medieval history in order to establish a reputation within his new academic environment, the young scholar was already preparing to chart a radically different course, away from the methods and assumptions of the field in which he was trained, as was evident in his 1905 inaugural lecture in Groningen titled 'Het aesthetische bestanddeel van geschiedkundige voorstellingen' ('The aesthetic element in historical presentation'). In it, Huizinga indicated his receptiveness to the 'ideographic' camp within the already notorious German *Methodenstreit* (the 'struggle over historical methods') although without rejecting influences from the social sciences.[11] Like the philosopher Wilhelm Dilthey – one of the primary opponents of the economic historian Lamprecht's defense of the 'nomothetic' position in this scientific struggle – Huizinga believed in the scientific approach to history while acknowledging that all historical knowledge derives from highly personal and subjective viewpoints.[12] As Wilhelm Windelband, another ideographic philosopher of history, put it, writing history implies awakening the forms of the past. This is what Huizinga intended when he devised the subtitle for *Herfsttij*: to focus on the 'the life and thought forms' of individuals rather than on

7 *Rechtsbronnen*.
8 Santing, 'De middeleeuwen ontsluierd', pp. 163-164.
9 Burke, *What Is Cultural History?*, p. 9.
10 Bulhof, 'Johan Huizinga', p. 207.
11 Oestreich, 'Huizinga', pp. 3-6.
12 Compare with Iggers, *The German Conception*, p. 138.

collective phenomena such as socioeconomic developments or political institutions.[13]

As in the 1905 essay, the medieval city only appears in *Herfsttij* as a setting for the emotional or violent outbursts of irrational crowds enjoying cruel executions or trial by combat, as a locus of loud sounds and strong light, but not one of cultural production. There seems to be only 'vigor' or 'fierceness' ('felheid') and little 'quest for a more beautiful life' ('zucht naar een schoner leven') within the city ramparts. Rather, it is the 'court state' ('hofstaat') that is 'the field upon which the esthetics of the life form can develop in full'.[14] Indeed, Huizinga seems to read the life forms of ordinary people exclusively through the lens of courtly culture. Examples include citing the 'Kerelslied', a Bruges song making fun of popular rebels at the end of the fourteenth century, or the 'proverbes del villain', burlesque proverbs about common people.[15] Huizinga remained a prisoner of his material and showed no interest in nonelite sources. As a result, city dwellers and the ordinary people in general appear mostly passive in Huizinga's scholarship. They might have listened to mendicant preachers but had no cultural, literary, or artistic agency of their own. This was reserved for the princely court in all its legendary Burgundian splendor. Even urban artists like Jan van Eyck were confined to court life and to the 'devotional silence' they apparently depict. What Huizinga deemed 'practical' or 'daily' life was shaped by 'the same forms as in theology', namely a scholastic realism in which concepts have a transcendental existence. But again, he considered these more commonplace 'life forms' only in the light of the most elitist types of sources and rarely used those produced outside the courtly or ecclesiastical environment, apart perhaps from the proverbs he found so interesting.[16]

What is more, Huizinga differentiated between 'the culture of the court, the nobility and the rich burghers' – the burghers are in fact only seldom associated with the court, in fact this is one of the few times Huizinga included burghers, even rich ones, in a reference to court life – which was passionate and lively on the one hand, and the sober and silent atmosphere of the Modern Devotion (*devotio moderna*) or of Van Eyck's paintings, on the other. But even if rooted in urban society, Huizinga claimed, Van Eyck's work should not be called *burgerlijk* (in Dutch this word, derived from *burger*

13 Oestreich, 'Huizinga', p. 8, paraphrasing Windelband's expression 'Neubeleben des Gebildes der Vergangenheit'.

14 *Herfsttij*, p. 35.

15 *Herfsttij*, p. 55.

16 *Herfsttij*, pp. 231, 237.

(burgher) does not carry the negative connotation the word *bourgeois* has) as it stemmed from courtly traditions in miniature painting. To Huizinga, even the fact that the urban life of Bruges, Ghent, and Brussels was 'sumptuous' and 'ripe' was apparently due to intense contact with court life. Only the Haarlem school of painters, notably Dirk Bouts, was really *burgerlijk*, but again in the mystic and religious sense of simplicity. Even more so than the work of the Flemish Primitives (*Primitifs flamands*), these works were as modest, stern, and silent as the IJssel cities of the eastern region of the northern Netherlands.[17]

In a 1915 essay, 'De kunst der Van Eycks in het leven van hun tijd' ('The art of the Van Eycks in the life of their times'), clearly written in preparation for his magnum opus, Huizinga did in fact address the 'urban' aspects of fifteenth-century Flemish painting, although summarily and dismissively.[18] No doubt anticipating a possible critique that the great Flemish painters also belonged to the urban world, Huizinga immediately set the tone by placing the Van Eyck brothers' art 'in the middle of court life'. For Huizinga, this was the only lens through which to view and understand the form and meaning of the fifteenth-century Flemish panel paintings that had fascinated him when he visited the legendary 1902 Bruges exhibition of the so-called Flemish Primitives – one of the first key moments in the genesis of *Herfsttij*. These artists were 'court painters' according to Huizinga. The *rederijkers* (rhetoricians), popular civic theater groups, were also briefly mentioned in relation to feast and celebration. Yes, allowed Huizinga, the *rederijkers* had emancipated *burgerlijk* festive culture from its ecclesiastical form; but only the princely court was capable of organizing a purely secular form of celebration with its own specific type of splendor. Only the chivalric was an alternative for the clerical.[19]

Of course Huizinga could not completely deny that the great art of the Burgundian century had its roots in urban society. However, in his estimation, the burghers of Ypres, Bruges, Ghent, Mechelen, and Louvain lived lush and luxurious lives under the influence of court culture and the nobility they sought to imitate. This cultural dynamic was quite different from the IJssel towns where the Modern Devotion inspired more sober sentiments and expressions.[20] Yet this entire line of Huizinga's reasoning

17 *Herfsttij*, pp. 271-272; See also Krul, 'In the Mirror', p. 360.

18 Consulted in the 2009 edition: Huizinga, 'De kunst der Van Eycks' (in Huizinga, *De hand van Huizinga*).

19 Ibid., pp. 215-218.

20 Ibid., p. 222.

seems rather confused and contradictory, as if Huizinga was answering anticipated criticism. In 1924, in his study of Erasmus, Huizinga returned to the distinction between cities of the southern and northern Netherlands. Huizinga explained that the cities of Holland and Zeeland could not compete with their Flemish and Brabantine counterparts, as they were too small to become centers of art and science. Holland's artists, like the virtuoso sculptor Claus Sluter, were thus irresistibly drawn toward the courtly and ecclesiastical centers of power that commissioned their work. However, returning to his view of the IJssel towns, Huizinga reiterated how during the final quarter of the fourteenth century these centers fostered a new spiritual movement, typical for the 'common character of the people of the northern regions' – the deeper form of religious life that was the Modern Devotion.

Huizinga's arguments found a fuller airing in 'Nederland's beschaving in de zeventiende eeuw' ('Dutch Civilisation in the Seventeenth Century') of 1941, which was clearly influenced by the Calvinist-tinged national mythology that is sometimes found even to this day in popular Dutch historical consciousness, and which emphasizes the typical burgher values of the Dutch Republic. In this common narrative, the Modern Devotion is, of course, represented as a 'proto-Reformation'. In 1934, Huizinga published an essay under the title 'Nederland's geestesmerk' ('The Netherlands's spiritual mark', a neologism[21] that might better be translated as 'the typical psychological character of Holland'), in short, a rather idealist and essentialist category. His assessment was that all Dutchmen were indeed *burgerlijk*: thrifty, not very rebellious, attached to their freedoms, and not militaristic.[22] But again, Huizinga was not interested in any actual social-historical description of the seventeenth-century Dutch ruling class, reflective of the same disinterest he had shown in late medieval urban merchants or guildsmen, whom he acknowledged only in their popular processions, which displayed the vivid colors and unchecked emotions he thought befitting simple townspeople lacking artistic or cultural agency.[23]

Because of his elitist tendencies and astonishing lack of interest in the majority of the population, historians with social scientific sensibilities have considered Huizinga guilty of aesthetic escapism. And while, after the 1980s, the return of narrative as a genre and the new cultural history have

21 De Berg, 'Geestesmerken', points out that the word had in fact already been used by the Protestant politician and journalist Abraham Kuyper in 1875, but Huizinga had been unaware of this and believed he had coined the term until a reader informed him otherwise.

22 *VW*, VII, p. 287.

23 Colie, 'Johan Huizinga', p. 622.

resulted in renewed interest in his work,[24] the earlier critiques remain valid. Huizinga was an antimaterialist in the sense that he implicitly considered socioeconomic history, including studies of urban space itself, largely irrelevant to cultural production. Without ever really repudiating quantitative history or positivism, Huizinga practiced an explicitly subjectivist approach to writing history. He consciously searched for freely creative cultural producers; ignoring economic influences, he found *Homo ludens* instead of *Homo economicus*, and preselected his questions and sources to achieve this goal. His pupil, Jan Romein, was the first to systematically criticize him for not exploring socioeconomic realities and their relevance to culture. Romein had been deeply inspired by his mentor as a cultural historian, but he was also a committed Marxist. In his view, culture was not a universal phenomenon but rather interacted with class positions.[25] Another important Dutch historian, Pieter Geyl, also reproached Huizinga for his failure – just like, for example, Burckhardt – to detect dynamic potential outside the realm of culture.[26]

As we have already seen, the most systematic epistemological influence on Huizinga was the work of ideographic and historicist idealists such as Dilthey and Windelband and, to some extent, the hermeneutic sociologist Georg Simmel.[27] However, the German historicist approach did not reject a socioeconomic focus to the degree that Huizinga did in his rigorous antideterminism. In the final assessment, Huizinga was simply not interested in the study of any social groups, including the nobility or other elites.[28] He did value the work of economic historians, but sometimes explicitly expressed his disinterest in social and economic facts,[29] although it is worth noting that he evoked them when they served his purposes. It would be somewhat anachronistic to reproach him on these grounds given that his contemporaries primarily formulated the connections between socioeconomic infrastructure and cultural superstructure in terms of mechanical Marxism or Lamprecht's failed attempt to devise general laws of history. Huizinga explicitly attacked historical materialism for its 'one-sidedness and schematizations' but he also praised Pirenne, whose

24 Tollebeek, *De ijkmeesters*, p. 179; Boone, '"L'automne du Moyen Age"', pp. 23-24.

25 Vermeulen, *Huizinga*; Hanssen, *Huizinga*, p. 268; Romein, *Op het breukvlak*, p. 586.

26 Hanssen, *Huizinga*, pp. 268-269; Geyl, *Huizinga als aanklager van zijn tijd*, p. 229; and other similar criticism for a lack of interest in politics and economy in Hugenholtz, 'The Fame', pp. 91-103.

27 Krul, 'Huizinga's definitie van de geschiedenis', p. 251; Weintraub, *Visions*, p. 209.

28 Peters and Simons, 'The New Huizinga', pp. 617-620.

29 Tollebeek, *De ijkmeesters*, p. 187.

intriguing if we consider that many historians of the medieval town were and are – as we were and are – absolutely fascinated by *Herfsttij*. When Jacques Le Goff prefaced the new edition of the *L'automne du Moyen Age* in 1975, he could not avoid a certain amount of skepticism, but he wrote with sincere enthusiasm that Huizinga, beyond approximations, amateurism, and an aesthetic approach, remains a master of thinking who still lights the way for historians.[41] According to Le Goff, Huizinga's masterpiece anticipated the work of the *Annales*. But what could be the connection between urban history and *Herfsttij*, where the town is everywhere and nowhere?

If we consider this book as just one piece in Huizinga's larger oeuvre – from his very first work devoted to Indian drama to his 'Dutch Civilisation in the Seventeenth Century' – Huizinga could certainly be regarded more as a 'thinker' than as a historian. One can identify his thoughts about cities by following the usual signposts of historians: the quotation of typical sources devoted to the analysis of words, scripturality, infrastructures, superstructures, etc., and then compile these together to draw conclusions about communal architecture, the place of guilds in the market, the development of the parliamentary system in municipal government, and so on. But disappointment would be the result. Equally frustrating would be any attempt to position Huizinga's work as a sort of forerunner to sociological approaches of history. In our view, this is certainly one of the reasons why he declined Lucien Febvre's invitation to write for the *Annales*. As Walter Simons wrote in his study 'The *Annales* and Medieval Studies in the Low Countries', Febvre was very enthusiastic regarding this prospect and even when Huizinga declined, Febvre tried anew. According to Febvre, Huizinga deserved to publish in his journal because he had the ability to draw connections between art, social structures, morals, collective or individual ways of thinking, etc.:

> Mais non! vous êtes trop modeste, et vous assignez aux *Annales* un but trop restreint! Il y a toute sorte de choses excellentes de vous qui sont faites pour les *Annales*! Tous les chapitres de votre *Déclin du Moyen Age* auraient pu y paraître les uns après les autres. Tout ce qui noue un lien entre l'art et l'économie, entre la pensée et la structure sociale, entre la

41 'Relisons donc Huizinga dans une perspective d'aujourd'hui. En nous rappelant que, hier, il déchira le voile d'une histoire orgueilleusement impassible et que pour nous, s'il peut être par ses à peu près, son esthétisme, son dilettantisme, un maître d'erreur, il est encore un ouvreur de portes qui mènent à l'histoire à faire' (Mettra, 'Entretien de Claude Mettra avec Jacques Le Goff', p. x).

> psychologie collective et les états sociaux rentre dans nos préoccupations. De l'économie pure, nous en avons; des historiens économistes, au sens étroit du mot, nous en avons: mais des hommes capables comme vous de nouer avec talent, un lien entre art, moeurs, état social, pensées collectives ou individuelles, il n'y en a pas des masses; et c'est par cela que personnellement, je tiens beaucoup à votre collaboration.[42]
>
> [Of course not! You are too modest, and you assign the *Annales* too limited a purpose! There are various sorts of excellent things you have written that are fit for the *Annales*! All the chapters of your *Decline of the Middle Ages* could have been published in it, one after the other. Everything that ties together art and economy, thought and social structure, collective psychology and social structure are of interest to us. Purely economic studies, we have them; economic historians in the strict sense of the word, we have them: but men like you who are able to connect art, habits, social groups, collective or individual thought, in a talented way [...] men of that kind are not that numerous. And this is why I personally would appreciate your collaboration.]

But Huizinga's way of thinking was not Marc Bloch's, and it was certainly no anticipation of sociological methods such as Pierre Bourdieu's. Structures are not at stake in Johan Huizinga's work.[43] As Huizinga himself declared when he evoked the morphology of history, cultural history should not serve sociology.[44] And in his work, we cannot find any attempts at the kind of comparative history so dear to Bloch. Indeed, Bloch's correspondence with Febvre indicates that he was not fond of Huizinga's work.[45] As Christophe de Voogd characterized him, Huizinga was as elusive as an eel in the hands of a fisherman. His ideas did not constitute the reflection of deductive thought found among historians for whom facts must be related in causal patterns. Rather, they were presented to the reader as in a medieval polyptych, using associations of images. And all of these metaphors, metonymies, musical images, etc. which so irritate many historians are not just figures of rhetorical style but rather the

42 Simons, 'The *Annales* and Medieval Studies in the Low Countries', p. 110, quoting Johan Huizinga, *Briefwisseling*, II, pp. 485, no. 1056.

43 See the reflections of Huizinga himself on cultural history in Huizinga, *De taak der cultuurgeschiedenis*. See also, Körner, 'Culture et structure', p. 55-63.

44 *VW*, VII, p. 76: 'Dat wil niet zeggen, dat de cultuurgeschiedenis zich nu toch maar in den dienst zou moeten stellen der sociologie. De cultuurgeschiedenis beschouwt de verschijnselen in hun eigen treffende belangrijkheid, die voor de sociologie slechts paradigmata zijn.'

45 *Marc Bloch, Lucien Febvre* [...] *Correspondance*, I, p. 462.

elements of the 'hermeneutic circle' defined by Dilthey.[46] If we want to grasp the conceptualization of the town in *Herfsttij*, we must enter the 'hermeneutic circle', isolate the parts necessary to understanding the whole, and consider his metaphors not as an embellishment of his writing, but as a mirror by which to view urban life.

Huizinga did not refer much to theory, as was common for historians at that time, and when he did it was with his own specific objectives, which were primarily 'esthetic'. His concrete methodological approach was to create an image of the period he was studying by selecting an ensemble of texts and images and trying to understand them as markers of the forms of life and thought within their complex relations. Huizinga's linguistic training served him well in his endeavor to study his textual sources as the vocabulary and syntax of social life, in order to detect the 'forms' of life and thought in a historical period.[47] And he had become interested in symbolism from reading Tylor's *Primitive Culture* as a young man.[48] He later eclectically borrowed various aspects of Dilthey's hermeneutics and Windelband's neo-Kantian philosophy on human sciences, as has been said. Influenced by Dilthey, Huizinga also thought that the *Geisteswissenschaften* should describe the basic values and philosophical outlooks of a culture or an epoch by relating art, ideas, politics, and economic activities to the cultural context to which they belonged as manifestations of life itself within a given historical period. Thus, the historian's purpose was to 'understand' ('verstehen') the mental structures of an era from visible signs in historical sources such as texts and images.[49] In an analogous manner, the neo-Kantian philosopher Heinrich Rickert had conceived of historical 'presentation' ('Darstellung') not only in terms of the reconstruction of history; for him the meaning of any fact could be apprehended only within the collection of empirical data from which it was drawn; its meaning could be grasped within the connecting and unity of facts – something Huizinga had enthusiastically agreed with in his 1905 inaugural lecture and theoretical manifesto for his later *Herfsttij*.[50]

46 De Voogd, *Le miroir de la France*, pp. 18-19.

47 Colie, 'Johan Huizinga', p. 612; Bulhof, 'Johan Huizinga', pp. 201-204.

48 Burke, *What Is Cultural History?*, p. 41.

49 Iggers, *The German Conception*, p. 141. As Dilthey wrote, 'the interpretation of the state of the soul [is linked to] the context of its entire life under the condition of its milieu'. The quotation is translated in Beiser, *The German Historicist Tradition*, p. 348, and see there generally, pp. 345-354.

50 Quoted here from 'Het esthetische bestanddeel van geschiedkundige voorstellingen', in Huizinga, *De hand van Huizinga*, p. 97. Huizinga refers to H. Rickert, *Die Grenzen der naturwissenschaftlichen Begriffsbildung* (Tübingen, Leipzig: Mohr, 1902), p. 313.

In its various forms and variants, German historicism deeply influenced Huizinga; it is impossible to understand his work outside this tradition.

At first sight, Huizinga's criteria for his hermeneutical corpus of texts could not have made him very attentive to urban 'forms', 'images', or 'colors' except through the mirror of elite courtly culture. But, while his sources were primarily drawn from French and Burgundian court chronicles, his history aimed to create a universal picture of medieval culture, as in the art of the Flemish Primitives, in which settings can be difficult to identify. When one looks at the background of the *Madonna with the Chancellor Rolin*, one sees an urban landscape, but which? A Burgundian town? A Flemish one? Autun, Ghent, Bruges, the heavenly Jerusalem? That does not matter; the city situated at the bottom of the hill near the river, where people cross the bridge to visit a market, a church, their home, where they moor boats, keep watch at the gate, etc., is not an identifiable town. It is, instead, the idea of the town, or more precisely the idea of the town in the fifteenth century, the crystallization of daily urban life and a spiritual ideal. In the first chapter of *Herfsttij* ('The Violent Tenor of Life') a few lines are devoted to the town:

> De stad verliep niet zoals onze steden in slordig aangelegde buitenwijken van dorre fabrieken en onnozele landhuisjes, maar lag in haar muur besloten, een afgerond beeld, stekelig van talloze torens. Zo hoog en zwaar de stenen huizen van edelen of koopheren mochten zijn, de kerken bleven met haar omhoogrijzende massa's de aanblik der stad beheersen.[51]

> [The city did not dissipate, as do our cities, into carelessly fashioned, ugly factories and monotonous country homes, but, enclosed by its walls, presented a completely rounded picture that included its innumerable protruding towers. No matter how high and weighty the stone houses of the noblemen and merchants may have been, the churches, with their proudly rising masses of stone, dominated the city silhouettes.]

No mention of belfries, guildhalls or marketplaces in this depiction. The town is dominated by churches, their height, their verticality, and their conquest of space by the peeling of their bells:

> Er was één geluid, dat al het gedruis van het drukke leven steeds overstemde, en dat, hoe bont dooreenklinkend, toch nooit verward, alles tijdelijk ophief in een sfeer van orde: de klokken. De klokken waren in

51 *Herfsttij*, p. 2 (*Autumn*, p. 2).

> het dagelijks leven als waarschuwende goede geesten, die met bekende stem dan rouw, dan blijdschap, dan rust, dan onrust kondigden, dan opriepen, dan vermaanden.[52]
>
> [But one sound always rose above the clamor of busy life and, no matter how much of a tintinnabulation, was never confused with other noises, and, for a moment, lifted everything into an ordered sphere: that of the bells. The bells acted in daily life like concerned good spirits who, with their familiar voices, proclaimed sadness or joy, calm or unrest, assembly or exhortation.]

These few lines are among the rare sentences that Huizinga devoted to the city; in this instance, a city in which he opened the door to the inhabitants' intimacy, their joy, their mourning, their faith, just from the sound of the bells. Another of Van Eyck's masterpieces has the same immediacy. When Van Eyck painted *The Arnolfini Portrait*, although he did not explicitly depict a specific town, Bruges is everywhere in his depiction of rich patricians. The town's wealth is evoked by the oranges gently placed on the windowsill, the amber of the rosary, the luxurious woolens, all alongside the domestic feelings of its inhabitants in the marriage setting, and the essentials of humanity symbolized by the rosary and the little brush: *Ora et labora* (pray and work).[53] These two instruments in the ordinary life of a fifteenth-century woman are hung around a mirror in which we can see Van Eyck himself and another man, perhaps his brother. Just as Van Eyck introduced us to this scene through reflection, the painting – characterized as a performative work or a witness-work by Jacques Derrida – can be compared to the *Herfsttij*. Not surprisingly, Huizinga's first choice of title for *Herfsttij* was *In de Spiegel van Jan van Eyck* (In the mirror of Jan van Eyck).[54]

The world of the fifteenth century – and the town is no exception – is viewed and vivisected via a mirror. The basis of Huizinga's *Herfsttij* is the image and representation; the book is a kind of *spiegel historiael* (historical mirror), a mirror through which Huizinga views the past. In this way, Huizinga saw past mere objects and simplistic facts to reveal the sense of a period. The world of contingencies was not his but values were. When

52 Ibid.

53 For more details, see Greilsammer, *L'envers du tableau*.

54 *VW*, III, p. 4. In his introduction he explains that he quoted especially Chastellain, Gerson, and Eustache Deschamps, not only because he knew them, but because they were the mirror of the spirit of their time.

he spoke of wealth and richness, Huizinga did not evoke the business of merchants and craftsmen, but the sin of greed, the 'impulse of nature and of the flesh'. Without chronological details, without any spatial cues, facts become an expression of a period rather than concrete evidence of it. In a recent compilation of his essays on medieval thought, Umberto Eco paid tribute to Huizinga, who perfectly understood the metaphysical symbolism of a medieval time in which everything was the announcement of another.[55] But Huizinga not only clearly explained how people of the Middle Ages converted their perception of beautiful things into a sense of divine communion, he also wrote *Herfsttij* as an immense analogy to medieval thought, using the same 'court-circuit de la pensée' (a sort of 'shortcut thought'). Hence, for example, he did not need to describe the activities of an urban merchant, he had only to evoke the sin of greed, knowing that readers would easily make the connection. Long before historians would reveal the role Franciscan brothers played in reconciling the faith of the merchant with the time of God, his image perfectly captured the dangers of the commercial economy of the Middle Ages and posed the question of how the quest for riches could be reconciled with faith.

We know that the cornerstone of Huizinga's historical reflection – *aanschouwelijkheid* – is a very difficult notion to translate, but 'perceivability' or perhaps 'illustrativeness' best indicates the sensitive evidence of the image.[56] Via the late-nineteenth-century neo-Kantian influence of thinkers like Windelband, Kant's aesthetical theory – not about art, but about sensitivity – comes to the fore. *Herfsttij* is a perfect demonstration of *historische sensatie* (historical sensation), as De Voogd noted in his doctoral dissertation *Johan Huizinga et les historiens français*.[57] Yet the evocation of the past with aesthetic and sensate elements runs the same risk that novelists do, namely, investing in the consciousness of their protagonists. For example, when Marguerite Yourcenar reflected later upon the writing of her *Memoirs of Hadrian*, she explained that the historical novel can only be a time regained, and is synonymous with the possession of an inner world.[58] The proximity

55 Eco, *Écrits sur la pensée au Moyen Âge*, p. 431.

56 *VW*, VII, p. 21: 'De aanschouwelijkheid is een hoofdvoorwaarde van de historische begripsvorming. In het natuurwetenschappelijk denken, zooals Windelband zegt, overweegt de neiging tot abstractie, in het historische denken die tot aanschouwelijkheid, dat wil zeggen "de individueele levendigheid van het denkbeeldig tegenwoordige voor het geestesoog."'

57 De Voogd, *Le miroir de la France*, pp. 240-241.

58 Yourcenar, 'Carnets de notes de *Mémoires d'Hadrien*', p. 527: 'De notre temps, le roman historique, ou ce que, par commodité on consent à nommer tel, ne peut être que plongé dans un temps retrouvé, prise de possession d'un monde intérieur.'

between these two points of view, that of a novelist and a 'historian', is confusing. A look at Huizinga's depiction of the Holy Innocents Cemetery in fifteenth-century Paris may clarify his theory:

> Nergens was alles wat de dood voor ogen riep zo treffend bijeen als op het kerkhof der Innocents te Parijs. Daar genoot de geest de huivering van het macabere in haar volste mate.[59]

> [Nowhere else was everything concerning death more completely brought together than in the Cemetery of the Innocents in Paris. There one experienced the macabre to the fullest.]

Huizinga used a series of adjectives and key words such as 'horror', 'death', 'horrible', 'bloody', 'pitiful', 'martyrdom', 'crude compassion', 'bones', 'skulls', 'decomposition', and 'death dance', etc., in just a few lines. Not only is the stage set, but we are vividly transported there; we can sense the atmosphere of fear, becoming immediately and intensely familiar with the idea of death in the fifteenth century. While this chapter is certainly not devoted to the city, the entirety of Paris and its inhabitants arise from the graveyard.

> Te midden van het voortdurende begraven en weer opgraven was het er een wandelplaats en een verenigingspunt. Men vond er winkeltjes bij de knekelhuizen en lichte vrouwen onder de arcade. Een ingemetselde kluizenares aan de zijde der kerk ontbrak niet. Soms kwam een bedelmonnik preken op de plaats, die zelf een preek in middeleeuwse stijl was. Soms verzamelde er zich een processie van kinderen: 12500 in getal, zegt de burger van Parijs, allen met kaarsen, die een Innocent naar de Notre Dame en weer terug droegen. Zelfs feesten werden er gegeven. Zozeer was het huiveringwekkende weer alledaags geworden.[60]

> [There amid the continuous burials and exhumations was a promenade and a meeting place. Small shops were found near the bare bones and easy women under the arcades. There was even an aged female recluse who lived in the side of the church. Sometimes a mendicant monk preached in that place that was itself a sermon in the medieval style. Many times processions of children assembled there; 12,500 says the Burgher of Paris, all with candles.

59 *Herfsttij*, p. 145 (*Autumn*, p. 169).
60 *Herfsttij*, p. 146 (*Autumn*, p. 170).

They marched from the Innocents to Notre Dame and back. Even festivities were held there. So much had the dreadful become the familiar.]

As we read this passage, even as we walk with the Parisians among the graves, we easily sense the vitality of the city: the multicolored costumes of prostitutes, the haggling among the shoppers and the din of voices calling back and forth, the acrobatic displays and the mourning rituals and prayers of the processions, as we taste the air filled with the mixed fragrances of wine and incense, mud and decay. When we read Huizinga, scents, colors and sounds interact, like in Charles Baudelaire's *Correspondances*. This synesthesia can be jarring in a work of historical writing. While we can allow that the text is certainly pleasingly evocative, it does not give us sufficient knowledge to explain the interaction between devotion and urban life at the end of the Middle Ages. But when Élodie Lecuppre-Desjardin studied the Joyous Entry of Margaret of York, Duchess of Burgundy, in Douai on 19 November 1470, she noted the same atmosphere of ecstatic thrill during the different mystery plays shown to the princess, the same riot of candlelight, bonfires, music, and intense emotions in this particular wet and windy night that appears in Huizinga's depiction of the Holy Innocents Cemetery. Indeed, *Herfsttij* made sense before the discoveries of archeologists proved that both the dead and the living coexisted in the city centers and that people were sincerely overwhelmed by emotions when they bid farewell – even if, in the 1970s, Philippe Ariès argued that medieval people did not love their children because they were so vulnerable to death![61]

In other words, Huizinga, as an esthetic thinker, successfully pinpointed universal feelings embodied by people of that time. When he explored the society of the fifteenth century, he chose to take on the mantle of a nobleman, not only because 'history from below' was not yet a method and not only because his major sources were chronicles and literature written for the aristocracy, but also because there were, for him, two influential wellsprings of medieval culture: Christianity and chivalry. Hence the introduction of Chapter 7, 'De betekenis van het ridderideaal in oorlog en staatkunde' ('The political and military value of chivalrous ideas'), is not devoted to the great knight Bertrand du Guesclin or to Duke Charles the Bold, but to a very important Ghent burgher: Philip van Artevelde. Huizinga wrote that we are wrong to imagine that men such as Artevelde reveled in *burgerlijk*

61 Ariès, *L'enfant*, p. 29.

simplicity. Rather, Artevelde lived a princely life with minstrels, banquets, luxurious clothing, gold plates, horses, and banners.[62]

The proximity of urban and courtly cultures in the late medieval Low Countries is now well established in scholarship. For example, a rich merchant like Pieter Lansaem, who died in Ypres in 1489, decided to appear on his grave marker not as a merchant with a purse in his hand, but as a knight with a sword.[63] Chivalric and religious ideals shaped urban culture because they were the universal ideals of the Middle Ages. Huizinga was wrong in ascribing the imitation of knights by the little people of Ghent, jousting from the backs of nags, to a childish spirit. But he was right in evoking this kind of behavior nevertheless. It was simply acculturation. Indeed, chivalric culture was so assimilated by urban people that it produced a particular kind of expression with urban tournaments, anthroponomy imitated from Chretien de Troycs' heroes, material culture shared by nobles, princes and rich burghers. And feudal ideology itself – based on the exchange of rights and duties and not servile allegiance – was certainly exemplified by urban acculturation in the north, where dukes and counts during their Joyous Entries had to promise to protect their towns before their city dwellers who in turn swore loyalty to their prince.

Thus, *Herfsttij* reads like a mirror of the Middle Ages in which towns did not escape from its sight. The civic landscape was distorted by the mirror's convexity, in which some elements are magnified and others disappear toward the edges. Huizinga was not a historian of whom one could expect an *histoire totale* taking into account the life and thought forms of all social classes, including the downtrodden peasants, urban workers, or even the rich merchants. Yet he introduced us to an aesthetic vision, one closer to the thought of Thomas Aquinas than to those of his contemporaries. According to Aquinas, beauty is an intelligible path to divine revelation. Let us treasure this way of writing history, itself inspired by medieval scholars, as means to help us to make sense of the Middle Ages, not as a particular period, but as a wonder, a revelation of the medieval way of life and thinking.

In the end, however, Huizinga's approach clearly had its shortcomings. Although his hermeneutic method certainly proved itself both fruitful and evocative, it was too singular. Huizinga's only lens for focusing his mirror was that of court culture; he almost entirely ignored the riches of the urban world of fifteenth-century Flanders, Brabant and Holland, and the sources it

62 This 'vivre noblement' of the urban Low Countries is recently better understood thanks to Buylaert, De Clercq and Dumolyn, 'Sumptuary Legislation'.

63 See Lecuppre-Desjardin, 'La ville, creuset des cultures urbaines et princières', pp. 289-304.

produced. But we should bear in mind the reasons for this limitation, namely, the central objective of Huizinga's book, an examination of the question of periodization and the distinctive forms of life and thought of the *siècle de Bourgogne*. While his was an incomplete approach to the problem, the methodological lessons to be drawn from the great Dutch scholar's way of seeing and visualizing later medieval culture will continue to remain crucial.

About the Authors

Jan Dumolyn (1974) is Senior Lecturer in Medieval History at the Henri Pirenne Institute for Medieval Studies, Ghent University. He has published widely on the political, social and cultural history of medieval Flanders and, in particular, on urban society, most recently having coauthored (with Andrew Brown) *Medieval Bruges, 850-1550* (Cambridge University Press, 2018).
Jan.Dumolyn@ugent.be

Elodie Lecuppre-Desjardin is Professor of Medieval History in the University of Lille (IRHiS). She is a specialist of urban society in medieval Low Countries, and of political and cultural history. Among numerous books and articles, she has recently published *Le royaume inachevé des ducs de Bourgogne* (Belin, 2016).
elodie.lecuppre@univ-lille.fr

4 The Forms behind the *Vormen*

Huizinga, New Cultural History, and the Culture of Commerce

Jun Cho

Abstract

This chapter draws on the insights of Huizinga's *Autumn of the Middle Ages* and the field of cultural history to argue that an investigation into the forms behind the *vormen* (forms) of the Burgundian court can shed light on a dimension of its culture that at once disrupts and affirms Huizinga's legacies. By revisiting chronicle episodes relished by Huizinga, and analyzing sources from the milieu that Huizinga cherished, this chapter shows how the famed cultural forms of the princely court also embodied commercial virtues as well as political functions. The reworking of 'magnificence' by Burgundian courtiers at the end of the fifteenth century reveals how a medieval understanding of magnanimity as an aristocratic and martial virtue gave way to magnificence as a princely and fiscal imperative. Thus, the 'forms of life' (*levensvormen*) expressed in the splendor of the Burgundian court were plays of magnificence, and in turn, testimonies of commercial prowess.

Keywords: Huizinga, new cultural history, Burgundian court, market culture, magnificence

It is the forms of life and thought that are used as evidence here.
To seize the essential content that resides in those forms –
will that ever be the task of historical inquiry? –[1]
– Johan Huizinga

1 Huizinga, *Herfsttij* (17th ed.), p. viii. I follow Walter Simon's translation in his review in *Speculum* 72:2, p. 491.

Arnade, Peter, Martha Howell, and Anton van der Lem (eds), *Rereading Huizinga: Autumn of the Middle Ages, a Century Later.* Taylor & Francis Group, 2019
DOI: 10.5117/9789462983724_CH04

1

For many students of medieval history, *The Autumn of the Middle Ages* has been a beloved work that seemed to capture the dreams, the ethos, even the senses of an age, so removed and so different from our own.[2] By brilliantly evoking the 'forms of life, thought and art in France and the Netherlands in the fourteenth and fifteenth centuries', Johan Huizinga painted a portrait of late medieval civilization that has continuously ignited interest in the period and colored popular, as well as scholarly, understanding of those centuries.[3] From his opening comment that life back then 'bore the mixed sense of blood and of roses', to his assertion that ideals took 'the path of the dream, a promise of escape from the gloomy actual', his ability to bring alive the 'otherness' of medieval culture has captivated modern minds.[4] Furthermore, while the initial reception of his work in his home country, the Netherlands, may have been lukewarm, the reputation and influence of his work flourished in the third quarter of the twentieth century, as it entered into the canons of Western Civilization courses, namely at the University of Chicago, and it was rediscovered as a pioneering work in new cultural history.[5]

In this author's estimation, the enduring attraction of Huizinga's *Autumn* also stems from a twofold reception of his work. First, it provided a vision of northwestern Europe in the fourteenth and fifteenth century as the final blossoming of a medieval chivalric culture, rather than the dawn of a new era. It was a vision of a world lost to us, rather than contiguous

2 Huizinga, *Waning*. The 1924 Hopman translation, an abridged version approved by Huizinga, has been the standard beloved version in the Anglophone world. The continuing influence of Huizinga's work, beyond the confines of the Western world, is attested by new translations in Chinese (2014), Korean (2010), Japanese (2001), increasing the number of languages the work has been translated into to 21, according to www.worldcat.org.

3 As, Peters and Simons, 'The New Huizinga', notes, 'art' was missing in the original Dutch title but added to the unpublished French and the abridged English editions, under Huizinga's guidance. Even the immensely popular HBO TV series *Game of Thrones*, set in a fantasy medieval world, bleak and violent, in which chivalry is a hollowed out ideal, seems to adhere to the overall tone of Huizinga's *Waning*.

4 Huizinga, *Waning*, pp. 25, 37; Burke, 'Huizinga', p. 23.

5 The history of its immediate reception is well documented in Hugenholtz, 'The Fame', pp. 91-103. He notes that it is a myth that Huizinga was dismayed by the cool reception and thus sought to buttress his credentials as an historian by attacking historicism, as was put forward by Ter Braak. Also summarized in Peters and Simons, 'The New Huizinga', pp. 614-617, and Burke, *What Is Cultural History?*, pp. 7-11, 41-50. Weintraub, *Visions*, is a veritable genealogy of 'old' cultural history, but as R.L. Colie notes in her review of the book 'of all the writers, only Burckhardt and Huizinga produced what are still recognized as model studies in the genre'.

to our own. Conceived as a work to place Van Eyck's artwork in historical context, *Autumn* was also a response to Burckhardt's characterization of Renaissance Italy as the birth of the modern world and the subsequent debate about the existence of a similar and parallel 'Northern Renaissance' in the Low Countries.[6] In contrast to Burckhardt, Huizinga imbued the fifteenth-century north with a tone of 'melancholy gravity' and 'general gloom' that was 'still medieval at heart'. At the same time, Huizinga pointed out that 'the distance separating Italy from the Western countries and the Renaissance from the Middle Ages' had been 'exaggerated'.[7] In the northern world, medieval civilization was famously 'in its last phase of life, as a tree with overripe fruits, fully unfolded and developed'.[8] This characterization by Huizinga, though at times misunderstood as 'nostalgia', was crucial, as it allowed the later Middle Ages to be viewed in its own right, through its own eyes, rather than distorted and dismissed by a modernizing lens.

Second, Huizinga's *Autumn* provided a vision of history different from the positivist tendencies of the early twentieth century and akin to the new concerns of the post-1960s, especially the 'cultural turn'. In this, Huizinga was an heir to the concerns and interests of Burckhardt, even if their conclusions differed markedly. Huizinga's 'path' to this approach to medieval history, as he relates himself, was more fortuitous than deliberate, but his commitment to 'cultural history' was unwavering.[9] Partially a result of his own unorthodox training as well as his fascination with all things medieval and discomfort with the historiography of his time, Huizinga's central quest was to gain a 'sense of a direct contact with the past', what he coined, 'historical sensation'.[10] The inspiration for this idea of history seems to be diverse: modern reviews have highlighted his embrace of diverse disciplinary approaches – from art history, anthropology, sociology and notably religious psychology – while Dutch commentators have pointed out the intellectual ferment of fin de siècle Netherlands.[11] In turn, Huizinga inspired a few,

6 Burckhardt, *Civilization of the Renaissance*. Tollebeek, '"Renaissance"'.

7 Huizinga, *Waning*, pp. 308, 318, 67.

8 Huizinga, *Autumn*, p. xix.

9 Huizinga, 'My Path to History', pp. 262-275. Yet he does charmingly and shyly mention that he had a life long 'secret vice', a keenness for heraldry, in all its manifestations, 'its helmets, coats of arms, shields, [...] what have you'. His thoughts on history are outlined in 'The Task' and 'The Idea' (originally delivered as a lecture in 1934).

10 Huizinga, 'The Task', pp. 51-55.

11 Peters and Simons, 'The New Huizinga'; Shaw, 'Huizinga's Timeliness', pp. 245-258; Bulhof, 'Johan Huizinga'; Krul, 'In the Mirror'. As for Dutch commentaries, see Kossmann, 'Postscript', and more recently Krul, *Historicus*. Peters and Simons, 'The New Huizinga', especially highlights the crucial role of André Jolles.

albeit important, intellectuals, such as Ernst Kantorowicz, Nobert Elias, and later Ernst Gombrich, Philippe Ariès, and Stephen Greenblatt.[12] By the centennial of his birth, Huizinga was well on the way to being embraced by the French Annales school and their turn to '*mentalité*', celebrated as a pioneer of 'new cultural history' in Anglo-American academia, and rehabilitated in his country of birth.[13] In fact, Huizinga firmly established the study of what he called 'cultural forms' ('cultuurvormen') or 'forms of life' ('levensvormen') – such as 'service, honour, fidelity, obedience, imitation, resistance, [...] vanity'[14] – as a valid and critical subject of historical inquiry. Thus, even when many historians disavowed his characterizations or conclusions on specific periods, topics, or figures, they have still fruitfully explored realms beyond what Huizinga himself imagined.

Yet, I argue, we have not quite 'disposed of his legacy' in the sense of utilizing and hence multiplying the 'talents' given to us by Huizinga, to paraphrase Rosalie Colie's critical yet warm reflection on his life and works half a century ago.[15] Contrary to many critiques of Huizinga in general and his *Autumn* in particular, Huizinga was not unaware of the political functions or stakes of chivalric and courtly ritual, or the sophistication of administrative and fiscal instruments, or the critical role of towns and commerce in this period. He sprinkled awareness of such historical trends, which were heavily researched by his contemporaries, and did not shy away from providing such analysis in his later works on different subjects – most conspicuously his report on American civilization that he published before his *Autumn*.[16] But in *Autumn*, he did not deem these subjects worth pursuing in his conception of the Burgundian cultural history he crafted. That said, a careful probing into the forms (documents) that reveal how the 'forms of life, thought and art' play out in the Burgundian court can lead us to apply Huizinga's insight into fields where he did not venture. Just as the works of Natalie Zemon Davis or Caroline Bynum have drawn on his approach to broach questions of political culture and gender, they can be likewise applied to questions of commerce. Such a fruitful cross-breeding of 'economic forms' and 'cultural forms' sheds light on a dimension of Burgundian court culture

12 Peters and Simons, 'The New Huizinga'; Jardine, 'The Afterlife'.

13 Breisach, *Historiography*, p. 425; Peters and Simons, 'The New Huizinga', pp. 616-617.

14 Huizinga, 'The Task', 66-67.

15 Colie, 'Huizinga', p. 630.

16 Huizinga, *America*. His writings on America, both before and after he visited the US in person, focused on an *economic* explanation of the peculiarities of American civilization, which he considered emblematic of modern civilization (unmoored from the weight of the past conspicuous in Europe).

that at once disrupts and affirms Huizinga's legacies.[17] In what follows, I would like to sketch one instance of how such cross-breeding might occur by examining an event highlighted by Huizinga himself and excavating the forms behind them.

2

In highlighting how 'life had still colors of a fairy tale' in the Middle Ages, Huizinga provided as evidence an incident related by Chastellain about Charles the Bold.[18] After a quarrel with his father the duke, Charles is stripped of his pensions and benefits. Despondent, Charles calls together his whole retinue, courtiers and household servants, and solemnly tells them he cannot retain them and asks for them to either leave until his status is rehabilitated or remain on their own resources. The crowd weeps and shouts in common that 'we all, my lord, will live and die with you'. Charles, moved by their loyalty, replies, 'Stay and suffer, and I will suffer for you, rather than see you in want.' Then 'lords, gentlemen, notable persons, all offer to him themselves, and their money, and all fine things', so much so that, as Huizinga playfully quotes, 'there was never a hen the less in the kitchen' and more interestingly, as Huizinga omits but is documented by Chastellain, there was 'accounting of expenses of *escrous* and the raising of *gages* and *pensions ordinnaires*'.[19]

Huizinga relished relating this story. As he noted, Chastellain must have touched up this incident. Chastellain himself was not present in that entourage nor did he name any person from whom he heard about it. Likewise, the lack of specific names and the amounts pledged calls into question the incident's veracity. Because Chastellain's focus was the personalities of the historical characters he depicted, he used most of his ink on the moving speech by Charles; there was scant consideration of exactly how Charles was able to overcome the loss of financial support from his father. Chastellain just seemed happy to report that it all ended well. It is a perfect example of Chastellain's narrative style: dramatizing the events as if they were an episode of a chivalric romance. Just like a band of knights, on a

17 This can also be considered as one way of reconciling the diverging interests of his senior and counterpart, Henri Pirenne, and Huizinga. On the fundamental disagreement yet mutual respect between the two historians, see Boone, '"L'automne du Moyen Age"'.

18 Huizinga, *Waning*, p. 15; *Autumn*, pp. 9-10; *Herfsttij*, pp. 7-8.

19 Chastellain, *Oeuvres*, IV, pp. 331-337.

quest together, tightening their bonds in times of troubles, the retinue of Count Charles pledged support to one another and thereby survived intact. This, according to Chastellain, was the important point, and this, according to Huizinga, was how Burgundian courtiers gave meaning to their affairs. And if even Chastellain was obliged to color this breach between the prince and his designated heir in 'the guise of a ballad', then to the uneducated, Huizinga exclaimed, 'how brilliant must royal life have appeared, when displayed in almost magical splendour!'[20]

However, both Huizinga and Chastellain were also clearly aware that these stories were deliberately cloaking their underlying details and that there was a financial underbelly that provided for the 'hen'. Huizinga immediately qualifies this story with the observation that 'in reality the mechanism of government had already assumed rather complicated forms', though he proceeds to elaborate that 'the popular mind pictures it in simple and fixed figures [...] which corresponds, more or less, to literary motifs'. Chastellain himself mentions the *escrous* and *gages* and *pensions ordinnaires*; as a supplicant and recipient of them, Chastellain was also clearly aware of the indispensable expenditures of the princely court and household.[21] Thus, behind the cultural form of a 'ballad' of errantry were measures and maneuvers taken to uphold the 'magical splendor' necessary to the comital retinue. What were they, and why were they rendered in this literary style?

It is difficult to pinpoint the exact events and affairs that are cloaked behind this story. If the reports of a Saxon diplomat are to be believed, the cutting of funding most likely happened in late 1463.[22] However, the one specific detail in the story, that Charles had 'left Sluis and arrived at Gorinchem' provides sufficient context.[23] Gorinchem was Charles' central base in Holland. After constituting his own court in 1456, and thus leaving the court of his father, Charles needed to secure revenue beyond the annual rent granted by his father. Charles had recently acquired lordship of this strategic town, as well as several others in Holland.[24] He had drawn close

20 Huizinga, *Waning*, p. 15.

21 Small, *George Chastelain*.

22 Vaughan, *Philip the Good*, p. 345.

23 Huizinga, *Waning*, p. 115.

24 The serious breach between the reigning prince, Philip the Good, and his heir apparent destabilized Burgundian politics in the mid-1460s. The political dimension was fueled by the rivalry and mutual suspicion between the newly ascendant Croy family and Charles, as well as Charles's frustration with his father's pro-French policies in the 1460s, notably the return of the Somme towns. But the financial dimension was Charles's effort to secure a stable revenue stream, independent of the annual rents granted by his father.

to several prominent Hollanders, including Anthon Michiels, who was previously the receiver-general of Holland and Zeeland, and members of the patrician Boschuysen family from Leiden.[25] Soon after arriving in Gorinchem he secured the right to be the heir of his father in Holland and Zeeland. In essence, though not all the details are clear, the surviving documents from the time reveal that Charles had been building up an independent power and revenue base, sufficient for the operation of his own court, by 1463.[26] The colorful paternal breach narrated in the chronicles most likely was an affirmation of this feat as well.

This interlocking of fiscal forms of revenue acquisition and the life forms of chivalric adventure conclude together in the visual sight of an orderly and prosperous household: one that does not lack provisions, one that could uphold the princely splendor. As Chastellain proclaimed, and Huizinga quotes, 'After the deeds and exploits of war, which are claims to glory, the household is the first thing that strikes the eye, and that which it is, therefore, most necessary to conduct and arrange well'.[27] Yet this raises the question anew of how to square these two forms: the literary and the fiscal. I suggest by reinterpreting one key 'cultural form' – magnificence, whose qualities Burgundian courtiers and Huizinga knew well – we can uncover the 'commercial form' that lurked within it.

3

As Huizinga grasped, the cultural forms of the era were not so much detached from the reality as a specific response to that reality. The response he identified for Burgundian court culture was one of 'escape' rather than 'reform' or 'detachment', but it was a response nonetheless that was a 'poetic solution' in which 'life is regulated as a noble game'. The chivalric culture of the court provides an 'aristocratic game' that also served a social function.[28] Huizinga was also explicitly aware of 'the political and military values of chivalrous ideas' and did mention some of the social hierarchical functions they served. Could not, therefore, the 'forms of life' of a Burgundian courtier also reconcile the chivalric with the commercial? If we follow the steps of

25 Van Steensel, 'Noblemen', p. 92. Most likely originally a member of the Michiel family of Lille who were confidents of Charles the Bold. Jan van Boschuysen joined the court not later than 1454, first as a valet. Buylaert, 'The "Van Boschuysen Affair"', p. 104.

26 Only the account of 1457 survives for the court of Charles the Bold during this period.

27 Huizinga, *Waning*, p. 39; Chastellain, *Oeuvres*, V, p. 364.

28 Huizinga, *Waning*, p. 37.

other new cultural historians and add the insight of Huizinga's later, more mature work, *Homo ludens*, the distance between the court and commerce, between the ceremonies and tournaments of chivalry and the bustling and hustling of the market may not be as far as we often assume.

In *Homo ludens*, Huizinga ascribed several formal characteristics to play: that it is voluntary (freedom), distinct from the 'ordinary', and 'played out' within certain time and places. The outcome of play is also uncertain, follows its own rules and 'creates order', and 'promotes the formation of groupings which tend to surround themselves with secrecy and to stress their difference from the common world'.[29] Each and every one of these qualities of play can be ascribed to the market and its exchange as much as to the competition of tournaments and rituals of ceremonies! It was not simply, as scholars have long agreed, that commerce depended on courtly extravagance and that courtly extravagance, in turn, depended on commerce. Rather, the court and commerce were parallel games that could be played out in similar ways.

To sketch a prime example of how this amalgam was realized in the Burgundian circles, I would like to draw attention to the Burgundian reimagining of the idea of 'magnificence'.[30] Even before it received full theorization in the Italian Renaissance, magnificence was an ideal that had gained currency since the European rediscovery of many of Aristotle's texts and their incorporation into the works of Thomas Aquinas.[31] In addition, especially thanks to its fascination with Alexander the Great, the Burgundian court was well aware of how the idea of magnificence was rendered in antiquity.[32] To the Burgundians, this 'magnificence' could be deployed to

29 Huizinga, *Homo ludens*, pp. 7-12.

30 Art historians have long considered 'magnificence' a major underlying theme in the Italian Renaissance. Ernst Gombrich first called attention to the idea in his 'The Early Medici', pp. 279-311. It was given scholarly elaboration by A.D. Fraser Jenkins in his seminal 'Cosimo de' Medici's', pp. 162-170. Scholars such as Dale Kent, Francis Kent, and James Lindow have examined how the idea justified and guided grand building projects in Renaissance Italy. See also, Goldthwaite, *Wealth and the Demand for Art*, pp. 206-208, 220-221. For the Burgundian Netherlands, Campbell, *Tapestry*, uses the idea of 'magnificence' to explain the phenomena of tapestries in princely circles, but doesn't elaborate on a specific Burgundian understanding of the concept.

31 On the circulation and reformulation of Aristotelian and Thomist thought in the Low Countries, see Vanderjagt, 'Burgundian Political Ideas'. For instance, a copy of Nicolas Oresme's French translation of Aristotle's *Nichomachean Ethics* is listed in the 1467 inventory of the ducal library in Bruges, and currently preserved as MS 9505-9506 in Brussels, Bibliothèque Royale.

32 The Burgundian fascination with Alexander the Great is well attested in the patronage of various manuscripts and tapestries that depicted Alexander the Great. Most famously, Philip the Good commissioned Jehan Wauquelin to compile a great history of Alexander the Great in 1448. Blondeau, 'A Very Burgundian Hero', pp. 27-42, provides an useful overview of the phenomena

lend legitimacy to a burgeoning dynastic power that lacked royal lineage or territorial integrity. Furthermore, when magnificence was firmly tied to great expenditure and largess, it would justify and channel the production and consumption of commercial wealth into a courtly virtue. This process of adapting and appropriating the concept of magnificence was worked out in Burgundian circles and realized in its court rituals.

The essential act of magnificence, as Aquinas unequivocally stated, was to do a great thing, which was reserved for a great man, and often for a singular occasion.[33] Still, Aquinas did not elaborate on how a magnificent deed could be accomplished. It was only in the second half of the fifteenth century, during the age of Burgundian splendor, that humanists in Italy advanced a theory of magnificence.[34] Theirs was a magnificence materially achieved by rulers who were great builders, whether of cityscapes, urban palaces, or public buildings – an idea that would be influential into the following century. The Burgundian court, I argue, was practicing a similar but distinct concept of magnificence, one more deeply rooted in medieval chivalric ideals but also reflecting commercial virtues, realized through singular occasions such as court festivals, urban processions, and public performances.

The Burgundian treatise on princely conduct and governance, *Instructions for a young prince* (*L'instruction d'un jeune prince*), perfectly captures the Burgundian attention to magnificence and its link to commerce.[35] The actual author is anonymous, but literary historians have generally attributed it to Ghillebert de Lannoy, though recently his brother, Hugo, has been suggested as the author as well.[36] Regardless of whether it was Ghillebert or Hugo, the Lannoy brothers were natives of Walloon Flanders, loyal vassals of the Burgundian dukes, and members of the Order of the Knights of the Golden Fleece, the prestigious and highest honor in the Burgundian court. They both had extensive experience as combatants in the Hundred Years' War, as diplomats in service of the dukes across Europe, and as governors

and considers that in the figure of Alexander the Great, the Burgundian dukes saw a model for their crusades (conquest of the east) and a justification of their territorial expansion and autonomy vis-à-vis the French monarchy.

33 Aquinas, *Summa Theologica*, II-II, Q. 134, A.1.

34 Giuniano Maio's *On Majesty* (1492) and Giovanni Pontano's *On Splendor* (1498) provided full theorization of the concept. Howard, 'Preaching Magnificence', sees the ideal appearing earlier in the fifteenth century and in wider fields such as oratory.

35 The modern critical edition is C.G. van Leeuwen's *Denkbeelden* and below I quote from his reproduction. The exact dating of the book is not known, though most scholars agree that it was sometime between 1435 and 1442.

36 Sterchi, 'Hugo de Lannoy', pp. 79-117.

of Burgundian territory, the fort of Sluis and the county of Holland and Zeeland, respectively.[37] As the title also notes, *Instructions* was written to be presented to a 'young prince', evidently Philip's son Charles the Bold, then still in his childhood. Though there is no evidence that Philip commissioned the work for his son, it retained a place in the library of Charles the Bold. A court painter lavishly illustrated the manuscript with a miniature of the treatise presented to the young Charles.[38]

Even more than the *Chronicles* of Chastellain, the *Instructions* provides a more courtly understanding of chivalric yet commercial ideals that resonated in Burgundian court circles. Whether Ghillebert or Hugo was the author, the Lannoy brothers were not systematic philosophers or scholastic clergymen in the mould of Aristotle or Aquinas. Rather they were practical men of the world – warriors, diplomats and statesmen, in service of a temporal lord. *Instructions* does not seek to strictly delineate the differences or analyze the relations among the various concepts presented in the treatise. Nor does it try to forge or develop a new definition, as the heavy debt to Aquinas and Aristotle shows. Rather the author of the text is trying to make classical virtues relevant and practically useful in the lives of his contemporaries in a changing world, to use inherited language to help the prince navigate the varied, murky landscape of the late medieval and early modern era.

In the *Instructions*' advice, we see a sense of magnificence derived foremost from a chivalric ideal in which martial courage and prowess are paramount, but is subtly transforming into a courtly notion of greatness in mind and deeds, projected through cultural projects, presented in public and dependent on great finance. After a short first chapter on 'fearing God as the first commandment of wisdom', the second chapter focuses on the personal virtues that a prince must attain in order to maintain justice as the first commandment of law. Lannoy mentions that a prince must have the 'four cardinal virtues' of 'prudence, justice, continence, and fortitude'.[39] In this sense, he is following a well-established medieval tradition for articulating the classical virtues of antiquity. Yet the small changes he makes are quite telling. Whereas Aquinas had stated that the three Christian virtues of 'faith, hope, and charity' were guiding principles

37 Loise, 'Ghillebert de Lannoy'; Wauters, 'Hugues de Lannoy'; Paviot, 'Ghillebert de Lannoy', pp. 42-45.

38 Jean Hennequart, *peintre et valet de chambre du duc*, was paid a sum of 11 £ 17 s. in September 1470 to illustrate *L'instrucion de joisne prince* and other parchments. *Compte*, vol. 3, no. 2310. The manuscript is preserved as MS 10967 in Brussels, Bibliothèque Royale, and MS 5104 in Paris, Bibliothèque de l'Arsenal.

39 Van Leeuwen, *Denkbeelden*, p. 12.

for the four classical virtues, Lannoy subsumed these three Christian virtues under an explanation of the first cardinal virtue of 'prudence'.[40] He also reshuffles the traditional arrangement of the four cardinal virtues used by Aquinas, switching continence to the third and fortitude to the fourth place (Aquinas's order was 'prudence, justice, fortitude, and continence'). This change of scheme, though minor, allows him to briefly discuss the first three and then permits him to dwell almost exclusively and most extensively on the fourth virtue of 'fortitude' which he explains is 'also called magnanimity, greatness of soul, or force of courage'.[41]

Lannoy's decision to let these qualities equal and also define the fourth and most important virtue of fortitude signals Lannoy's intent to join several ideas under one rubric. Formally, Aquinas had divided fortitude into several parts made up of magnanimity, magnificence, patience, and perseverance.[42] Aquinas narrowly used the term magnanimity as 'stretching forth of the mind to great things' while magnificence was, for him, literally 'to do something great'. Likewise, patience was considered to 'safeguard the good of reason against sorrow', while perseverance was to 'persist long in something good until it is accomplished'. Such distinctions or precisions are lost on Lannoy, for in his explanation:

> Magnanimity is the fourth of the virtues which we must greatly honor, because no knight of great renown has ever undertaken valor in arms, worthy of memory, without its company, aid and comfort. This virtue according to our language means that force of courage or boldness that belongs especially to princes and knights. Because of her nature, she is reinforced against all that can befall: against lance, bombardment, cannon, torment of sea, harshness of winter, fervor of summer, and great number of enemies, and cities, forts, castles enclosed in walls.[43]

For Lannoy, the various elements of fortitude that in Aquinas's telling combined to make it a cardinal virtue are effaced and we are left with one

40 Ibid. In Aquinas's terminology, the three virtues of 'faith, hope and charity' are 'theological' virtues. They retain a different category since they are considered to reflect the nature of the divine and thus are gifts of God rather than merits attained by human endeavor. Lannoy seems to do away with such distinctions and offers 'faith, hope and charity' as a companion to assist prudence, the 'foundation' of all virtues.

41 Van Leeuwen, *Denkbeelden*, p. 12: 'force que aulcuns nomment magnanimité, haultesse de coeur ou force de courage'.

42 Aquinas, *Summa Theologica*, II-II, Q. 128.

43 Van Leeuwen, *Denkbeelden*, p. 14.

martial virtue, namely, magnanimity. It is a chivalric virtue shared by the knight and his prince, equipping them to undertake hardship and gain renown. Though this virtue needs to be tempered by 'reason and justice', still neither 'the spilling of blood' nor even 'death' can stop a knight from the pursuit of 'honor and great fame'.[44]

Yet this traditional notion of magnanimity as a martial virtue would face difficulty in the face of changed reality, and Lannoy switches the emphasis from 'force of courage' toward the 'greatness of soul'. The traditional path for a knight to glory is martial, but as Lannoy's fifth chapter on war makes clear – most likely based on his experience of the Hundred Years' War – he sees war as detrimental to the common good and urges the prince to keep the peace.[45] Thus, addressing the prince directly, Lannoy shifts this fourth virtue (fortitude rendered as magnanimity) away from simple courage and martial prowess into a series of recommendations that implore the prince to pursue loftier achievements.[46] Much of the advice emphasizes the need to exercise justice and magnanimity and to be generous and gracious to his vassals and people: the prince should keep his word to his subjects, the prince should not harshly punish, the prince should listen to all sides, etc.[47] Though Lannoy does not specify the deeds by which the prince may gain renown, the practical dimension of the fourth virtue is not to pursue martial feats but to practice acts that benefit the common good and elevate the prince, positioning him as a higher authority.

This turn from fortitude to magnanimity opens the way to a discussion of largess and liberality, concepts that were often confused and fused with magnificence. In his *Ethics*, for example, Aristotle discussed magnificence after liberality, commenting that 'the magnificent man [...] can discern what is suitable, and spend great sums with good taste. [...] The magnificent man will therefore necessarily be also a liberal man'.[48] Lannoy also emphasized that 'largess and liberality in all things belong to princes and grand lords, because they are praised and acknowledged'.[49] The bestowal

44 Ibid.

45 Ibid., pp. 30-32.

46 Furthermore, according to C.G. van Leeuwen, compared to Lannoy's other treatise, *l'Enseignement de vraie noblesse*, it is from this point onward that Lannoy adds a specifically princely dimension to this fourth virtue.

47 Van Leeuwen, *Denkbeelden*, pp. 14-15. As part of his advice regarding the good deeds that the prince should strive for, Lannoy enters into a long digression about the ancient knightly virtue of 'francise', which the prince, also as a knight, should also hold and maintain.

48 Aristotle, *Nichomachean Ethics*, 1122a-b.

49 Van Leeuwen, *Denkbeelden*, p. 16.

of gifts, and generosity more generally, constitutes magnificence. But as Aquinas articulated, the gifts princes distributed should not be understood as mere distributions of wealth: 'The magnificent man also makes gifts of presents [...] but not under the aspect of gift, but rather [...] in order to honor someone, or in order to do something which will reflect honor on the whole state'.[50] So, Lannoy next hastened to add that the prince should avoid 'men of base condition' and 'keep company and enjoy pleasures and festivities with noble men, sages and the well-known'.[51] It was the prerogative and the privilege of the prince to bestow gifts to honor his subjects, and doing so lavishly yet artfully would be the true mark of magnificence.

For even greater effect, Lannoy invoked the example of the Philosopher and Alexander the Great: 'as testified by Aristotle, who in the advice that he made to King Alexander, pointed out that, for a prince who gives generously, there is no need to build a strong castle'.[52] This had a double effect. First, it brought discussion of the fourth virtue around full circle. As courage was a necessary component of magnanimity, largess was a necessary component of magnificence, and furthermore, in his metaphor and in practical terms, such magnificence was greater than the initial martial aspect: largess bests a fortress. Second, it invoked the magnificence of King Alexander's court, a subject of fascination in Burgundian circles. For the Burgundian dukes, Alexander the Great was the historical embodiment of princely magnificence. Philip the Good had commissioned a series of tapestries that depicted scenes from the *Romance of Alexander* (*Roman d'Alexandre*), while Charles the Bold himself had sponsored the French translation of a biography of Alexander by Quintus Curtius, and had it read to him at night.[53] By conflating the virtues of fortitude and magnanimity, then associating the latter with liberality and largess while evoking the example of Alexander, Lannoy paved the road from a martial and chivalric virtue of fortitude into a courtly and princely virtue of magnificence.

Lannoy was well aware that the practical dimension of realizing such magnificence was finance. In the seventh chapter, where he takes up the subject of princely finances, Lannoy states that 'he who knows the greatness and magnificence which belongs to the prince, ought to know that conduct of his estate belongs to very great finance'.[54] Rather than treat finance as a

50 Aquinas, *Summa Theologica*, II-II, Q. 113. A.3.

51 Van Leeuwen, *Denkbeelden*, p. 16.

52 Ibid.

53 Cockshaw, 'Les manuscripts', pp. 6-9; Vaughan, *Charles the Bold*, pp. 163, 181-182.

54 Van Leeuwen, *Denkbeelden*, p. 35: 'Qui congnoist la haultesse et magnificence qui appartient aux princes, doit sçavoir que a la conduite de leur estat appartient moult grans finances.'

matter not befitting the prince (and better relegated to subordinate officials), he implores the kings and princes to diligently attend to the supervision and government of their finances.[55] He goes on to summarize the traditional (and unrealistic) view that the prince should finance himself from 'his own provisions and his traditional domains'.[56] Extraordinary means of revenue such as gifts, favors, or levying tax or aides or extractions on the people can only be justified for proper defense or benefit to the people or the marriage of princely children.[57] Turning more specifically to the question of expenditure, he cautions that 'war can consume all finance', but he easily justifies money spent on the accoutrements of the court and courtly life, such as clothing, horses and harnesses, equipping the guards, charity and alms, generous gifts to nobles and ambassadors and messengers.[58] These things were the stuff of magnificence, and princes needed to manage their finances to make these prerogatives and privileges possible.

4

This reworking of 'magnificence' as a princely virtue, incorporating commercial values and financial prerogatives, becomes fully realized as a governing idea in the circles of Charles the Bold. The most prominent formulator and propagator of such understanding was Guillaume Fillastre the Younger, chancellor of the Order of the Golden Fleece during the reign of Duke Charles. By the time of his appointment as chancellor of the order in 1461, Fillastre was the Bishop of Tournai, having secured the position through the support of Philip the Good.[59] He was also part of the 'second generation' of Burgundian intellectuals who were educated in classical and Christian learnings, in conversation with Italian humanists, and responsible for writing promulgations, ordinances, and treatises which spelt out the political thought of the Burgundian court.[60] Whereas Lannoy showed the way, by separating virtues of nobility from Christian ones, by conflating magnificence with fortitude and magnanimity, and by contemplating the

55 Van Leeuwen, *Denkbeelden*, p. 35.
56 Ibid.: 'vivre du leur et de leurs anciennes demaines'.
57 Ibid.
58 Ibid., pp. 37-38.
59 Prietzel, *Guillaume Fillastre*, provides the fullest account of his life. Prietzel has also compiled and edited his writings, with introductions, in his *Guillaume Fillastre: Ausgewählte Werke* (hereafter *Werke*) and I quote from his reproductions.
60 Vanderjagt, 'Classical Learning', pp. 269, 272.

importance of magnificence in the extended treatment of its substance, Fillastre cemented the change by elevating magnificence as the premier virtue and ordering other virtues along lines that would have been unrecognizable to Aristotle or Aquinas, despite his evident debt to their works.

In 1468, at the first chapter of the Order of the Golden Fleece with Charles the Bold as sovereign of the order, Guillaume Fillastre presented a sermon on princely virtues notable for some novel aspects. This sermon became the basis for Fillastre's *Book of the Golden Fleece*, presented and dedicated to Duke Charles.[61] Drawing on the traditional three Christian virtues and four cardinal virtues which Lannoy had combined, Fillastre presented a new scheme of virtues. As Huizinga happily recounted, the original inspiration for the name 'Order of the Golden Fleece' was the ancient myth of Jason and the Argonauts, whose story seems to have fascinated Philip the Good and appealed to his retinue's sense of camaraderie.[62] However, the pagan origin of the name was problematic, especially as Duke Philip began to contemplate leading a crusade. Thus, within the first decade, Jean Germain of Tournai, the first chancellor of the order, sought to 'Christianize' the symbolism of the order by incorporating the biblical fleece of Gideon. By 1468, when Charles had become Burgundian duke, Fillastre drew on both strands, classical and Christian, but synthesized them in his own way and reordered them into a hierarchy of virtues fit for his prince. Some of his steps are not surprising. He recounted the legend of the Golden Fleece and claimed it as history and not myth, and thus the work of God. He provided an interpretation of the story as an allegorical representation of the redemptive work of Jesus and asserted that six virtues were embodied in the symbol of the 'golden fleece'. The number six itself was not random, but rather the result of a conscious effort to combine both classical and Christian ideals and reconcile the works of his predecessors. Based on mentions of fleece in both ancient mythology and in biblical stories, Fillastre formulated a scheme in which the fleece of different biblical and historical figures represented cardinal virtues: the fleece of Jacob, Gideon, Mesa (King of Moabs), Job, David, as well as Jason. 'Each of the said [six] fleece accords with a virtue belonging to the estate of the nobility'.[63]

The most important aspect is Fillastre's forceful, novel designation of 'magnanimity' or 'magnificence' as the first and most important virtue. 'The first is the fleece of Jason, which, among the six, is the one named or

61 *Werke*, pp. 42-48.

62 Huizinga, *Waning*, pp. 85-86.

63 *Werke*, pp. 256-258.

can be named the golden fleece [...] by this fleece, we shall declare the noble virtue of magnanimity'.[64] The immediate content of this magnanimity does not seem to different from Lannoy's understanding: 'The magnanimous man does not fail to expose himself to peril or fortune for a great or right cause', that is, magnanimity is not merely the 'greatness of soul' in the strict sense of the original Greek, as carefully differentiated by Aristotle, but foremost a general motivation for and manifestation of great deeds, that is, magnificence.[65] As for Lannoy, magnificence here is a greatness that subsumes under its rubric traditional martial virtues such as courage and fortitude.[66] Also similar to Lannoy, it is constituted by aiming for lofty goals, by giving generously and liberally, and avoiding bad company. In addition, Fillastre, as the religious chancellor of the knightly order, drew on Christian fathers, such as St. Ambrose and St. Augustine, as inspiration behind his expansive definition.[67] Most of all, this allows Fillastre to claim, without reserve, 'magnificence' as the first virtue among all virtues, the virtue that animates and makes possible the other virtues.

The novelty and importance of this expansive understanding of magnificence as a governing virtue can be seen in two major aspects. First, Fillastre not only elevated 'magnificence' to the first virtue, he also backed it up by placing 'justice' as the second virtue, the fleece of Jacob. 'Prudence', which was Aquinas' first secular virtue and which Lannoy had used to subsume the three Christian virtues (faith, hope, and charity) is relegated to third position, the fleece of Gideon. Then 'fidelity', 'patience', and 'clemency' follow as fourth, fifth, and sixth, the fleeces of Mesa, Job, and David. This new ordering by Fillastre reveals an underlying current already present in Lannoy's treatise, that is, the prime purpose of a prince is administering justice. But this justice, especially in the absence of any appeal to papal or ecclesiastical authority, can only be exercised and legitimized by the magnanimity or magnificence of the prince!

Second, the common denominator upholding 'magnificence' and 'justice' is the Burgundian understanding of the 'common good' ('bien publique') and 'commonwealth' ('chose publique').[68] For Fillastre, as was for most late medieval writers familiar with Aristotle's *Ethics*, justice was not merely about retributive measures for criminal matters, nor limited to protection from

64 *Werke*, p. 257.

65 *Werke*, p. 44.

66 *Werke*, p. 428: 'magnanime, quant on voit qu'il a le couraige déterminé a quelque grant fait'.

67 *Werke*, p. 267.

68 Vanderjagt, *Qui Sa Vertu*, pp. 45-73, provides a broader treatment of these ideas in Burgundian political thought.

external threats. Justice concerned the 'preservation of the commonwealth, for the peace and security of his people and his land, resist injustice and disorderliness', that is, what is now called governance.[69] As Vanderjagt has argued, this secular form of justice, worldly in its promise and perspective, was the good work to be done by the prince, separate from the good news proclaimed by the Church and the judgment to eternal life administered by the Pope. It was for a common good that was very much a 'material one [...] within history and time'.[70] The second virtue, justice, was one bestowed directly by God to the ruler, manifest in his magnificence and magnanimity which made possible the exercise of this justice, and in turn, made magnificence a virtue rather than a vice.[71] Such coupling of reason and power, justice and magnificence, implicit in Lannoy, was made explicit by Fillastre. Justice was the purpose of governance, and magnificence the source of this justice.

In his *First Book of the Golden Fleece*, Fillastre recounted the recent history of the Burgundian dukes, not in a strictly chronological manner, but rather to emphasize their 'magnanimity', in particular that of Duke Philip the Good. He didn't fail to mention the battles young Philip partook in, but he further highlighted how Duke Philip aggrandized and pacified the Burgundian realm and had his eyes firmly on the crusade.[72] In this context, one of the most famous and notorious of Burgundian ceremonies, the Feast of the Pheasant at Lille in 1454, underscores the Burgundian understanding of magnificence. The extravagance and ostentation of the feast, both in contemporary records and later popular memory – a 'fantastic ornament' in which 'a blasé aristocracy laughs at its own ideals' in Huizinga's memorable words[73] – seems to defy comprehension.[74] Even the climax and naming of the feast, a taking of vows before a roasted pheasant, has eluded comprehension for its historical inspiration. Yet, as Normore has recently argued, the feast was a prime site in which magnificence as an ethical virtue was demonstrated and instilled among Burgundian courtiers.[75]

69 *Werke*, p. 54, n. 148, and examples at p. 294.

70 Vanderjagt, *Qui Sa Vertu*, p. 69, 49-51. See also Spufford, *Monetary Problems*, pp. 139-141 in which he discusses how the governing circle around Duke Philip and Charles understood their right of coinage as a means of guaranteeing the common good, rather than a means of self-interest.

71 *Werke*, p. 55, and examples at pp. 267, 277.

72 *Werke*, pp. 268-289.

73 Huizinga, *Waning*, p. 89.

74 Belozerskaya, *Rethinking the Renaissance*, reaffirms this extravagance, but in a positive sense, as a Burgundian practice of magnificence that dazzled contemporary European nobility.

75 Normore, *Feast for the Eyes*, pp. 102-30. Normore specifically emphasizes the ethical dimension of 'magnificence' tied to the virtue of 'temperance' and how the feasting was fraught with the danger of being either excessive or inadequate, both failures of 'magnificence'.

Furthermore, as Fillastre's reworking of 'magnificence' proclaims, it was a perfect representation of Burgundian 'magnificence' as a political and financial statement, the very mark of ducal governance. The political message was clear: the feast was both a victory lap after suppressing the Revolt of Ghent the year before and as a pledge to lead a crusade against the Turks who had just taken Constantinople. The material promise was apparent: the eye-startling and mouth-watering abundance of the feast was a show-case of Burgundian wealth and capacity. Both, in Burgundian terms, were a reminder of the 'magnificence' of the Burgundian duke that made possible the 'justice' in Flanders and a pointer to his ability to bring about the same in the Holy Lands.

On a final note, the gradual evolution and development of Burgundian understanding of 'magnificence', from an emphasis on encapsulating traits such as fortitude or courage to an emphasis on the projection of political and commercial greatness, can be seen in Jean Molinet's compilation of the twelve 'magnificences' of Charles the Bold.[76] Writing after the death of Charles on the battlefield of Nancy, and based on the notes of his predecessor Chastellain, Molinet (often considered the last of the Burgundian chroniclers) gave the most explicit formulation of this new Burgundian understanding of 'magnificence'. Molinet employed 'magnificence' as a noun and not an adjective – grounding it as a conceptual anchor. Furthermore, unlike previous authors, there are only two military feats in Molinet's list of magnificences: the 'subjugation of Ghent' in 1467 and the siege of Neuss in 1474-1475.[77] The remainder are court ceremonies or public occasions such as the chapters of the Order of the Golden Fleece in Bruges and Valenciennes, 1468 and 1474 respectively; the wedding of Charles to Margaret of York in Bruges, July 1468; the meeting with the emperor at Trier, in late 1473; and the reception of the Order of the Garter in Ghent, 1470, among others. This was not for the lack of military endeavors or territorial expansion, as Charles had also recovered the Somme towns, defeated the rebellion in Liège, and taken possession of the Duchy of Guelders and parts of Alsace. Furthermore, from a military perspective, the siege of Neuss was actually a failure, as Charles had to cease the siege without a surrender and because the siege prevented him from coordinating an invasion of France with his brother-in-law, Edward IV. Thus, already in the eyes of the Burgundian chronicler, it was the court gatherings, with their public performances, presentations of ducal splendor,

76 Molinet, *Chronique*, pp. 170-171.

77 Respectively, the first and final magnificence. The twelve 'magnificences' are not in chronological order, but they do not seem to be ordered in terms of significance either.

organization of orderly processions, occasions for largess, manifestations of princely sovereignty, and all the accoutrements which embodied the commercial prowess of the Low Countries, that constituted 'magnificence'.

Seen in this light, princely magnificence is a cultural form that has a commercial content and a political function. The 'form of life' in the court – the public procession in colorful liveries of fine and luxurious cloth, the splendid arrangement and decoration of the banquet hall in the courtyard, the brilliant display of tapestries and silverware and the lavish feast – were plays of magnificence, and in turn, testimonies of commercial prowess. Furthermore, the ceremonies and rituals in which luxurious liveries were distributed, splendid tapestries were hung, and banquet and jousts were hosted, were plays of gifts to the duke's retinue, to his guests in attendance, and to the populace in audience. They were the 'largess' of the prince, which had the market embedded with them, and their seeming ostentatiousness actually constituted the 'magnificence', of the prince, from which flowed the 'justice' that secured the 'common good'.

Conclusion

Huizinga's insights applied to evolving Burgundian definitions of 'magnificence' provide an approach to revisiting Huizinga's *Autumn*. Foremost, it permits us to reassess Huizinga's characterization of fourteenth- and fifteenth-century northwestern Europe, in its own eyes. If the 'form of life' in the Burgundian court exhibited the symptoms of an 'overripe' medieval culture in decay, this exploration of the forms behind the forms (*vormen*) and their integration into the cultural idea of 'magnificence' allows us to recast these processions, banquets, and tournaments as simultaneously embodying burgeoning commercial ideals of wealth production and consumption. If Huizinga's call was for a 'cultural history' that pursues 'historical sensation', then this understanding of 'magnificence' provides a form (*idea*) in which the weeping and bonding of Charles the Bold and his men can also signal the confidence of a newly constituted court, funded, orderly and prosperous, as a play of fiscal and commercial acumen as well as chivalric heroism and fealty. Through the display of material goods that realized princely magnificence, the Burgundian court was not just 'escaping' the uncertain reality of continuous commercialization but also 'reforming' the commercial world it confronted. Such a process unfolded in conversation with ancient and medieval traditions and contemporary Italian experiments, but it was also firmly Burgundian. Finally, if a 'cultural form' such as 'magnificence'

their generation in the Low Countries and elsewhere, possessed qualities reflecting the training of professional historians of the era: a bedrock commitment to the traditional auxiliary sciences (diplomatics and paleography especially) and to heuristics.[1] Pirenne, as the older one of the two, was already the acclaimed Belgian historian when Huizinga's book appeared; he was author of a multivolume history of Belgium, at once a crowning scholarly achievement and also a commercial success. The publication of each of Pirenne's volumes was celebrated; in 1912, the publication of volume four coincided with the commemoration of his 25 years of professorship at Ghent University. It was the perfect occasion for a public and scientific homage organized in the Royal Academy in Brussels on 12 May 1912 and attended by Huizinga. At that moment, Huizinga was professor in Groningen and served as a member of the academy's committee. The ceremony offered Pirenne the occasion to thank the audience, in the guise of scientific modesty essential to the scholarly persona he had carefully constructed.[2] Hence, the following typical quote: 'My work has advanced as if a gently flowing stream, without friction, without struggle, without obstacles. It is a place to take one's pleasure, not a place to win glory' ('Mon travail s'est avancé comme une eau qui coule sur une pente douce, sans heurts, sans luttes, sans obstacles. Il y a lieu de s'en réjouir, il n'y a pas lieu d'en tirer gloire').[3] Formulated in 1912, this statement reflects an optimistic view of a society and its immediate future, which first darkened and then suddenly vanished two years later when World War I broke out and many of Pirenne's and Huizinga's intellectual certainties were fractured and even destroyed.

Pirenne and Huizinga had met personally for the first time in 1908, when Huizinga visited Ghent to join the historical methods seminar Pirenne (and even more his colleague Paul Fredericq) had introduced in Ghent, which was based on a German model Pirenne had adapted from his postdoctoral years there.[4] In 1917 Huizinga wrote again to Pirenne, who was held prisoner/hostage in Germany because of his opposition to the German occupier's policy of imposing Dutch as the sole language of instruction at Ghent University. At that occasion Huizinga recalled the good times enjoyed in Ghent in 1908, the dinner with other Ghent colleagues at Pirenne's home, and the visit to the Ghent Altarpiece (the *Adoration of the Mystic Lamb*), a

1 I have elaborated this in Boone, '"L'automne du Moyen Age"', pp. 29-30.

2 The attention to the phenomenon of the scholarly persona is quite recent and a result of the 'cultural turn', as applied to Pirenne: Keymeulen, 'Henri Pirenne', pp. 77-80.

3 Pirenne, *Manifestation*, p. 52. Put in context in Boone and Keymeulen, 'Personne ne songe à l'Europe'.

4 Huizinga, *Briefwisseling*, I, p. 99, no. 68. Tollebeek, *Writing the Inquisition*, pp. cii-ciii.

very large and complex 15th-century polyptych altarpiece painted by the Van Eyck brothers in the cathedral, where both men had met Hypolite Fierens-Gevaert, an international expert in the paintings of the so-called Flemish Primitives. It was the first public exhibition of these paintings in Bruges in 1902 that is thought to have played a fundamental role in sparking Huizinga's fascination with the Burgundian period.[5]

During the fateful summer of 1914, Pirenne traveled to Groningen on 1 July to receive an honorary doctorate for which Huizinga had acted as sponsor.[6] He already had received two such doctorates in Germany: in Leipzig in 1909 and in Tübingen in 1911, both of which he would return in protest against the German invasion of Belgium in August 1914. The ceremony took place without Huizinga present as he had to face a personal tragedy, the death of his wife on 21 July. The letters Huizinga wrote during this period testify to his grief and despair.[7] There is, however, one exception: on 7 August he wrote to Pirenne, addressing him for the first time with the words 'cher collègue et ami', in order to express what he described as 'l'indignation que nous a suscitée l'outrage brutal et cynique dont les Belges souffrent aujourd'hui' ('the brutal and cynical assault that the Belgians have now suffered has enraged us').

As a matter of fact the German army had crossed the Belgian frontier on 4 August, thereby starting World War I on the Western Front. As Huizinga continued in the same letter:

> Je conçois quelle douleur doit être la vôtre, vous qui avez donné l'expression historique à l'âme belge, qui avez aidé par cela à former la nationalité même qui est aux prises maintenant. Et c'est votre sol natal: Verviers, le pays liégeois qui a été envahi! Et sans doute plus d'un de vos quatre fils est à l'armée.[8]
>
> [I imagine the pain that must be yours, you who have given expression to the Belgian soul, who have helped to construct her identity, which

5 Huizinga, *Briefwisseling*, I, p. 202, no. 190. Huizinga recalls that during the visit to the chapel where the painting was then mounted (the original Vijdt chapel), 'était assis un monsieur au visage important, et vous dîtes à M. Frédéricq: tiens, c'est Fierens'. Apart from visiting the Bruges exhibition, reading works like *La Renaissance septentrionale* (published in 1905) by Hippolyte Fierens-Gevaert (1870-1926, professor in Liège and conservator in the Fine Arts Museum in Brussels) have been important for Huizinga. In the latter's experience meeting Fierens at that particular occasion must have been a strong 'historical sensation', a case of intellectual serendipity of which Huizinga was particularly fond.

6 Lyon, *Henri Pirenne*, pp. 187, 203; Huizinga, *Briefwisseling*, I, p. 162, no. 141.

7 Tollebeek, '"Au point sensible"', p. 415.

8 Huizinga, *Briefwisseling*, I, p. 164, no. 145.

is now threatened. And even your birthplace: it is Verviers, the land of Liège, which has been invaded. And doubtlessly more than one of your four sons must be in the army.]

The illness of his wife, together with a general feeling of decline and of the loss of values, loomed even larger in Huizinga's life during the years preceding and during World War I as he prepared *Herfsttij*. Not only had he lost his wife in July 1914, on 28 October of the same year he had accepted a professorship in Leiden, and thus had to leave Groningen and the intellectual landscape in which he had lived and where he had been so happy. In between these two dates the war broke out, which would profoundly change Western society and culture, shattering the bourgeois society of the late nineteenth and early twentieth centuries, forcing elites to reexamine if not redefine their sense of modernity.[9] As such, *Herfsttij* can be regarded with good reason as a 'book of remembrance' about Huizinga's personal life and the political world in which he lived.[10] Even though *Herfsttij* was published in 1919, Huizinga had worked on it during the war years. The effects of the great war reverberated not only with respect to Huizinga's new personal life (after his wife's death and the move to Leiden) but also to his public life, made plain by the photo dated in the summer of 1915 showing Huizinga participating in military exercises in formal dress on the dunes of Katwijk, in order to be able to defend his country, if necessary.[11]

The small world of Dutch medievalists reacted to the publication of the book *Herfsttij* with a certain embarrassment, for its aesthetic spirit, literary character, and the choice of sources placed it far outside the norm for medievalists of the day. They were then battling to gain status for their field at a time when the country's 'Golden Age' of the sixteenth and seventeenth centuries was at the center of historical studies.[12] In such an intellectual context, Huizinga's voice was a disturbing one, and the success his book had in literary circles did not render the situation less embarrassing. The influential archivist from Utrecht, Sam Muller, had made it clear in his review of Huizinga's book for the cultural magazine *Onze eeuw* (Our century) that literary praise was rather dangerous for a historian.[13] Muller's critique was based on the fact – evident in several chapters of *Herfsttij* – that Huizinga had used a narrow range of sources

9 Keymeulen, *Het fenomeen Pirenne*, pp. 10-12, 151-153.

10 The notion of a 'book of remembrance' with regard to *Herfsttij* was coined by Krul, 'In the Mirror', pp. 370-371.

11 Van der Lem, *Johan Huizinga*, p. 137.

12 Concerning the early reception of *Herfsttij*, see Hugenholtz, 'The Fame', pp. 236-239.

13 Muller, 'Het boek van professor Huizinga'.

that provided a perspective only on one sector of society and had remained largely blind to the economic and political sources of the period. In a letter to his publisher Huizinga dismissed Muller's review as 'rather silly'.[14] It was not only Dutch medievalists who rebuked Huizinga. The Utrecht medievalist Frits Hugenholtz (1922-1999), a student of Huizinga and one of the editors of his collected works, recalled how the reading of Huizinga's book was not encouraged at all when he studied medieval history at Ghent University in 1947-1948 under Pirenne's successors there.[15] Indeed, François Louis Ganshof, an avid positivist, while polite to Huizinga, established no professional relationship with him at all.[16] Isolated from the intellectual circles of his immediate colleagues, Huizinga sought his inspiration elsewhere. Many of Huizinga's critics, Pirenne included, had identified the Swiss historian Jacob Burckhardt (1818-1897) and his major work *Die Kultur der Renaissance in Italien* (1860) as both precursor and a source of inspiration for *Herfsttij*.[17] Burckhardt's notion of 'renaissance' indeed was of a great importance in Huizinga's publications. But as Jo Tollebeek made clear, although Burckhardt and Huizinga shared an almost 'medically' inspired take on cultural history, there remained a fundamental difference: Burckhardt emphasized its therapeutic aspects while Huizinga stressed the impression of sickness and decline.[18]

2 The Burgundian State in Historical Perspective: Huizinga and Pirenne

As already mentioned, Henri Pirenne provided Belgium with a master narrative of its history that gave a central role to the dukes of Burgundy. According to Pirenne, the political unification of the principalities of the former Low Countries under the dukes was the forerunner of the political process that had, in the course of the nineteenth century, resulted in two sovereign states, the kingdoms of Belgium and of the Netherlands. Pirenne thus replaced the somewhat pessimistic view of the action of the dukes of Burgundy, which had dominated Belgian historiography of the nineteenth century, with a much more positive assessment of their role in history. In

14 As quoted in Hugenholtz, 'The Fame', p. 239.

15 Ibid., p. 240.

16 Trüper, *Topography of a Method*, p. 173, n.140.

17 See the references in the letters Huizinga wrote in response to some observations in that sense made by Pirenne (whose outgoing letters unfortunately were not preserved): Huizinga, *Briefwisseling*, I, pp. 233-234, no. 271.

18 Tollebeek, '"Renaissance"', pp. 361-363.

the traditional pessimistic view, the dukes were considered responsible for the dismantling of a political order. This viewpoint was most prominently formulated in the thesis of Pirenne's old teacher in Liège, later colleague in Ghent, and 'comrade-in-arms' during their partly joint exile in Germany, Paul Fredericq.[19] Although he later revised this interpretation,[20] paradoxically Pirenne had then done relatively little research on the history of the dukes.[21] Rather, the second volume of his *Histoire de Belgique*, which covers the period from the beginning of the fourteenth century to the death of Duke Charles the Bold in 1477, is primarily based on narrative and literary sources, chronicles written by authors such as Froissart, Chastellain, d'Escouchy, La Marche, Monstrelet, Commynes, and many others – the same sources Huizinga relied on in *Herfsttij*. To a large extent this selection was quite 'natural' for both authors since these sources were readily available in text editions at the beginning of the twentieth century. Diplomatic sources and state and city financial records – the archival material historians of the Burgundian period use today – were not yet being mined.[22] Pirenne's and Huizinga's very different approaches and conclusions about the Burgundian period starkly illustrate how two talented historians could diverge intellectually while using many of the same sources. Both men were, of course, very much aware of their differences in interpretation. In a letter dating from 1930 Pirenne reacted to the copy of an article on the Burgundian unification process that Huizinga had sent him with the following remark[23]:

> Je dirais volontiers qu'étant donné votre point de vue, vous avez raison. Mais, en envisageant le sujet d'une manière plus concrète, dans les faits plutôt que dans les idées, dans ce que les ducs ont fait sans peut-être avoir voulu le faire, on le voit apparaître, me semble-t-il, d'une manière un peu différente. Il y a, en somme, plusieurs vérités pour une même chose: c'est un peu, comme en peinture, une question d'éclairage. L'essentiel est de faire réfléchir.[24]
>
> [I would freely concede that, given your point of view, you are correct. But, looking at the subject more concretely, by way of facts more than ideas,

19 Fredericq, *Essai sur le rôle politique*, passim. Concerning Fredericq, see Tollebeek, *Fredericq & zonen*, passim.

20 Carlier, 'Contribution à l'étude de l'unification', pp. 8-11.

21 Uyttebrouck, 'Henri Pirenne et les ducs', pp. 87-91.

22 See several contributions in the collection of essays edited by Paravicini et al., *La cour de Bourgogne*, pp. 21-106.

23 The article in question is Huizinga, 'L'état bourguignon', passim.

24 The citation was published in Huizinga, 'Henri Pirenne'.

by way of what the dukes did instead perhaps of what they wanted to do, one sees things, it seems to me, a little differently. There are, in short, many truths for the same thing: it is a little, as in painting, a question of lighting. The essential thing is to force careful reflection.]

Huizinga commented on this letter when he cited it in his *in memoriam* concerning Pirenne after the latter's death in 1935: Pirenne, he insisted, was a 'robust realist', in no way a critic of positivism.[25]

So, what were exactly the points of difference between the two scholars? Did their opinions concerning the dukes of Burgundy remain in conflict into the 1930s, almost fifteen year after Huizinga's book? Huizinga's growing reputation in part offers an answer. As the author of *Herfsttij*, which enjoyed surging popularity and translations into many languages, Huizinga was regularly invited to deliver talks and publish essays on Burgundian history. In 1933, for example, Huizinga was again preparing essays on Burgundian history and on the character of the Dutch state. In that same year, as the rector of Leiden University, Huizinga had tackled a difficult case of plagiarism of which his colleague Herman Colenbrander was accused and whose 'victim' happened to be Henri Pirenne.[26] Because Huizinga neither obtained Colenbrander's admission of guilt nor succeeded in dismissing him from his position, Huizinga was in a less than happy mood when he departed for Berlin. There he was supposed to deliver two speeches on 27 and 28 January 1933, two days before the fatal elections that resulted in Adolf Hitler's chancellorship of Germany. On 27 January he spoke on the theme 'Die Mittlerstellung der Niederlande zwischen West- und Mitteleuropa' ('The middle position of the Low Countries between Western and Central Europe') for the Deutsche Hochschule für Politik, Grundfragen der internationalen Politik, funded by the Carnegie chair for foreign policy. On 28 January in Berlin he delivered a paper entitled 'Burgund: eine Krise des romanisch-germanischen Verhältnisses' ('Burgundy, a crisis in the Romance-Germanic relationship') at Humboldt University. Both texts were published but one of them became yet another nightmare for Huizinga.[27] In April of the same

25 'Deze woorden moet men uit den mond van dezen robusten realist, weinig gericht op bespiegeling en vreemd aan scepticisme, allerminst opvatten als een vertwijfeling aan de positieve kenniswaarde der historie' (Huizinga, *VW*, V, p. 504).

26 On the Colenbrander case, see Boone, '"L'automne du Moyen Age"', pp. 44-45.

27 The first one was edited in the series of 'Vorträge des Carnegie Lehrstuhls für Aussenpolitik und Geschichte an der Deutsche Hochschule für Politik, 5' (Leipzig-Köln: B.G. Teubner, 1933) reedited in Huizinga, *VW*, II, pp. 284-303. The second lecture was published in the leading German review *Historische Zeitschrift* 148 (1933), pp. 1-28, reedited in Huizinga, *VW*, II, pp. 238-265.

year, 1933, a conference of the International Student Service took place in Leiden, hosted by Huizinga as rector and therefore honorary president of the meeting. The German delegation was headed by Dr. Johann von Leers (1902-1965), author of several aggressive anti-Semitic publications in full accordance with the Nazi ideology.[28] When Huizinga made it clear to Dr. Von Leers how much the Leiden academic community disapproved of his ideas, the German delegation left Leiden.[29] Back in Berlin, Von Leers retaliated by requiring the editors of the *Historische Zeitschrift*, who had agreed to publish Huizinga's paper, to add a postscript stating that had they been aware in time of the incident in Leiden, they would have refused Huizinga's contribution. In return, the editors of the leading Dutch history journal, *Tijdschrift voor Geschiedenis*, renounced their subscription to the *Historische Zeitschrift*. And in the last letter he ever sent to Huizinga, an aged Pirenne wrote to offer his support of Huizinga, his tone echoing that of letters of encouragement Huizinga had sent him in the fateful summer of 1914:

> Votre belle attitude à l'égard de la brutalité hitlérienne a été digne d'eux. L'Historische Zeitschrift vous a exclu honoris causa et nous avons tous applaudi ici à la riposte si méritée de la Tijdschrift voor geschiedenis. Jusqu'où les aberrations du racisme entraîneront-elles ces malheureux allemands? Qui donc a dit: 'Der Weg der Menschheit geht von Humanität, durch Nationalität, zur Bestialität'?[30]

> [Your admirable stand in the face of the brutality of Hitlerism suits them perfectly. *Historische Zeitschrift* has banned you 'honoris causa' and here we have all applauded the entirely justifiable response of the *Tijdschrift voor geschiedenis*. Just how far will these miserable Germans take their racism? Who was it that said, 'Mankind's journey goes from humanity, through nationality, to bestiality'?]

This may seem an aside when considering the different ways Pirenne and Huizinga viewed the Burgundian state. Yet the discussion of what Pirenne called 'le point sensible de l'Europe' and Huizinga the 'Mittlerstellung' of the former Low Countries was in fact an extremely sensitive one after the major

28 On him, see Sennholz, *Johann von Leers*, passim. Von Leers was a high-ranking SS official, former collaborator of Joseph Goebbels, who fled after the war to Italy, Argentina, and finally Egypt, were he converted to Islam, continued his anti-Semitic activities, and died in 1965.

29 Van der Lem, *Johan Huizinga*, p. 229.

30 Huizinga, *Briefwisseling*, II, p. 492, no. 1064; the citation is drawn from a poem by the Austrian poet Franz Grillparzer (1791-1872).

disruption of public life caused by World War I. The extreme right-wing parties in Europe that came to power in many countries in the 1930s, especially the fascist and ultra-Catholic movements, demonstrated – as the extreme right still continues to do in postwar Europe – a particular need to appropriate history or parts of 'national' history for political and propaganda needs. With regard to the Burgundian chapter of the Low Countries, the most obvious framing was the great-Netherlandish vision, which imagined a return to the unity of the former Dutch-speaking provinces (covering the 'Flemish' part of present day Belgium and the Netherlands). In the hands of the Dutch historian Pieter Geyl, a vigorous opponent of Henri Pirenne, the argument was based on cultural, more precisely linguistic, unity.[31] But an even more political and ideologically loaded attempt was mounted by the Francophone and ultra-Catholic party Rex (referring to Christus Rex). From the very beginning of World War II its leader Léon Degrelle expressed the desire to rekindle the Burgundian state as a kind of super Belgium reaching from the Meuse in the north to the Somme in the south.[32] In the course of the war, Degrelle became more and more involved in open collaboration with the Nazi regime, foremost as leader of the Waffen SS division La Wallonie with which he fought on the Eastern Front.[33] The old crusader ideal that in the course of the fifteenth century had been promoted by the dukes of Burgundy was effortlessly transposed into a crusade against godless Bolshevism. During these military expeditions the references to Burgundy became very visible: the Burgundian cross (or the cross of St. Andrew) was used as a military emblem and after the defeat organizations of former soldiers of Degrelle's division still referenced Burgundian history. In 1978 they still baptized the organization of veterans as 'les Bourguignons' while their journal bore the title '*Le Téméraire*', referring to Duke Charles the Bold's commonly accepted surname.[34]

3 Huizinga and Pirenne: The Great Divergence or the Burgundian State Reconsidered

Pirenne and Huizinga offered startlingly different assessments of the legacy of the dukes of Burgundy in the history of the Low Countries. Huizinga

31 Tollebeek, *Een slapeloos doordenken van alle dingen*, pp. 87-89.

32 Velaers and Van Goethem, *Leopold III*, pp. 435, 437, 439.

33 Littell, *Le sec et l'humide*, pp. 10-22.

34 Boone, 'The Dukes of Burgundy', p. 351. It should be noted that some authors refer to the contemporary surname 'le Hardi', see Cauchies, *Louis XI*, pp. 147-159.

tackled the Burgundian issue in some additional publications, including those that were the result of the public talks he delivered in Berlin in 1933, and then in a series of major articles focusing on 'a national consciousness' in Dutch history. He first dealt with the problem in a text published in the general cultural and literary journal *De Gids* (first published in 1837 and still in circulation) in 1912.[35] It is clear that this publication was meant as a forerunner of *Herfsttij* because it drew heavily on the literary texts and chronicles from the Burgundian period. The tone is set in the very first sentence, which refers to how the bells of Ghent welcomed the entry of Duke Philip the Bold and of his wife Margaret of Flanders in January 1386 as the new count and countess of Flanders, thus symbolizing the advent of the new Burgundian dynasty in the county of Flanders. In Huizinga's estimation, the ringing of the bells also marked the birth of a nation – or better, twinned nations: Belgium and the Netherlands.[36] Time and again Huizinga stresses that external circumstances not linked in a direct way to the action of the dukes – the economic and what he calls 'ethnographic' or cultural conditions – could have taken history in a different direction, if it had not been for the ambitions of the dukes and thus for their political will to unite a number of principalities in the Low Countries. Another fundamental element Huizinga stresses is how the Burgundian dukes elicited a shared sense of political loyalty to the Burgundian dynasty. In creating the sense of a Burgundian party the dukes cultivated a self-identity that diverged from the effects the French royal institutions and administration (finance included) had. In general, the dukes and their party sought to establish their own *bien public*. But their efforts remained vague and imprecise, based as they were on feelings and sentiment and not a precise plan. Even a clear terminology and nomenclature were lacking. The 'Burgundian state', Huizinga advises, is a creation of modern historiography but not a phenomenon contemporaries recognized – made plain by the ducal desire for a royal title named after regions like Lotharingia or Frisia. Royalty would befit their rank and ambition, hence the importance to the dukes of devices, emblems, catchphrases, and blazons, in brief, all the outward elements to which *Herfsttij* so eagerly refers. After 1477, Huizinga argued, the loss of the duchy of Burgundy proper to the French made the relationship between France and Burgundy more straightforward and clear – reviving the old Lotharingian kingdom was out of the question. What is more, the action of the Estates General in 1482, after the death of the last direct heir to the Valois dukes of Burgundy, Mary

35 Huizinga, 'Uit de voorgeschiedenis', passim; Huizinga, 'L'état bourguignon', passim.
36 Huizinga, 'Uit de voorgeschiedenis', p. 97.

of Burgundy, reinforced Burgundian identity even more as it gave voice to unity from below. Huizinga concludes that a true Burgundian nation of the Low Countries existed only from in the period from 1477 (marked by the death of Duke Charles the Bold and the loss of the duchy of Burgundy) to 1572 (the revolt of the northern provinces of the Low Countries against King Philip II of Spain, the Habsburg heir to the Burgundian Netherlands).[37] He even references the third volume of Pirenne's *Histoire de Belgique* to explain the growing opposition over the course of the sixteenth century between the subjects' consciousness of a common political identity and the ruling Habsburg dynasty's ambition to exert absolute power over them.[38] In that confrontation, the heritage of the dukes of Burgundy receded and gave way to two heirs: a true nation in the form of the Calvinist Republic of the Northern Netherlands, and the Southern Low Countries, where only the name and the symbols of Burgundy remained.

As already mentioned, Pirenne did not write extensively about the dukes of Burgundy apart from the two volumes of his *Histoire de Belgique* that covered the period from the late fourteenth century to the arrival of the Duke of Alba in 1567 after the violent 'wonder year' of 1566. Pirenne's wider scholarly contribution was an enormous *corpus*, ranging from edited sources to important monographs, although they only scarcely touch upon the Burgundian period.[39] It is therefore difficult, if not almost impossible, to extract from that corpus an argument that he interpreted the Burgundian dukes' policies and actions as a prelude to Low Country cohesion and ultimately the emergence of the Belgian state. After all, it was only in a single article published in German and English in 1909 (a French version was published posthumously in 1986), that Pirenne wrote about 'the formation and constitution of the Burgundian state'.[40] As befitting any modern scholar (but not all of his contemporaries), Pirenne started by interrogating the very subject at hand by pointing out that the term 'Burgundian state' is a late-nineteenth-century invention. Nevertheless, the designation, to Pirenne, is 'not arbitrary but based on historic fact and tradition'.[41] Much like Huizinga, Pirenne stressed the remarkable longevity

37 Huizinga, 'L'état bourguignon', p. 162.

38 Ibid., p. 208.

39 Uyttebrouck, 'Henri Pirenne et les ducs', pp. 87-89. Among the sixteen books Pirenne wrote, none is dedicated to the dukes; of his 163 articles or chapters in collective works, only 4 are.

40 Pirenne, 'The Formation', pp. 477-502, in German: Pirenne, 'Die Entstehung', and in French: Pirenne, 'La formation'. The French version represents the text as presented at the International Congress of Historical Sciences of Berlin, held in 1908.

41 Pirenne, 'The Formation', p. 478.

and resilience of Burgundian symbols and signs: briquet, flags, military symbols, indeed the very name of the 'cercle de Bourgogne' as favored in the sixteenth century by Charles V. But it was the creation of centralizing institutions throughout their territories which Pirenne deemed the most profound and influential step undertaken by the dukes of Burgundy. Already in the second volume of his *Histoire de Belgique* (1908) Pirenne came to see Philip the Bold's new chamber of account in Lille as 'le point de départ d'une ère nouvelle dans l'histoire constitutionelle de la Belgique' ('the start of a new era in the constitutional history of Belgium').[42] In a nutshell, the strong French model of institutionalization the dukes introduced in the Low Countries was the cornerstone of success. The Burgundian model established in Lille was repeated in Vilvoorde/Brussels (1404) in the wake of the incursions and later annexation of the duchy of Brabant and also in The Hague after the dukes gained the county of Holland-Zeeland (1446).[43] Local inhabitants contested these annexations, yet, almost a century later during the great 1477 crisis the Burgundian state underwent after the unexpected death of Duke Charles the Bold, subjects reacted in these areas by opting to optimize rather than flatly reject ducal administration and institutions – a remarkable turnaround given the previous history of conflict. Ducal institutions, Chambres des Comptes above all, were also the very spaces where the Burgundian memory was recorded and organized. Indeed these late medieval archives constitute – England aside – some of the world's richest princely archives of the medieval world.[44] Even though Pirenne had not worked systematically in these repositories, he was nevertheless well aware of their richness, hence the emphasis he placed on the importance of Burgundian institutions. Pirenne underscored three mayor hybrid elements that characterized the Burgundian 'state'. First: that it was not a monarchy but a princely 'state' legally dependent on two monarchies (the king of France and the German emperor) to which the Burgundian dukes owed fealty; second, the linguistic diversity given that its territories were 'a frontier state between two tongues' but one rich with cultural exchanges; and third, open borders and geographical diversity.[45] The realization of a 'Burgundian state', according to Pirenne, was the result of an ongoing process of political, social and economic forces that began in the early Middle Ages and which the Valois dukes and their Habsburg successors brought to fruition. As Pirenne

42 Pirenne, *Histoire de Belgique*, II, p. 372.

43 See, with abundant references to the literature, Boone, 'L'état bourguignon', pp. 137-142.

44 Cockshaw, 'Les archives', pp. 43-54; Vaughan, *Valois Burgundy*, pp. 32-47.

45 Pirenne, 'The Formation', p. 479.

observed, 'as it appeared at the time of Philip the Good and as it remained under Charles V at the time of its fullest development, the Burgundian state may be defined as a plurality of autonomous territories forming a monarchical unity'.[46] Pirenne stressed that political unification was not merely the result of ducal politics, no matter how ambitious these were. Rather, the 'nascent capitalism and the economic individualism which was developing along with it' loomed large, at least in these cities (in the county of Holland and especially in Antwerp) open to innovation, as opposed to the cities of Flanders (Ghent and Bruges), caged by their privileges of the past.[47] Political development and economic growth went hand in hand, creating new centers of opportunity and development.[48] In a dialectical relationship with ducal political and institutional innovations a nascent commercial, capitalist economy birthed the performative Burgundian and Habsburg state. That it came to an end during the reign of King Philip II of Spain was not a surprise, since Spanish Habsburg authority despised the civic and regional interests of Low Country cities and their provincial institutions. In the struggle against Philip II the 'Burgundian state' became a nation, yet one located in the northern Low Countries. The Republic of the United Provinces ushered in 'unheard-of prosperity' while the Catholic southern Low Countries 'drawn into the decadence of Spain, was to vegetate in obscurity'.[49]

4 The Burgundian 'State': A Failed State or an Anachronism?

The divergence between Huizinga and Pirenne to a large extent hinged on whether the dukes were striving for 'a monarchical unity' among a plurality of principalities (Pirenne) in distinction to their French royal cousins or whether a national state emerged only when, ironically, the Valois Burgundy dynasty expired (Huizinga). In this latter vision even Duke Philip the Good was denied both a role in and the idea for a systematic plan to construct political unity (Huizinga). In subsequent historiography notions of the state remained ambiguous, but nevertheless anybody working on the Burgundian Low Countries was heir to the ideas and the language put in play by these

46 Ibid., p. 495.
47 Ibid., p. 496.
48 As such his findings express at an early stage the idea of the tension between center and periphery that was to have a great future in economic history; for an overview, see Boone, 'Centre et périphéries', pp. 363-364.
49 Pirenne, 'The Formation', p. 502.

scholars. The English historian Richard Vaughan (1927-2014), to whom we owe four excellent, widely used biographies of the four Valois dukes, did implicitly assume the notion of state – made evident in the subtitles of his monographs.[50] Gradually, of course, he realized that its priori acceptance was problematic because both England and France, by comparison, featured statist attributes wholly absent in Burgundy: a capital city, a royal authority, a national language, and a territorial name, among the most important.[51] These insights are not original, as it was no less than Pirenne who had pointed them out. In French historiography the notion of 'state' appeared to be less problematic when used in reference to the Burgundian polity, at least until recently (especially in the scholarship by Lecuppre-Desjardin) as Bertrand Schnerb's work argues in conformity with the work of Bernard Guenée. In a country that for centuries was characterized by a strong central state from Louis XIV to the Fifth Republic, what a state meant was clear. Such a designation was even readily applied to lesser French princely entities; one speaks commonly of the 'État savoyard', the 'État breton', the 'État bourbonnais' or the 'État angevin'.[52] The English historian John Elliott (born 1930), expert on early modern Habsburg Spain, popularized the notion of 'composite monarchies' in part because of his familiarity with the Burgundian antecedents. Helmut Koenigsberger (1918-2014) had earlier coined the term when grappling with a single ruler who governs diverse territories as if they were separate kingdoms, in accordance with local traditions and legal structures.[53] The categorization of a state as composite permitted historians to combine a methodological approach from above that also admits considerable political power from below, as in the work of American historian/sociologist Charles Tilly.[54]

As applied to medieval history, political terms like 'composite monarchies', the tension between power from above versus power from below, the 'new institutional economics' and their emphasis on the effects of state institutions in both the public and private sphere (monetary stability, judicial and commercial certainties, etc.), and the concept of 'empowering interactions', as in the work of Pierre Bourdieu and Anthony Giddens, help

50 Vaughan, *Philip the Bold*, *John the Fearless*, *Philip the Good*, and *Charles the Bold*, passim.

51 Vaughan, 'Hue de Lannoy', p. 335.

52 Schnerb, *L'état bourguignon*, p. 8; the definition by Guenée is a minimal one: 'il y a Etat dès qu'il y a, sur un territoire, une population obéissant à un gouvernement, dans ce cas, il va de soi qu'il y a eu aux XIVe et XVe siècles en Occident des Etats dont il convient d'étudier les structures' (Guenée, *L'occident aux XIVe et XVe siècles*, pp. 62-63).

53 Elliott, 'A Europe of Composite Monarchies', p. 51.

54 Most prominently in Tilly, *Coercion*.

to frame recent works on the Burgundian Netherlands.[55] For example, in 2014 Dutch historian Robert Stein published a synthesis (an English version followed in 2017) that emphasized the role of institutions and the dialectic relation between princes and subjects in the ultimate creation of three states covering the territory of the Burgundian Netherlands.[56] In 2016 Élodie Lecuppre-Desjardin provided us with a study of the aborted dream of the dukes of Burgundy for monarchical legitimacy, in which she clearly channels Huizinga as she stresses that political fantasies became only realizable after 1477 and the demise of Charles the Bold's political ambitions on the battlefields of Grandson, Murten and Nancy.[57] As with those before her, Lecuppre-Desjardin clearly wrestles with the elusive notion of a Burgundian state, finally proposing to replace it with the 'grande principauté de Bourgogne' (namely, a collection of principalities or a composite state indeed – the principality of Burgundy) in a laudable effort to integrate the French principalities – the duchy and county of Burgundy proper – into a more capacious notion of statehood. With respect to law, the 'grande principauté' was a fiction. Yet the intellectual maneuver to incorporate the French principalities into any consideration of whether or not a 'Burgundian state' existed is as clever as it is welcome, as it forces us to explore the dukes' endeavors beyond national boundaries.

In conclusion: we are fated to adhere to the old opposition between Pirenne and Huizinga on the Burgundian state and to revisit it again in assessing the differences in interpretive approach between Lecuppre-Desjardin, closer to Huizinga's sensibility, and that of Stein, who, like Pirenne, pay abiding attention to institutions and state building. Is it still only a matter of 'plusieurs vérités pour une même chose' ('many truths for the same thing') or of 'une question d'éclairage' ('a question of lighting')? To a certain extent, this is still the case. Nevertheless, the huge body of work since Pirenne and Huizinga has enriched yet complicated how we confront the question. To quote Wim Blockmans, one of today's experts on state formation and historian extraordinaire of the Burgundian era, 'historians find it mostly as difficult as the general public to think about public authority in the past without referring implicitly or explicitly to the states as they exist in their own days'.[58] This was true for Pirenne and Huizinga almost

55 For a recent evaluation of the theoretical approach to statebuilding, see Holenstein, 'Introduction', pp. 25-31.

56 Stein, *Magnanimous Dukes*, passim.

57 Lecuppre-Desjardin, *Le royaume inachevé*, pp. 15, 337-344.

58 Blockmans, 'Citizens and Their Rulers', p. 281.

a century ago and this applies to us as well. Knowing this, today's strains put on the political states as they developed in the course of the nineteenth and twentieth centuries by local and regional levels as well as supranational constructions (NATO, the European Union, the United Nations), should not only be treated as the threat as they often are – globalization, Brexit, and the other hot button subjects of today's political discourse notwithstanding. They are, rather, products of the more mundane process of historical evolution and of the dialectics inherent in any political system of power. In this respect, the experiences of the principalities once ruled by the dukes of Burgundy and the way historians like Huizinga and Pirenne looked upon them and wrestled with their essence, are both a constant reminder of history's lessons and the source of inspiration.

About the Author

Marc Boone studied history at the University of Ghent. Since 2012, he has served as dean of the faculty of arts and philosophy. He has held invited professorships in Dijon and Paris (EHESS and Paris IV) and is a member of the Royal Academy of Belgium for Arts and Sciences and former president of the European Association for Urban History. His most recent books are *À la recherche d'une modernité civique. La société urbaine des anciens Pays-Bas au bas Moyen Âge* (Editions de l'université de Bruxelles, 2010; Japanese version in 2013) and, with Bruno Blondé and Anne-Laure van Bruaene as co-editors, *City and Society in the Low Countries, 1100-1600* (Cambridge University Press, 2018).
Marc.Boone@ugent.be

Part II

Art, Literature and Sources in *Autumn of the Middle Ages*

6 Art History and Huizinga's *Autumn of the Middle Ages*

Diane Wolfthal

Abstract

The visual arts, and in particular the landmark exhibition of Flemish art in 1902, were instrumental in the formulation of Huizinga's *Herfsttij der Middeleeuwen*. This chapter analyzes Huizinga's ideas concerning the visual arts, explores their impact on art historical thinking, and evaluates whether research since the publication of his book supports or refutes his conclusions and methodology.

Keywords: F.W.N. Hugenholtz, Horst Gerson, Millard Meiss, art, art history, Jan van Eyck, Claus Sluter, Melun Diptych

Art is central to Johan Huizinga's *Autumn of the Middle Ages*. Painting sparked the idea for the book and two chapters focus on the visual arts. My essay first briefly reviews Huizinga's involvement with art in the years leading up to his writing of the book, and then analyzes its ideas about art and its effect on the discipline of art history. In particular, I will assess the conclusion of Edward Peters and Walter P. Simons that 'given Huizinga's expressed interest in the visual arts, it is remarkable that his work left little or no mark in the field of art history. [...] [A]rt historians in the Netherlands, Belgium, and France largely ignored it. Nor has it made much of an impact on art history in the United States'.[1]

1 I would like to thank Peter Arnade and Martha Howell for inviting me to participate in this volume, and Douglas Brine and Anton van der Lem for their helpful suggestions on an earlier draft of this chapter. Peters and Simons, 'The New Huizinga', p. 615.

Arnade, Peter, Martha Howell, and Anton van der Lem (eds), *Rereading Huizinga: Autumn of the Middle Ages, a Century Later*. Taylor & Francis Group, 2019
DOI: 10.5117/9789462983724_CH06

1 Huizinga's Involvement with Art, Artists, and Art Critics

Huizinga was deeply stirred by art, and it remained critically important to him throughout his life. He was an amateur artist, critic, exhibition organizer, museum policy expert, and friend of artists and art critics, and these diverse roles directly affected *Autumn of the Middle Ages*.[2] He made drawings to help him to visualize the past. His reading notes include sketches ranging from arms and armor to architectural details, and when he taught, he often drew on the blackboard. As early as the 1890s he composed historical drawings with a 'klare lijn' ('clear line') derived from such illustrators as Aubrey Beardsley and Benjamin Rabier.[3] He was deeply influenced by the 'Movement of the 1880s', which adhered to the principle of 'art for art's sake', a tenet that he embraced in his classic text. He was an attentive reader of the movement's journal *De Nieuwe Gids*, which published innovative writers, poets, art critics, and artists beginning in 1885.[4] Huizinga was later part of the circle that produced the art and literary magazine *De Kroniek*, which was founded in 1895, and differed from *De Nieuwe Gids* in its inclusion of political essays.[5] Among those active in both journals was Jan Veth, the art critic and portraitist who became Huizinga's lifelong friend.[6] Through *De Kroniek* Huizinga also met André Jolles, who was writing about Renaissance art in the 1890s.[7] It was Jolles who suggested in 1903 that Huizinga should investigate Jan van Eyck, so that the two could coauthor a publication on the subject. Ten years later, Jolles queried Huizinga, 'Is the Burgundian harvest ripe yet?'[8] A flurry of exhibitions of fifteenth-century Flemish art, beginning with one held in Bruges in 1902, deeply impressed Huizinga as did Jacob Burckhardt's *Die Kultur der Renaissance in Italien*, published in 1860, which

2 For Huizinga's art, see Puigarnau, 'Johan Huizinga', p. 435, figs. 15-17, 24; Peters and Simons, 'The New Huizinga', p. 610; Haskell, 'Huizinga and the "Flemish Renaissance"', p. 471, fig. 254. For Huizinga's relationship to art throughout his career, see Kempers, 'De verleiding van het beeld'; Tollebeek, 'De middeleeuwen dromen'.

3 Puigarnau, 'Johan Huizinga', p. 435, figs. 15-17, 24; Peters and Simons, 'The New Huizinga', p. 610; Haskell, 'Huizinga and the "Flemish Renaissance"', p. 471, fig. 254; Koops et al., *Johan Huizinga 1872-1972*, fig. 2.

4 Otterspeer, *Reading Huizinga*, p. 31; Kempers, 'De verleiding van het beeld', pp. 32-33.

5 Gerson, 'Huizinga und die Kunstgeschichte', p. 350; Kempers, 'De verleiding van het beeld', pp. 39-41.

6 Haskell, 'Huizinga and the "Flemish Renaissance"', p. 472; Kempers, 'De verleiding van het beeld', pp. 36-39.

7 Peters and Simons, 'The New Huizinga', p. 611; Kempers, 'De verleiding van het beeld', p. 36.

8 They had a falling out when in 1933 Jolles became a Nazi. See Peters and Simons, 'The New Huizinga', pp. 608, 611.

relied heavily on visual culture to understand Renaissance Italy.[9] It should not be surprising, then, that Huizinga's inaugural lecture at Groningen University in 1905 explored the aesthetic element in historical thought and his belief that art should serve as a primary source for understanding history.[10] In 1916 Huizinga published an article on the art of the Van Eycks, which became the basis for a chapter in *Autumn of the Middle Ages*, and it was early Netherlandish painting that sparked the idea for the book. As he related, when he was walking along the canal one day:

> The notion came to me that the late Middle Ages were not the herald of something that was to come, but the fading away of something that has passed. This thought, if one can speak of it as a thought, revolved above all around the art of the Van Eycks and their contemporaries, which considerably occupied my mind at that time.[11]

In fact, art was so important to Huizinga's conception of the book that the word appears in the subtitle of his authorized English translation.[12]

2 Huizinga's Ideas on Fifteenth-Century French and Flemish Art

Huizinga, then, was an artist, art lover, and art critic, but he was not a trained art historian. Rather, in *Autumn of the Middle Ages* he employs art as a cultural historian who believes that the best way to understand a society is to rely on a range of sources, including the visual culture. But Huizinga also focuses on images because he assumes that they are remembered better than words; he notes that when Egypt is invoked, people think first

9 Bouwsma, '*The Waning of the Middle Ages* by Johan Huizinga', p. 45 ('relied heavily on'); Kempers, 'De verleiding van het beeld', p. 45. See Peters and Simons, 'The New Huizinga', pp. 598-599, for additional exhibitions and a reenactment of a tournament in 1907.

10 Huizinga, *Waning* (1968; first edition 1924); Huizinga, *VW* VII, pp. 3-28.

11 For the article, see Peters and Simons, 'The New Huizinga', p. 598. For the quote, see Haskell, 'Huizinga and the "Flemish Renaissance"', p. 475. For a slightly different translation, see Otterspeer, *Reading Huizinga*, p. 191.

12 Huizinga, *Waning*. Huizinga continued to publish on art throughout his life, authoring a monograph on Jan Veth in 1927, a book on Dutch culture that focused, in part, on art in 1941, and reviews of thirteen of the fourteen volumes on early Netherlandish painting by the great connoisseur Max J. Friedländer between 1924 and 1937. For these, see Kempers, 'De verleiding van het beeld', pp. 36-37, 44-50, and Peters and Simons, 'The New Huizinga', p. 598, n. 35.

of its art.[13] Art is also central to his study because he believes that, 'the basic characteristic of the late medieval mind is its predominantly visual nature. [...] Thought takes place exclusively through visual conceptions. Everything that is expressed is couched in visual terms'.[14] It is not surprising, then, that *Autumn of the Middle Ages* explores a wide range of objects, from paintings by Jan van Eyck and sculpture by Claus Sluter to French and Flemish illuminations, castles, tapestries, woodcuts, murals, *Vierges ouvrantes*, and such multimedia complexes as the Cemetery of the Innocents in Paris.[15] Huizinga also focuses on art because he judges it 'far ahead of literature', except in the fields of comedy and erotica.[16] Furthermore, he examines the visual culture in conjunction with historical accounts because he seeks to explain why fifteenth-century Flemish paintings are so serene whereas contemporary chronicles are filled with violence.[17] In doing so, he radically changed the perception of fourteenth- and fifteenth-century northern France and the Low Countries.

Although Huizinga makes art a centerpiece of his book, he seems to have read few art historical publications.[18] He does mention – and disagree with – Émile Mâle's theory that fifteenth-century paintings stem from performances.[19] In addition, he seconds the idea, proposed by earlier scholars, that a distinct style developed in Haarlem, which differed from that of Flanders, but he attributes this difference to class, not, as had previously been suggested, geography.[20] Not only does Huizinga rarely cite art historical literature, but he also seldom adopts art historical methodology. For example, although the major categories of art historical investigation at the time were archival research, connoisseurship, and iconography, that is, the study of the subject matter of art, Huizinga shows little interest in

13 Haskell, 'Huizinga and the "Flemish Renaissance"', p. 474; Huizinga, *Waning*, p. 240.

14 Huizinga, *Autumn*, p. 341; Huizinga, *Herfsttij*, *VW*, III, p. 353: 'De grondtrek van den laat-middeleeuwschen geest is zijn overmatig visueel karakter. Er wordt in gezichtsvoorstellingen gedacht. Alles wat men uitdrukken wil, wordt neergelegd in een zichtbaar beeld.' See also Huizinga, *Waning*, pp. 271-272.

15 Huizinga, *Autumn*, pp. 23, 338, 365, also mentions such later artists as Velázquez, Rembrandt, Murillo, Emmanuel de Witte, and Steinlen. Huizinga also discusses costumes and banners at length. In the first edition, Sluter is hardly mentioned, but later editions redress this oversight. See Krul, 'Realism, Renaissance, and Nationalism', p. 287.

16 Huizinga, *Autumn*, pp. 347 (quote), 361. Huizinga, *Herfsttij*, *VW*, III, p. 358: 'De schilderkunst is hier in middelen van uitdrukking de litteratuur verre voor.' See also Huizinga, *Waning*, p. 276.

17 Huizinga, *Autumn*, p. 294.

18 Huizinga does cite art historical publications, including those by Betty Kurth, A. Kleinclausz, and Paul Durrieu. See ibid., p. 432, n. 13, n. 25; p. 433, n. 38; p. 436, n. 25; p. 438, n. 76.

19 Ibid., p. 165.

20 Ibid., pp. 315-316.

any of these approaches.[21] To the contrary, his writings about art consist largely of either descriptions or personal opinions, and his judgments are often denigratory. Gerard David's Justice panels are 'rather weak as far as composition is concerned'.[22] Claus Sluter's sculpture is 'too expressive, too personal'.[23] Breughel's paintings are 'bizarre and burlesque'.[24] Broederlam's St. Joseph is a 'caricature' and Flemish tapestries are 'overcrowded'.[25] Jan van Eyck's compositions lack rhythm and express 'no new ideas'.[26] In his Ghent Altarpiece, Eve has breasts that are 'too high' and is 'naively' painted, the singing angels show 'overly emphasized, distorted' faces, and their music stand has 'pedantic ornaments'.[27] Huizinga's criticisms, in short, are much too negative, but they are also at times much too broad. He asserts that early Flemish paintings lack originality because they were bound by traditional compositional types, and he dismisses late Gothic architecture and ornament as a build-up of sterile details: 'The flamboyant Gothic is like an endless organ postlude; it breaks down all forms by this self-analyzing process; every detail finds its continuous elaboration, each line its counter line. It is an unrestrainedly wild overgrowth of the idea by the form; ornate detail attacks every surface and line'.[28]

Besides outright condemnation, Huizinga also often undercuts praise with criticism. He admires the 'skill, the fabulous perfection of the details' of Van Eyck's art, and the 'most profound characterizations' of his portraits,

21 Peters and Simons, 'The New Huizinga', p. 615, justly observe that 'Huizinga's training and talents were those of a historian and an artist; he was not, however, a historian of art.'

22 Huizinga, *Autumn*, p. 376. Huizinga, *Herfsttij*, *VW*, III, p. 384: 'zijn vrij zwak van compositie'. See also Huizinga, *Waning*, p. 302.

23 Huizinga, *Autumn*, p. 309. Huizinga, *Herfsttij*, *VW*, III, p. 321: 'te expressief, te persoonlijk'. Huizinga, *Waning*, p. 245.

24 Huizinga, *Autumn*, p. 363. Huizinga, *Herfsttij*, *VW*, III, p. 373: 'het bizarre, het burleske'. Huizinga, *Waning*, p. 291, translates this as 'From the "genre" to the burlesque is but a step.' Huizinga, *Waning*, p. 291.

25 Huizinga, *Autumn*, pp. 177, 301. Huizinga, *Herfsttij*, *VW*, III, p. 185: 'van de caricatuur'. This does not appear in Huizinga, *Waning*.

26 Huizinga, *Autumn*, pp. 319, 376. Huizinga, *Herfsttij*, *VW*, III, p. 331: 'Nieuwe gedachten spreekt zij niet uit.' This does not appear in Huizinga, *Waning*.

27 Huizinga, *Autumn*, pp. 342, 373. Huizinga, *Herfsttij*, *VW*, III, 'die al te uitdrukkelijke grimas, die ietwat beuzelachtige versiering van den muzieklessenaar' (p. 354), and 'in de kleine, te hoog geplaatste borsten' and 'naïef' (p. 381). See also Huizinga, *Waning*, pp. 272 and 299.

28 Huizinga, *Autumn*, pp. 300-301. For lack of originality in compositions, see p. 318. Huizinga, *Herfsttij*, *VW*, III, p. 312: 'De flamboyante gothiek is als een eindeloos orgelnaspel: zij lost alle vormen op in zelfontbinding, geeft aan elk détail zijn voortgezette doorwerking, aan elke lijn haar tegenlijn. Het is een ongebonden woekeren van den vorm over de idee; het versierde détail tast alle vlakken en lijnen aan.' See also Huizinga, *Waning*, pp. 237-238.

but he denounces the 'exaggerated execution' of the *Madonna with the Chancellor Rolin*.[29] Similarly, he applauds the 'mysterious darkness' of Van Eyck's *Annunciation* (National Gallery of Art, Washington, DC), but criticizes its 'anecdotal details' and its painter's 'unbounded lust for detail'.[30] He commends the illuminator of King René's *Le cueur d'amours espris* for 'succeeding in depicting a radiant sunrise and the most mysterious effects of dusk', but terms the master 'strange'.[31]

At times Huizinga's judgments seem to be based on a distaste for religious imagery, which may stem from his Protestant upbringing. He terms the carvers of *Vierges ouvrantes* 'shameless' for 'turning everything holy into pictorial images'.[32] He describes the expression of the Madonna of the Melun Diptych as 'bizarre and inscrutable' and the angels as 'stiff', and condemns the diptych as a whole for showing 'decadent godlessness' and a 'blasphemous nonchalance toward the sacred'.[33] Only the portrait panel of this diptych escapes his criticism and is termed 'vigorous'.[34] The fact that Huizinga rarely cites art historical publications may stem from the Catholic viewpoint of W.J.H. Weale, Émile Mâle, and others. Willibald Sauerländer, for example, termed Mâle's approach 'a wonderful vindication of the old Catholic France'.[35]

Indeed what Huizinga seems to admire most about French and Flemish art is the depiction of ordinary details from everyday life, not religious themes. 'We delight', he writes, 'in the copper kettle [in the Ghent Altarpiece] and the view of the sunny street. In these details, which were only a secondary concern for the artist, the mystery of everyday things blossoms in its quiet

29 Huizinga, *Autumn*, pp. 331, 334. Huizinga, *Herfsttij*, *VW*, III, p. 344: 'de diepste karakterschildering'; p. 346: 'de overmatige geacheveerdheid werkelijk storend werkt'. See also Huizinga, *Waning*, pp. 264, 266.

30 Huizinga, *Autumn*, p. 336. Huizinga, *Herfsttij*, *VW*, III, 'de geheimzinnigste donkerte', 'anecdotische details' (p. 348), and 'ongebondensten lust tot détailleering den vrijen loop laten' (p. 347). See also Huizinga, *Waning*, p. 267.

31 Huizinga, *Autumn*, p. 347. Huizinga, *Herfsttij*, *VW*, III, p. 358: 'Een stralende zonsopgang is reeds gelukt aan den meester, die koning René's Cuer d'amours espris illustreerde.'

32 Huizinga, *Autumn*, p. 179. Huizinga, *Herfsttij*, *VW*, III, p. 187: 'Zonder de geringste spottende bedoeling kon de gemeenzaamheid met al het heilige en de zucht tot verbeelden ervan leiden tot vormen, die ons onbeschaamdheden zouden kunnen schijnen.' This statement is omitted in Huizinga, *Waning*.

33 Huizinga, *Autumn*, p. 182. Huizinga, *Herfsttij*, *VW*, III, p. 190: 'de bizarrerie van de hermetische gelaatsuitdrukking, de stijve roode en blauwe engelen', 'van décadente goddeloosheid', and 'een blasphemische vrijmoedigheid met het heilige'. See also Huizinga, *Waning*, pp. 153-154.

34 Huizinga, *Autumn*, p. 182. Huizinga, *Herfsttij*, *VW*, III, p. 190: 'forsche'. See also Huizinga, *Waning*, p. 153.

35 Sorensen, 'Mâle, Émile'.

glow. Here we sense the direct emotional stirring about the miraculous quality of all things'.[36] He exults in the 'tender and delicate' calendar pages of the *Très Riches Heures*, judging September dreamlike, March somber and majestic, and December magnificent, with 'gloomy towers [...] rising threateningly above the dried foliage'.[37] Most telling are his comments about the 'Adoration of the Magi' in the *Très Riches Heures*. The cityscape in the background is praised for showing 'all the atmospheric and rhythmic perfection of a dreamlike softness', but the religious scene in the foreground is criticized as 'bizarre and pompous'.[38]

The repeated invocation of the notion of dreams stems from Huizinga's belief that art was produced to create a beautiful life. In line with the 'Movement of the 1880s', Huizinga values art for art's sake, that is, the type of imagery whose primary function is to be admired for its great beauty. He bemoans the fact that fifteenth-century northern art is tied to 'practical' functions, such as serving as tombs and altarpieces, or displaying the splendor and magnificence of the donor.[39] He suggests that the reason for these mundane functions is that in northern culture 'the theoretical analysis of beauty is deficient'.[40] Here and elsewhere he judges northern art by Italian Renaissance values. He prefers the 'strict, simple, naturalness of Donatello' to Sluter's prophets on the Moses Fountain, and contrasts the restraint, unity, and harmony of Italian art to the 'disharmony' of the Dijon altarpiece by Jacques de Baerze and Melchior Broederlam.[41] He further asserts that a 'composition of an important action, or of a presentation with movement and many persons, a feeling for rhythmic construction and cohesion is required above all. Giotto had once possessed it and Michelangelo was to

36 Huizinga, *Autumn*, p. 337. Huizinga, *Herfsttij*, *VW*, III, p. 350: 'zelfs daar verblijdt ons haast nog meer het koperen keteltje en de doorkijk in de zonnige straat. Het zijn de détails, die voor den maker louter bijwerk waren, welke hier doen bloeien in zijn stillen schijn het mysterie van het alledaagsche, de onmiddellijke aandoening over het wonder van alle dingen en zijn beeldwording'. See also Huizinga, *Waning*, p. 268.

37 Huizinga, *Autumn*, p. 352. Huizinga, *Herfsttij*, *VW*, III: 'teerste en fijnste uitingen der miniatuurkunst' (p. 362), 'sombere torens [...] dreigend uitstekende' (p. 363). The first part of the quote does not appear in Huizinga, *Waning*, but the second part does, on p. 280.

38 Huizinga, *Autumn*, p. 350. Huizinga, *Herfsttij*, *VW*, III, p. 363: 'bizarre, pompeuze aanbidding der koningen in de Très-riches heures de Chantilly verrijst het gezicht op Bourges in verdroomde teerheid, volmaakt van atmosfeer en rythme'. See also Huizinga, *Waning*, p. 279.

39 Huizinga, *Autumn*, pp. 296, 299, 306-307, 311. Huizinga, *Herfsttij*, *VW*, III, p. 308: 'praktische'. See also Huizinga, *Waning*, p. 234.

40 Huizinga, *Autumn*, p. 324 (quote). Huizinga, *Herfsttij*, *VW*, III, p. 336: 'De theoretische analyse van het schoone is dus gebrekkig.' This quote does not appear in Huizinga, *Waning* .

41 Huizinga, *Autumn*, p. 301. Huizinga, *Herfsttij*, *VW*, III, p. 312: 'strenge, sobere natuurlijkheid', 'een disharmonie'. See also Huizinga, *Waning*, p. 238.

correctly handle it again'.[42] Although he briefly notes that Albrecht Dürer, Quentin Massys, and Jan van Scorel all admired the Ghent Altarpiece, this is overshadowed by a long quote, attributed to Michelangelo, that criticizes Flemish art.[43]

Huizinga became mildly interested in iconography after he read Erwin Panofsky's article on *The Arnolfini Portrait*, which he first cites in his fourth edition.[44] Huizinga foreshadows Meyer Shapiro's seminal article that connected the mousetrap in the Merode triptych with the metaphor, propounded by theologians, of Christ as the bait by which God caught the devil.[45] But since he relegates this observation to a footnote in the fourth Dutch edition and it appears in neither English translation, it remained unnoticed by art historians. Huizinga is especially attentive to the history of secular subjects, and spends several pages discussing the iconography of the Nine Worthies, and of such macabre themes as the Three Living and Three Dead, the Dance of Death, and the Art of Dying.[46]

But Huizinga's arguments are sometimes contradictory. For example, he asserts that 'the fine arts [...] do not openly lament', yet he describes Sluter's 'profound and dignified depiction of grief' in his mourners.[47] He also often flattens the complexity of the situation, for example, when he disregards the ideas of the art historians Gustav Friedrich Waagen and Heinrich Gustav Hotho, among others, to argue that the Van Eycks should be viewed solely as the product of court culture.[48] Sometimes his assertions contradict the evidence, as when he insists that the sitter portrayed in *The Arnolfini Portrait* 'is not at all Italian'.[49] But his conclusions are sometimes just. He reminds readers how much art has been lost, especially secular art, such as hunting

42 Huizinga, *Autumn*, p. 375. Huizinga, *Herfsttij*, *VW*, III, p. 384: 'Maar om een gewichtige handeling, een bewogen voorstelling met veel personen op te zetten, was bovenal dat gevoel voor rythmischen opbouw en eenheid noodig, dat eertijds Giotto gekend had, en dat opnieuw door Michel Angelo werd begrepen.' See also Huizinga, 'Renaissance and Realism', p. 301.

43 Huizinga, *Autumn*, pp. 320-321.

44 Ridderbos, *Schilderkunst in de Bourgondische Nederlanden*, p. 18.

45 Huizinga could have seen the Merode triptych in the exhibition in Bruges of 1907. See *Exposition de la Toison d'Or*, p. 54, cat. nr. 181. As a source for this concept Huizinga cited Peter Lombard; for Huizinga's interpretation of the mousetrap, see Huizinga, *Herfsttij* (4th ed.), p. 437; Krul, 'Realism, Renaissance, and Nationalism', p. 428, n. 100.

46 Huizinga, *Autumn*, pp. 76-77, 165-167.

47 Ibid., pp. 295 and 310. Huizinga, *Herfsttij*, *VW*, III: 'Want de beeldende kunst [...] weeklaagt niet' (p. 306), 'de diepste en waardigste verbeelding van den rouw' (p. 322). See also Huizinga, *Waning*, pp. 232 and 245.

48 Huizinga, *Autumn*, p. 315. See also Ridderbos, 'From Waagen to Friedländer', p. 234.

49 Huizinga, *Autumn*, p. 312. Huizinga, *Herfsttij*, *VW*, III, p. 324: 'schijnt wel het minst Italiaansche'. See also Huizinga, *Waning*, p. 247.

and bathing scenes. He also recognizes the power of art, for example, when, during peace negotiations in 1384, John of Gaunt demanded that tapestries showing battle scenes be replaced with those depicting the Passion.[50]

Perhaps his most striking disagreement with art historians of his time is his characterization of fifteenth-century northern art.[51] He belittles its realism and argues that it is entirely medieval in content, concluding that the 'desire to depict everything as corporeally as possible is, above all, the perfect product of a genuinely medieval spirit'.[52] But his fundamental point, which he repeatedly asserts, is his denial that early Flemish art was a beginning, or that it even held the seeds for a new Renaissance style. Instead he continually emphasizes not only its continuity with the past, but also what he sees as its decadent, decaying, and sterile character.

3 Reactions of Art Historians

Sparse evidence exists concerning art historians' early reception of *Autumn of the Middle Ages*. The first recorded reaction may be a review in *Repertorium der Kunstwissenschaft*, dated 1925, by Richard Hamann, a professor of art history at the University of Marburg, which compared Huizinga's book to Burckhardt's *Die Kultur der Renaissance in Italien* and disputed the Dutch historian's theory that Jan van Eyck's painting was medieval in character.[53] Four years later, Aby Warburg recorded in his diary his lack of interest in the book, 'werde leider Huizinga lesen müssen' ('I will unfortunately have to read Huizinga').[54] But his comment also makes clear that Warburg viewed the book as critically important, a must-read. Yet from the 1920s through the 1940s, to my knowledge, only two art historians cite it and neither engages with its ideas. First Georg Troescher lists it in his bibliography, and then G.J. Hoogewerff simply mentions that it brought attention to the north Netherlandish portrait of Lysbeth van Duvenvoorde.[55]

As F.W.N. Hugenholtz has observed, *Autumn of the Middle Ages* was 'an unusual book, that, notwithstanding its sales figures, became

50 Huizinga, *Autumn*, p. 297, for example.

51 Ibid., pp. 310, 319.

52 Ibid., p. 329. Huizinga, *Herfsttij*, *VW*, III, p. 342: 'want juist hun nauwgezet realisme en hun streven om alles zoo lichamelijk mogelijk in beeld te brengen is de volkomen uitgroei van den echt middeleeuwschen geest'. See also Huizinga, *Waning*, p. 263.

53 For Hamman, see Sorensen, 'Hamman, Richard'.

54 Puigarnau, 'Johan Huizinga', pp. 419, 428, 435.

55 Troescher, *Claus Sluter*, p. 342; Hoogewerff, *De Noord-Nederlandsche Schilderkunst*, pp. 50-51.

influential much more slowly than one might have supposed'.[56] He notes that although it was most popular in the Netherlands, its reception there among historians was cool. In addition, since few art historians outside the Netherlands read Dutch, their initial reaction was largely delayed because it was dependent on translations; the German edition appeared in 1924, the English in 1924, and the French in 1932. Since it was reprinted 'much more often' in German than in any other language besides Dutch, it should not be surprising that apart from one Dutch scholar (Hoogewerff), all early commentators on the book – Hamann, Warburg, and Troescher – were German.[57]

Hugenholtz mused, 'If the Dutch historians totally failed to understand the greatness of *Herfsttij*, did the historical profession outside the Netherlands immediately perceive its real value? Not at all'.[58] The same holds true for art historians. In 1953, Panofsky, in his influential *Early Netherlandish Painting*, praised Huizinga's 'masterful chapters' on the late medieval 'preoccupation with the macabre' and cited *Autumn of the Middle Ages* as his source for the spectacles worn by Sluter's prophet.[59] But whereas Huizinga criticized early Netherlandish art for its accumulation of detail, which he largely viewed as meaningless, Panofsky assumed that such elements were meaningful and sought to explain them as integral parts of consistent iconographic programs.[60] Furthermore, Panofsky adopted the view, shared by most twentieth- and twenty-first-century art historians, that early Netherlandish art continued many aspects of the past, but also embraced a new approach to style and meaning.[61]

Beginning in the 1960s, *Autumn of the Middle Ages* is mentioned more frequently in art historical publications.[62] It not only sparked two exhibitions at university museums in the United States but was also cited in the bibliography of Hans H. Hofstätter's survey of late medieval art, which

56 Hugenholtz, 'The Fame', pp. 91, 92.

57 Ibid., p. 91.

58 Ibid., p. 98.

59 Panofsky, *Early Netherlandish Painting*, I, pp. 389, n. 2, and 391, n. 3.

60 For this comparison, see Lloyd, 'Disguised Symbolism', pp. 14-15.

61 Although Haskell suggests that Panofsky's theory of concealed or disguised symbolism stems from Huizinga's desire to read medieval thinking into fifteenth-century Flemish paintings, this cannot be proven. See Haskell, 'Art and History', pp. 4, 6.

62 Peters and Simons, 'The New Huizinga', p. 616, mention the 'veneration' expressed by Karl Weintraub, and the turn by art historians to cultural history. To this may also be added the expansion of the higher education system in the United States and the concomitant increased number of publications in art history.

appeared in German, French and English editions.[63] A quote from Huizinga also appeared in the Italian and English versions of *The Complete Paintings of the Van Eycks*, and his book is listed in the bibliography of the catalog for the most influential exhibition of Flemish art of the decade.[64] Perhaps most revealing of the book's reputation, however, is its presence in *A Basic Bibliography on the Fine Arts*, published in 1960.[65]

The most significant art historical study of *Autumn of the Middle Ages* in this decade, however, was Horst Gerson's. In 1966, a year after he accepted the art history chair at the University of Groningen and became director of its Institute for Art History, Gerson presented an inaugural lecture, which, in part, discussed the book. Gerson's paper called attention to Huizinga's lifelong involvement with art and artists, noted his personal approach to art, and summarized his writings on visual culture.[66] Concerning *Autumn of the Middle Ages*, Gerson criticized Huizinga's neglect of the Master of Flémalle and Rogier van der Weyden, noting that they were more influential than Jan van Eyck. Gerson also condemned Huizinga's failure to recognize that the fine arts began to detach from crafts in the fifteenth century, and that art history is a distinct discipline from history with its own goals and methodologies.

From the 1970s until the present, *Autumn of the Middle Ages* has been mentioned in a wide range of publications on French and Flemish art, especially in the United States. Sometimes the book is only cited in the bibliography, but when it is mentioned in the text the reactions are varied.[67] At times it is roundly criticized. The most famous example occurred in 1974, when Millard Meiss wrote that Huizinga 'was not an art historian and the bibliography [...] contains few books on art'. Meiss also censured Huizinga for

63 The two exhibitions are 'The Waning of the Middle Ages', Pomona, CA, 1965, and 'The Waning Middle Ages', Lawrence, KS, 1969; Hofstätter, *Spätes Mittelalter*, p. 252.

64 *Flanders in the Fifteenth Century*, p. 419; Faggin, *The Complete Paintings of the Van Eycks*, p. 11; Faggin, *L'opera completa dei Van Eyck*, p. 11.

65 Lucas, *Art Books*, p. 31.

66 For his inaugural lecture, see Sorensen, 'Huizinga, Johan'. For his published paper, see Gerson, 'Huizinga und die Kunstgeschichte', and for other versions, see Grasman, *Gerson in Groningen*, pp. 110-111.

67 To cite only a few examples of publications that mention *Autumn of the Middle Ages* in the bibliography only: Troescher, *Claus Sluter*, p. 342; Metropolitan Museum of Art, *The Secular Spirit*, p. 284; Musper, *Netherlandish Painting*, p. 131; Purtle, *The Marian Paintings*, p. 209; Schreckenberg, *Claus Sluter*, p. 148; Šebková-Thaller, *Sünde und Versöhnung*, p. 149; Van Os, *The Art of Devotion*, p. 186; Harbison, *The Mirror of the Artist*, p. 179; Avril, *Jean Fouquet*, pp. 130 and 425; Grandmontagne, *Claus Sluter*, p. 550; Ketelsen und Neidhardt, *Das Geheimnis des Jan van Eyck*, p. 257; Blum, *The New Art of the Fifteenth Century*, p. 290.

his low estimation of northern art and noted that the book 'continues to be widely read and enjoyed, so that his judgments remain more influential than they deserve to be'. Meiss concluded that Huizinga 'often clutches at straws and his book [...] contains more nonsense than any good historical book I know'.[68] But other art historians expressed adulation. Ernst Gombrich, who first heard Huizinga lecture at the Warburg Institute in 1937, later praised his originality in reinterpreting Jan van Eyck in terms of what he knew of fifteenth-century culture.[69]

Art historians frequently express both praise and criticism. A typical example is Wim Swaan, who ventriloquizes Huizinga when he writes of 'the final harvest of the Gothic style', notes that the Middle Ages 'waned', and quotes the historian's characterization of the period as one of violent contrasts, when 'life bore the mixed smell of blood and roses'.[70] In contrast to Huizinga, however, Swaan denies that the art of the time lost 'creative vigour' in this period.[71]

Some consider Huizinga a central figure for the discipline of art history. He appears in W. Eugene Kleinbauer's book on the methods of art history, in the *Dictionary of Art Historians*, and in an encyclopedia on Dutch art.[72] Others see him as an important cultural historian. In 1993, Francis Haskell devoted more than 30 pages to Huizinga in his chapter on historians who write about fifteenth-century Flemish art.[73] Haskell begins the chapter in the late eighteenth century and ends with Huizinga's interest in art, his views about art, and his opposition to the ideas of such art historians as Louis Courajod, Hippolyte Fierens-Gevaert, and Karl Voll, who all viewed early Netherlandish painting as the beginning of the Renaissance in the north. Haskell praises Huizinga for his evocative writing, filled with sounds and smells, but criticizes him for omitting bourgeois art and for rarely discussing specific artworks within the contexts of his other themes. For example, in his discussion of the violent tenor of fifteenth-century life, Huizinga makes no mention of the gory Justice paintings of Bouts and David, and although dreams are a recurrent theme, they are never related to the art of Bosch. Haskell concludes, 'Huizinga's response to fifteenth century art was original,

68 Meiss, *French Painting in the Time of Jean de Berry: The Limbourgs*, I, pp. 40, 433, n. 16.

69 Gombrich, *Ideals and Idols*, p. 45. For the date of the lecture, see Gombrich, 'The High Seriousness of Play', p. 139.

70 Swaan, *The Late Middle Ages*, pp. 7, 22.

71 Ibid., p. 7.

72 Kleinbauer, *Modern Perspectives*, p. 147; Sorensen, 'Huizinga, Johan'; Kempers, 'Huizinga, Johan (1872-1945)', p. 187.

73 Haskell, 'Huizinga and the "Flemish Renaissance"', pp. 431, 468-498.

and the ingenuity with which he drew on his impressions of it in order to interpret the character of a whole civilization remains as stimulating as it was sophisticated – and perhaps misguided'.[74]

Haskell returned to the subject of Huizinga in a later article that suggested that the works of Hippolyte Taine and John Ruskin foreshadowed *Autumn of the Middle Ages* and that explored Panofsky's ideas in the light of Huizinga's. Perhaps Haskell's most valuable accomplishment, however, is his attempt to try to recreate Huizinga's experience of visiting the 1902 exhibition of Flemish art. Haskell notes that no paintings by Rogier van der Weyden were displayed and only a small work by the Master of Flémalle, which may explain Huizinga's focus on Jan van Eyck. Furthermore, most of the exhibited works were second-rate paintings by unoriginal artists, which may have sparked Huizinga's theory that early Netherlandish painting is sterile and derivative. The presence of Hans Memling's *Shrine of St. Ursula*, a carved and gilded wooden reliquary containing oil-on-panel inserts, may also have suggested 'a chivalrous fairy story', which would have reinforced Huizinga's interest in chivalry.[75] In short, Haskell's analysis helps explain the development of Huizinga's views on early Netherlandish painting and culture, especially since he began reading fifteenth-century chronicles and poetry only after he saw the exhibition of 1902.

Although some art historians have criticized *Autumn of the Middle Ages*, others have recognized its seminal importance. Lucy Freeman Sandler terms the book one of the 'defining works of history, [...] works that reach out beyond the world of professional scholarship even as they change it', and Susie Nash agrees that it is an 'influential and evocative text'.[76] In addition its writing style is often praised. Larry Silver commended its 'incomparable prose', and Sherry Lindquist admired its 'evocative, romantic' tone.[77]

Nor were Gerson and Haskell the only art historians to engage with the substantive issues raised by Huizinga's study. Hugo van der Velden's book on a votive portrait by Gerard Loyet takes as its starting point some of Huizinga's ideas: that our knowledge of art cannot rest solely on surviving objects, that fifteenth-century art was produced to serve the patron, that no clear boundary distinguishes art from craft, and that the importance of

74 Ibid., p. 488.

75 Haskell, 'Art and History', pp. 12, 14 (quote).

76 Sandler, Review of Michael Camille, *Master of Death*, p. 485; Nash, *Northern Renaissance Art*, p. 327.

77 Silver, *Marketing Maximilian*, p. 270; Lindquist, *Agency, Visuality and Society*, p. 85.

panel painting to the Burgundian dukes has been vastly overrated, whereas their interest in 'pomp and splendour' cannot be rated highly enough. Van der Velden concludes that Huizinga's 'materialistic interpretation of early Netherlandish art [...] has much to recommend it'.[78]

In 2014, Bernhard Ridderbos placed Huizinga's *Herfsttij* at the center of his analysis of Flemish fifteenth-century painting, terming it the most praised cultural study written in Dutch.[79] In his introduction, he summarizes Huizinga's book and its reception among art historians, suggesting that it was often ignored because its treatment of art was both brief and superficial.[80] Subsequent chapters, which focus on a single painter, begin with an examination of Huizinga's ideas about the artist. Ridderbos asserts that the inspiration for his book was the *Herfsttij*, which he termed a stimulating and admirable study, which both intrigued and irritated him.[81] For example, he notes that although Huizinga praises the 'lofty, dignified seriousness and the deep peace' of Memling's art, he does not otherwise mention him.[82] Ridderbos attributes this neglect to the fact that Memling's paintings were not commissioned by courtly patrons, the focus of Huizinga's book.

But the vast majority of references to *Autumn of the Middle Ages* are brief. Lotte Brand Philip cites Huizinga's descriptions of Burgundian 'mechanical marvels' to support her theory of a machine-operated Ghent Altarpiece.[83] Michael Komanecky refers to Huizinga's description of the medieval Satan.[84] Lynn F. Jacobs is captivated with Huizinga's characterization of the fifteenth century as a time of vivid and contrasting colors.[85] Gregory Clark cites Huizinga as a source for a statement from Philip the Good upon the death of his one-year-old infant.[86] Catheline Périer-d'Ieteren points to Huizinga as an early proponent of the idea that the northern Netherlands had stylistic features that were distinct from those of Flanders.[87] Sherry Lindquist commends his notion that the boundary between the religious and secular spheres is porous, and views Huizinga as an early pioneer in

78 Van der Velden, *The Donor's Image*, pp. 3, 4 (quote), 5, 285 (quote). For Huizinga, also see pp. 6, 104, 155, 250.

79 Ridderbos, *Schilderkunst in de Bourgondische Nederlanden*, p. 13.

80 Ibid., p. 12.

81 Ibid., p. 20.

82 Huizinga, *Autumn*, p. 294; Ridderbos, *Schilderkunst in de Bourgondische Nederlanden*, p. 247.

83 Philip, *The Ghent Altarpiece*, p. 114.

84 Komanecky, 'Introduction', p. 10.

85 Jacobs, *Early Netherlandish Carved Altarpieces*, pp. 70 and 281, n. 70.

86 Clark, *Made in Flanders*, p. 158, n. 30.

87 Périer-d'Ieteren, *Dieric Bouts*, p. 23.

the recognition of the importance of the patron in the production of art.[88] *Autumn of the Middle Ages* is even invoked by historians of modern Jewish art as a methodological model.[89]

Sometimes even Huizinga's critics build on his ideas. Boudewijn Bakker invokes Huizinga's discussion of the writings of Denis the Carthusian, a close adviser to Philip the Good, Duke of Burgundy, in order to interpret the illuminations of the Limbourg Brothers. Rather than conclude, with Huizinga, that the Burgundians had no art theory, Bakker argues that Denis, among others living in the late Middle Ages, 'defined beauty as exceptional, awe-inspiring, and picturesque'.[90] Umberto Eco agreed, warning that 'one must be careful not to equate an imprecision of language with the absence of a sense of a state of aesthetic contemplation'.[91] Bret Rothstein supports Huizinga's views that fifteenth-century Flemish art proliferates and is a 'feast for the eyes', but disagrees with his view that painters lack originality. Rothstein concludes that 'Huizinga's pejorative tone seems at odds with both the sophistication and the undeniably religious sentiment' of their art.[92]

Art historians often cite Huizinga's discussion of late medieval attitudes toward death. Albert Châtelet invokes them in the context of what he terms the fifteenth-century Netherlandish fear of death.[93] Carol M. Richardson and Douglas Brine support Huizinga's idea that northern European art shows a preoccupation with death, especially compared to contemporary Italian works.[94] By contrast, Ashby Kinch concludes that art historians have moved away from Huizinga's negative conception of the fifteenth century as obsessed with death and instead now see images of death in a positive light, 'as a powerful late medieval engagement with one of life's central questions'.[95]

Several art historians criticize Huizinga's interpretation of the relationship between images and religious devotion. Benjamin Lloyd asserts that Sluter's detailed treatment of his sculpture should not be viewed as a sign of decay and an impediment to religious practice, but rather as an enhancement of Christian devotion.[96] Jeffrey Hamburger censured Huizinga on three

88 Lindquist, *Agency, Visuality and Society*, pp. 85, 195.
89 Cohen, 'An Introductory Essay', p. 3.
90 Bakker, 'Conquering the Horizon', p. 207.
91 Eco, *Art and Beauty in the Middle Ages*, p. 12.
92 Rothstein, *Sight and Spirituality*, pp. 176-178.
93 Châtelet, *Early Dutch Painting*, p. 87.
94 Richardson, 'Art and Death', p. 224; Brine, *Pious Memories*, pp. 19, 247, n. 85.
95 Kinch, *Imago Mortis*, p. 4.
96 Lloyd, 'Disguised Symbolism', pp. 14-15.

separate occasions, asserting, 'The nexus between popularization and vulgarization received canonical status in Johan Huizinga's *Waning of the Middle Ages*'.[97] John R. Decker disagreed with Huizinga's view that art offered, to use Decker's term, 'half-crazed mental games' to superstitious devotees, and Michael Camille agreed that Huizinga did not satisfactorily explain the mystical interpretation of images.[98] Claude Schaefer quotes at length Huizinga's interpretation of the Melun *Madonna* as godless, before rejecting it, noting that the donor, Étienne Chevalier, was a pious Christian and that the diptych was commissioned for a church.[99]

Another type of criticism was voiced by Marina Belozerskaya, who condemned Huizinga for his Italian bias and argued that he failed to recognize the huge demand for Flemish luxury goods, including art, across Europe, especially in Italy, and instead saw the Burgundian culture as decadent and declining.[100] In addition, recently Ethan Matt Kavaler critiqued Huizinga's view of late Gothic architecture as representing the death of an old style.[101]

Despite the many art historians who mention *Autumn of the Middle Ages*, it is also important to note those who do not. The early art historians Friedrich Winkler, Charles de Tolnay, Hermann Beenken, and Leo van Puyvelde fail to cite it, the most extensive monograph on Jan van Eyck by the noted Belgian scholar Elisabeth Dhanens never refers to it, and the comprehensive Belgian bibliography on early Netherlandish painting, published in 1984, omits it.[102] In addition, those art historians who see themselves as scientific – and this includes especially those who specialize in technical studies – have little use for Huizinga's romantic, evocative, and imaginative portrayal of fifteenth-century northern culture.

Art historians are divided on Huizinga's fundamental argument as to whether fifteenth-century Flemish and northern French art are Gothic or Renaissance. Often architecture and manuscript illumination are categorized as medieval, whereas panel painting is more often termed Renaissance. But frequently Gothic and Renaissance are viewed as styles that coexisted at the same time and place, and art historians have shown

97 Hamburger, 'The Visual and the Visionary', pp. 165, 166; Hamburger, *Nuns as Artists*, p. 222; Hamburger, *The Visual and the Visionary*, p. 113.

98 Decker, *The Technology of Salvation*, p. 93, n. 55.

99 Schaefer, *Jean Fouquet*, p. 150.

100 Belozerskaya, *Rethinking the Renaissance*, pp. 2, 8, 12, 41-45, 66. See also pp. 34, 40.

101 Kavaler, *Renaissance Gothic*, especially pp. 3-4, 23.

102 Winkler, *Die altniederländische Malerei*; De Tolnay, *Le Maître de Flémalle*; Beenken, *Hubert und Jan van Eyck*; Van Puyvelde, *Van Eyck*; Dhanens, *Hubert and Jan van Eyck*; Comblen-Sonkes, *Guide bibliographique*.

that the reasons why a particular style was chosen often had more to do with politics, religion, or socioeconomic class rather than with aesthetic taste.[103] Moreover, most art historians envision fifteenth-century visual culture, especially Flemish painting, not as a sterile end, but rather as a fertile beginning that exerted a tremendous influence not only on later northern art, but also on the visual culture of Italy. Finally, art historians also disagree with Huizinga's interpretation of the realistic details in early Netherlandish painting and instead view the enrichment of religious imagery with everyday motifs as a way to make art come alive for fifteenth-century viewers. But even those who reject Huizinga's most basic premise often admire his work. James Snyder's *Northern Renaissance Art* terms *Autumn of the Middle Ages* 'fascinating', praises its interdisciplinary approach, and supports its portrayal of 'a rich tapestry of a world'.[104]

Conclusions

Are Peters and Simons right, then, to conclude that *Autumn of the Middle Ages* 'left little or no mark on the field of art history'?[105] Wessel Krul, pointing to Huizinga's lack of interest in iconography, agrees that 'art historians have in general taken little notice of his work'.[106] Haskell's conclusion is similar, although a bit more nuanced:

> Above all, as far as I can see, no art historian now agrees with the central tenet of his book to the effect that the magnificent art of fifteenth-century Flanders [...] represents not an innovative 'Renaissance' but an autumnal, if ostentatious, decline from the Middle Ages [...] but Huizinga's view has either been explicitly rejected – as by the distinguished connoisseur of Northern Art, Horst Gerson, in an otherwise appreciative appraisal – or (more usually) totally ignored.[107]

Certainly art historians have rejected Huizinga's central argument that fifteenth-century art was purely retrospective. They have also spurned his theory of biological determinism, that is, his view that cultures are

103 Kavaler, *Renaissance Gothic*. Linda Neagley is currently writing a book exploring the meanings of buildings in Normandy that juxtaposes Renaissance and Gothic styles.
104 Snyder, *Northern Renaissance Art*, p. 16.
105 Peters and Simons, 'The New Huizinga', p. 615.
106 Krul, 'In the Mirror', p. 377.
107 Haskell, 'Art and History', pp. 3-4.

born, mature, and die. Nor did they embrace his style of writing. For most art historians it seemed too novelistic and impressionistic to convey ideas based on reason and supported by evidence. As E.H. Kossmann concludes, Huizinga's 'major works are not based on hypotheses, checked, rejected, reworded, and reworked, but on theses, visions, elucidated, enlarged, commented upon rather than demonstrated'.[108] Furthermore, few of Huizinga's art historical ideas have held up over time.

Autumn of the Middle Ages at first attracted little attention, initially because few art historians read Dutch. Then, when Panofsky's tightly argued, profusely illustrated, and heavily footnoted studies became the model for art history, Huizinga's book seemed inadequate, especially the abridged English version and those editions that were not illustrated.[109] Most art historians viewed it as irrelevant to the disciplinary questions that most concerned them and most disagreed with Huizinga's personal judgments about northern art, which seemed so overwhelmingly negative. Furthermore, although Huizinga foreshadowed the recent art historical turn away from positivism and toward a broader range of study objects and an embrace of interdisciplinarity, the new materialism, emotions, and erotica, there is no evidence that he was a direct source for those approaches. Long ago Huizinga proclaimed that 'the historical sense is increasingly being displaced by the visual', but Bram Kempers justly reminds us that historians' use of art rarely convinces art historians.[110] *Autumn of the Middle Ages* is to a great extent no exception to that rule.

Yet Peters, Simons, Krul, and Haskell underestimate Huizinga's influence. Art historians continued to read *Autumn of the Middle Ages*, continued to cite it, and continued to respond to a wide range of issues raised by the book. Many were persuaded by Huizinga, especially by his non-art-historical observations, particularly his portrayal of the *mentalité* of the time. Typical responses are those of Craig Harbison, who agreed with Huizinga that the period was characterized by 'many, often conflicting forces', and James Snyder, who saw the 'serious melancholy and pessimism of the age that Huizinga described so vividly in his classic text'.[111] More importantly, Huizinga helped bring attention to early Netherlandish art, and offered an interdisciplinary model that made clear the wide range of sources that could illuminate

108 Kossmann, 'Postscript', p. 231.

109 The first and second Dutch editions were not illustrated.

110 Huizinga, 'De kunst der Van Eycks' (citation in *VW*, III, p. 436); Kempers, 'De verleiding van het beeld', p. 31.

111 Snyder, *Northern Renaissance Art*, p. 105; Harbison, 'Iconography and Iconology', p. 401.

Burgundian culture, from chronicles and romances to theological tracts and images. Art historians, in short, followed the general pattern outlined by Hugenholtz for historians. Most of their comments, he noted, 'are little more than short notices. [...] Moreover, in reading [them] [...] I became very much aware of the difficulty of drawing general conclusions from reactions which in many respects turned out to be highly idiosyncratic'.[112] Art historians were not swayed by Huizinga's major art historical arguments, but many were stimulated by his scintillating book, which bristled with new ideas and observations and captivated readers with its vivid and eloquent prose. This remains his fundamental contribution to the field.[113]

About the Author

Diane Wolfthal is David and Caroline Minter Professor of Humanities, Professor of Art History at Rice University. Diane Wolfthal's books include *In and Out of the Marital Bed: Seeing Sex in Renaissance Art* (Yale University Press, 2010), *Picturing Yiddish: Gender, Identity, and Memory in Illustrated Yiddish Books of Renaissance Italy* (Brill, 2004), *Images of Rape: The 'Heroic' Tradition and Its Alternatives* (Cambridge University Press, 1999), and *The Beginnings of Netherlandish Canvas Painting* (Cambridge University Press, 1989). She also coauthored *Princes and Paupers: The Art of Jacques Callot* (2013) and *Corpus of Fifteenth-Century Painting in the Southern Netherlands and the Principality of Liège: Early Netherlandish Paintings in Los Angeles* (KIK-IRPA, 2014). She is a founding coeditor of *Early Modern Women: An Interdisciplinary Journal*. Her two major current projects are 'Household Help: Servants and Slaves in Europe and Abroad, 1400-1700', under contract to Yale University Press, and an exhibition, 'Medieval Money', for the Morgan Library and Museum in New York.
dbw2@rice.edu

112 Hugenholtz, 'The Fame', p. 93.
113 Note Umberto Eco's words: 'The number of occasions on which I have quoted from Huizinga shows how fruitful I have found him to be.' See Eco, *Art and Beauty in the Middle Ages*, p. 123.

7 Did Germany Have a Medieval *Herbstzeit*?[1]

Larry Silver

Abstract

German courts of the Holy Roman Empire are not frequently associated with the autumnal values portrayed for France and Burgundy by Johan Huizinga. Only around 1500 does court patronage around Habsburg Emperor Maximilian I or in major provinces, such as Saxony or Bavaria, truly emerge in German-speaking lands, and it has often been associated with a 'Northern Renaissance' around the principal artistic figure of Albrecht Dürer. But because Maximilian was heir and ruler of the Burgundian Netherlands through his marriage in 1477 to Mary of Burgundy, he truly participated in that same chivalric culture so firmly established under the Valois. This chapter examines the adoption of Burgundian court culture as an essential instrument of statecraft by Emperor Maximilian and his 'theater state' around 1500, while also noting a rare, earlier instance of sophisticated court culture on German soil in the art of the anonymous Housebook Master or Master of the Amsterdam Cabinet.

Keywords: *Goldenes Rössl*, Housebook Master, Maximilian I, Mary of Burgundy, Hans Burgkmair, tournaments, Golden Fleece

German courts of the Holy Roman Empire are not frequently associated with the autumnal values portrayed for France and Burgundy by Johan Huizinga. Only around 1500 does German court patronage emerge, especially

1 References to Huizinga's masterwork below will refer to the translation by Rodney Payton and Ulrich Mammitzsch: Huizinga, *Autumn of the Middle Ages*. Like the translators, I want to acknowledge my own profound debt to Prof. Karl Weintraub of the University of Chicago, who introduced me to Huizinga in general and to that great book in particular. See his own publication, Weintraub, *Visions of Culture*, pp. 208-246.

Arnade, Peter, Martha Howell, and Anton van der Lem (eds), *Rereading Huizinga: Autumn of the Middle Ages, a Century Later.* Taylor & Francis Group, 2019
DOI: 10.5117/9789462983724_CH07

Illustration 7.1 **Anonymous Parisian goldsmith, *Goldenes Rössl* (Little Golden Horse), c. 1405, gold, silver, enamel, precious stones. Altötting, Schatzkammer der Heiligen Kapelle**

around Habsburg Emperor Maximilian I, or in such major provinces such as Saxony or Bavaria, and it has often been associated with a 'Northern Renaissance' around the principal artistic figure of Albrecht Dürer.[2] But because Maximilian was heir and ruler of the Burgundian Netherlands after his marriage in 1477 to Mary of Burgundy, he also truly participated in that same chivalric culture so firmly established under the Valois dukes. Thus

2 Michel, *Emperor Maximilian I* (exhibition catalog with a full bibliography); Müller et al., *Apelles am Fürstenhof.* The definitive study of Maximilian is the five-volume study by Hermann Wiesflecker, *Kaiser Maximilian I.: das Reich Österreich und Europa an der Wende zur Neuzeit*, especially vol. 5: *Der Kaiser und seine Umwelt. Hof, Staat, Wirtschaft, Gesellschaft und Kultur* (1986).

this chapter will examine the adoption of Burgundian court culture as an essential instrument of statecraft by Emperor Maximilian, who cultivated a 'theater state' around 1500; it will also note another rare, earlier instance of sophisticated court culture in fifteenth-century Germany: the art of the anonymous Housebook Master.[3]

Courts inevitably intermarried, so the first main instance of a literal transplant of French court culture onto German soil resulted from just such a royal marriage. The most spectacular and luxurious surviving example of Parisian court art was a 1405 new year's gift to French King Charles VI from his consort Queen Isabeau of Bavaria: the *Goldenes Rössl* (Little Golden Horse), a miniature sculpture ensemble of enamel, ivory, and gold, plus pearls and precious gemstones.[4]

It depicts in miniature a Huizinga fantasy world, combining courtly ceremony with religion. This *Goldenes Rössl*, or 'Little Golden Horse', as it has come to be named from a notable detail, actually features the Virgin Mary, draped in white robes, with her Son, surrounded by angels while seated beneath a golden sun in a raised garden bower. Flanking the Madonna at her feet, three further childlike saints – John the Baptist and John the Evangelist in white, plus red-robed St. Catherine of Alexandria (her martyr's palm in gold is extended by the Christ Child) – suggest that this garden vision occurs in a truly heavenly setting. The central holy figures are adored further below by two profile kneeling figures, arrayed according to rank. The king, Charles VI, dressed in royal robes with fleurs-de-lis but also wearing the armor of a knight, appears on the favorable viewer left. Opposite him, a page holds his helmet and royal crown; between them lies the king's prayer book at his prie-dieu, or prayer stool. Below them all at base of this precious object stands the eponymous little white horse, attended by another standing page in livery.

Almost all the Huizinga *Herfsttij* elements are here, starting with the ceremonial hierarchy of figures on different levels according to their sanctity or worldly status. Luxury abounds in the materials themselves, such as the enormous brooch of ruby and pearls worn by the Virgin, but they also gesture toward current court values of exquisite workmanship

3 For the cultural concept of the theater state, see Geertz, *Negara*; for European royal ritual and ceremony, see Geertz, 'Centers, Kings, and Charisma'.

4 Baumstark, *Das Goldene Rössl*. The work entered the Bavarian ducal collection in 1405 and remained there until 1506 before being donated to the pilgrimage church in Altötting as a pious bequest (Eikelmann, 'Zur Geschichte des Marienbildes'). For the court tradition of new year's gifts, see Buettner, 'Past Presents', pp. 598-625, esp. 607, fig. 6.

in metalwork, *email en ronde bosse*.[5] Almost all other extant French luxury decorative arts creations of the period, such as Jean de Berry's *Reliquary of the Thorn* (London, British Museum, Waddesdon Bequest), combine superb craftsmanship and precious materials with religious dedications (though many other worldly luxuries, such as jeweled brooches, have surely been lost for their valuable components). Just as in the religious imagery of Jan van Eyck, noted by Huizinga, heavenly queenship is signaled by worldly trappings of wealth, status, and power, including the angelic attendants around the holy figures and the strict hierarchy of placement (note again that the king appears by the favorable right hand of the Virgin and receives the inclination of Madonna and Child).[6] Luxury reinforces devotion; courtliness on earth reflects the hierarchy of heaven.

The theme of the Madonna in the enclosed garden, often a garden of roses without thorns, a space redolent of her purity, enjoyed a long and lively representation in the visual arts of the later Middle Ages, in part connected to the love imagery of the bride in the Song of Songs.[7] Of course, this trope already informs the secular allegory, *Roman de la Rose*, in thirteenth-century France and sparked the lively *querelle* about chastity and chivalry in connection with that work.[8] But fifteenth-century German painters were also attracted to showing the holy figures in an enclosed garden or bower. Chiefly they worked along the Rhine: the anonymous Master of the Garden of Love (c. 1410/1420; Frankfurt, Staedel Institute), Stefan Lochner of Cologne (c. 1445/1450; Cologne, Wallraf-Richartz Museum), and even Martin Schongauer of Colmar (1473; Colmar, St. Martin's Church).[9]

But the world of Huizinga might be even more pertinent if Willibald Sauerländer's claim about the *Goldenes Rössl* is correct. He argues that this ensemble actually enacts a wishful fantasy quite at odds with the reality of the court of Charles VI, where the dashing knight-king of Isabeau's miniature

5 Eikelmann, 'Goldemail um 1400'; Meiss, *French Painting in the Time of Jean de Berry: The Late Fourteenth Century*, I, pp. 141-146, noting (p. 142) that '[l]ike contemporary paintings the little sculptures consist of a peculiar blend of naturalistic and fanciful forms. [...] [In] the context of the *joyaux* the objects that are in fact natural [the jewels] appear fanciful, whereas the artificial forms – that is, the simulated animals, flowers, and human beings – are the more "naturalistic."'

6 Huizinga, *Autumn*, pp. 333-335; Kahsnitz, 'Kleinod und Andachtsbild'. Jan van Eyck's small *Madonna at the Fountain* (1439; Antwerp, Koninklijk Museum) could be added to this list; Purtle, *The Marian Paintings*, pp. 157-167.

7 Vetter, *Maria im Rosenhag*; Falkenburg, *Fruit of Devotion*, esp. pp. 16-37.

8 Huizinga, *Autumn*, pp. 133-140.

9 Vetter, *Maria im Rosenhag*, frontispiece, figs. 22-23; see also Landolt, *German Painting*, pp. 67, 126. On Lochner, see Julian Chapuis, *Stefan Lochner*, pp. 88-94, comparing it to metalwork, expressly to the *Goldenes Rössl*. On Schongauer, see Heinrichs, *Martin Schongauer*, pp. 129-158.

was replacing a monarch who in real life increasingly was susceptible to mental illness and violence. Sauerländer sees their two royal children Jean (b. 1398) and Catherine (b. 1401) as also depicted by their childlike name saints in this votive image, thus patron saints who can act as advocates before the Madonna and Child.[10] Thus within the blend of courtliness and devotion which shaped the *Goldenes Rössl*, another Huizinga autumnal quality emerges – the ready familiarity of venerated saints as companions and intercessors, described by Huizinga in his chapter, 'The Depiction of the Sacred'.[11] And we recall that this image did not begin as a church donation, but instead as a private, if royal, commission. Thus, while still subordinated in kneeling posture and profile location below the holy figures, King Charles VI nevertheless appears before them as equal in size, granted free access to their presence.

Of course, the *Goldenes Rössl* is not a work produced in Germany, but a masterpiece of the French royal court in Paris. For the most part, the smaller, less centralized German courts within the patchwork quilt of the Holy Roman Empire did not commission such works. But one major exception of courtly imagery is the work made by an anonymous artist from the Middle Rhine, called the Housebook Master, whose work has demonstrable connections to at least one court, Heidelberg, in 1480.[12] He illustrated a dedication page for a 1479 manuscript, *Die Kinder von Limburg* (Heidelberg, Universitätsbibliothek MS Cod. pal. germ. 87), a courtly romance text translated into German by the court minstrel at the Heidelberg court of the Elector Palatine. Like the *Goldenes Rössl*, that manuscript was presented as a new year's gift for 1480, the date that appears on the presentation page by the Housebook Master. There the author, Stabius, kneels before his youthful patron – presumably also the patron of the artist, temporarily or not – Philip the Sincere (Philipp I, der Aufrichtige, 1448-1508). With an air of courtly elegance, he wears an ermine-trimmed robe and fashionable pointed shoes. Even the contents of that text smack of late medieval issues, involving the children of Duke Otto of Limburg, whose daughter must be rescued from captivity by the sultan and returned to a world of arms and love to marry a king's son.

The same courtly fashions (especially in footwear) reappear in an isolated silverpoint drawing (Berlin, Kupferstichkabinett) of *Standing Lovers*, in

10 Sauerländer, 'Kinder als Nothelfer'; see also Rehm, 'Isabeau de Bavière', esp. pp. 24-25.

11 Huizinga, *Autumn*, pp. 190-202.

12 Filedt Kok, *Livelier Than Life*, esp. 245, no. 118, plate V, for the dedication page with a patron, Elector Palatine Philip the Sincere; Hess, *Meister*, pp. 45-46. The original Dutch title of Filedt Kok's important exhibition catalog, *'s Levens Felheid*, directly refers to Huizinga's first chapter of the *Herfsttij*.

Illustration 7.2 Master of the Amsterdam Cabinet [Housebook Master], *A Pair of Lovers*, c. 1480-1485

Gotha, Schlossmuseum

which a long-tressed youth (who resembles Philip the Sincere in the dedication miniature) turns to his ladylove to present her with his feathered hat, perhaps as a gift or love token.[13] This world of courtly love is marked by youth, beauty, true love, and fidelity.

Another drawing, sketchier but plausibly associated with the Housebook Master (Berlin, Kupferstichkabinett) shows a lavish banquet, with a lord seated in the center below a brocaded cloth of honor and surrounded by an entourage comprising more humbly dressed townspeople; Aby Warburg identified the subject as the young Maximilian I, then King of the Romans rather than emperor, enjoying a peacemaking banquet after his release from imprisonment in Bruges (16 May 1488).[14] Whether we acknowledge that specific identification, let alone the claim that it was an eyewitness record of the event, the ceremonial aspect of this scene and its clear social hierarchy of dress, placement, and setting certainly point to the world of the court and to such miniatures as the celebrated January feasting page of the *Très Riches Heures* by the Limbourg Brothers for Duke Jean de Berry (1413-1416).[15]

The verso of the Berlin banquet drawing shows the same aristocrat, this time even more closely resembling extant portraits of the young Maximilian, celebrating mass with an attendant in a private oratory, separated off by a curtain. Such scenes certainly derive from earlier staples of Flemish manuscripts made for the Burgundian court, especially under Duke Philip the Good (d. 1467).[16] They proclaim both piety and a visible social hierarchy for such rulers.

Perhaps more to the point about courtliness in the Housebook Master's work is his marvelous set of drawings of courtly genre scenes in the eponymous volume known as the 'Housebook' (Schloss Wolfegg, Collection Waldburg Wolfegg).[17] That curious title was applied in the nineteenth century, because this mixed volume (with several artists) seemed to encompass issues related to the household of a knight's castle, though in fact it includes

13 Filedt Kok, *Livelier Than Life*, pp. 250-251, no. 121; *From Schongauer to Holbein*, pp. 55-57, no. 15. Hess, *Meister*, pp. 24-25, separates the drawing out, associating it with the drypoints of the eponymous Master of the Amsterdam Cabinet. See also the panel painting (Gotha, Schlossmuseum), *A Pair of Lovers*, fashionably dressed, ascribed to the same artist; Filedt Kok, *Livelier Than Life*, p. 270, no. 133; Hess, *Meister*, pp. 104-113.

14 Filedt Kok, *Livelier Than Life*, pp. 254-256, no. 124; Hess, *Meister*, pp. 50-52; *From Schongauer to Holbein*, pp. 59-62, no. 17; Warburg, 'Zwei Szenen'.

15 Normore, *Feast for the Eyes*, pp. 143-144, plate 1 and passim.

16 Smeyers, *Flemish Miniatures*, pp. 296-297, figs. 9-11.

17 Filedt Kok, *Livelier Than Life*, pp. 218-244, no. 117; Waldburg Wolfegg, *Venus and Mars*, esp. 'Chivalrous Life', pp. 44-74.

Illustration 7.3 Housebook Master, *Standing Lovers*, c. 1485, silverpoint drawing

Berlin, Kupferstich-kabinett

considerable imagery about warfare and astrology (the Children of the Planets) in addition to scenes of jousting and courtship. The heraldry of the book's owner remains unidentified and might even be satirical: a sawed-off golden tree trunk on a blue background, whose shield sits below a jousting helm surmounted by a fierce griffin.[18] The lively bifolio drawing of a military

18 Maria Lanckorónska identified the coat of arms of the frontispiece as that of the castellan of the Schalksburg, a knight of the Ergenzingen family known as Ast (bough), whose castle was owned by the counts of Württemberg by the fifteenth century. Filedt Kok, *Livelier Than Life*, pp. 220-221, citing Maria Lanckorónska, *Das mittelalterliche Hausbuch der fürstlich Waldburgschen Sammlung* (Darmstadt: Roether, 1975).

encampment (fol. 53r-53r1) shows a wagon camp (*Wagenburg*), originally based on Hussite tactics and popular in late-fifteenth-century warfare amid the emerging presence of individual handguns, which could be fired from inside the wagons like from a portable fortress.[19] Such firearms can also be seen along with crossbows among the weapons carried in a preceding fold-out page of an army on the march, led by drum and fife (fol. 51v-52r1). That procession also includes a banner with the device of Emperor Frederick III, 'AEIOU'.[20] The camp tents are punctuated by heraldic banners and shields, which also indicate the central presence of Emperor Frederick III (r. 1452-1493), accompanied by his chancellor Adolf II of Nassau (d. 1475), elector and bishop of Mainz, plus a background tent with the same tree trunk arms as the manuscript owner. This scene has often been identified with the 1475 siege of Neuss near Cologne by Frederick III, when he attempted to blunt the expansion of Duke Charles the Bold of Burgundy; certainly it fits that period. Thus the late-fifteenth-century Holy Roman Empire and its Middle Rhenish region emerge as plausible cultural settings for the Housebook images.

The seven courtly scenes of the Housebook, clustered in a single gathering, contain no text, but like the military scenes later in the volume they feature images, lightly tinted, that all extend over two pages. The first scene is a *Bathhouse* (fol. 18v-19r) located within a walled garden, where a fountain sculpture spouts as courtly couples stroll or sit, while reading aloud (with falcon on arm). On the right side of the image appears the bathhouse, where a quartet of figures soak together, visible through a window. At the left a well-dressed young man wears the insignia of the Order of the Jug, a knightly order established in Aragon and favored by Frederick III, on his white stole.[21] Meanwhile, a lutenist plays for a listener outside, and beside a set table wine is chilling. Even the pets are exotic: a monkey teases a hunting dog. This world of pleasure and leisure corresponds closely to the ideal image of luxurious, untroubled courtly behavior. The following drawing, again as if in echo of Flemish manuscripts, specifically of the boating parties of May scenes from the Labors of the Months,[22] shows a *Castle* (fol. 19v-20r) surrounded by water in an open landscape. Class distinctions are evident here: nobles with

19 Rogers, 'Tactics and the Face of Battle', esp. p. 216; Hall, *Weapons and Warfare*, pp. 108-113; more generally, Vale, *War and Chivalry*. This scene has often been identified with the 1475 siege of Neuss by Frederick III.

20 Lhotsky, 'AEIOV', pp. 155-193.

21 Waldburg Wolfegg, *Venus and Mars*, pp. 72-74; Coreth, 'Orden von der Stola', pp. 34-51.

22 See Smeyers and Van der Stock, *Flemish Illuminated Manuscripts*, pp. 62-63, on the Antwerp, Mayer van den Bergh Breviary, c. 1510.

laurel crowns or other sophisticated headwear stroll as couples, while their servants fish or fowl in the water around them. The moat also contains birds of privilege, swans. In both of these initial courtly drawings the princely buildings provide the appropriate settings for these charming fantasies of courtly behavior, akin to images of bathhouses and gardens of love in late medieval manuscripts, such as the allegorical *Roman de la Rose*.

The following two pages of the Housebook feature knightly tournament contests. Nothing speaks more to the world of Huizinga than jousting, or *pas d'armes*.[23] Of course, these contests were the peacetime preparation of the mounted knight for cavalry combat in actual war. The first double page of the Housebook (fol. 20v-21r) shows a joust with tipped lances, or coronels, the most elite of jousts.[24] The principal antagonists on their caparisoned mounts, with decorated shields and horse cushions, are wearing the heaviest (and costliest) of all armor with a *Stechhelm*, a thick helmet with only a narrow slit for viewing; even the horses wear bits of armor.[25] At the right margin a second for the mounted knight also wears the insignia of the Order of the Jug on his red outfit. Around the jousters, a crowd observes on foot and on horseback, the latter group as couples who wear the same fashionable headwear, footwear, and costly costumes already seen in other drawings. Many are seen from behind. The start of the event is being signaled from horseback by a trumpeter, as a court fool, wearing a costume with asses' ears and a pointed dunce cap, rides behind him with a flute.

The next double page (fol. 21v-22r) shows a joust at full tilt, viewed only by men on horseback, many of them wearing helmets; their tinted costumes mirror the contestants, showing that they are retainers. This contest is *Scharfrennen* with pointed, untipped lances, lighter armor, and specific, hatlike helmets that did not cover the full face; it more closely simulates the danger of what might occur on the field of battle, involving hitting the opponent's shield without the goal of unhorsing him.[26] That this event might take place in a camp setting is further suggested by the lively horse race across the top of the sheets.

A final pair of pictures in the Housebook takes up the other significant peacetime training-ground for the knight: the hunt, whose site, a game

23 Huizinga, *Autumn*, pp. 88-91; Vale, *War and Chivalry*, pp. 63-99.

24 Waldburg Wolfegg, *Venus and Mars*, pp. 54-56.

25 Beaufort-Spontin and Pfaffenbichler, *Meisterwerke der Hof-, Jagd- und Rüstkammer*, p. 88, no. 20; Pyhrr, LaRocca, and Breiding, *The Armoured Horse*. A *Stechhelm* adorns the coat of arms of the original owner.

26 Beaufort-Spontin et al., *Meisterwerke der Hof-, Jagd- und Rüstkammer*, pp. 90-91, no. 21; Vale, *War and Chivalry*, pp. 70-87.

preserve, still remains a place of privilege and wealth, protected strictly against poaching by lesser classes. On the first image (fol. 22v-23r), couples ride horses together, women sitting sidesaddle, in pursuit of a stag in the lower left corner.[27] The leader of the hunt, who turns to face the group, again wears the insignia of the Order of the Jug. A background setting includes productive lands with a village, a watermill, and fields ploughed by hard-working peasants, but it also shows a hilltop castle in the upper left. The entire scene is reminiscent of the seigneurial supervision deeply encoded into the Labors of the Months images, beginning with the much-imitated Limbourg Brothers' *Très Riches Heures* (1413-1416; Chantilly), where the August page shows a hunt with falcons across the foreground before a background castle and ploughed fields, plus a stream where peasants swim to cool off.[28] Hunting, especially hawking, is more commonly shown in association with May in aristocratic illustrated manuscript calendar cycles.

In the last of the courtly genre scenes of the Housebook (fol. 23v-24r) two noble couples consort arm-in-arm within the confines of a castle, surrounded by laborers outside the stable. Women outnumber men here, and the real hunt is a courtship, as a pair of ladies set out in the middle distance. At the horizon, one peasant is caught by a trap and hangs upside by his leg from a tree; near him another man hides in a bush shelter from a woman who clearly is searching for him. This scene is more socially mixed as well as comically fanciful, but its audience remains aristocratic, more appropriate to the lords of such a castle (and owners of such a volume) than to their servants.

Taken together, then, the charming drawings by the anonymous Housebook Master use themes, especially of knightly tournaments and the stag hunt, which also suggest a lively world of court culture and activity, including the markers of the knightly Order of the Jug, then favored in imperial Germany.[29] His imagery of warfare also situates his imagery around the later 1470s, even if the identification of the *Wagenburg* does not necessarily specify the 1475 action at the siege of Neuss by Emperor Frederick III. And the imperial device of AEIOU reinforces his associations with the imperial court. In similar fashion, his drawings that seemingly involve a young Maximilian

27 For more on the association of the stag as a noble quarry with courtly behavior, see Thiebaux, 'The Medieval Chase', pp. 260-274; Thiebaux, *The Stag of Love*.

28 Huizinga, *Autumn*, p. 352, plates 32-33. For an analogous aristocratic view of the peasantry, see Camille, 'The Lord's Lands'.

29 Hess, *Meister*, esp. pp. 42-44. See Huizinga, *Autumn*, pp. 92-97, for knightly orders.

Illustration 7.4 Albrecht Dürer, *Wedding of Maximilian of Habsburg to Mary of Burgundy* (Small Triumphal Chariot), c. 1516-1518, woodcut

I at banquet and at mass might not be expressly linked to events in Bruges in 1488, but already that young prince, the heir and successor as emperor to Frederick III, was already deeply involved in the crossover between Burgundy and the Empire, since he married the heiress of Duke Charles the Bold in August, 1477, mere months after Charles's death in January. Their betrothal, however, was arranged already in 1473 at a ceremonial meeting between Charles the Bold and Frederick III at Trier, where the splendor of the Burgundians was on full display.[30] Thus Maximilian was already an object of interest during that watershed period of the Housebook Master's activity. Moreover, using the presentation page miniature (1480) of the *Kinder von Limburg* manuscript as an indication of work at the Heidelberg court of Philip the Sincere, we can at least connect and date our master to an actual court, one that promoted humanistic learning as well as romances.

30 *Splendours of the Burgundian Court*, pp. 264-315, esp. pp. 264-265.

But the true heir to Huizinga's Burgundy and its theater state was Maximilian of Habsburg (1459-1519), later Emperor Maximilian I (officially titled as of 1508 with a coronation in Trent). Huizinga tersely characterizes the mid-century Burgundian splendor under Duke Philip the Good in his 'preference for chivalry and splendor, in his crusade plans, in the old-fashioned literary forms he protected'.[31] Maximilian adopted that heritage in 1477 with his wedding to Mary of Burgundy, sole heir of Charles the Bold, the recently deceased son of Philip the Good, who truly set the cultural model for court splendor.[32]

While the patronage of Philip the Good has only been addressed episodically, the crusade remained especially important to him, particularly in the year after the fall of Constantinople, when at his legendary Feast of the Pheasant in Lille (17 February 1454), he led the Order of the Golden Fleece, his own Burgundian order founded in 1430, in vows to go on crusade and even to duel the Grand Turk in single combat, if necessary.[33] Philip's productive scriptorium generated numerous illuminated manuscripts for him on the subject of the crusades, a cause that held special pride for the House of Burgundy, since his father in his own youth had gone on crusade as Count of Nevers, leading the disastrous Battle of Nicopolis in 1396.[34] Moreover, part of the enduring splendor and dynastic identity of the dukes of Burgundy emerged in their elaborate tombs, beginning with the Dijon complex at the Chartreuse de Champmol of the original Duke of Burgundy, the Valois brother of the king of France, Philip the Bold (d. 1404), designed by sculptor Claus Sluter.[35] Indeed, Maximilian I maintained virtually all of these pastimes, the 'serious play' of chivalry for Huizinga. Little wonder that later generations would dub Maximilian, 'the last knight' (*Der letzte Ritter*).

A sense of how much the chivalric world mattered to Maximilian emerges from his (unfinished) *Triumphal Procession* imagery, first dictated by the emperor to his private secretary Marx Treitzsaurwein and later realized in the form of luxury illuminations (originally over a hundred meters long!) by Albrecht Altdorfer of Regensburg and in woodcuts (unfinished) by Hans

31 Huizinga, *Autumn*, p. 288; see Smith, *Philip the Good, Duke of Burgundy*.

32 Mary died in a riding accident in 1482, though Maximilian made many images, including posthumous portraits, in devotion to her memory; see Roberts, 'The Chronology'.

33 Huizinga, *Autumn*, pp. 95-97, 101, 106; Moodey, *Crusader Histories*, pp. 106-110, 125-148; Vaughan, *Philip the Good*, pp. 143-145, 266, 297-298; ibid., pp. 160-162, for the Order of the Golden Fleece. On court feasts, see Normore, *Feast for the Eyes*, passim.

34 Huizinga, *Autumn*, pp. 1, 86; Vaughan, *John the Fearless*, p. 4. For the manuscripts: Moodey, *Crusader Histories*, passim.

35 Huizinga, *Autumn*, pp. 307-310; Lindquist, *Agency, Visuality and Society*, esp. pp. 139-147.

Burgkmair and other graphic artists from Augsburg.[36] These images were representations only of an ideal parade; Maximilian delighted both in the traditions of illumination, like Philip the Good, but he had also discovered the possibility of media outreach and utilized the printing press not only for distribution of texts but also for multiple images of woodcuts.[37] Of course, the idea of a triumphal procession stems from victory marches with armies, captives, and booty by imperial generals or else a ruler's ceremonial arrival, or *adventus* into ancient Rome; elements of that classical heritage, frequently invoked by rulers in Renaissance Europe, are also still retained in Maximilian's program, which in fact includes images on floats (or banners in the Altdorfer miniatures) of military victories before a trophy car and a march of conquered enemies.[38]

More revealing, however, of his chivalric orientation from Burgundian models are the initial stages of that visual *Procession*. Crucially, these initial woodcuts, complete with careful portraits of court officers, were designed and supervised by Hans Burgkmair, the principal illustrator for many of Maximilian's proposed book projects.[39] The *Triumphal Procession* actually begins with an ensemble of Maximilian's assistants in the hunt, his lifetime consuming passion.[40] Peacetime skills in hunting link up with wartime ability to ride and use arms, and one set of designs by Augsburg artist Jörg Breu for glass paintings at a hunting lodge of Maximilian pair hunt scenes with images of his celebrated military campaigns.[41] The ambitious emperor, who also fancied himself an expert in many leisure fields, even planned to author several books on this subject, as a roster of titles dictated to Treitzsaurwein indicates: 'Hunting', 'Falconry', 'Fishing'. He did manage to compile a 'Secret Hunting Book' and a 'Tyrol Hunting Book', to record the naturalist details of his favorite sites and techniques for hunting in his home region.[42]

First place in the *Procession* belongs to falconry, an ancient courtly pastime but also the most public and safest of hunts, open to women

36 Michel, *Emperor Maximilian I*, pp. 224-249, 268-271, nos. 53, 68; Silver, *Marketing Maximilian*, esp. pp. 169-195. Burgkmair et al., *Triumph of Maximilian I*; Altdorfer, *Der Triumphzug Kaiser Maximilians I*, passim.

37 Eisenstein, *Printing Press*.

38 Strong, *Art and Power*, esp. pp. 65-91.

39 Silver, 'The "Papier-Kaiser"'; for the Altdorfer miniatures of the *Procession*, see Michel, '"For Praise and Eternal Memory"'.

40 Schack, *Der Kreis um Maximilian I*, passim.

41 Cuneo, 'Images of Warfare'; Silver, 'Glass Menageries', pp. 121-127.

42 Michel, *Emperor Maximilian I*, pp. 314-319, nos. 90-93. Rupprich, 'Das literarische Werk Kaiser Maximilians', esp. p. 49.

participants, so also occasions for festive party atmospheres; thus falcon hunts also served Maximilian, according to his fictionalized autobiography *Weisskunig* (see below) as a neutral site where he could be approached.[43] Mary of Burgundy also was an avid hunter, and her premature death resulted from an equestrian accident while she was hawking. More hazardous larger animals follow, game characterized in the *Weisskunig* as 'princely hunting': stags, chamois, ibex, boar, and bears. Game preserves that fostered these animals in the region were restricted to princes and nobles, who used dogs to drive the quarry and fired crossbows, as illustrated in several Lucas Cranach images, a 1506 woodcut and a 1529 painting, commemorating a stag hunt (perhaps around 1497) with Emperor Maximilian, Saxon Duke Frederick the Wise, and other notables (Kunsthistorisches Museum, Vienna).[44] A particular challenge to crossbow marksmanship was the ibex, a 'noble creature' in the words of the *Weisskunig*, poised on mountain crags at a distance from the hunter.

The next hunt in the *Procession* is devoted to stags. Maximilian hunted them both on horseback (*parforce* hunting; shown in the Cranach painting) or within enclosures (park hunting). Stag hunts ended with aristocratic ritual, with the quarry dressed by the master and distributed according to rank, down to servants and dogs. The implements of this ritual consisted of specialized hunting knives: Maximilian's personal set was forged by his royal knifesmith, Hans Sumersperger.[45] Because of their high status as quarry, stags also occupied a special niche in medieval allegories of love.[46] More dangerous still were the two hunts that follow in the *Procession*: boars and bears.

All of these animals and their hunts formed the main subject of one more Maximilian text, another quasi-autobiographical allegory, called *Theuerdank* (Lofty thoughts, 1517).[47] Here the dangers of the hunt form a courtly romance quest, which ends with the hero's (a lightly disguised young Maximilian) successful courtship of his future queen, Ehrenreich (Rich-in-honor). That series of hunts and other adventures in the wilds of

43 Turner, *Lure of Falconry*. See lost Eyckian courtly images: one, preserved in a copy at Versailles of Netherlandish nobles at play with falcons; Post, 'Ein verschollenes Jagdbild Jan van Eycks', pp. 120-132; the other, a fishing party (drawing copy; Louvre), Kurz, 'Fishing Party', pp. 117-131.

44 Sternelle, *Lucas Cranach*, passim.

45 Thomas, 'Hunting Knives', pp. 201-208.

46 Thiebaux, *The Stag of Love*.

47 Michel, *Emperor Maximilian I*, pp. 285-287, no. 73; for Maximilian's literary texts more generally, especially in a courtly context, see Jan-Dirk Müller, *Gedechtnus*, passim.

Illustration 7.5 Hans Burgkmair, *Theuerdank as Champion of Fortune*, woodcut from *Theuerdank* (Augsburg: Johann Schönsperger, 1517), ch. 118

forests and mountains leads to a series of successful jousts with rivals at Ehrenreich's court. This rhymed text was lavishly printed in the new typeface Fraktur, which imitated scribal flourishes and Gothic script, and was fully illustrated with woodcuts by Leonhard Beck, Hans Burgkmair, and Hans Schäufelein. In general *Theuerdank* conforms nicely to the elaborate earlier Franco-Burgundian stagings of tournaments and court entertainments described by Huizinga as a 'heroic dream'.[48] Even more appropriately, immediately after the nuptials are celebrated, the eponymous hero must go on

48 Huizinga, *Autumn*, pp. 70-120.

crusade to fulfill his ultimate vow in a story 'to be continued', whose text is left blank after a heroic image of his equestrian portrait as an armored knight with the red cross banner of St. George.

In the *Triumphal Procession*, after a cluster of mounted valet attendants (cupbearer, cook, barber, and tailor), the next segment features floats with court performers, chiefly musicians.[49] Here Maximilian particularly adhered to the Burgundian court model, renowned across Europe, and he is documented as being constantly surrounded by musicians.[50] He sponsored court composers, led by Heinrich Isaac and Ludwig Senfl, after the model set with Dufay and Binchois and their disciples in Burgundy. And his *Triumphal Procession* has served countless modern musicologists, by showing the forms of instruments and the performing ensembles of Renaissance-era musicians.[51] The floats proceed as groups: lutes with viols, for *Hausmusik*, often with singers; winds (shawms, trombones, and krummhorns) for festive occasions; portable organ (played by Paul Hofhaimer, court organist, choir director, and composer at Innsbruck); 'sweet melody' (drums, strings, and winds), and a concluding choir, headed by George Slatkany, bishop of Vienna, who headed the chorus at court and founded the renowned Vienna Boys Choir. Other court entertainers then follow on their own floats: fools and jesters (led by Kunz von der Rosen, also subject of an etched portrait by Daniel Hopfer of Augsburg).[52] Finally, the festive masqueraders, dressed in costumes and carrying torches, follow, but they actually form the celebratory conclusion of tournaments and thus formed one of Maximilian's special interests, to be discussed after the tournaments below.

Jousting and tournaments, Maximilian's other great passion, like that of the dukes of Burgundy, as delineated by Huizinga, formed the next major element in his *Triumphal Procession*.[53] As with the hunt, the peacetime combat of jousting was considered the most appropriate training for warfare, especially under the late medieval knightly tradition of cavalry combat in armor. These knights are variously armored, according to each kind of specialized tournament combat.

49 Cuyler, *The Emperor Maximilian and Music*; Senn, 'Maximilian und die Musik', pp. 73-85.

50 *Splendours of the Burgundian Court*, pp. 302-303; Wangermée, *Flemish Music and Society*, esp. pp. 115-182; Brown, *Music in the Renaissance*, esp. pp. 24-92; though trained in Burgundy with Gilles Binchois, Johannes Ockeghem served three French kings from the early 1450s until the end of the fifteenth century, when he lived in both Bruges and Antwerp. See also Belozerskaya, *Luxury Arts*, pp. 187-225, for a recent general overview.

51 Henning, *Musica Maximiliana*; Munrow, *Instruments*, passim.

52 Michel, *Emperor Maximilian I*, p. 309, no. 87.

53 See note 23, above; *Splendours of the Burgundian Court*, pp. 296-299.

First out are the foot combatants, raised to the level of noble jousters by Maximilian himself, who even participated in this event (later, fencing competitions would emerge from this form of combat). Weapons used included flails, pikes, lances, halberds, and battle-axes, as well as swords and shields of various kinds. Next came the mounted combats, *Stechen* and *Rennen*, already distinguished above for their different helmets and degree of danger within the drawings by the Housebook Master. About Maximilian, it should also be noted that the emperor engaged personally and deeply with the design of armor for both tournaments and display as well as military use, and all histories of late medieval armor point to how 'Maximilianic' armor ushered in a new, Renaissance design that conformed far better to the rounded contours of the body.[54] Leading armorers for the emperor included the Helmschmied family in Augsburg as well as Konrad Seusenhofer in Innsbruck.[55]

Maximilian took his tournaments seriously enough to record their outcomes and to plan an illustrated book – again lightly fictionalized – about himself as the triumphant jouster *Freydal*.[56] This tournament-centered text can be regarded as the prequel to *Theuerdank*, or at least its fuller articulation of the concluding section on jousting as part of the courtship for his princess bride. It has little plot, but instead follows a sequence of tournament combats – *Rennen*, followed by *Stechen*, then foot combat (*Gefecht*) – ending with their respective concluding fancy-dress balls or masquerades, 64 in all. The manuscript that collected designs for the images, pasted-in miniatures in tempera and watercolor (Kunsthistorisches Museum, Vienna), encompasses fully 255 sheets. A list at the front of the codex includes the roster of names of ladies for whom Freydal ran each of his tournaments, then his opponents, arranged according to event (though not with locations). Like most of his publication projects, this one also remained unfinished, though Albrecht Dürer did complete five woodcuts for the illustrations (c. 1516), one of each element of the tournament, including

54 Michel, *Emperor Maximilian I*, pp. 326-331, nos. 96-100; Silver, *Marketing Maximilian*, pp. 153-155; Thomas, 'Harnischstudien I', pp. 139-158; Thomas and Gamber, *Innsbrucker Plattnerkunst*, passim.

55 Hans Burgkmairs family in Augsburg enjoyed close connections to the Helmschmied family, including nearby residence, so Burgkmair's imagery of Maximilian in armor, such as his magnificent 1508 woodcut, *Maximilian on Horseback* (Michel, *Emperor Maximilian I*, pp. 348-352 nos. 111-113) always features up-to-date armor design; Falk, *Hans Burgkmair*, pp. 74-76. Cf. Terjanian, *Princely Armour*.

56 Michel, *Emperor Maximilian I*, pp. 282-284, no. 72. One of the miniatures is dated 1515 and initialed with the monograph NP, perhaps Nikolaus Pfaundler of Innsbruck.

the masquerade (*Mummerey*) by torchlight.[57] Each one, however, shows the latest fashionable armor with a pleated skirt (*Faltenrock*),[58] plus a golden crown helmet for Maximilian, and each has inscribed names for each of his opponents, so we have names to attach to the Dürer images. Similar tournament books were prepared for other chivalric rulers, such as Lucas Cranach's Saxon patron, Johann Friedrich the Magnanimous (1521-1534), and Cranach produced several large woodcuts of tournaments for the court, complementing his *Stag Hunt* (c. 1506).[59]

As Dürer's torch-lit masquerade dance indicates, tournaments were periods of public display and luxury for Maximilian, as for his Burgundian predecessors.[60] Indeed, that same Burgundian model would continue to influence ceremonial occasions later in the century, particularly in Tudor England.[61] Tournaments also were often held on festive occasions, such as an imperial diet, or a princely marriage, such as the great double wedding in Vienna in 1515, when Maximilian married his grandchildren to the ruling family of Hungary.[62] The *Freydal* images also provide a roster of some fantastic costumes worn by the masked participants: fools, hunters, peasants, monks, mountain men, plus a numerous foreigners – Turks, Hungarians, Russians, Burgundians, Italians, and Spaniards – and such animals as birds or apes. Music, of course, accompanied all these festivities.

Ceremony in Burgundy often centered around that most exclusive, noble, closed circle, the knightly Order of the Golden Fleece, established by Philip the Good in 1430.[63] A book of statutes for the order was written by Guillaume Fillastre (d. 1473), bishop of Tournai and abbot of St. Bertin at Saint-Omer,

57 Schoch, Mende, and Scherbaum, *Albrecht Dürer*, no. 272.1-5. A woodblock for the last of these is preserved in Berlin. These woodcuts distinguish the German *Rennen* from the foreign/ Italian (*welsch*) *Gestech*, which occurs across a barrier.

58 Compare the datable *Faltenrockharnisch*, ordered in 1512 by Charles, grandson and successor (as Charles V) of Maximilian and made by Konrad Seusenhofer in Innsbruck (Hofburg, Vienna); Beaufort-Spontin and Pfaffenbichler, *Meisterwerke der Hof-, Jagd- und Rüstkammer*, pp. 94-95, no. 23.

59 The earliest tournament woodcut is dated 1506; three later ones are dated 1509. Koepplin and Falk, *Cranach*, I, pp. 191-206, 227-229, nos. 108-112; the hunt woodcut is ibid., p. 241, no. 138. See also the tournament book by the Cranach workshop and the tournament woodcut imitating Dürer's *Freydal* woodcut of *Rennen*, ibid., pp. 230-231, nos. 115- 117.

60 *Splendours of the Burgundian Court*, pp. 292-295.

61 Yates, 'Elizabethan Chivalry'; Kipling, *Triumph of Honour*; Anglo, *Spectacle, Pageantry*; Anglo, *Great Tournament Roll*.

62 Wiesflecker, *Kaiser Maximilian I*, V, pp. 391-393, enumerates many of these occasions.

63 In addition to sources cited above at n. 33, see *Splendours of the Burgundian Court*, pp. 186-193; Blockmans and Prevenier, *Promised Lands*, pp. 74-75; See also Cockshaw and Van den Bergen-Pantens, *L'Ordre de la Toison d'Or*, passim.

who became the order's second chancellor in 1461. Appropriately for the courts of Philip the Good and Charles the Bold, those protocols – plus coats of arms and representations of the knightly members – soon turned into illuminated manuscripts from the last quarter of the fifteenth century, today preserved in major European national libraries (Vienna, Brussels, London, Copenhagen, The Hague).[64]

Maximilian did not merely adopt the Order of the Golden Fleece; he assumed its leadership. In 1477 after the death of Charles the Bold in 1477 and his marriage in that same year to Mary of Burgundy, he became sovereign of the order, as ruler of the Burgundian region. He then proposed his son Philip the Fair (1478-1506) for membership as a toddler in 1481. Maximilian's hostile relations with the proudly independent nobles of the Low Countries led to his replacement as sovereign in favor of his son in 1484; in 1491 the teenage Philip the Fair took on the office; he, in turn, then admitted to the order in 1501 his own newborn son Charles (1500-1558), the future Emperor Charles V, after Maximilian I. Charles would become sovereign of the order after assuming his majority in 1516.

Moreover, like the other proud members of the order, including his son and grandson, Maximilian proudly wore the chain insignia of the Golden Fleece in many of his state portraits across his lifetime, especially by his principal painter Bernhard Strigel. The chain is particularly prominent in both the painted (Vienna; Nuremberg) and printed posthumous images of the emperor, produced shortly after his death in 1519 by Albrecht Dürer.[65]

Maximilian also fostered a knightly order of his own with just the same motivation that fired Philip the Good. He took St. George as a personal patron saint, particularly because of his association with the Crusades; the 1508 pendant to his own equestrian woodcut by Hans Burgkmair was a mounted *St. George* killing the fabled dragon and rescuing the imperiled princess.[66] The print is inscribed 'St. George, Vanguard of the Army of Christians' ('Divus Georgius Christianorum Militum Propugnator'), making clear the crusade associations of both the saint and his contemporary imperial imitator in the pendant print. Maximilian's father, Emperor Frederick III, had already founded a knightly order of St.

64 Smeyers, *Flemish Miniatures*, pp. 365-367; *Splendours of the Burgundian Court*, pp. 192-193, for Fillastre manuscripts. A fine survey of the history of the order with display of its principal treasures: Fillitz, *Trésors de la Toison d'Or*, pp. 114-121, nos. 32-35.

65 Michel, *Emperor Maximilian I*, pp. 292-295, nos. 75-78; Luber, 'Dürer's Maximilian Portraits', pp. 30-47; for other portraits of Maximilian, see Michel, *Emperor Maximilian I*, nos. 2, 9, 11, 13, and 16 (Archduke Charles with the chain).

66 Silver, 'Shining Armor', pp. 8-29.

George in 1467, centered at his palace in Wiener Neustadt, and intended largely as a counter to the advances of the Ottoman Turks into Habsburg borderlands. Maximilian expanded the order into a lay brotherhood, which could combine chivalric allegiance to the ruler with pledges to pursue a crusade.[67] On his massive woodcut *Arch of Honour*, devised by Dürer and his workshop (c. 1515-1518), Maximilian included a pair of woodcuts devoted to his patronage of the Order of St. George as well as his intention to lead them on to a crusade.[68] They show the emperor under the red cross banner of the saint with his knights; accompanying verses proclaim, 'Knightly friendships he did forge / By strengthening the Order of St. George.' The second image verses declare: 'With earnestness and diligence / he came to Christendom's defense. / For soon he planned a new Crusade / and asked all princes for their aid.'

Many of Maximilian's varied chivalric interests are also reprised in his (also unfinished) allegorical autobiography, *Weisskunig* (White king [or Wise king]), another text dictated to Marx Treitzsaurwein with woodcut illustrations by Hans Burgkmair, Leonhard Beck, and several other artists.[69] Of all his literary legacy, Maximilian planned for this text to be his historical memoir, including accounts of his numerous battles, albeit with names of rival kings disguised by colors. With such a text he could elevate his deeds to the level of Burgundian literary models by their several publicist historians of that court, its chivalry, and war: Georges Chastellain (d. 1475), Olivier de La Marche (d. 1502), and Jean Molinet (d. 1507).[70] Maximilian was the first Holy Roman Emperor to employ court chroniclers, usually polymaths such as Ladislaus Sunthaym and Johannes Stabius, especially engaged with researches into his genealogy, itself often dependent on Burgundian family trees.[71] Philip the Good read recast histories (centered on Charlemagne) and histories of the crusades (especially the First Crusade and its knightly paragon, Godfrey of Bouillon), but also the legendary life of an ancestor, the first Burgundian duke, Girart de Roussillon (text by Jehan Wauquelin

67 Silver, *Marketing Maximilian*, pp. 114-126, including a discussion of the elaborate printed *Prayerbook* that Maximilian devised for the use of the Order of St. George.

68 Michel, *Emperor Maximilian I*, pp. 373-375, no. 124; Silver, 'Power of the Press', pp. 45-62; Schauerte, *Ehrenpforte*, esp. pp. 153, 325-327, for the St. George Order.

69 Michel, *Emperor Maximilian I*, pp. 288-289, no. 74; *Splendours of the Burgundian Court*, p. 356, no. 170.

70 For the literary culture surrounding *Weisskunig*, Müller, *Gedechtnus*, esp. pp. 130-148, and on the allegorizing of the concept of 'knight', in both *Theuerdank* and *Weisskunig*, ibid., pp. 212-233, especially in relation to La Marche and Molinet.

71 Michel, *Emperor Maximilian I*, pp. 162-173, nos. 17-23; Silver, *Marketing Maximilian*, pp. 41-76; Tanner, *Last Descendants*, esp. pp. 67-130; see also pp. 146-161 on the Golden Fleece.

Illustration 7.6 Hans Burgkmair, *Equestrian Portrait of Emperor Maximilian I*, 1508, woodcut

Chicago, Art Institute

along with a *History of Alexander*).[72] In similar fashion, *Weisskunig* depended heavily on earlier literary models, particularly German romances, *Heldenbücher*, also systematically copied out and preserved on instructions from Maximilian himself.[73]

The first part of *Weisskunig* lays out the youthful education and training of the prince, which conditioned the kinds of enduring pastimes that we have already seen for Maximilian – all vividly laid out in multiple woodcut illustrations by Burgkmair and Leonhard Beck. With proper panegyric excess, its text credits him with expertise in almost every possible physical and mental activity. But even as a youth he played with toy cannons, crossbows, archery, and tabletop jousting, according to a Burgkmair woodcut. Pictures of an older *Weisskunig* show in sequence his mastery of all these weapons in the hunt and tournament. His love of calligraphy led him to foster not only beautiful manuscripts but also the Fraktur font seen in the *Theuerdank*, his printed Prayerbook, and other printed works.[74] His interest in art is represented with a marvelous double portrait of his visit (with a hunting dog) to Burgkmair's studio, where he supervises the painter at his easel, delineating precisely the kinds of subjects that we know already from Cranach's court art: animals from the hunt as well as armor and weapons. But *Weisskunig* also visits armorers, cooks, musicians, and he supervises the torch-lit masquerades so basic to *Freydal*.

Where Maximilian truly retains and enhances the model of his Burgundian predecessors is in his tomb ensemble. Tombs already formed a special artistic legacy of the dukes of Burgundy. As early as 1381 Philip the Bold, founder of the Valois dynasty, stipulated with sculptor Jean de Marville the designs of his tomb, destined for the Chartreuse de Champmol outside Dijon, and carved (1384-1410) by Claus Sluter and Claes van de Werve of Haarlem.[75] Completed after his death (1404), the magnificent tomb features underneath its recumbent painted and gilded effigy a remarkably varied and animated set of 40 miniature alabaster figures, representing the Carthusian monks who made up the real-life funeral procession as mourners (*pleurants*). The

72 Moodey, *Crusader Histories*, esp. pp. 174-239 for Godfrey and Charlemagne and for general literature, pp. 53-78: 'Generally the Burgundian authors who reworked these stories for the court replaced Arthurian characters with Crusade-era heroes' (p. 59). The 1448 *Girart de Roussillon* manuscript, text by Wauquelin, is in the Austrian National Library, Vienna, ms. 2549; Smeyers, *Flemish Miniatures*, pp. 300-307; Thoss, *Das Epos des Burgunderreiches Girart de Roussillon*.

73 Silver, '"Guten Alten Istory"'.

74 Strauss, *The Book of Hours*.

75 *Splendours of the Burgundian Court*, p. 342, no. 153; Lindquist, *Agency, Visuality and Society*, pp. 138-148; Jugie, 'Tomb of Philip the Bold', pp. 223-235; Prochno, *Kartause von Champmol*, passim.

same model was again realized posthumously (1443-1470) at Champmol for the next Burgundian duke, John the Fearless (d. 1419), carved by Jean de la Huerta and Antoine le Moiturier to be part of an ongoing dynastic ensemble in Dijon to rival that of the French monarchs near Paris at St. Denis.

But the strongest Burgundian model for what Maximilian would aspire to exceed with his own tomb appeared with alternate mourners – this time relatives of the deceased, in splendid contemporary court dress and not expressly mourning – that surround the tomb of Isabella of Bourbon (d. 1465), Mary of Burgundy's mother and second wife of Duke Charles the Bold.[76] While the original tomb ensemble in the former abbey of St. Michael in Antwerp was damaged during iconoclastic riots of 1566, ten figures – five men and five women – out of an original 24 survive (now in the Rijksmuseum in Amsterdam). Cast in bronze by Renier van Thienen of Brussels, they were probably designed in wood by carver Jan Borman in accord with a newer concept, kinship, featuring ancestors around the tomb, together with their brightly colored coats of arms. This concept depends on recent models of the region from the time of Philip the Good: the tombs of Joanna of Brabant (Brussels, 1457-1458) and Louis of Male (Lille, 1454-1455). For Mary of Burgundy herself, who was sole heir of Burgundy, gilded family trees, rather than either actual mourners or these kinds of kinship figures, adorn the sides of her tomb, 1488-1502, but she was surely responsible for this design of the tomb of her mother, Isabella.[77] Unfortunately, almost none of the individual figures can be identified by name, though Bavarian imperial rulers of the Netherlands are featured.

Isabella's genealogical figures are notable for their opulent court dress, yet they stand a mere 55 cm high.[78] When Maximilian began to design his own tomb in 1502 (eventually installed in the Innsbruck Hofkirche by Ferdinand II, 1566-1583, but designated in his will for his father's St. George's church in Wiener Neustadt), he seized on the basic idea of being surrounded by ancestors, cast in bronze and dressed in appropriately luxurious and historically appropriate costume and accompanied by their coats of arms; however, to assert his own imperial grandeur, he proposed to have fully 40 over-life-sized ancestor mourner figures, both male and female, by his side (28 were finally completed and installed, but only eleven were completed at the time of his

76 *Splendours of the Burgundian Court*, p. 207, no. 34; Scholten, *Isabella's Weepers*; Morganstern, *Gothic Tombs*, pp. 140-149.

77 For Mary of Burgundy's tomb, also realized by Jan Borman (gisant) and Renier van Thienen (sides), see Roberts, 'The Chronology'.

78 Scholten, *Isabella's Weepers*, pp. 31-45; compare Van Buren, *Illuminating Fashion*, passim.

death).[79] The tomb also was to include portrait busts of Roman emperors (21 executed out of 34 planned), matching the ones included on his *Arch of Honour*, as well as statuettes (23 completed out of a planned 100) of the Habsburg ancestors whom he claimed as venerated saints and planned to gather in an illustrated book publication with woodcuts by Beck.[80] In addition to his father Frederick III and other Habsburg imperial ancestors and a few sainted royals of dubious connection, Maximilian included the Burgundian dukes themselves, both his son Philip the Fair (who predeceased him in 1506), but also his father-in-law Charles the Bold and his father Philip the Good. Maximilian's fanciful ancestry even outdoes the boldest Burgundian claims: King Arthur, Theodoric the Ostrogoth, but also Burgundian prototypes Charlemagne and Godfrey of Bouillon. Among the women relatives, direct ancestral connections are stronger, including both of his wives (Bianca Maria Sforza as well as Mary of Burgundy) plus his mother, grandmother, sister, and daughter (Margaret of Austria, regent for Maximilian in the Burgundian Low Countries). As laid out by his supervising court artist Jörg Kölderer, on an elaborate colored pen drawing on parchment (1528; Kunsthistorisches Museum, Vienna) and more elaborately on separate folios for individual figures, close to designs already realized and still planned for individual statues (National Library, Vienna, codex 8329), these chosen ancestors essentially replicate the ones enshrined as statues on floats in Altdorfer's *Triumphal Procession* parchment.[81] Also like the earlier Burgundian tomb projects as well, Maximilian's funeral complex took generations to complete, even in its partially realized outcome, in part because of its massive scale but also because of a series of different bronze casters for the figures, first painter Gilg Sesselschreiber (who chiefly drew up sketches) and later the more capable Stefan Godl. Like all of Maximilian's projects, even though it involved some of the finest contemporary designers (including Albrecht Dürer) and carvers (Veit Stoss, Hans Leinberger), this one, too, remained incomplete. But more fully than any of his other many emulations of the recent Burgundian heritage, it shows his ability to use the courtly splendor of art and display as a major instrument of statecraft.

79 Michel, *Emperor Maximilian I*, pp. 360-368, nos. 119-122; *Splendours of the Burgundian Court*, p. 343, no. 156; Egg, *Die Hofkirche in Innsbruck*, passim; Scheicher, 'Das Grabmal Kaiser Maximilians I'; Seipel, *Werke für die Ewigkeit*, passim.

80 For Maximilian's elaborate genealogical researches and claims for sainted ancestors, see Michel, *Emperor Maximilian I*, pp. 165-173, nos. 19-23; for the Roman emperor busts, see ibid., pp. 366-368, nos. 121-122. For the wider projects of genealogy, including the tomb, *Procession*, and related projects, see Silver, *Marketing Maximilian*, pp. 41-76.

81 For Kölderer and his role on the tomb project, see Scheichl, 'Who Was (or Were) Jörg Kölderer?', esp. pp. 86-87.

About the Author

Larry Silver is the Farquhar Professor of Art History, emeritus, at the University of Pennsylvania. An art historian of early modern paintings and graphics in Northern Europe, he has published monographs on Rembrandt, Rubens, Dürer, Bruegel, and Bosch, on the origins of pictorial genres in the Antwerp art market, and another study, *Marketing Maximilian* (Princeton University Press, 2008), on the imagery created for that Holy Roman Emperor, which forms the basis of his chapter in this volume.
lasilver@sas.upenn.edu

8 The Making of *The Autumn of the Middle Ages* I

Narrative Sources and Their Treatment in Huizinga's *Herfsttij*

Graeme Small

Abstract

This study investigates Huizinga's engagement with the sources and his application of method in more detail than has previously been attempted, finding the former to be far deeper and more extensive than is commonly realized and the latter to be more coherent and sustained than is usually claimed. In the process we situate Huizinga's research questions, methods and conclusions in the wider context of late-nineteenth and early-twentieth-century Western historiography. *Waning* emerges from this investigation, not so much a 'deeply puzzling book' as a remarkably ambitious exercise in 'cultural history', understood by Huizinga as a real alternative to 'political history' in the wider field of *algemene geschiedenis* (general history).

Keywords: late medieval narrative sources, Burgundian literature, Middle French Literature, Middle Dutch literature, Neo-Kantian method, cultural history, *algemene geschiedenis*

What follows is an exploration of the research that went into *Herfsttij der Middeleeuwen* (1919), setting the text in its time and in relation to Huizinga's other writings, drawing on his unpublished notes and published correspondence, and above all focusing attention on the narrative sources he used: which ones and how many; why and how he chose those sources rather than others; and the ways in which they functioned in the book in relation

Arnade, Peter, Martha Howell, and Anton van der Lem (eds), *Rereading Huizinga: Autumn of the Middle Ages, a Century Later.* Taylor & Francis Group, 2019
DOI: 10.5117/9789462983724_CH08

to his theses and methods.[1] In the process, this investigation is intended as a contribution to the study of how medieval European history could be written in the early twentieth century. Often we emphasize the exceptional and original qualities of both Huizinga and *Herfsttij*, and rightly so. Here, however, we will argue that the book was in many ways a highpoint of the 'autumntide' of nineteenth-century historical scholarship and methodology: a seemingly timeless classic that was much more of its time than is commonly recognized.

1 Understanding the Past: Reading, Seeing, and Feeling

Huizinga's enthralling writing in *Herfsttij* was influenced by the contemporary style of fin de siècle novelists and the belletrist talents of the authors of older universal and romantic histories. He rated *Herfsttij* as his chief (*voornaamste*) publication, and its unparalleled popular success (reputedly the biggest selling work of medieval history of all time) was surely a factor in the ten nominations (1939-1945) which he received for the Nobel Prize for Literature.[2] If *Herfsttij*'s prose seems as captivating today as it did when the world was a century younger, it is worth remembering that it does so despite the challenges to the harmony of the text posed by multiple translations, abridgments and new editions.

Insofar as they have been the subject of comment, Huizinga's research and reading have seemed rather less impressive. It has even been said that *Herfsttij* was based on just a handful of court chroniclers and poets.[3] Huizinga is partly to blame for the impression he was not the most assiduous of readers. In his autobiographical essay 'My Path to History' (1943), he emphasized how little he read ('I was no great bookworm, nor have I become one'); how instrumentally he read ('apart from the work in hand, I read very little, much too little'); how hastily he read primary sources ('the speed with which I tackled the subject [Erasmus] and selected information […] is something I cannot recommend to any serious historian').[4] The one and only description he has left us of his reading process for *Herfsttij* conjures up an image of languid days spent, not in the academic world of the university

1 Krul, 'In the Mirror', p. 354; Peters and Simons, 'The New Huizinga'.

2 For this and what follows, see Peters and Simons, 'The New Huizinga', pp. 587-591; https://www.nobelprize.org/nomination/archive/ (accessed 18 May 2017); Huizinga, 'My Path to History', p. 272 (where *voornaamste* is translated as 'best known'); *VW*, I, p. 38.

3 E.g., Cantor, *Inventing the Middle Ages*, p. 378; Pleij, 'Huizinga's *Herfsttij*', p. 9.

4 For this sentence and the next, see Huizinga, 'My Path to History', pp. 251, 273-275.

or Royal Library (where we can now say from his unpublished notes that many of his books were in fact sourced), not in his note-filled, book-lined study (where 'Huizinga as reader', dressed in a suit and tie, was generally photographed or drawn), but in the more leisurely environment of an attic room one hot summer in the family's holiday house near Middelburg, with the chronicler Jean Froissart for company.[5] Huizinga likened his research to the carefree flight – of a butterfly? A bumble bee? – 'across the garden of an age, alighting upon a flower here and there and then moving on'.[6] The fact that he was not particularly explicit (in *Herfsttij* itself, at least) about the methods which lay behind the selection of his sources, and the manner of his reading, has led some commentators to doubt whether the book had any method at all.[7]

But Huizinga's reading was wide as we shall see. It was also born of a method which he never imposed on his reader of *Herfsttij*, but which he did set out in a variety of other places, and which we will attempt to situate here in its contemporary context. This method consisted of seeing and feeling the past as though it were a living presence for the historian. How strange this sounds to historians today, we who have been trained in models of explanation and expectations of proof that bear the influence of the natural sciences. Of historians who adopted laws of proof and hierarchies of causes, he would later ask, long before Hayden White and others:

> Do you historians not recognise the strongly subjective element in all historical cognition, in the formulation of the question, in the selection and sifting of the material, in the interpretation and synthesis of the data ascertained?[8]

Instead, he argued in his inaugural lecture at Groningen in 1905 (which was something of a blueprint for key elements of his method), history should strive for an *understanding* of the past.[9] In the case of *Herfsttij*, the all-important subtitle of the book identified 'the forms of life, thought and art in France and the Netherlands in the fourteenth and fifteenth centuries' as the subjects at hand. Understanding them would require

5 For lists of books consulted, with libraries and even shelf marks identified, see Universiteitsbibliotheek Leiden, Huizinga-archief (hereafter UBL Hui.) 52: P.14. For UBL Hui., see Van der Lem, *Inventaris*.

6 Huizinga, 'My Path to History', p. 275.

7 Aston, 'Huizinga's Harvest', p. 7; Lyon, 'Was Johan Huizinga Interdisciplinary?'

8 Huizinga, 'The Task', p. 49; cf. White, 'Fictions of Factual Representation'.

9 Huizinga, 'The Aesthetic Element'.

complete immersion in the sources of the age. Only by these means could direct contact with the minds of individuals in the past be achieved, and the 'forms of life and thought' be as deeply known to the historian as if she or he had experienced them.

All one's senses might be recruited in this total engagement with a 'living past', so that reading had the power to produce a form of synesthesia – an idea that had appealed to Huizinga since his student days at Groningen and Leipzig.[10] The deeply read historian who truly lived with and understood his subjects, defined as individuals and their actions, could smell the scent of blood and roses that seemed to characterize their age, or hear the ringing of bells that measured the time of their daily lives (to borrow two well-known images from *Herfsttij*). This was not a simple reimagining of the past, as one might see at the theater or in a medieval fair, but an experiencing of the past as it was brought to life 'by the slightest historical document, whether in word or in image'.[11] Thus experienced, the past created 'an almost (do not laugh) ecstatic sensation of no longer being myself, of overflowing into the world around me, of touching the very essence of things, the experience of Truth through history'.[12]

Huizinga applied his highly subjective method of seeing and feeling the past through total immersion in its sources for the first time in *Herfsttij*, and it produced some astonishing passages. At one point he places us before Jan van Eyck's painting of the marriage of the Bruges-based Lucca banker Giovanni Arnolfini, and invites us to consider the self-portrait which the painter created in that work by means of his reflection in a mirror, accompanied by the inscription 'Johannes de Eyck fuit hic, 1434'. Huizinga comments: 'Jan van Eyck was here. Just a short time ago. The deep silence of the chamber still reverberates with the sound of his voice'.[13] A more complex example demands that we look at (rather than listen to) the past. Huizinga invites the reader to behold the court chronicler Chastelain: 'The crude Fleming whom Chastelain was is revealed here under his enveloping *houpelande* [courtier's tunic], which was splendid in gold with a pattern of red squares'.[14] The physical details and phrasing suggest that Huizinga has a court portrait of Chastelain before his eyes, perhaps like Van Eyck's *The Arnolfini Portrait*.

10 Huizinga, 'My Path to History', p. 271; Otterspeer, *Reading Huizinga*, pp. 148-165. See also Huizinga, *Autumn*, p. 243.

11 Huizinga, 'Bernard Shaw's Saint', p. 214.

12 *VW*, II, p. 566.

13 Huizinga, *Autumn*, p. 312.

14 Huizinga, *Autumn*, pp. 109-110; 'Hier komt de ruwe Vlaming, die Chastellain was, onder de prachtige houppelande van goud en rood granaatpatroon te voorschijn' (original: *VW*, III, p. 118).

'Heavy garments, all dark red and gold' in that painter's *Adoration of the Mystic Lamb* did indeed encapsulate for Huizinga the 'dazzling bombast' of 'Burgundian court style'.[15] But then we recall there is no known court portrait of the Burgundian chronicler, nor any record of one that has been lost.[16] Huizinga, we realize, is asking us to look at Chastelain in real life, popping up before us in his finery as if he were the subject of a portrait. The painter who captures the chronicler's character and the form and colors of his costume can only be Huizinga, or possibly the reader who stands beside him, responding to his invitation to look at this pompous courtier. He and we are no longer ourselves. One of us seems to have become Jan van Eyck; perhaps, indeed, we all have.[17]

It is precisely at this point of deepest subjectivity that the 'historical imagination' reaches 'the highest attainable objectivity': 'living pictures in the theatre of the mind'.[18] As Huizinga put it in his notes, 'when I have understood something, I have an affinity with it. It is actually a picture book'.[19]

Direct contact with the past had by then become a visual experience made more possible than ever by accessible reproductions of old masters in print, and by the major exhibitions of late medieval art that were then so popular, not least the famous Bruges exhibition of 1902 which first engaged Huizinga in the work of the brothers Van Eyck, and which began the process of reflection, and sometime later the research, that produced *Herfsttij*.[20] 'Our historical sense organ has become increasingly visual', wrote Huizinga,

15 Huizinga, *Autumn*, p. 342. Also used in the Archangel Gabriel's 'brocade coat dark red and gold' in Van Eyck's *Annunciation*, now in Washington (ibid., p. 335).

16 The one chronicle miniature depicting Chastelain dates to the early sixteenth century, and represents him not as a courtier, but in the dark sober gown of the learned man: see Small, *George Chastelain*, p. 242.

17 For another use of this technique, see Huizinga, 'The Aesthetic Element', p. 241 (Herodotus on Xerxes), discussed in Otterspeer, *Reading Huizinga*, pp. 148, 171.

18 Huizinga, 'The Aesthetic Element', p. 237.

19 UBL Hui. 52: B.3. Such was his affinity with Chastelain's way of thinking that at one point, without warning, he even begins to write in the chronicler's distinct style and in his exact words, possibly from memory, certainly without quotation: 'if [the people] occasionally grumble and denounce the authorities, "povres brevis, povre fol peuple", with one word the lord will restore them to calm and reason' (Huizinga, *Autumn*, p. 66; original version: *VW*, III, p. 71). No reference is attached to this pseudo-quote, but it mirrors a series of related passages in Chastelain's chronicle which refer to the 'povre peuple' (Chastelain, *Oeuvres*, V, pp. 270, 297, 275, 476), the 'povre fol peuple' (ibid., p. 325), the 'povres brebis' (ibid., pp. 264, 268), and 'leur folle gouverne' (ibid., p. 356).

20 Huizinga, *Autumn*, p. 293. On the the exact pictures Huizinga was inspired by in 1902, see Haskell, 'Art and History', pp. 12-14.

and it was the art of the late medieval period that led him to reflect more deeply on the cultural history (and therefore the narrative sources) of the time – a process sharpened by his engagement with Jacob Burckhardt's *Civilization of the Renaissance in Italy* (1860), and by contemporary debates surrounding the respective merits of Italian, Burgundian and French art as harbingers of modernity.[21]

Huizinga agreed that visual images were superior to narrative sources in terms of their capacity to bring the period to life, due to their intense realism and accessibility to the viewer. Direct speech in Froissart's chronicles bore some resemblance to the effects of light in a painting as a way of enabling us to see the past more clearly (he kept a large file of examples in his notes, enthusiastically observing of one: 'That's amazingly exact! And modern').[22] Unfortunately and typically, however, Froissart used the technique far too often. Chastelain was the 'one author above all in whose work we notice the same crystal-clear view of the external manifestations as in Van Eyck'.[23] Yet even Chastelain at his best could not surpass Van Eyck at his worst.[24]

For all its superior potential, however, visual art was not without its shortcomings as a source. Fewer paintings survived than works of literature, and whole genres (such as erotic painting) had vanished.[25] Painting seemed to capture more of the religious than the secular forms of life and thought of the age (although Huizinga thought this point could be easily exaggerated).[26] Above all, he would later say, literature made it 'possible for us to appraise the spirit as well as the form' of an age, which was something the work of the Van Eycks could never do.[27] If we only had access to the visual art of an age and not its narrative sources, we would therefore risk misunderstanding its 'forms of life, thought and art'. The cultural historian required both – a point Huizinga returned to in a work that was, as we shall see, very closely related to *Herfsttij*, his long essay 'Dutch Civilisation in the Seventeenth Century'.[28]

21 Huizinga, *Autumn*, p. 295; Kaegi, 'Das historische Werk Johan Huizingas', pp. 14-24.
22 This sentence and next, see Huizinga, *Autumn*, p. 347; UBL Hui. 114: D.2, F.4.
23 Huizinga, *Autumn*, p. 347.
24 Ibid., p. 342.
25 Ibid., pp. 295, 373. As Pleij has observed ('Huizinga's *Herfsttij*', p. 13), he paid relatively little attention to lacunae which also existed in the literature. He even seemingly forgot (though he took note of it in his reading) that his main source, Chastelain's chronicle, also exists in fragments: UBL Hui. 52: G.1.
26 Huizinga, *Autumn*, p. 332.
27 Huizinga, 'Renaissance and Realism', p. 297.
28 Huizinga, 'Dutch Civilisation', p. 9.

It helped that in Huizinga's view, all 'imaginative activity' – whether history, poetry or art – emerged from the same 'original response and the emotion that accompanies it', which a contemporary – whether historian, poet, or artist – could experience.[29] 'Only when the stage of actual composition is reached, does the differentiation between, say, poetry and history begin to emerge.' Behind the many different kinds of creative composition lay common forms of 'spontaneous everyday thinking', as one commentator on Huizinga's method has put it: the habits of mind ('response and emotion') which came naturally to contemporaries, and which were revealed, for example, in the 'unselfconscious observation' a painter, poet, or historian might drop into his or her work, almost universal and eternal in quality, recognizable to the human mind in any age; or in the conventional range and complexity of styles they were inclined to adopt self-consciously, and which were much more the product of the time and place of their formulation.[30] This is what Huizinga meant by the 'forms of life and thought' which lay embedded within the visual images and narrative sources of the age, and which it was the cultural historian's task to recover and understand. Once retrieved, the many examples illustrative of these habits of mind were loosely assembled by what he called his 'mosaic method', in which the fragmentary 'illustrative details' were linked up with each other within categories of interpretation that had occurred to the historian, and which were added to and refined over time.[31] These categories were given physical existence in the envelopes in which Huizinga kept his little strips of notes, like so many mosaic fragments, as Anton van der Lem explains in the present volume. At a certain point in the gathering of this harvest, the cultural historian felt sufficiently directed by the sources, and sufficiently well-equipped with material lifted from them, to start writing his or her 'morphology of the human past'.[32]

As even the most cursory reading of *Herfsttij* will attest, the principal characteristics of those 'forms of life, thought and art' in the fourteenth and fifteenth centuries turned out to be very clear indeed to Huizinga.

29 For this sentence and the next, see Huizinga, 'The Aesthetic Element', p. 230.

30 Bulhof, 'Johan Huizinga', p. 208; Huizinga, *Autumn*, pp. 349-351. Bulhof's specialization in the work of Wilhelm Dilthey, discussed further below, makes her (not coincidentally) one of the best early readers of Huizinga's method.

31 'In order to begin an analysis, there must already be a synthesis present in the mind. A conception of ordered coherence is an indispensable precondition even to the preliminary labour of digging and hewing' (Huizinga, 'The Task', p. 25). On the 'mosaic-method', see *VW*, IV, pp. 124-125.

32 Huizinga, 'The Task', p. 60.

It is important to remember at this point the tenor of his findings. The dynamism of the high Middle Ages had turned in this closing phase to atrophy and exhaustion, manifested in empty and incessant formalism, all of which could be seen in the three main areas the book concerned itself with.[33] Within the court and civic elite first of all, 'forms of life were elaborated into beautiful and uplifting games and the wild growth of these games into empty display'.[34] In spiritual thought and practice, there was an 'unlimited desire to bestow form on everything that is sacred, to give any religious idea a material shape'.[35] Art (whether visual or literary) partook of an 'endless system of formal representation', leaving 'nothing unformed, unpresented, or undecorated'.[36] In all three areas there was evidence of the 'coming of the new form' – a new form that was simpler and less fraught, whatever its precise manifestation. But that evidence remained slight and inconclusive.

Whatever we think of Huizinga's understanding of the period and the methods he used to reach it, both must be seen in relation to the times and places of their formulation. The one common denominator in the chairs he held at Groningen (1905) and Leiden (1915) while he was writing *Herfsttij* was their attachment to the field of 'general history'. His normally benevolent mentor and predecessor at Groningen, Pieter J. Blok, chose an event held to celebrate his own long career in history to tell Huizinga, among the other celebrants from the small world of Dutch medievalists who had traveled for the event to Noordwijk close to Leiden, that 'it was high time [he] published something of real importance' in the field. The subject matter and approach of *Herfsttij* constituted an entirely legitimate response to that challenge, issued in the autumn of 1909.[37]

Huizinga's approach was in keeping with German traditions in the philosophy of history which he encountered for the first time, not (it would seem) during his brief period of study in Leipzig in 1894-1895, where Karl Lamprecht was then teaching, and whose controversial ideas on cultural history were nonetheless of some value to Huizinga, but in preparing his Groningen inaugural ten years later, when he was introduced to the work of the main critics of Lamprecht by his then colleague, the psychologist

33 On the nature of 'general formalism': Huizinga, *Autumn*, p. 281.

34 Huizinga, *Autumn*, p. 45

35 Ibid., p. 173

36 Ibid., p. 300.

37 Huizinga, 'My Path to History', p. 273. For a photograph of Blok's villa at Noordwijk, a key location in the genesis of *Herfsttij*, see Huizinga, *Mijn weg*, p. 74.

Gerardus Heymans.[38] Foremost among those who influenced Huizinga were Wilhelm Dilthey, Georg Simmel, Wilhelm Windelband, Heinrich Rickert and Eduard Spranger.[39] To take only the historicist tradition exemplified by Dilthey, now recognized as Huizinga's 'fundamental epistemological inspiration', he found there solid support for his view that history was a science of the mind distinct from the natural sciences – a science in which the principle goal was to arrive, not at an explanation of the past, but at an empathetic understanding which enabled the historian to grasp the mental constructs of individuals in earlier times.[40] In Dilthey too he found encouragement to read poetry and study art as means of understanding the individual mind. Here he found comfort for his belief that the historian might come to understand a writer better than that writer understood him- or herself, and that such a level of knowledge of the individual in history would shed light on the spirit of whole. His desire to see the past in terms of images was further bolstered by the neo-Kantian concept of 'graphical history'.[41] The 'decisive hermeneutic step' which is discernible in the historical philosophy of Dilthey is that of 'the historian merging into the historical actor', a method which led Huizinga to place the reader in the shoes of Van Eyck in the passage cited above.[42] All of these ideas were fundamental in Huizinga's treatment of the narrative sources in *Herfsttij*, and they help us to understand his confidence that a process of total immersion in the *Weltanschauung* (worldview) of his individual narrative sources would permit him, and his readers, to see their age in the round.

Huizinga's choice of subject matter was also profoundly shaped by the types of views he found expressed in the field of general history, which by his time was increasingly taught as an amalgam of national entities.[43] His first response to Blok's unrefusable invitation was to explore 'my vague ideas on the Middle Ages' through the specific lens of Burgundian culture, his interest already piqued by the art of the time, as we have seen. He began work almost immediately on a series of undergraduate lectures on the

38 A number of valuable discussions of Huizinga's method in general (rather than more specifically on how those methods apply in *Herfsttij*) now exist, particularly Tollebeek, *De toga van Fruin*, pp. 205-225; De Voogd, *Le miroir de la France*, pp. 220-263; Strupp, *Johan Huizinga*, pp. 43-119; Krumm, *Johan Huizinga*, pp. 61-70.

39 Tollebeek, *De toga van Fruin*, pp. 199-257.

40 De Voogd, *Le miroir de la France*, p. 1; Hodges, *The Philosophy of Wilhelm Dilthey*.

41 Strupp, 'A Historian's Life in Biographical Perspective', p. 110.

42 Plamper, *The History of Emotions*, p. 45.

43 Cohen, 'Huizinga als Leids hoogleraar', p. 194.

subject at Groningen (1909-1910). To judge from his text, and especially from his surviving notes, Huizinga's research for his classes drew heavily on two examples of general histories in the national tradition which had both been published just seven years earlier.[44] These works were volume 2 of Henri Pirenne's *Histoire de Belgique*, and volume 4 of Ernest Lavisse's *Histoire de France* (part 1 of which was written by Alfred Coville, part 2 by Charles Petit-Dutaillis).

For anyone wishing to understand how Huizinga, a virtual novice in the subject in terms of his research and publications, was able to launch himself into the age of Burgundy, there is nothing more instructive than to read the chapters which these leading works of general history devoted to the intellectual life, letters, and art of the period, and which Huizinga annotated in detail. Here we find precisely the sort of view we mainly associate with Huizinga today, but which at that time had become part of the mainstream of general historical thinking, influenced by liberal or confessional ideas about the late Middle Ages as a stagnant period preceding the Renaissance and the Reformation, but subsequently given a particular inflection by the relevant national past in each case. So, intellectual and spiritual atrophy was rampant in a French fourteenth century already blighted by war, as Coville judged it:

> The lyrical poem is pure artifice, a learned game from which the soul is almost always absent. There is a certain falseness and pedantry in that literature, as there is in chivalric manners. The poetry of the Middle Ages thus seems to be nearing the end of its career, just like chivalry.[45]

The cultural life of the fifteenth century seemed little better to Petit-Dutaillis, at least until signs of renewal began to appear:

> They continue to moralize endlessly, to love allegory, and as for the maniacal obsession with form, the writers of the fourteenth century are surpassed by those of the fifteenth. But here comes something new, isolated great talents are emerging to the fore [...] one of these great men, Villon, created modern lyric poetry.[46]

44 On his use of general histories to prepare his teaching, see Huizinga, 'My Path to History', p. 264.

45 Coville, *Les premiers Valois*, p. 439.

46 Petit-Dutaillis, *Charles VII*, pp. 208-209.

In the Burgundian Low Countries, where there had been relative peace and prosperity compared to France, and which was also the precursor of his beloved Belgium, Pirenne found fewer grounds for pessimism. Nevertheless, the fifteenth century was an anxious age of extremes which filled up

> minds with disquiet and anxiety, of which there were numerous symptoms. The portraits of the era represent serious, unsmiling faces. Among the people sinister stories circulate about poisonings and other crimes, which are only fueled by the frequency of political assassination. The appetite for blood and torture proved to be terrible.[47]

Translated into Dutch, any one of these passages from the most up-to-date historical syntheses of the time could be dropped with barely a ripple into some easily chosen part of *Herfsttij*.

Much the same is true of many of the judgments of the narrative sources of the period which we find in our three influential general histories. For Coville, Deschamps's poetry suffered from a 'laborious technique' which instilled 'fatigue and revulsion' in readers who rarely encountered in its verses the 'formulation of a simple expression'.[48] For Pirenne, Chastelain's language was 'full to the brim with emphatic pomp'.[49] In the work of Robert Gaguin, thought Petit-Dutaillis, 'humanism was only just announcing itself; but it was announcing itself'.[50] Late medieval atrophy, excessive formalism and mental extremes, all alleviated by glimmers of a new dawn, were therefore standard fare in the latest and most eminent works of 'general history' of the day. It was these challenging, rebarbative phenomena which Huizinga set out to understand better, by employing an approach for which he had found intellectual justification in the thought of leading German thinkers of the past decade or two.[51]

As historians turned away in greater numbers from the chronicles which had formed the backbone of the great histories of the Burgundian dominions written in the mid-nineteenth century, and looked instead to recently cataloged archival documents, the rich harvest of editions of the

47 Pirenne, *Histoire de Belgique*, II, pp. 435-436.

48 Coville, *Les premiers Valois*, p. 407.

49 Pirenne, *Histoire de Belgique*, II, p. 425.

50 Petit-Dutaillis, *Charles VII*, p. 443.

51 Cf. Krul, 'In the Mirror', p. 355, on his belief that Huizinga 'offered a vision of a period in History which until then had lacked a recognisable identity', except possibly in the dramatic vision of novelists like Huysmans (ibid., pp. 364-365).

narrative sources that had been built up over the preceding years was in danger of going to waste.[52] And yet the rich harvest was there, 'filling the warehouses of scholarship': 'sources are published that are not sources as such', Huizinga later lamented, 'but standing pools'.[53] This was the main body of material Huizinga would use. The boldness of his enterprise is accentuated when we compare his goals with those of a rare fellow worker in the field, Pierre Champion. Champion's two-volume, 850-page *Histoire poétique du XVe siècle* appeared just five years after *Herfsttij*, and was apparently written without the independent French scholar knowing anything of the Leiden professor's efforts.[54] Like Huizinga, Champion set out to show the value of literature as a source, convinced that historians had neglected these important documents in which a society's morals and sentiments found expression.[55] In his review of the book, Huizinga saw Champion as a coworker of sorts, noting that 'something of the hand and eye of the age has passed into him'; Champion's study was full of serious, accurately captured scenes, 'like the work of a fifteenth-century painter'.[56] But *Histoire poétique* was simply a series of forays – some long, some short – into the history of the literature of the age: 'a *spicilegium* of the biographies of those whom I considered the most representative of that time'. Huizinga's, by contrast, was a cultural history of an age seen through its art and literature; it aspired to be, not a gathering of ears of corn after the harvest had been collected (*spicilegium*), but rather the gathering and sifting, weighing and measuring of the whole harvest itself.

52 Cf. Huizinga, 'Bernard Shaw's Saint', pp. 229-230, reflecting majority views among historians about narrative sources (in this instance on the subject of Joan of Arc), which 'embroidered a humanistic and historiographic pattern with elaborate miraculous details [...] and quite a bit of rhetoric, so that these most original and primary sources must, remarkably enough, be considered among the least reliable'. See also Hugenholtz, 'Le déclin', p. 44.

53 Huizinga, 'The Task', pp. 25-26. The one historian who would still draw on the narrative sources at this stage was Huizinga's friend Pirenne in volumes 1 and 2 of his *Histoire de Belgique*, which Huizinga praised for 'the sense of a direct contact with the past': cf. Huizinga, 'The Task', p. 53; Boone, '"L'automne du Moyen Age"', p. 43, n. 63.

54 Champion's *Histoire poétique* was published in 1923. The first French review of *Herfsttij* did not appear until 1925, and only then of the 1924 German translation. Champion's brother Édouard was asked if the family publishing house would be interested in producing a French edition of *Herfsttij*, but the approach was not made until January 1923. I am assuming that Pierre Champion did not read Dutch; if he did, and he had indeed read *Herfsttij*, the complete absence of any mention of it in his *Histoire poétique* would be a remarkable oversight. Supporting detail for this observation is in De Voogd, *Le miroir de la France*, pp. 46, 293-294.

55 Champion, *Histoire poétique*, I, pp. vii-xi.

56 *VW*, III, pp. 573-574.

2 Sources in Quantity

In light of the methodological positions he adopted it comes as no surprise to discover that Huizinga was among the least quantitative of historians, believing that 'in the number the story is vanquished, and no picture is born'.[57] Yet to achieve a better understanding of his priorities and methods, it is helpful to take a broadly quantitative approach to his harvest of the narrative sources. In arriving at the statistics which follow, the text and critical apparatus of the 1996 Payton and Mammitzsch translation have been used to count up passages where there is clear evidence – by quotation, paraphrase or some other form of direct reference – of Huizinga's engagement with a single anonymous narrative source (e.g., the *Cent nouvelles nouvelles*); with one of the many works of a single identifiable author (e.g., the large number of poems of Eustache Deschamps); or with a published collection of a particular document type (e.g., the *ordonnances des rois de France*). The results of this inquiry have been checked against an online version of the fullest Dutch edition of *Herfsttij* from Huizinga's collected works (1949). It would be unrealistic to attach too much credence to the apparent precision of this exercise for a number of reasons, not least Huizinga's tendency to present his illustrative material from the most frequently cited authors by author name, rather than by the separate titles of the individual works they wrote. Although he was quick to spot editorial and even authorial errors, he rarely paid close attention to the specific circumstances of a single work's creation or reception: it was often simply the mind of the author that interested him. Given that almost nothing in the book came from an unpublished archival or manuscript source, however, the approach does provide a good indication of its source base.

In total, *Herfsttij* (in the version we have used) contains 1672 direct quotations, paraphrases or some otherwise meaningful form of reference taken from a total of 86 different sources from the period, identified either as a single anonymous work, a single published collection of a source type, or as one or other of the works attributable to a single known mind. The inclusion of the second and third categories in this list means that the total of 86 is a considerable underestimate of the total number of individual sources Huizinga read, from royal letters to entire chronicles in multivolume editions. Virtually all of the main categories identified in the present-day Narrative Sources from the Medieval Low Countries (NaSo) project can be located among Huizinga's materials, including 'chronicles, circumstantial literature,

57 *VW*, VII, p. 142.

correspondence, diaries-memoirs, exempla, fiction, genealogies, hagiography, historical notes, histories-gesta, necrologia-obituaria, pamphlets-treatises, poems, sermons [and] travel literature'.[58]

This wide range and considerable volume of material was absorbed in the period from the Groningen lectures to the submission of the manuscript early in 1919.[59] Huizinga claimed that the work had taken longer (or maybe that was just how it felt to him): when Jan Romein, one of his best pupils, excitedly announced he had read the book in just twelve evenings, Huizinga replied with a smile of regret that he had worked on it for twelve years.[60] The reading program appears to have begun with a frenzy of work for the Groningen lectures on Burgundian culture, for at least 32 of the 86 sources which appear in *Herfsttij* were consulted and cited in Huizinga's notes for those classes, including almost all of his principal sources. There were interludes in this reading program when Huizinga was engaged in other research, including his essay on American culture (reading for which took up the summer of 1917, for example), and his history of Groningen University.[61] These works, which he described in his correspondence of the time as being of second rank, were welcome interludes in May and June especially, when (as he wrote in a letter to Pirenne) he found he often lacked the concentration to push on with 'mon "grand" livre sur la fin du moyen-âge'.[62] There were inevitably delays too, as Huizinga hunted down the materials he felt he needed with the help of the Leiden librarians and his network of scholarly contacts in the Netherlands.[63] The work on *Herfsttij* remained his main preoccupation throughout these years. In 1917 he told Pirenne (once again) that he was exhausted by the project, having feared more than once that 'I have conceived of a work that is too great and too heavy for my strength'.[64]

Measuring Huizinga's reading in terms of sources cited, time spent and anguish expressed gives the lie to his self-deprecating comments written

58 NaSo was established by the universities of Ghent, Louvain and Groningen and is published by the Belgian Royal Historical Commission. The genres missing from Huizinga's source base but present in NaSo are annals and king lists (more early than late medieval); encyclopedia; and memorial books.

59 On the submission of the manuscript (which does not survive, unlike Huizinga's notes) see Hugenholtz, 'Le déclin', p. 45.

60 Romein, 'Huizinga als historicus', p. 272.

61 Huizinga, *Briefwisseling*, I, p. 207.

62 Ibid.

63 Gustave Cohen, the then recently appointed professor of French at Amsterdam, for example, whom Huizinga contacted through a younger Leiden colleague in Romance Philology, Kornelis Sneyders de Vogel, with a list of books he needed: UBL Hui. 52:2 (14 December 1917).

64 Huizinga, *Briefwisseling*, I, p. 200.

many years later, and shows just how absurdly wide of the mark is the statement that he fired the book off one summer after reading a handful of chronicles.[65] The work for *Herfsttij* may well have been the largest single research investment of his career; it filled hundreds of envelopes and continued to pay dividends in his publications as late as the 1930s. But in at least two respects, criticisms that have been leveled at Huizinga's reading do find some vindication in a quantitative analysis of his sources.

There is no doubt, first of all, that Huizinga cited some sources far more than others, and that this tendency could make his source base seem narrower than it really was. Two authors in particular stand out in the crowd of 86 sources, together making up nearly 25 percent of all 1672 references: George Chastelain (d. 1475), official chronicler, poet, and counselor of the last two Valois dukes of Burgundy; and Eustache Deschamps (d. 1406), poet and royal officer of various kinds (*bailli*, court usher).[66] After this leading pair (in which first and second places are nevertheless clearly differentiated), a tight bunch of three authors comes next, all of them mentioned around half as often as Chastelain. They are the theologian and chancellor of the University of Paris Jean Gerson (d. 1429); the chronicler and poet Jean Froissart (d. after 1404); and the Burgundian ducal household officer, memoirist and poet Olivier de La Marche (d. 1502).[67] Together this threesome accounts for a further 19 percent or so of the references to narrative sources. Somewhat on his own is Chastelain's successor Jean Molinet (d. 1507), with just over 4 percent of references (meaning that the two official poet-historians of the dukes of Burgundy between them account in total for 17 percent of the references to narrative sources in *Herfsttij*).[68] Just behind Molinet comes the unlikely pairing of Denis the Carthusian (d. 1471), the Roermond theologian and mystic who mostly lived in seclusion from the world, and the anonymous author of the *Journal d'un bourgeois de Paris* (d. after 1444), who recorded the busy life of the French capital in a period of great turmoil.[69] Between them, then, eight authors make up around 54 percent of all references in *Herfsttij*, spread across the majority of the narrative source categories recognized by NaSo.

65 Cantor, *Inventing the Middle Ages*, p. 377.

66 Chastelain's works are mentioned 216 times, Deschamps's 193 times. Chastelain is referred to in all but one of the fourteen chapters of the first edition of *Herfsttij*, while Deschamps appears in nine out of fourteen.

67 Gerson is mentioned 115 times, and is present in all but one of the chapters; Froissart 100 times, in all but three chapters; de La Marche (d. 1502) 95 times, and at least once in all but two chapters.

68 There are 69 references from Molinet spread across all but two chapters.

69 Denis is mentioned 57 times across eleven chapters, and the anonymous Parisian 43 times across nine chapters.

As a result of this intense concentration on a core group of witnesses, the remaining 46 percent of references come from a far larger supporting cast. Measured in terms of citations, this crowd of narrative sources can be divided into four. Ahead of the rest is a group of six authors cited between 25 and 35 times, appearing on average in around half the chapters of the book, and together accounting for 10 percent of all references. They are: the nobleman and memoirist Jacques Du Clercq (d. 1501), the nobleman, minor officer and chronicler Enguerran de Monstrelet (d. 1453), the leading courtier and memoirist Philippe de Commynes (d. 1511), the jurist, bishop and polemicist Jean Juvenal des Ursins (d. 1473), the monk and chronicler Michel Pintoin (also known as the Religieux de Saint Denis) (d. 1421), and the court poet and musician Guillaume de Machaut (d. 1377). Thereafter comes a larger group of 23 sources which are each mentioned between 10 and 22 times, accounting for roughly 19 percent of the total number of references (i.e., considerably less than Chastelain and Deschamps combined), and which are listed here in an appendix. They are followed by a larger bunch still, consisting of 38 narrative sources which are mentioned more than once but fewer than ten times, accounting for just over 10 percent of all references in *Herfsttij*, most of them spread over two, three or four chapters. The remaining 7 percent or so are single references to a single source.

The second criticism that can be leveled against Huizinga arises from the infrequency of citations to some of the materials mentioned in the preceding paragraph, to which we might add the charge that he simply left things out altogether: not just individual sources, but whole categories of sources. As we shall see, infrequent mentions of a source do not necessarily indicate that the work in question is unimportant in Huizinga's scheme of things: on the contrary, authors who play a key role in shaping his understanding of the age might be mentioned on as few as a dozen occasions (such as the poet François Villon [d. after 1463]). But there is no getting round the fact, as Karin Tilmans has observed, that *Herfsttij* cites just one Dutch-language history among the many chronicles and memoirs which it draws on, most of the rest being in Middle French, with just a few in Latin.[70] To this charge Herman Pleij adds another: the absence of comment on an entire branch of Middle Dutch literature of the time produced by the chambers of rhetoric (urban literary associations which met regularly in the towns and cities of northern France and the Low Countries to compete with one another in the writing of verse, members of which participated officially in many

70 Tilmans, 'Chroniqueurs en kroniekschrijvers', p. 54.

civic occasions, such as princely entry ceremonies or processions).[71] Closely linked to this lacuna is a third which Jelle Koopmans has emphasized: with the exception of a single mention of the Middle Dutch play *Marieken van Nimwegen*, there is no discussion of the theater of the time, arguably one of the most important developments in the literary life of the regions concerned, and a genre that was performed in both Middle French and Dutch.[72] To these gaps we might add others from the court literature of the age, despite the fact this was clearly Huizinga's favorite field of investigation. The large number of lengthy prose renderings of earlier verse epics which the Burgundian court commissioned warrants barely a mention (as Claude Thiry has observed).[73] The same could be said of the many translations of classical historians which were made for the Burgundian court. As a result, there is no place for some of the most famous names of Burgundian court literature: no Jean Wauquelin, no David Aubert, no Jean Miélot.

3 The Criteria of Source Selection

Setting aside the gaps and peaks for a moment and concentrating instead on the total number of narrative sources cited, it is worth noting that there was probably no better decade than the first of the twentieth century to be looking for materials to write the type of project Huizinga envisaged. Ironically, just as historians were turning their backs on the narrative sources, these years witnessed the publication of four surveys which captured the rich crop of editorial work from the previous century, as well as the latest writing on each of the sources cataloged. The least frequently cited of these reference works in Huizinga's notes are Pirenne's *Bibliographie de l'histoire de Belgique* and volume 2.1 of Gröber's *Grundriss der romanischen Philologie*, both of which appeared in 1902.[74] The substantial body of material assembled in volume 4 of Auguste Molinier's *Les sources de l'histoire de France*, entitled *Les Valois, 1328-1461* (1904) was a far more informative guide than the previous standard works by August Potthast and Ulysse Chevalier, and it was heavily used throughout the decade-long project.[75] In the very

71 Pleij, 'De verguizing'.

72 Huizinga, *Autumn*, p. 18; Koopmans, 'Einde van het *Herfsttij der Middeleeuwen*?'

73 Thiry, 'Le printemps des temps nouveaux', pp. 223-224.

74 Gröber, *Grundriss der romanischen Philologie*, II, part 1, pp. 1126-1159; Pirenne, *Bibliographie de l'histoire de Belgique*. References to Gröber occur throughout the notes, but those relating to Pirenne only appear in UBL Hui. 52: L.5.

75 On this major work see, most recently, Guyot-Bachy, 'Auguste Molinier'.

year he started work in earnest, the best scholarly guide Huizinga could possibly have hoped for appeared in the shape of Georges Doutrepont's *La littérature française à la cour des ducs de Bourgogne* (1909). To judge from Huizinga's notes, Doutrepont quickly became his *vade mecum*, to such an extent that on one occasion we catch the words of the Louvain philologist falling virtually unchanged from the Leiden historian's pen.[76] Never before had it seemed quite so possible to grasp the literature of the entire age. The availability of Gröber, Molinier and Doutrepont helps explain the range and volume of Huizinga's reading, but it also makes the task of explaining his peaks and gaps all the more necessary.

The source surveys which Huizinga used were organized, much like the general histories which had directed his initial reading, along national lines. In Doutrepont's case, the national framework was given a particular slant by his adherence to the *Mouvement wallon* and his authorship of several works on the 'lettres françaises de Belgique'.[77] But Huizinga himself deliberately excluded national considerations from his criteria for source selection. Molinier's listing of Burgundian chronicles alongside Italian or German works under a separate rubric of *chroniques étrangères* seemed particularly strange to him: how could any contemporary ever have considered the house of Burgundy, with its profound engagement in the political life of the kingdom, to be a foreign power, as different as France from Belgium in his own day?[78] The first outcome of Huizinga's reading program for *Herfsttij* was his rejection of the imposition of anachronistic national conceptions on the age of Burgundy, a line of thinking he expounded in a paper read to an audience at Utrecht in 1911 where Pirenne himself – his new friend, but also the godfather of Belgian history, the man who had done more than anyone to identify Burgundy with his own nation state – sat in the audience.[79]

It is important and relevant to recall how deeply ingrained national frameworks of scholarship had become by 1909, and therefore how significant an action it was to step outside them. Scientific discussion and public debate surrounding the visual art of the fifteenth century had become polarized

76 Cf. Doutrepont, *La littérature française*, pp. 304-305: 'De plus, à entendre le poète (Martin Le Franc), ils (les seigneurs) font monter leurs jongleurs, leurs bouffons de cour au rang de conseillers et de ministres. Tel est, par exemple, Coquinet, le fou de Bourgogne'; Huizinga, *Autumn*, p. 12: 'A poet (Martin le Franc) complains that princes promote their jesters or musicians to the position of councillor or minister as indeed happened to Coquinet the Fool of Burgundy' (original text in *VW*, III, p. 15).

77 Guiette, 'Georges Doutrepont'.

78 *VW*, II, p. 112.

79 Tollebeek, 'At the Crossroads of Nationalism'.

around such concerns.[80] The 1902 Bruges exhibition of Burgundian art had been followed in 1904 by a Parisian counterblast, an exhibition of *les primitifs français*; two years later, Hippolyte Fierens-Gevaert formulated a Belgian retort, *La Renaissance septentrionale et les premiers maîtres des Flandres* (which Huizinga read and annotated). Not that Huizinga was entirely exempt from the sentiments which he endeavored to filter out of his criteria for source selection. As we shall see, patriotism (conceived of as an apolitical form of nationalism) can be discerned in the treatment of narrative sources. But the nationalism of his own day remained outside his terms of reference.

This fact may also explain why the politics of the fifteenth century, which were so often interpreted through the nationalist lens of modern works of general history, were also of little concern to Huizinga in *Herfsttij*. If one were to look at the narrative sources of the fifteenth century from a political angle, he noted, a false impression of the age would result; sources of this type were 'not [...] substantially different from a description of the ministerial and ambassadorial politics of the eighteenth century'.[81] Political concerns came and went; studying them, Huizinga seems to imply, did not bring the cultural historian any closer to the 'forms of life, thought and art' of a given age. This point too is significant. In a field of history (*algemene geschiedenis* [general history]) that was increasingly dominated by the national narrative, Huizinga was making a bid for the importance of cultural history. A decade later he would define 'the task of cultural history' more clearly.[82] In *Herfsttij*, however, he was content to formulate a worked example of his developing thinking.

Huizinga's principal concern in selecting his sources was squarely in line with his own methodology, derived from readings in the philosophy of history. Literature was valued in terms of its proximity to life – life as it was lived at court, in smart academic circles, on the streets of Paris or in the noble manor. His desire to obtain a direct connection with life by means of the literature of the time is already clear in the preface to his work, where he acknowledged the importance of his core sources 'in which their expressions are the preeminent mirror of the spirit of their age'. The idea that sources might serve as mirrors or as photographic plates is recurrent in *Herfsttij*.[83] Their authors struck him as being the most representative of their time,

80 For this and what follows, see Haskell, 'Huizinga and the "Flemish Renaissance"', pp. 443-467.

81 Huizinga, *Autumn*, p. 15.

82 A point well made in Otto, 'Vormen van het ondermaanse', p. 49.

83 Huizinga, *Autumn*, pp. 63, 200, 349, 350.

thinkers who were unoriginal and conservative.[84] This perspective may help us understand the complete or relative absence from Huizinga's source base of some of the most original and distinguished thinkers of the day in the fields of theology or philosophy, such as Jean Buridan or Nicolas Oresme.[85]

Because Huizinga saw life clearly through the eyes of these sources, he developed a personal relationship with them. He formed views on the character of his authors which he revealed in complicitous asides to the reader, drawing us into his understanding of their minds. Jean Molinet was 'Good old Molinet', in contrast to his predecessor, 'that pompous Polonius Chastelain' with his 'solemn verbosity [...] his style a little schoolmasterish'.[86] The anonymous Parisian was 'a conventional fellow, rarely given to the enjoyment of cleverly turned phrases or mental games'.[87] It was important to Huizinga to know details about the personal lives of his subjects. He bothered in his notes to jot down the date of Charles d'Orléans's wedding, and retained the fact that the Burgundian official Pierre Bladelin was childless, or that Guillaume de Machaut was blind in one eye.[88] His notes on Jean Gerson bring all of these elements together. Huizinga collected the details of Gerson's career as one would expect, but he also noted down details from his background which might not seem important to another kind of historian: the fact that Gerson was one of five brothers, for example, one of whom died, the other three becoming monks.[89] Gerson – 'honest, pure and well-meaning' – was a prolific theologian whose traditional views might be considered representative of majority positions in the thought of his time.[90] His reforming agenda and his status as a 'public intellectual' led him to pronounce on a great many aspects of daily life, one of Huizinga's key concerns.[91] Given his career and standing, Gerson had personal dealings with many other people whom Huizinga was interested in – the relatively obscure preacher Jean de Varennes, for example.[92] In short, Gerson gave

84 For example, Denis the Carthusian (UBL Hui. 27 I, p. 84) or Gerson (UBL Hui. 114: G.3).

85 Courtenay, 'Huizinga's Heirs', pp. 25-27.

86 Huizinga, *Autumn*, pp. 323, 93, 168.

87 Huizinga, *Autumn*, p. 244.

88 UBL Hui. 27 I, p. 17; ibid., 52: V.12.

89 Historians have since studied the importance of Gerson's family context in the formation and expression of his spiritual beliefs, in particular relations with his female relatives: Ledwidge, 'Relations de famille'.

90 Hübner, 'Der theologisch-philosophische Konservatismus des Jean Gerson'.

91 Hobbins, 'The Schoolman as Public Intellectual'.

92 On Jean de Varennes, Huizinga's information was gleaned from notes in the editions of the works of Jean Gerson and Jean Froissart: UBL Hui. 52: S.10. The earliest monograph on the subject was Vauchez, 'Un réformateur religieux dans la France de Charles VI'.

Huizinga an unrivalled vantage point over the spiritual life of the age. By dint of looking through his eyes for so long, he happened in this case to develop a personal affinity with the source – something that did not happen in Huizinga's relationship with Chastelain or Deschamps.

It follows that narrative sources which were at any kind of remove from the life of the age must have seemed less rewarding to Huizinga, and that this must have had a bearing upon his selection and treatment of his material. Here we begin to understand the omission or relative neglect of certain sources. It was possible to glean useful details from the impersonal financial document set down by the bureaucrat and stored in the archive, for example, and Huizinga certainly drew on Léon de Laborde's archival sources on arts and letters at the Burgundian court (a foundational work in the field).[93] But the legal document which resulted from a quite different set of human interactions, recording within its own confines both the extremes and norms of life, was surely much more promising as a narrative source to Huizinga than most financial records.[94] Hence the value to *Herfsttij* of Charles Petit-Dutaillis's rich collection of letters of remission in his *Documents nouveaux sur les mœurs populaires et le droit de vengeance* (1909), for example.[95] Huizinga was perfectly aware that narrative sources (including letters of remission) did not necessarily record life as it had actually been lived, but rather gave an account of life which contemporaries were prepared to accept or entertain.[96] This had no negative bearing on the value of such materials for his investigation whatsoever – indeed, quite the opposite. By the same token, how useful to Huizinga were the lengthy prose renderings of earlier verse epics and the translations of classical histories which figured prominently in the library of the dukes of Burgundy? It was possible to say something about the 'forms of life and thought' of the later Middle Ages on the basis of how a contemporary reimagined Chrétien de Troyes's stories of the twelfth century, or how Quintus Curtius Rufus's first-century *Histories of Alexander the Great* were translated.[97] But there were surely more obvious routes to that goal through the vast, freshly cataloged canon of literature from the time.

93 Cited 27 times across six chapters of *Herfsttij*. Huizinga identified potentially useful publications of financial accounts using Molinier, but no subsequent notes taken from these materials survive: UBL Hui. 52: R.3.

94 E.g., Huizinga, *Autumn*, pp. 27-29.

95 Cited seven times across four chapters.

96 E.g., Huizinga, *Autumn*, pp. 8 (Jouffroy), 54 (Chastelain's invented speeches).

97 Of David Aubert's lengthy *Perceforest*, for example, he paraphrased Doutrepont's observation (*La littérature française*, p. 49) that the work was a 'chivalric encyclopedia': UBL Hui. 52: V.22. But for negative comment on the *mises en prose*, see Huizinga, *Autumn*, p. 354.

Prose romances and translations of classical histories did at least have two features which sat well with Huizinga's preference for literature that was close to life. In the first instance, neither was written in verse. Huizinga felt that the prose of the era was 'relatively and generally better than the poetry'.[98] Both could serve as a lens for isolating forms of life and thought, of course. But in verse it was the limitations of the age, its excessive formalism and atrophy that were more likely to be revealed in the endless word play, overcomplicated rhyming schemes and other literary constructions of fifteenth-century poems.[99] Critics have pointed out in reply just how creative, innovative and imaginative the contemporary poets could be.[100] Once again, Huizinga was very much of his time in agreeing with the widely held judgments of his day about the 'hollow words and doggerel' of the fifteenth century.[101] But it should be said he also showed particular interest in the values of innovation and novelty which these poets cherished; more than that, indeed, he tried to understand them. These traits, he concluded, were prime examples of the quest for ever more intricate 'forms of thought' which characterized the age: 'the devices employed by Molinet to gain the praise of his contemporaries as an inspired rhetorician and poet appear to us like the last degenerative phase of a form of expression shortly before its demise. [...] But this is precisely what the contemporary admired as something new.'[102] Simply pointing out further instances of poetic innovation therefore leaves Huizinga's main point unaddressed, and possibly strengthened.[103]

The other feature which kept de-rhymed romances and translations of classical histories closer to life in Huizinga's view was the fact they were written in the vernacular. Despite the likelihood that Latin texts constituted 70-80 percent of all available reading in the fourteenth and fifteenth centuries, vernacular narrative sources predominate in *Herfsttij*.[104] Huizinga certainly did not eschew Latin sources. Latinity was a key issue in relation to the Renaissance, and it was important to Huizinga that French humanists practiced Latin letters in ways which, all things considered, 'were already linked to the large international intellectual movement' and were 'in no way inferior to later products' (one of the many ways in

98 UBL Hui. 114: L.3; Huizinga, *Autumn*, p. 341.

99 Huizinga, *Autumn*, p. 353.

100 Koopmans, 'Einde van het *Herfsttij der Middeleeuwen*?'; Thiry, 'Le printemps des temps nouveaux'.

101 *VW*, III, p. 574.

102 Huizinga, *Autumn*, pp. 380-381

103 As in Rigolot, 'Les rhétoriqueurs', p. 14.

104 Bozzolo and Ornato, 'Les lectures des français'.

which he thought Burckhardt had overemphasized the exceptionalism of the Italian Renaissance).[105] But it is interesting to note that he also kept a file on the mistakes which contemporaries made in Latin: their lack of familiarity with the language was a matter of importance to him.[106] He seems to have believed that one could not see the contemporary mind quite so clearly when it cloaked itself in the ill-fitting garb of Latin. Even in the case of a practiced Latinist like the Bishop of Chalon Jean Germain, Huizinga regretted in his notes that the Livy-esque style of his language had a leveling effect which tended to deaden the author's particular traits and nuances.[107] When the authors of French vernacular prose texts played around with clever neo-Latinisms, they added to the wearisome pile of examples which demonstrated the atrophy and excessive formalism of the age.[108]

The value of the vernacular over Latin in Huizinga's method makes the relative absence of Middle Dutch literature all the more puzzling, for here too the narrative sources were just as close to life. It is surprising how rarely it is pointed out that Huizinga's education and training took place at the feet of some of the leading specialists of Middle Dutch language and literature of the day, giving him no doubt an awareness of the possible consequences of neglecting this area in his investigations. At secondary school he was taught by Jan te Winkel, who was already by that stage the editor of several Middle Dutch texts, not least the great thirteenth-century poet Jacob van Maerlant. In 1908 Te Winkel would embark on the publication of a seven-volume history of the development of Dutch literature which came to serve as a handbook to the whole field, just at the time in fact that Huizinga was embarking on his own research for *Herfsttij*.[109] Even though the teacher did not inspire much personal affection in the pupil, Te Winkel's influence was enough to encourage Huizinga to study the field of *Germanistik* at Groningen.[110] Huizinga remembered his Groningen university tutors warmly when he came to write his autobiographical essay, and they too included such experts of Middle Dutch language and literature as Willem van Helten, author of a

105 Huizinga, *Autumn*, pp. 383-384, 74.

106 UBL Hui. 114: L.2.

107 Huizinga, *Autumn*, p. 387; UBL Hui. 114: J.1.

108 Huizinga, *Autumn*, pp. 387-388. Of one of these examples in his notes, Huizinga observed: 'One can hear Rabelais sniggering' (UBL Hui. 114: K.6).

109 Te Winkel, *De ontwikkelingsgang der Nederlandsche letterkunde*. See also Van Driel, 'Kalme gemoedsrust'. The most recent syntheses of the field are Van Oostrom, *Wereld in woorden*, and Pleij, *Het gevleugelde woord*.

110 Huizinga, 'My Path to History', p. 248.

Middelnederlandsche spraakkunst (1887) based on over 150 sources.[111] The syllabus for the undergraduate degree which Huizinga followed was based on a German academic model for the study of *Philologie* which 'emphasized the essential unity of the cultural manifestations (linguistic, literary, artistic, religious, etc.) of the national spirit (*Volksgeist* or *Nationalgeist*) during a particular period of its existence'.[112] So from an early stage Huizinga, who had been trained in 'Dutch studies' rather than simply as an historian, was in the habit of considering multiple forms of creative composition (poetry, history, painting) as a single object of study. All of this reminds us once again of how much Huizinga's *Herfsttij* owed to the times and places of its gestation.[113] But in this one respect, Middle Dutch literature, Huizinga did not take a route suggested by his schooling and university education, despite the strong likelihood it would have been more obvious for him to use such sources than their Middle French counterparts. The latter do not seem to have figured formally in his education at all.[114]

The intellectual reasons for Huizinga's choice are clear enough. His research goal in *Herfsttij* was to understand the work of the Van Eycks, and it was this inquiry that led the cultural historian into the narrative sources:

> The literature that is at the same level as the art of Jan van Eyck is courtly, or at least aristocratic, is written in French, and is read and admired by the same circles that place their orders with the great painters.[115]

With the union of the Low Countries under the Burgundian dukes in the second quarter of the fifteenth century, the earlier Dutch literature of the courts of the counts of Holland or the dukes of Brabant became part of the cultural patrimony of the new dynasty – a process which must have been facilitated by the fact that French literature had long been a major influence on Dutch courtly texts anyway, with very little traffic in the

111 On Van Helten and Simons, teachers of Huizinga at Groningen, see http://www.dbnl.org/auteurs/auteur (accessed 23 May 2017). A detailed account of Huizinga's time in Groningen, although not touching on the issue of Middle Dutch, is Krul, *Historicus*, pp. 62-122.

112 Van Essen, *E. Kruisinga*, especially pp. 37-49.

113 Even his study of Sanskrit, which can seem surprising to us now, was a mainstream element of the Groningen curriculum in postgraduate study which he followed, and a subject which Van Helten had specialized in since 1889.

114 Medieval French literature was one of the specialisms of the Groningen professor of French, Anton van Hamel, and he published on Villon. But he was more interested in the high Middle Ages than Huizinga's period. Huizinga does not mention attending Van Hamel's classes. On Van Hamel, see: http://www.dbnl.org/tekst/_jaa003190801_01/_jaa003190801_01_0014.php.

115 Huizinga, *Autumn*, p. 332.

opposite direction.[116] A leading specialist of the Middle Dutch literature of the period finds that with certain nuances, Huizinga's ideas are broadly applicable to writing at the Dutch court around 1400.[117] The new Burgundian court brought texts like Froissart's or Chastelain's to the fore, as Huizinga observed in his notes, all of them writing in French.

> What had the Dutch been writing? Their little provincial histories. Is it the rise of a dynasty (or rather the beginning of a period in general) that always awakens such historians [as Froissart and Chastelain]?[118]

Huizinga knew what the main Dutch-language histories were and jotted down bibliographical references in his notes, but he had clearly decided there was not much point in devoting a great deal of attention to a form of court literature that was secondary in nature: a part of the cultural life of the age, but at one remove from its core, the core defined as the world of Van Eyck.[119]

In criticizing Huizinga for neglecting Middle Dutch literature, posterity has not always remembered that he shared Henri Pirenne's positive estimation of the importance of Flemish prose as practiced by writers of the mystical tradition, not least Jan van Ruusbroec ('that founder of Flemish prose').[120] The Dutch-language literature of the mystic tradition was primarily associated with the cities rather than the court, and the supplementary charge that Huizinga overlooked the Dutch literature of the towns and cities is also generally made without taking this important point into account. But what of that other strand of urban Middle Dutch literature, the work of the *rederijkers*? Herman Pleij has laid the blame for the poor estimation and neglect of the work of the rhetoricians among modern scholars of literature at Huizinga's door. Despite their importance in the cultural landscape, Pleij argued, Huizinga barely mentioned the rhetoricians in *Herfsttij*; worse still, he tarnished them by implication with all the characteristics he detected

116 Van Oostrom, 'Middle Dutch Literature', p. 75

117 Van Oostrom, 'De oude orde in verval?', p. 207.

118 UBL Hui. 121 IV: 4.

119 The notes are in UBL Hui. 50: H.6. In coming to this conclusion he was once again in step with (although rather less harsh than) Pirenne, who thought that the few rhymed chronicles that continued to be written in Dutch for aristocratic audiences in the fifteenth century were 'of puerile banality': Pirenne, *Histoire de Belgique*, II, p. 418. Cf. UBL Hui. 27 I, pp. 78-79: 'the Dutch element in Burgundian culture is not the main part'.

120 Pirenne, *Histoire de Belgique*, II, p. 419. Huizinga cited Ruusbroec 11 times in two of the chapters of *Herfsttij*.

in the work of the court rhetoricians such as Chastelain and Molinet.[121] And it is certainly true that the *rederijkers* crop up only twice in *Herfsttij*, first as the industrious agents of the autonomous development of urban festivals in the fifteenth century which had previously been the preserve of the church, and later as a 'perfectly old-fashioned form' of the 'humanist club spirit' that figured in Italian civic life.[122]

But once again, we must not isolate Huizinga's views from the context of his time, even if nowadays we no longer read his fellow travelers from a century ago. Pirenne's view of 'secular literature' in Middle Dutch was more explicitly pejorative than any Huizinga actually expressed, it must be said.[123] Behind Pirenne's poor estimation of the *rederijkers* and the archery guilds which sponsored Middle Dutch theater lay the views of founding figures of the study of rhetorician theater itself, such as the Flemish nationalist Prudens van Duyse, who considered the decadence of *rederijker* literature to be the result of the unhealthy French influence of the Burgundian court.[124] We know from his notes that Huizinga used Van Duyse for his Groningen lectures. Although Huizinga was also aware of the efforts of Gerrit Kalff to rehabilitate the reputation of the rhetoricians and commented on the subject in his lecture notes, the views of Van Duyse and his ilk persisted.[125] Doutrepont, whom Huizinga was also reading, repeated them.[126]

The emphasis Doutrepont placed on theater as spectacle, rather than theater as literature, was a further disincentive to Huizinga when it came to selecting this material as a source for *Herfsttij*. For Huizinga, 'literary history [was] cultural history'.[127] The essentially transient, visual, auditory and rarely recorded nature of performance added a further layer to obscure the historian-interpreter's chances of seeing 'the forms of life and thought' of the age through theater, whether that of the amateur *rederijkers* or of the emerging professionals.[128] Even the transient cultural phenomenon of the *entremets* (table decorations and live entertainments at a court banquet) could still be studied to some extent by the cultural historian because it could be described as 'applied literature', that is to say: based loosely on a

121 Pleij, 'De verguizing'.
122 Huizinga, *Autumn*, pp. 303-304, 389.
123 Pirenne, *Histoire de Belgique*, II, p. 420.
124 Van Duyse, *De rederijkkamers*, I, p. 118; Dewulf, 'The Flemish Movement', p. 25.
125 Kalff, *Geschiedenis der Nederlandsche letterkunde*; UBL Hui. 27 I, p. 68.
126 Doutrepont, *La littérature française*, p. 350.
127 Huizinga, 'Historical Ideals of Life', p. 65.
128 In his notes Huizinga distilled Doutrepont's remarks at pp. 345-346 as follows: 'How the fifteenth century sees theater: spectacle. Not literature.' UBL Hui. 114: V.7.

narrative source, such as the *Vows of the Pheasant*.[129] Despite having included theater in his extensive reading program and also spoken on the subject in his lectures on Burgundian culture in 1909-1910, Huizinga decided it could not be integrated in *Herfsttij*.[130]

Blaming Huizinga for 'the vilification of the rhetoricians' is misguided for a second reason, one that is bound up with the original conception of *Herfsttij*. When he started out on his exercise in cultural history, Huizinga's intention had been to understand the art of the Netherlands of the seventeenth century. He hoped to achieve this goal by going back to the fifteenth century and the world of the Van Eycks, before moving on to Rembrandt and the apogee of the Dutch 'Golden Age'. A detailed plan of the intended book included a large opening section on 'Burgundian culture', and this was the subject of Huizinga's Groningen lectures (which themselves began with a section on the Dutch culture of the seventeenth century).[131] This initial phase of work on Burgundy developed into *Herfsttij* – an enormous first chapter that developed beyond its original purpose and became a separate entity. It was not until 1930 that Huizinga began to set down his ideas on the later period, and these did not take final form until his long essay 'Nederland's beschaving in de zeventiende eeuw' ('Dutch Civilisation in the Seventeenth Century') of 1941. We might therefore say that *Herfsttij* and 'Beschaving' were two seeds planted at the same time, but which germinated years apart.

When he eventually came to write the later work, Huizinga was in no doubt that 'the basis of seventeenth-century Dutch culture was urban society'; 'as trade and industry became the main sources of wealth, so culture, too, assumed an increasingly urban aspect'; the main actors in this civilization were the magistrates and townsmen of Dordrecht, Haarlem and Leiden. Last but not least,

> two forms of association, the civic guards and the chambers of rhetoric, both going back to the late Middle Ages, were chiefly responsible for providing the social framework in which cultural activity could take place.[132]

So Huizinga did have a central role to ascribe to the *rederijkers*, but it was one that came later in the story, and one which only found full expression in the

129 Huizinga, *Autumn*, p. 305.
130 UBL Hui. 52: L.6; ibid., 27 I, pp. 30-31.
131 Van der Lem, *Het Eeuwige*, p. 74.
132 Huizinga, 'Dutch Civilisation', pp. 41, 17, 20, 42.

geographical context he was then writing about, the northern Netherlands at their cultural apogee.

Huizinga clearly accepted the view expressed by Van Duyse and other Dutch specialists of his time that the cultural life of the Burgundian Netherlands two centuries earlier had been dominated by the court. In his notes for *Herfsttij* he observed that the late medieval rhetoricians were '*not yet* truly *burgerlijk*, but an imitation of aristocratic manners' (emphasis mine); compared to Chastelain, their works were labored and contrived.[133] We would adopt a different position today.[134] But in the context of *Herfsttij* and the time of its formulation, it seemed clear that the *rederijkers*, much like Dutch court literature of that time, were a secondary cultural phenomenon. Instead of blaming Huizinga for the maligning of the *rederijkers*, perhaps we ought to underline his willingness, in the face of established opinion, to state so clearly their key role in the long-term cultural development of the Low Countries.[135]

4.a Sources in Time

Having considered Huizinga's overarching goals and method as they are suggested by his treatment of narrative sources in *Herfsttij*, and having then assessed his narrative source base in relation to his criteria for selection, we can now turn in a final section, divided into two parts, to offer an interpretation of the principal functions which the narrative sources performed in the book. These functions will be broadly categorized as chronological and geographical, both of which arose from his intention to write a substantial work in the field of *algemene geschiedenis* (general history), interpreted by Huizinga as cultural history.

To grasp the importance of time in Huizinga's disposition of his narrative sources, the best place to start is with a work he mentions very little by an author he thought less significant as a cultural figure than more mainstream figures like Jan Brugman or Denis the Carthusian. The work is the *Imitation of Christ* by Thomas à Kempis (d. 1471).[136] Huizinga deemed *Imitation* to be 'the most powerful and beautiful work of that period', a remark which in

133 UBL Hui. 114: R.3. In his Burgundian culture lectures he was more positive: rhetorician literature was a 'joyous phenomenon' in cultural history: ibid., 27 I, p. 68.

134 Mareel, 'Urban literary patronage'.

135 Van Bruaene, *Om beters wille*, p. 173.

136 UBL Hui. 27 I, p. 84.

itself demands that we consider it more fully. The main point about the work was that it was timeless, 'not limited to one cultural epoch; it departs from all culture and belongs to no culture at all'; a 'book for all the ages' that could have been understood in any time, not just the age of Burgundy when it happened to have been created.[137] The fact that such a work could exist in Huizinga's scheme of things, a work that was out-of-time as it were, reveals his belief in the existence of universal forms which can be expressed in a universally accessible way.[138] Because the 'forms of life and thought' captured in the *Imitation of Christ* belonged to all periods, our access to it is unmediated. This barely mentioned work is therefore pivotal in Huizinga's application of methods he had assimilated and developed from German traditions of the sciences of the mind. The existence and character of the *Imitation* affirm the possibility that we can attain direct contact with a previous age. By the same token, this timeless narrative source throws into sharper relief the characteristics of the time-bound world that surrounds it.

A second, larger group of individual narrative sources or categories of source in *Herfsttij* performs a similar but simpler role. Huizinga repeatedly makes contemporary cultural references which function as so many points of contact between the world inhabited by his reader (imagined as the product of an enlightened liberal education of the nineteenth century) and the age of Burgundy. Sometimes the references are very general in nature ('the most intimate empathy [...] which we, in conjunction with cruelty, still know from Russian literature'), others are quite specific (Emerson, De Maupassant, Zola, Anatole France).[139] That Huizinga expressly looked for such references to include in his works, rather than adding them as instinctive asides, is suggested by a note to himself to look up detailed confirmation in Balzac's novel, *Le médecin de campagne* (1833), of a point which he wished to make about mourning practices.[140] So while we can agree that *Herfsttij* was 'a superb panoply of literary allusion', we might add that the likely intention was to make the 'forms of life and thought' of the fourteenth and fifteenth century more accessible by means of comparisons with the cultural present or recent past.[141] Sometimes the connection is articulated through a series of linked examples situated at different points in time. In one case Huizinga exemplifies a form of thought which we might call 'the French martial spirit'

137 Huizinga, *Autumn*, pp. 265-267.

138 Cf. Otterspeer, *Reading Huizinga*, p. 58, who does not use this example.

139 Huizinga, *Autumn*, pp. 47, 22, 151, 230-231, 363; UBL Hui. 114: L.3.

140 UBL Hui. 52: O.7.

141 Otterspeer, *Reading Huizinga*, p. 68.

by connecting four examples together, beginning in the later Middle Ages and moving progressively to the present: Jean de Bueil (d. 1477), author of a fictional account of a young warrior, *Le jouvencel*, was the narrative source for the fifteenth century, which Huizinga equated with the musketeer of the seventeenth century, presumably (though he does not say so) as celebrated by Alexandre Dumas (d. 1870).[142] Next came the *grognard* of the Napoleonic wars, a figure mythologized by Jules Michelet in a passage which bears a striking (and probably not coincidental) resemblance to Huizinga's technique here.[143] Finally, we are brought up to the present day with the figure of the *poilu* of contemporary newspaper reports from battlefronts less than 200 miles to the south of Leiden.[144] Like steps of a ladder reaching down through time, characters or types drawn from narrative sources (as well as the visual arts) known to an educated public thereby linked the contemporary reader to the forms of life and thought of earlier ages.

Thus far our examples of the temporal use of narrative sources reveal Huizinga's concern to create the possibility of contact with, and understanding of, a living past which can be visually called to mind. A third group of narrative source has a different conceptual role, to do with the issue of periodization – a major concern of this work of *algemene geschiedenis*. Although *Herfsttij* is ostensibly concerned with the fourteenth and fifteenth centuries, the book is peppered with references to a wider chronological period which begins as early as the twelfth century, and fades as late as the eighteenth.[145] Relating a story about the poet-prince René of Anjou, for example, Huizinga observes: 'Is this medieval? Is it Renaissance? Or is it not eighteenth century?'[146] The *terminus a quo* is clearly the high and proud civilization of the central Middle Ages, the age of John of Salisbury and Abelard, subjects on which Huizinga would write in later years as something of a prequel to *Herfsttij*.[147] From an early stage in his teaching he

142 Huizinga, *Autumn*, p. 80.

143 Michelet, 'Introduction à l'histoire universelle', pp. 48-49. For Michelet the martial spirit of the French is personified by the medieval figure of the 'gamin', and later by the *grognard* of Napoleon's armies. It is likely Huizinga is directly echoing his reading of this specific passage of Michelet. For Huizinga's first formulation of the point, see UBL Hui. 52: W.6. For his admiration for Michelet, see De Voogd, *Le miroir de la France*, pp. 139-147.

144 In another example (Huizinga, *Autumn*, p. 365), this time visual, the description of a peasant home by Chastelain gives rise to a chain of references linking the art of the past to the here and now, passing through Breughel (d. 1569), Rembrandt (d. 1669), Murillo (d. 1682) and on to Théophile Steinlen (d. 1923).

145 Tollebeek, '"Renaissance"', p. 362.

146 Huizinga, *Autumn*, p. 209.

147 Nauta, 'Huizinga's Lente'.

had come to the view that the twelfth century was a period when Western civilization 'took on its definitive form, its configuration'; when 'new forms and foundations of mental activity and social life were developing [...] forms and foundations that still serve as supports for the present day'.[148] In his notes for *Herfsttij* there are similarly clear remarks about the twelfth century as a highpoint.[149] The idea is present in the book itself, for example, in his comments on the 'high flowering of the court lyric' in the twelfth century, and the 'different turning' that began to be apparent in the thirteenth-century *Roman de la Rose*.[150]

Determining the *terminus ad quem* of what we might call Huizinga's macro chronological framework is more problematic. That the eighteenth century constituted some kind of loosely defined endpoint emerges from several comments. This was the time when exponents of Romanticism could regard the cultural forms of the Middle Ages as something recognizably different from those of their own age, for example.[151] In another passage Huizinga states that the 'stereotypical commiseration of the Third Estate' which we find in late medieval narrative sources will last into the eighteenth century, in the work of La Bruyère (d. 1696), Fénelon (d. 1715) and the Marquis of Mirabeau (d. 1789).[152] The seventeenth century was a period when the nobility still dominated public life and the Third Estate was reduced to the role of spectators, a point surely linked to his comment elsewhere that the Third Estate would remain an undifferentiated mass in which laborers and bourgeoisie were still lumped together into the eighteenth century – all points Huizinga could trace in the late medieval narrative sources.[153]

If Huizinga did not feel inclined to specify the precise end date of the macro chronological framework which he staked out around *Herfsttij*, this is most likely to have been deliberate. The effect of this soft frame around the core subject matter of the book was to challenge periodizations which placed emphasis on the Renaissance (or indeed the Reformation) as a major watershed between medieval and modern. Of the witch craze, for example, Huizinga would write: 'no humanism, no Reformation prevents this madness'.[154] So the period from the twelfth to the eighteenth centuries

148 Huizinga, 'Abelard', p. 179.

149 UBL Hui. 52: V.14: 'So we can see that the Renaissance, modern culture, everything germinated in the twelfth century.' Cf. Otterspeer, *Reading Huizinga*, pp. 52-54.

150 Huizinga, *Autumn*, p. 127.

151 Ibid., p. 61.

152 Ibid., p. 67.

153 Ibid., pp. 51, 61, 64.

154 Ibid., p. 286; cf. ibid., p. 210: 'even the Renaissance did not change the ideal of holiness'.

was a continuum along which the Renaissance was simply an additional point, not a rupture or an entirely new start. Despite Huizinga's very clear statements to that effect throughout *Herfsttij*, with all their implications for Burckhardt's paradigm, this most important argument has been misunderstood or underestimated surprisingly often, from the earliest readers onward.[155]

Turning, finally, to our chronological observations about the nature of the narrative sources of the fourteenth and fifteenth centuries themselves, it has been noted that Huizinga's depiction of their worldview was static, as though 'forms of life, thought and art' at the beginning of the fourteenth century were the same as those which prevailed at the end of the fifteenth. Illustrating the anxiety contemporaries felt about matters of precedence and etiquette, for example, Huizinga laid out a series of examples stretching from Froissart's account of the Battle of Crécy (1346) to the descriptions given by Jean Molinet and Thomas Basin of the execution of Louis de Luxembourg in 1475, as if the 'forms of life and thought' evinced in these events were ultimately the same.[156] Some of his footnotes list examples from a multiplicity of authors which he had clearly gathered together in one of his envelopes with little or no thought given to the time of the formulation of the texts in question, as though they were examples of a 'ubiquitous zeitgeist' which could be found in almost any narrative source from – say – 1300 to 1500, so long as it was sufficiently close to life.[157] Once again, moreover, a trait which critics have deplored in the book turns out to have been the result of a deliberate choice on Huizinga's part. In his notes on the work of Molinet, Huizinga revealed that he was sensitive to the dynamism of the period: 'things have changed a lot between 1400 and 1480', he noted.[158] But his deliberate insistence on the static nature of thought emerges clearly in a criticism he makes of Eustache Deschamps's editor, Gaston Raynaud, who had suggested that the strong pessimism of a late poem by Deschamps may have been the result of purely personal circumstances (the effects of

155 In November 1919 Henri Pirenne's sole criticism to Huizinga was that he had seen the Renaissance too much through the eyes of Burckhardt. Huizinga replied: 'I don't really see how my book could have given an impression of dependence on B., I thought rather I had reacted against him' (Huizinga, *Briefwisseling*, I, p. 271). A more recent commentator who at the very least underestimates the force of Huizinga's objections to Burckhardt is Bouwsma, '*The Waning of the Middle Ages* Revisited', p. 327, by stating that Huizinga 'far from attacking Burckhardt's conception of the Renaissance wholesale [...] accepted and reiterated its general validity'.

156 Huizinga, *Autumn*, p. 45.

157 Van Oostrom, 'De oude orde in verval?', p. 204.

158 UBL Hui. 114: M.7

old age, his withdrawal from court). Why could it not simply have been a true reflection of the forms of life and thought of the time more generally, asked Huizinga?[159] As he wrote elsewhere in *Herfsttij*, 'the medieval image of society is static, not dynamic'.[160]

Huizinga's representation of a static period has been ascribed to his readings in cultural anthropology, which marked him out from many in the historical profession of his day and are part of the image of Huizinga's exceptionalism. By comparison with history, anthropology was 'more concerned with analyzing a particular society at a given period of time than with investigating social change and movement'.[161] But if Huizinga was indeed an 'ethnographer of the past' and 'the atemporal nature of [his] study is, indeed, its most striking feature', we cannot agree that this conclusion must have come to him exclusively via the discipline of anthropology.[162] The static image of late medieval 'forms of life, thought and art' in *Herfsttij* made an important historical point about time, namely, that forms change slowly. It mattered that Molinet 'worked à la Froissart', as Huizinga observed in his notes.[163] By strongly emphasizing continuities which he detected in the narrative sources of the fourteenth and fifteenth centuries, a time which he located within a macro framework extending two or three centuries on either side, Huizinga mounted a double challenge to prevailing notions of periodization which might in consequence be said to have exaggerated the theme of change encapsulated in the term 'Renaissance'. This was a significant contribution to the field of general history at the time, and need not have arisen from his undeniably important interest in anthropology.

4.b Sources by Place, or *genius loci*

Huizinga did nevertheless see 'the coming of the new form' as an important theme of his book. The argument was largely made in geographical terms, by discerning particular cultural forms in narrative sources which he portrayed as being typical of the places where they originated. The organization of narrative sources in a geographical disposition also allowed him to reinforce his general thesis about the weight of the Italian Renaissance in cultural history.

159 Huizinga, *Autumn*, p. 124.
160 Ibid., p. 63.
161 Aston, 'Huizinga's Harvest', p. 15.
162 Bulhof, 'Johan Huizinga', pp. 201-202.
163 UBL Hui. 50: M.3.

The first point to address is the place of Italian narrative sources in *Herfsttij*. For a book which challenged the hitherto widely accepted modernity of Italian cultural forms in 'general history' (a fact which did not go unnoticed in Italy), it is remarkable how little space is accorded to the Italian narrative sources of the period.[164] Huizinga lectured on the topic of the Italian Renaissance at Delft in 1908 and contemplated offering his colleague Colenbrander an essay on the subject for the journal he was involved in for much of his career, *De Gids*. But at that stage he felt he had not yet studied the primary sources closely enough.[165] References to Italian narrative sources of the period do occur in *Herfsttij* and can be significant. Huizinga refers at one point to Denis the Carthusian's citation of Petrarch on the theme of the loss of Jerusalem, and doubtless took pleasure in discovering the difficulty which Denis had in conveying the Italian poet's sophisticated style.[166] Ariosto, Poggio Bracciolini, Boccaccio, Bartolomeo Fazio and Bandello are all mentioned, and there was also some room for Dante, reputedly Huizinga's favorite author.[167]

But all of these references are made in passing. Key characteristics of the Italian Renaissance would be revealed in *Herfsttij* through a profound engagement with the narrative sources, not of Italy, but of northern Europe. This was done by highlighting the common forms of life and thought that could be said to connect the two cultural *milieux*. Hence comparisons such as that of the *rederijkers* with the 'club spirit' of Italian humanists mentioned above, or views such as the following expressed in *Herfsttij*: that 'there is actually no essential contrast between the allegory of the Middle Ages and the mythology of the Renaissance'; that 'the beautification of life that the Florentines expanded on are nothing but old medieval forms'; that 'medieval and Renaissance elements' were 'intertwined'.[168] Looking in the other direction, Chastelain – the archetypical figure of Burgundian culture – was capable of writing which was humanist in nature, his description of the qualities of Charles the Bold (for example) being entirely in keeping with 'Burckhardt's Renaissance man'.[169] In short, Huizinga's holds up a

164 Varvaro, 'Riconsiderando l'*Autunno del Medioevo*', pp. 786-787.

165 Huizinga, *Briefwisseling*, I, p. 94. Huizinga also taught on the subject of Florence at Leiden in 1917.

166 Huizinga, *Autumn*, p. 385.

167 Otterspeer, *Reading Huizinga*, p. 30.

168 Huizinga, *Autumn*, pp. 246, 39, 75.

169 Ibid., pp. 43, 74. UBL Hui. 52: C.3: 'His worship of the moral element in history is already truly humanist'; 'Chastellain's oratory is already pure Renaissance.'

Burgundian mirror to the Italian Renaissance and invites us see how little the latter's likeness is altered when we do so.[170]

To a far greater extent than the broad geographical terms of the subtitle suggest, the center of gravity of *Herfsttij* was solidly planted in the core of the Burgundian lands. The great bulk of the citations in the book are from narrative sources which originated, not simply in 'France and the Netherlands' in general, but more specifically in the southern Netherlands and northern France, or in those parts of the wider kingdom of France which experienced Burgundian influence for a significant part of the relevant period (Paris, for example, where the anonymous Parisian chronicler recorded Burgundian influence over the city for more than three decades [1400-1437]). Eustache Deschamps was not, as Huizinga observed in his notes, a Burgundian servant at any point in his career, but he did jot down the fact that Deschamps lived for several years in Brussels and wrote about his time in the city, as though it were fitting that this old-fashioned poet should have gravitated toward the geographical center of what would become the Burgundian world.[171] Also observed in his notes is the fact that Froissart was from a family of Valenciennes merchants, and that Denis the Carthusian, although cloistered in Roermond, was an advisor to the Burgundian court on spiritual matters. Nine of the main sources of the hundreds of direct references and citations in the book came from works by writers who were Burgundian court servants or administrators for all or much of their careers. Together this group makes up at least one-third of all references to a specific source in *Herfsttij*. Of Huizinga's top six sources, in fact, only Jean Gerson had no obvious connections with the geographical center of gravity in the Burgundian world of northern France and the southern Netherlands (although even he received Burgundian patronage for a while).[172] Geographically speaking, then, there is a certain degree of homogeneity in the seemingly diverse and rich narrative source base of *Herfsttij*, the great bulk of which is located at the splendid court and among the rich burghers of Burgundy, the stamping ground of 'the pompous spokesmen of the heavily draped Burgundian ideal

170 UBL Hui. 114: I.3: 'Is Italian humanism really so different from the Burgundian *quattrocento*?' In this passage of his notes he also briefly compares Poggio Bracciolini's *Facetiae* to the *Cent nouvelles nouvelles*, and Coluccio Salutati to the rhetoricians.

171 UBL Hui. 52: G.1.

172 Ibid. 114: G.3, where Huizinga notes his belief that Gerson 'remained Burgundian' even after the scandalous and profoundly divisive murder of Louis of Orléans in Paris in 1407. It would be more accurate to say Gerson worked hard to maintain peace in the troubled times after the murder (Brown, *Pastor and Laity*, p. 9). So Huizinga imagined Gerson to be more Burgundian than he really was, just as he did with Deschamps.

[…] the old-fashioned minds of French literature'.[173] Here we have the most important *genius loci* of the whole book. And this essentially *old* world shared fundamental characteristics with the civilization of Renaissance Italy – a comparison which Huizinga used to emphasize the oldness that was in the Renaissance, rather than any newness that might have been in Burgundy.

But the picture is more variegated in tone. To grasp how Huizinga's sense of *genius loci* could also introduce a degree of nuance into *Herfsttij*, we need to be cognizant of his technique of building an argument through contrasts.[174] Throughout the book, authors of narrative sources (or important figures within those sources) are consistently contrasted with one another to show how the new form was emerging alongside the old: the modern, pragmatic hero of *Le jouvencel* stood in sharp contrast to the archaic, chivalric figure of Jacques de Lalaing, for example. Jean Gerson was one of the 'new men', 'a man of realities and a psychologist, very different from the impersonal [Denis the Carthusian]', the latter being capable of 'truly medieval' thinking.[175] The old and new are in tension with one another, albeit that the weight of examples falls far more heavily in the former category.

When we examine these contrasting pairs or groups in more detail, it soon becomes apparent that the figures most associated with medieval 'forms of life and thought' are usually from the core of the Burgundian lands, while the newer figures come from the wider Francophone world (including the two pairs we have just mentioned: the 'realistic knightly figure' of *Le jouvencel*, 'the voice of the new age' such as 'could not yet be fashioned by Burgundian literature').[176] The further south we go from the core of Burgundian influence into the kingdom of France, in fact, the more modern the narrative sources become:

> The modern authors, such as Villon, Cocquillart, Henri Baude, as well as Charles d'Orléans and the author of 'L'amant rendu Cordelier', are those whose minds are unencumbered by all this [classicism], even if still dressed in medieval form.[177]

Chastelain the quintessential Burgundian was repeatedly found to be the antithesis of new(er) men of the French-speaking south: Villon who

173 Huizinga, *Autumn*, p. 389.
174 Otterspeer, *Reading Huizinga*, p. 17.
175 UBL Hui. 52: G.5; Huizinga, *Autumn*, p. 385.
176 Ibid., pp. 80-81, 113.
177 Ibid., p. 389; see also ibid., p. 330 for similar comment on Villon and d'Orléans.

'manages to add a new touch'; Commynes, with his 'modern characteristics', an escapee from the old chivalric north who abandoned the antediluvian Charles the Bold for the modern Louis XI.[178] Robert Gaguin could don the pretentious Latinate style preferred by some of the pompous Burgundians, 'but he moves more freely without that splendiferousness'.[179]

France could not yet be said to be modern, of course – nowhere could, not even Florence. Among France's intellectuals were men like Jean de Montrueil and Pierre Col, defenders of that 'abundantly medieval work' *Le roman de la rose*, who contrasted with more consistently modern figures on the other side of the Rose debate, such as Gerson or Christine de Pizan (with her 'clean and simple talent').[180] But largely speaking the coming of a new form was far more apparent in France than it was in Burgundy broadly defined, the latter having lost contact with the former's 'lighter and more harmonious spirit'.[181] France 'occupies the middle ground' between Italy and the Burgundian lands.[182]

But variegation is not only to be found to the south in *Herfsttij*. Another contrasting form was also coming in the north, specifically in the northern Netherlands, a region that was distinct in key respects from the Burgundian heartlands of Flanders, Hainaut or Brabant.[183] To understand the place of the northern Netherlands in *Herfsttij*, we may begin by picking out instances where Huizinga accentuated the parallels and even similarities which he found in 'forms of life and thought' he saw in that region, and those which he found in the French narrative sources – as if the distinct *genius loci* of each had more in common with the other than it did with the core of Burgundian civilization geographically located between them. Huizinga relates Commynes's lack of chivalric delusion to the fact that he had a mother from Zeeland, Margaret of Arnemuiden, for example.[184] The point would seem a strange, were it not for the fact that the statement is immediately related to the claim that the 'knightly spirit seems to have died away early in Holland'.[185] French spirituality, to take another example, had much in common with

178 Ibid., pp. 118, 158-159, 168, 283; UBL Hui. 52: D.1; 114: I.3; *VW*, III, pp. 575-577.

179 Huizinga, *Autumn*, p. 393.

180 Ibid., pp. 358, 138.

181 Ibid., p. 305. Cf. the suggestive remarks of Thiry, 'Le printemps des temps nouveaux' on the possible influence here of the work of Gustave Lanson. However, we have found no references to Lanson in Huizinga's reading notes for either his lectures or the book.

182 Huizinga, *Autumn*, p. 388.

183 Huizinga's sense of Holland's distinctiveness grew from his initial comments on the subject in his 1909-1910 lectures down to the completion of *Herfsttij*.

184 Huizinga, *Autumn*, p. 118; UBL Hui. 52: N.3.

185 Huizinga, *Autumn*, p. 118.

the beliefs of the *devotio*, the only difference being that in the latter's case, the 'spirit' was normalized 'into a new life form'.[186] It was not surprising (but worth noting) that the all-seeing Frenchman Gerson defended the Netherlandish Congregation of Windesheim at the Council of Constance.[187] In his wisdom, according to Huizinga, Gerson saw that the *devotio* emerged from sentiments which were shared by his own flock, but its adherents had developed a discipline which 'his French sheep lacked'.[188] High-profile migrants from France to the northern Netherlands also interested Huizinga, as if the similarities of 'forms of life and thought' in each outweighed trifling differences between them, such as language. Thomas Basin, Bishop of Lisieux, took exile in the north from Louis XI and later became Bishop of Utrecht, the diocese where he completed some of his histories which Huizinga compared, for the absence of Burgundian forms of thought within them, to the memoirs of Commynes.[189] Huizinga made a great deal of effort to track down a copy of the works of Alain de La Roche, also known as Alanus de Rupe, who began public life as a Dominican in Brittany, and who was 'one of the most noticeable types of the French, more extreme devotion'.[190] As Huizinga noted when he was finally able to write about de La Roche, Alain wound up in Zwolle in the northern Netherlands with the brethren of the Common Life, among whom, it is implied, he and his French spirituality found a home-from-home.

In these ways, Holland was therefore on its way to becoming quite distinct from the southern Netherlands in *Herfsttij*; less obviously medieval in the Burgundian sense at least, and in ways that paralleled or even resembled forms of life and thought in France. In the southern Netherlands, the court and the rich burghers who imitated them were the dominant cultural force.[191] In the north, small towns and the lesser nobility were to the fore. The solemn spirituality of the northern Netherlands was recognized by authors

186 Ibid., p. 221.

187 Ibid., pp. 223-224.

188 Ibid., pp. 221-224.

189 Ibid., p. 72; UBL Hui. 52: L.3.

190 Huizinga, *Autumn*, p. 232. He kept a record in his notes of the unsuccessful attempts of the Leiden University librarian, Scato G. de Vries, to locate a copy of the book in libraries at The Hague, Amsterdam, Utrecht, Groningen, Arnhem, Deventer, Delft and Haarlem: UBL Hui. 52: G.9. Further notes at ibid., A.4; A.15.

191 Huizinga, *Autumn*, pp. 315, 332. It has been pointed out (e.g., Krul, 'In the Mirror', p. 372) that Huizinga never 'offered any proof that cultural life among the middle classes and among those who by their language stood apart from the dominant elite was actually derivative'. While this is true, the point must now be reconsidered against a growing body of work on relations between city and court, including new discoveries relating to the Ghent background of Huizinga's most important source, Chastelain: Brown and Small, *Court and Civic Society*; Small, *George Chastelain*.

of narrative sources from the south, and Huizinga sought confirmation of that claim in the judgment of the arch-Burgundian Chastelain.[192] In painting, too, there were fundamental differences. Dirk Bouts was a northerner from Haarlem who worked in the south, where the rich and showy Burgundian world generated demand for his talents. But 'the simple, stringent, reserved qualities of his art' belonged to the north: they were genuinely *burgerlijk*, in contrast to the 'aristocratic conceits, the pompous elegance, pride and glitter of the southern masters'.[193] His form of art was comparable to the forms of life and thought one found among the quiet Dutch towns far from the court, where the *devotio* (and its narrative sources) found 'serious' adherents among the men and women 'of the middle class who sought spiritual support in the Fraterhouses and among the Windesheimers'.[194]

It has been observed elsewhere that Huizinga began to reflect on the nature of a specifically Dutch culture during his time as a school teacher in Haarlem (1897-1905), and that this line of thought developed most strongly in his publications of the 1920s and 1930s.[195] Here we see that *Herfsttij* was also an important stage in the development of his thinking. The distinct place for the Netherlands which he carved out in the book posed a challenge to his original idea of writing a history of seventeenth-century Dutch civilization with roots in the Burgundian period, but in the end he resolved that problem by deciding that Burgundy had been a loose union of territories which had not exerted fundamental cultural influence over the Dutch.[196] Burgundy is virtually absent from 'Beschaving'. His feelings of pride for *burgerlijk* Holland and his projection of its separate cultural identity back to the fifteenth century might also seem to be in contradiction with the views he formulated on the anachronism of tracing modern national identities to the past in his field of general history. But perhaps this, too, could be resolved, to Huizinga's satisfaction at least. Nationalism as a political force was distinct from patriotism, and the latter could even be the subject of study for the cultural historian.[197] In adumbrating this viewpoint in *Herfsttij*, before

192 Huizinga, *Autumn*, p. 223, n. 15; Cf. ibid., p. 203: 'those in the south accept contradictions more readily'.

193 Ibid., pp. 315-316.

194 Ibid., pp. 313-314.

195 Van der Lem, *Het Eeuwige*, pp. 118-170, 199-229, 316-323.

196 For this sentence and the next, see Huizinga, 'Dutch Civilisation', pp. 26-27.

197 Cf. Krul, 'In the Mirror', p. 367. I would argue instead that there is a logical progression from Huizinga's views in *Autumn* to those of his 1940 essay, 'Patriotism and Nationalism in European History': two clearly contrasting terms, the first of which 'undoubtedly belongs to the positive domain' (p. 152), while the latter 'flourishes almost entirely in the sphere of competition and opposition' (p. 154).

developing it more fully in his subsequent publications (and indeed in his role as a public intellectual during the dark years of the 1930s), Huizinga made an important contribution to long-term debates about Dutch identity.

So, recognizably new forms were not just emerging under Tuscan skies, where their emergence was perhaps not so uniquely important as Burckhardt and his many followers had said. New forms were coming too, albeit in different guises, in un-Burgundian France and an un-Burgundian northern Netherlands. Even at the very core of the old Burgundian civilization of the southern Netherlands and northern France it was occasionally possible to catch a fleeting glimpse of more modern, less medieval 'forms of life, thought and art', in the unguarded moments of self-expression by the most commonly cited authors of our narrative sources. But mostly speaking, 'that literature does not yet know a single modern thought'; 'those poets have no future'.[198] Burgundy would be the supernova of the Middle Ages, shining brightly but in fact already past the end of life, increasingly incapable of bearing the crushing weight of its own gravity, and brilliantly foreshadowing the black hole into which all that was medieval eventually disappeared.

Conclusion

In the field of general history to which Huizinga's chairs were attached when he was writing *Herfsttij*, views of the past were being shaped, as they always are, by contemporary political forces. The research for *Herfsttij* produced a reaction against such developments, at least to the extent that Huizinga's patriotism could be considered distinct from the nationalism of some of his contemporaries. The book offered cultural history as an alternative to a nationally oriented vision of general history. The methods of the project were first adumbrated in Huizinga's Groningen inaugural of 1905, and were set out more fully in a programmatic essay on the 'Task of Cultural History' nearly a quarter of a century later. Half of the intervening period was taken up with researching and writing *Herfsttij*, the key work in which Huizinga developed his thinking. His major finding was that the Italian Renaissance should no longer be accorded the primacy which Burckhardt had given it half a century earlier – a point he made without engaging in detailed study of the Italian narrative sources. While recognizing the ambition of his project and the originality of his thought, we have sought here to show how the directions he took were shaped by developments within the discipline at

198 UBL Hui. 52.: A.5; Huizinga, *Autumn*, p. 331.

that time, and not just in the general culture of his age (as is sometimes said in discussions of Huizinga): by the general histories of France and Belgium which helped him to launch his research, and which he partly reacted against; by the industrious editors and bibliographers of the nineteenth and early twentieth centuries who supplied him with material which other historians were beginning to neglect; by the German philosophers of history who gave clarity and authority to his method. Huizinga's was thus one face in a crowd of great scholars, albeit a distinctive one. His distinctiveness has increased as those who once surrounded him have gradually faded, some more, some less, from our sight.

Appendix: Authors, Narrative Sources or Collections of Narrative Sources Mentioned between 10 and 25 times in *Herfsttij*

Jean de Bueil, *Le jouvencel* (22), Christine de Pizan (19), *Le livre du chevalier de La Tour Landry* (18), Jean Lefèvre de Saint-Rémy (aka Toison d'Or) (16), Thomas Basin (15), Jean Meschinot (15), Jean de Montreuil (15), Jean de Roye (15), René d'Anjou (13), Alain Chartier (13), Philippe de Mézières (13), François Villon (13), Eleanor of Poitiers (12), *Cent nouvelles nouvelles* (12), Nicolas de Clemanges (12), Robert Gaguin (12), Mathieu d'Escouchy (12), *Lettres de Louis XI* (11), *Livre des trahisons* (11), Jan van Ruusbroec (11), Pierre de Fenin (10), *Le pastoralet* (10), *Quinze joyes de mariage* (10).

About the Author

Graeme Small is Professor of Medieval History at Durham University, UK. He has published books on Burgundian historiography, court and civic society in the Burgundian Low Countries (with Andrew Brown), and more recently on the kingdom of France in the late Middle Ages: *Late Medieval France* (Macmillan International Higher Education, 2009).
g.p.small@durham.ac.uk

9 The Making of *The Autumn of the Middle Ages* II

The Eagle and His Pigeonholes: How Huizinga Organized His Sources

Anton van der Lem

Abstract
Having published in Dutch in 1998 the Inventory of the Archives of Johan Huizinga, I offer readers of this chapter the opportunity to become acquainted with Huizinga's papers and working method, especially regarding *Herfsttij der Middeleeuwen*. There are many more notes made by Huizinga while preparing his magnum opus than have been published. After a short history of his papers' arrival at the Leiden University Library, I elaborate on Huizinga's sources and note-taking. Regrettably, his library has been dispersed, but it is the objective of the Special Collections Department to re-collect the books that Huizinga owned.

Keywords: archives, note-taking, (private) libraries

Many authors studying the works of Johan Huizinga have made use of his papers in the Huizinga archive in the Leiden University Library, and many continue to do so. They come primarily from the Netherlands or Belgium and rarely from other countries, which is unsurprising given that he made his notes in Dutch. Despite the publication of the inventory of his archives, Huizinga's working method has not yet been studied.[1] Given that Graeme Small's essay in this volume concerns the content of Huizinga's notes on his Burgundian and French sources, I will limit myself to the form of his notes and other practical matters.

1 Van der Lem, *Inventaris*.

Arnade, Peter, Martha Howell, and Anton van der Lem (eds), *Rereading Huizinga: Autumn of the Middle Ages, a Century Later*. Taylor & Francis Group, 2019
DOI: 10.5117/9789462983724_CH09

Leiden University Library recently launched an initiative to reconstitute Huizinga's private book collection, with the aim of discovering what he owned and how he used his library, especially the manner of his note-taking from the books he borrowed or possessed and how this work was expressed and reflected in his archival papers.[2] The next step after this project will be the creation of a Huizinga website, to be available by open access in both Dutch and English. The site will present Huizinga's archives in the round, including his published articles and books (in searchable form, in Dutch and in translation), a calendar of his life and times, his correspondence, portraits, pictures, literature, etc. In this way we hope to serve a much larger audience than could ever be accommodated in the library's Special Collections Reading Room.

1 Huizinga's Archives and Books

Several photographs provide an impression of Huizinga's study. The first was probably made in Groningen, where he held the chair of general and Dutch history (1905-1914) In the background we can discern what appear to be the pigeonholes where he kept his notes in envelopes, and the manuscripts of his university lectures.

At the end of 1914 Huizinga moved to Leiden, where he taught general history from 1915 until 1941. Depictions of his study, first at the Witte Singel 32, and from 1935 in his new home at the Van Slingelandtlaan 4, only show books. The picture of the study in his house at the Van Slingelandtlaan, probably taken immediately after the move, shows a study in perfect order. Thanks to digital techniques we can now enlarge the photograph and pick out the titles of individual books. Huizinga kept no books outside his study, as his daughters reported. We may surmise that he kept his papers behind the intriguing curtains which can be seen hanging just behind his chair. What happened with his manuscripts and books?

2 Exiled out of Leiden

Huizinga was cruelly torn from his quiet study when he was arrested on 7 August 1942, along with eight other Leiden professors, by the Nazi occupying forces. The group was transported to the former Roman Catholic seminary of St. Michielsgestel, north of Eindhoven in the southern part of

2 Van der Lem, *Een bibliotheek*, and Van der Lem, 'Lees met beleid'.

Illustration 9.1 Huizinga in his study as a professor in Groningen

Huizinga archive in Leiden University Library

the country, where they were kept as hostages in forced residence. In the event of an attack on Nazi targets by the underground resistance movement in the Netherlands, the occupier would respond by executing hostages. This actually happened shortly after the arrival of the Leiden professors, on 15 August, when five hostages from Rotterdam were shot. One can imagine the impact this had on all the prisoners, especially the newcomers.

Illustration 9.2 Huizinga's study in Leiden, Van Slingelandtlaan 4, 1935 or later

Huizinga archive in Leiden University Library

Huizinga was about to turn 70 years old on 7 December 1942, and his health was not good. For these reasons he was set free on 25 October, but not allowed to return to Leiden. It is likely he remained an object of suspicion as one of the leading figures of the intellectual and moral resistance to the Nazi regime at Leiden University. He was only released on the condition that he would take up residence in one of the eastern provinces of the Netherlands, either Gelderland or Overijsel. He gratefully accepted the offer from the Leiden professor R.P. Cleveringa of a house in the village of De Steeg, east of Arnhem, which his colleague used for weekends and holidays. Here Huizinga settled with his second wife, Augusta (Goes) Huizinga-Schölvinck, and their little daughter, Laura Maria, born 4 November 1941. Huizinga thanked Cleveringa for his generous gesture, not only for the convenient residence, but especially 'because I feel it as a distinction to be allowed to live in the house of the man who before and above all others has defended the honor of our beloved Leiden'.[3] This

3 J. Huizinga to Rudolf and Hiltje Cleveringa-Boschloo, 29 October 1942: 'dat ik het als een eer voel, juist het huis van hem te mogen bewonen, die vóór en boven alle anderen de eer van ons dierbaar Leiden heeft opgehouden', in Huizinga, *Briefwisseling*, III, p. 381.

was a reference to Cleveringa's impassioned speech on 26 November 1940 against the dismissal of Jewish personnel at Leiden University by the Nazi regime. Cleveringa's words remain an inspiration, and are commemorated by Leiden University every year by the organization of lectures all over the world at the end of November.[4] The sojourn of the Huizinga family in De Steeg was supposed to be only temporary; the family intended to return to Leiden after the war, even though Mrs. Huizinga frequently suggested that they remain in De Steeg.

All of the family's furniture, books, and papers remained in Leiden. During their absence, the house in Leiden was rented by lawyers, who were acquaintances of Cleveringa. It is not known whether the furniture and the books were stored on site or elsewhere, or whether the books simply remained on their shelves. Exiled in De Steeg, Huizinga missed his library. One of his last students, Miss Suze Kuenen, provided him with books from Leiden, but nowhere in Huizinga's letters is there any mention of access to his own books in his study at Van Slingelandtlaan. For this reason we may suppose that the books were stored elsewhere, and were inaccessible. Were this not the case, it would have been relatively easier to provide the exiled Huizinga with books from his own collection. Huizinga died quite unexpectedly at De Steeg on 1 February 1945. As late as 25 January he was working on a declaration intended for publication at Leiden University after the liberation of the country.[5]

It follows, crucially, that Huizinga never took any decision regarding the fate of his archives and his private collection of books. It was some time after the war, in the autumn of 1946, before his widow could reestablish herself with Laura at their former Leiden address. In the Leiden University Library archives there is no record of the offer, acceptance, or date of receipt of Huizinga's papers. The only evidence we have so far takes the form of a letter by Auguste Huizinga-Schölvinck, in which we learn that it was her task to organize the papers and grant them to the University Library in the summer of 1947.[6] The archives were kept there and were given almost no attention until 1972, when the centennial of Huizinga's birth was celebrated in an international conference in Groningen. In advance of that occasion

4 R.P. Cleveringa (1894-1980), professor of law at Leiden University 1927-1941 and 1945-1958. On 27 November 1940, a day after his speech, Cleveringa was arrested and dismissed as professor; he was released in September 1941.

5 Huizinga archive, no. 136. This item is not mentioned in the *Inventaris*, as no.136 was donated by Mrs. Laura M. Conley-Huizinga after the publication of the inventory. Cf. Huizinga's letter to F.M. van Asbeck, January 1945.

6 Auguste Huizinga-Schölvinck to Werner Kaegi, June 1947, The Hague, Literatuur Museum.

A.E. (Dolf) Cohen, professor of medieval history in Leiden, ordered an inventory to be made of the contents of the archives.[7] Although this inventory was nothing more than a brief list and description, it was used by the first investigators of the archives and for that reason has been preserved in the much more detailed inventory published in 1998.

3 The Notes for *Herfsttij*

Two sheets of paper contain the titles of a number of books Huizinga read for *Herfsttij*, bearing the shelf numbers of the libraries where he found them: the Royal Library in The Hague and his own University Library at Leiden.

As historians know well, to read a book profitably means making notes, whether one owns the book or not. This truth also applies to Huizinga. Even in the case of books he owned, Huizinga made his notes on separate pieces of paper rather than directly on the page itself, except for the correction of printing errors or the occasional line drawn in the margin – always very thin, and in pencil. Only one of the books from his partially reconstituted collection is interleaved with blank pages on which Huizinga wrote many remarks, namely his edition of the *Annales Egmundani* (Annals of the monastery of Egmond), one of the most important medieval monasteries of the County of Holland.[8] The book deals with the early history of the County of Holland up to 1205, and was used extensively by Huizinga for one of his first studies as an historian on the subject of the emergence and development of Haarlem.[9]

When preparing to take notes on an article or book, it was Huizinga's practice to take a sheet of paper and cut it lengthwise. He then made his notes, most of them in the form of simple quotations, always preceded by an indication of the source: author and/or title, volume and/or page. When he had finished his reading he cut the paper horizontally into separate parts, which in Dutch might be described as *snippers* or *strookjes*, in French *fiches*; in Latin, the word *cedulae* would be appropriate, in German *Zettel*. In English we might use the terms *strips* or *slips*. Then he divided the slips among his envelopes, each envelope containing slips relating to a separate subject, and each with its own caption or title. 350 such envelopes were

7 Koops et al., *Johan Huizinga 1872-1972*. A.E. Cohen contributed his paper on Huizinga as professor at Leiden University.

8 *Annales Egmundani*. Huizinga's copy: UBL: HUIZIN 2003.

9 Huizinga, 'De opkomst van Haarlem', with many references to *Ann. Egm.*, his customary abbreviation.

Illustration 9.3 List of books in Huizinga's handwriting of books returned to the Royal Library in The Hague and the University Library of Leiden

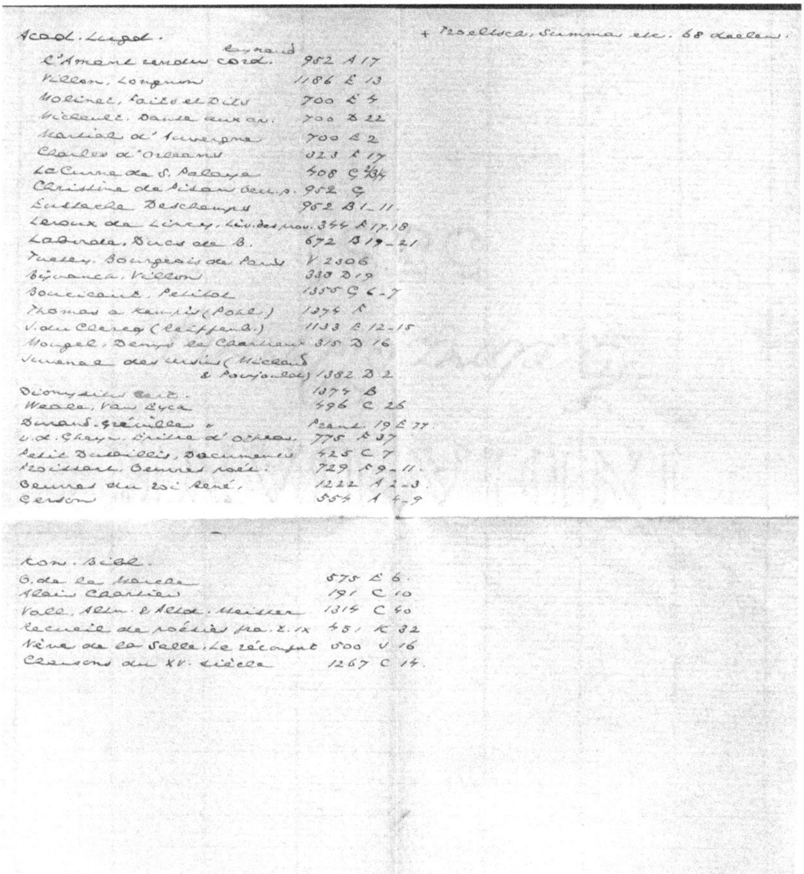

Acad. Bibl. + Passelecq, Summa etc. 68 deelen.

Raynaud
L'Amant rendu cord. 952 A 17
Villon, Longnon 1186 E 13
Molinet, Faits et Dits 700 E 4
Michault. Danse aux av. 700 B 22
Martial d'Auvergne 700 E 2
Charles d'Orléans 323 E 17
La Curne de S. Palaye 408 G 2/34
Christine de Pisan Oeuv. p. 952 G
Eustache Deschamps 952 B 1–11.
Leroux de Lincy, Liv. des prov. 344 E 17.18
Laborde, Ducs de B. 672 B 19–21
Tuetey. Bourgeois de Paris V 2306
Bijvanck, Villon 330 D 19
Boucicaut, Petitot 1355 G 6–7
Thomas a Kempis (Pohl) 1374 E
J. du Clercq (Reiffenb.) 1133 E 12–15
Mougel, Denys le Chartreux 315 D 16
Juvenal des Ursins (Michaud & Poujoulat) 1382 D 2.
Dionysius Cart. 1374 B
Weale, Van Eyck 496 C 26
Durand-Gréville Prent. 19 E 77.
v.d. Gheyn. Épître d'Othéa. 775 E 37
Petit Dutaillis, Documents 425 C 7
Froissart. Oeuvres poét. 729 E 9–11.
Oeuvres du roi René. 1222 A 2–3.
Gerson 554 A 4–9

Kon. Bibl.
O. de la Marche 575 E 6.
Alain Chartier 191 C 10
Vale, Altn. & Altd. Meister 1314 C 40
Recueil de poésies fra. t. IX 451 K 32
Nève de la Salle. Le réconfort 500 V 16
Chansons du XV. siècle 1267 C 14.

Huiz 52 II

Huizinga archive in Leiden University Library

created for *Herfsttij* alone.[10] When he was ready to start writing his text, Huizinga took the strips out of their envelopes and decided which ones he

10 Huizinga archive, no. 52, running from A.1., 'Aard van het rechtsgevoel' [character of the sense of justice], to Z.1., 'Zalig de armen' [blessed the poor], and no. 114, from A.1., 'Aard der allegorie, vooral Chastellain' [character of allegory, esp. Chastellain], to Z.4., 'zwart en grijs' [black and grey].

Illustration 9.4 Inserted page in Huizinga's copy of the *Annales Egmundani*, with his remarks

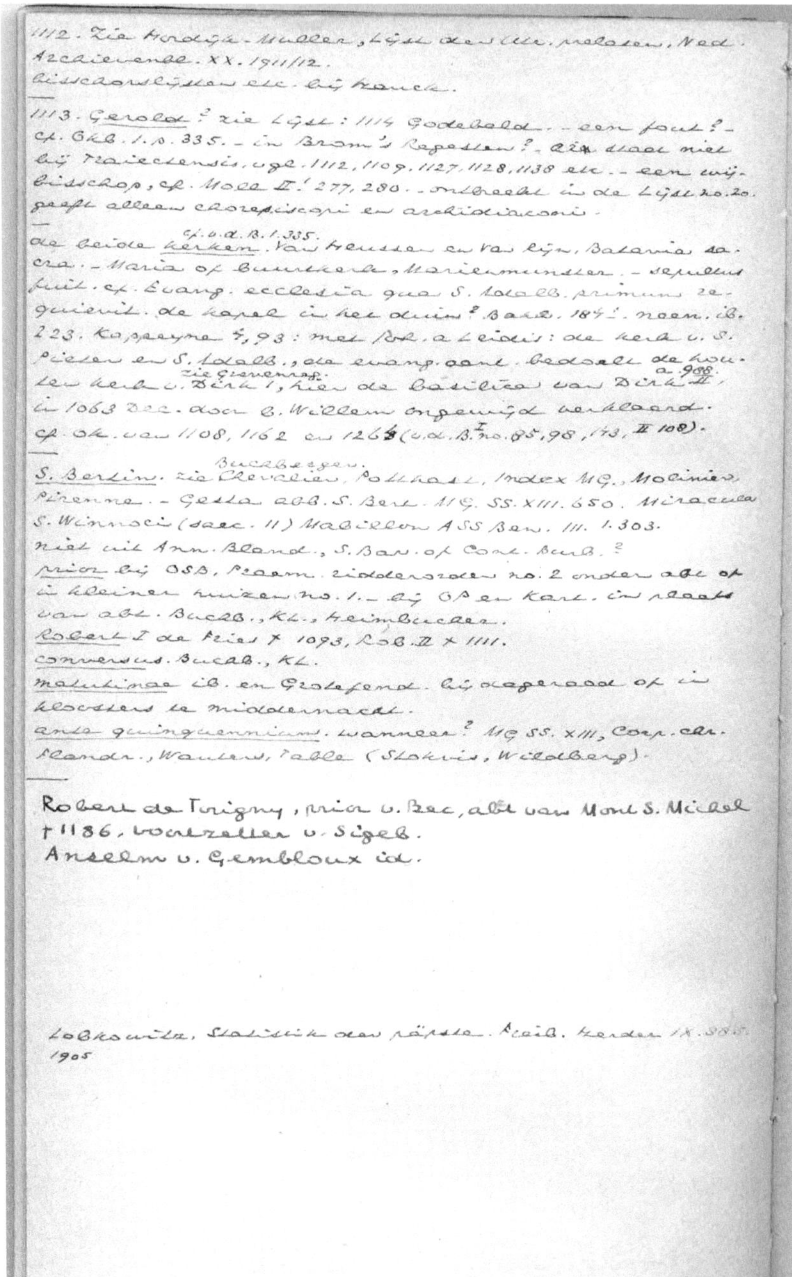

1112. Zie Hordijk-Muller, Lijst der Utr. prelaten, Ned. Archievenbl. XX. 1911/12.
bisschopslijsten etc. bij Hauck.

1113. Gerold? zie Lijst: 1114 Godebold. – een fout? – cf. OkB. I. p. 335. – in Brom's Regesten? – [illegible] staat niet bij Traiectensis, vgl. 1112, 1109, 1127, 1128, 1138 etc. – een wij-bisschop, cf. Moll II.¹ 277, 280. – ontbreekt in de Lijst no. 20. geeft alleen chorepiscopi en archidiaconi.

cf. o.d. B. I. 335.
de beide kerken. Van Heussen en van Rijn, Batavia sacra. – Maria of Buurkerk, Mariënmunster. – sepultus fuit. cf. Evang. ecclesia qua S. Adalb. primum requievit. de kapel in het duin? Bast. 184?. neen. ib. 223. Kappeyne [illegible], 93: met Rob. a Leidis: de kerk v. S. Pieter en S. Adalb., de evang. eerst bedoelt de houten kerk v. Dirk I, hier de basiliek van Dirk II, a. 988. zie Grevenrag. in 1063 [illegible] door b. Willem ingewijd verklaard.
cf. Ok. van 1108, 1162 en 1263 (o.d. B. I no. 85, 98, 143, II 108).

S. Bertin. zie Chevalier, Buchberger, Potthast, Index MG., Molinier, Pirenne. – Gesta abb. S. Bert. MG. SS. XIII. 650. Miracula S. Winnoci (saec. 11) Mabillon ASS Ben. III. 1. 303.
niet uit Ann. Bland., S. Bav. of Cont. Burb.?
prior bij OSB, Praem. ridderorden no. 2 onder abt of in kleinere huizen no. 1. – bij OP en Kart. in plaats van abt. Buchb., KL., Heimbucher.
Robert I de Fries † 1093, Rob. II † 1111.
conversus. Buchb., KL.
matutinae ib. en Grotefend. bij dageraad of in kloosters te middernacht.
ante quinquennium. wanneer? MG SS. XIII, Corp. chr. Flandr., Wauters, Table (Stokvis, Wildberg).

Robert de Torigny, prior v. Bec, abt van Mont S. Michel † 1186, voortzetter v. Sigeb.
Anselm v. Gembloux id.

Lobkowitz, Statistik der päpste. Freib. Herder IX. [illegible]
1905

Huizinga archive in Leiden University Library

Illustration 9.5 Notes from La Marche and Molinet in the envelope 'Entremets'

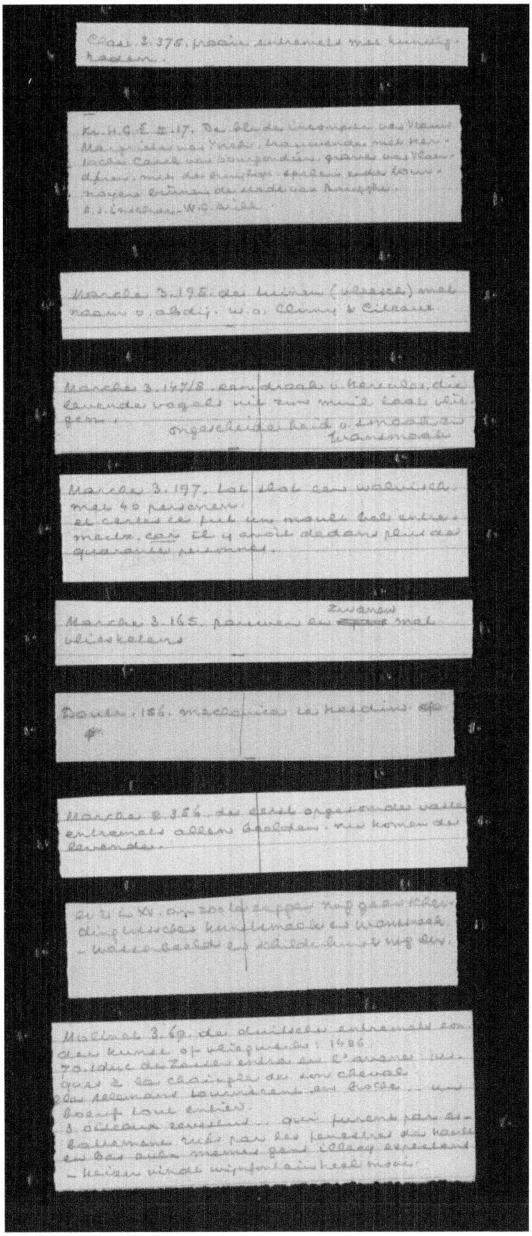

Huizinga archive in Leiden University Library

would use. He put the appropriate strips with his quotes or ideas in what he considered to be the right order. When he had quoted or otherwise used a strip, he would draw a small vertical line across the text (see again ill. 5). Once he had written his text, he put all the strips – both used and unused – back into the envelope. Some envelopes contain just a few strips, while others were crammed with many of them.

Huizinga alighted upon this working method very early in his career, though not during his time as a student, nor in the period when he taught history at a secondary school in Haarlem (1897-1905). The complete manuscripts of his history lessons are in the archives, but there are no strips of notes among them.[11] The first of his manuscripts to contain strips kept in envelopes are his studies on the ancient history and culture of India (especially on ancient Indian medicine).[12] The strips turn out in this instance to have been written on the reverse side of a manuscript of his own biography of Hendrik Kern, the leading contemporary Dutch specialist of Sanskrit (and much else besides).[13] The biography of Kern was written for a series intended for the general public, and for that reason it was not annotated. It is typical of Huizinga that he should have kept a printed copy of this biography with his own handwritten references, as if to record for himself – or for any subsequent queries he might receive – the sources upon which his account was based.[14] It is also probably no coincidence that the *Annales Egmundani* is the only book we have found so far with interleaved blank pages, as if Huizinga was, in his early career, still searching for the appropriate working method for his research and subsequent writing. He probably discovered that it would not be possible to interleave every usable book, and that he therefore had to find a more appropriate and flexible form of note-taking. In the end, that method turned out to be his strips and envelopes, much like the documents and folders of our present-day word-processing software.

Huizinga's strips give rise to a number of potential insights. The 'spent' strips with the material scored through may be used to document the time of publication of his manuscript. His very refined use of the Dutch language resulted in terms which can be found nowhere else in his published work, for instance the expression *plat symbolisme* (vulgar symbolism). Typing this expression into a digital search machine leads us exactly to the place where he

11 Huizinga archive, no. 11.

12 Huizinga archive, no. 34 II: Oldindian medicine. The captions on the envelopes 3.1. Demonologie II, 3.2. Dood, 3.3. Dosa IV, 3.4. Dosa-systematiek V, 3.5. Physiologie VI, suggest that there must have been many more envelopes.

13 J. Huizinga, 'Hendrik Kern'. Huizinga archive, no. 34 IV: Hendrik Kern, with two earlier manuscripts.

14 UBL: HUIZIN 5 ned 1 (2).

used it in *Herfsttij*. For all the many used strips, there are just as many (or even more) which he did *not* use in the book. What does this process of selection of material imply for the preparation, construction, and completion of *Herfsttij*? From his early beginnings in reading for *Herfsttij* Huizinga intended to keep his range of subjects as wide as possible. No historian knows in advance what will be usable and what will not; at best, one has only a vague idea of how the finished text will look. Better, therefore, to take too many notes than too few. The number of narrative sources Huizinga ultimately used was very large, but, of course, they are only a minor part of the total number of sources available: on the subject of the later Middle Ages, as for so many others, there is simply 'too much to know'.[15] In his preface to *Herfsttij*, Huizinga declared that he had limited himself to authors who were representative of many of their contemporaries, but this statement should not be taken to mean that he left these other authors unread. Of the historians, he preferred Chastellain and Froissart; of the poets, Eustache Deschamps; of the theologians, Jean Gerson and Denis the Carthusian, because in their works the mirror of their time was best reflected. The envelope with subject title 'Froissart' contains no fewer than 51 strips. But this envelope only contains strips relating to Froissart as a person, or to his work in general; hundreds of other strips bearing quotations from the works of Froissart are to be found in other envelopes.

Unfortunately there is no manuscript of *Herfsttij der Middeleeuwen*, nor of any other article or book published by Huizinga up until the manuscript of *Homo ludens* in 1938. Huizinga did not use a typewriter, preferring to submit his manuscript in his own very clear handwriting. Perhaps the manuscript remained at the publishing house after it was printed, or was discarded, but most likely it was returned to the author, who had written his manuscript on only one side of the sheet. After receiving his manuscript back from the publisher, Huizinga cut it once more into appropriate pieces to create fresh paper for new notes. As a result, and by happy coincidence, it is possible to reconstitute three quarters of one page of *Herfsttij*. It is possible that after his second marriage (4 October 1937), his wife, aware of his growing fame, convinced him that he had to safeguard his manuscripts for generations to come. Such a possibility would explain why the manuscripts of Huizinga's later books have been rescued from the effects of the author's careful use and reuse of paper.

As a result of Huizinga's working practices, the majority of his strips have a text on the reverse side. Investigators who are familiar with Huizinga's work are often able to identify the content of these textual fragments. To

15 Blair, *Too Much to Know*.

Illustration 9.6 The only left page of the manuscript of *Herfsttij der Middeleeuwen*. One-quarter of the pages is missing because of reuse of the reverse

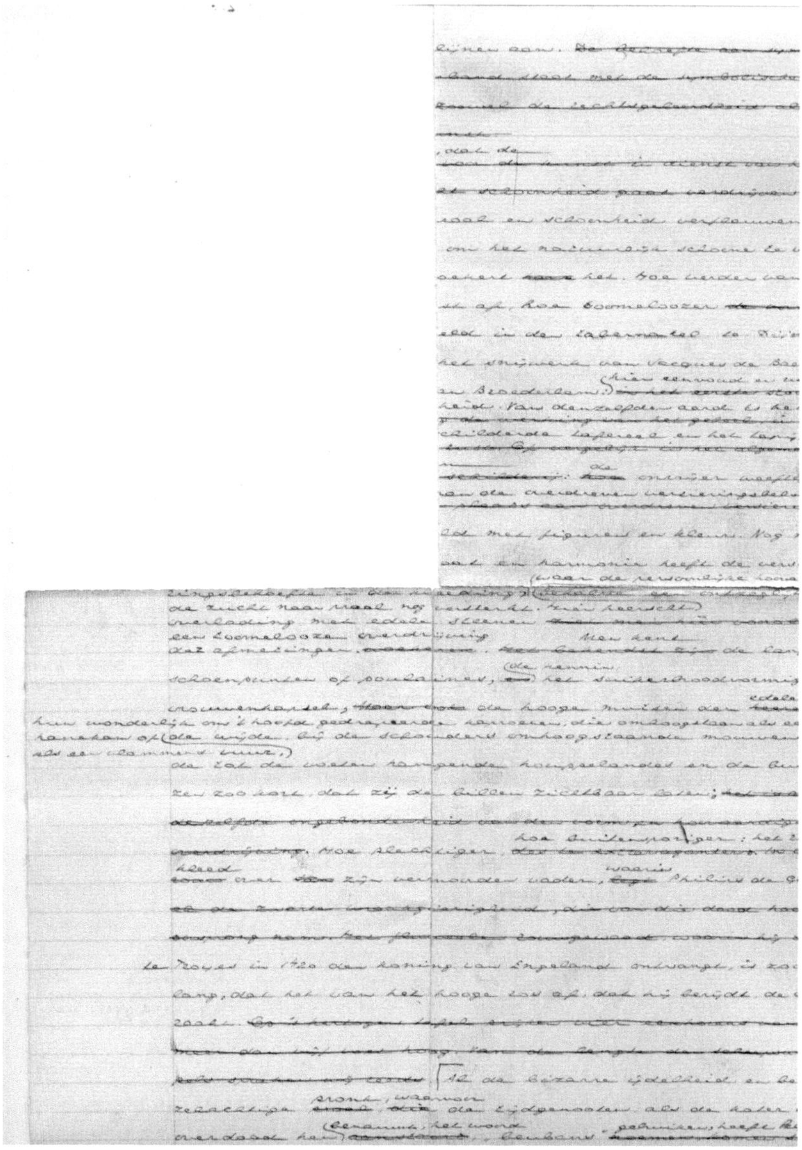

Huizinga archive in Leiden University Library

encourage more such discoveries, the published inventory of the archives indicates where material on the reverse side of the strips has been identified.

Illustration 9.7 Huizinga as a student in his study in his elderly home

Huizinga archive in Leiden University Library

4 What Is Not in the Archives

In addition to Huizinga's notes for his published works, the archives also contain his lecture notes from his student days at Groningen University. Alas, there are no papers relating to his private reading of ancient and modern literature, for instance of Shakespeare or Balzac, or even contemporary literature. His appreciation of Shakespeare is, however, obvious

Illustration 9.8 Balzac's *Lettres à l'étrangere* (Paris: Calmann-Lévy, 1899), with the title written by Huizinga himself

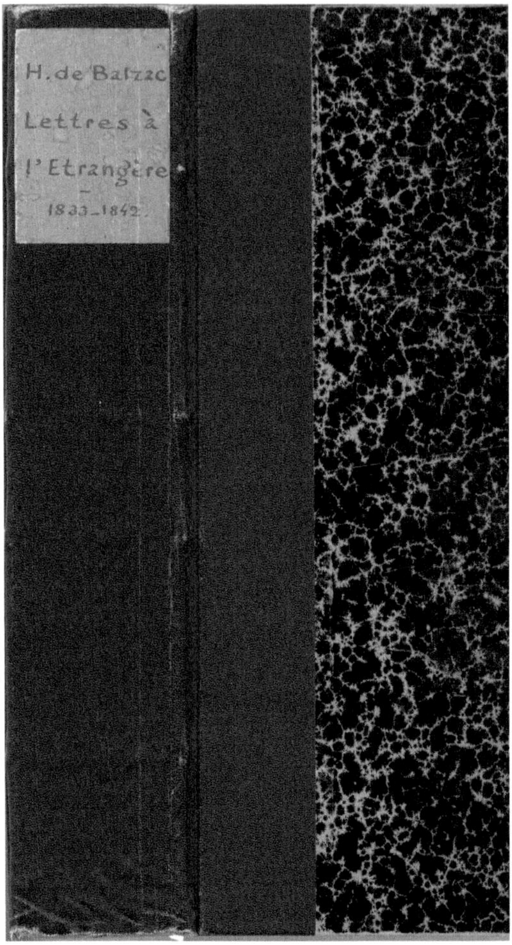

Huizinga archive in Leiden University Library

from Shakespeare's portrait hanging above Huizinga's student desk. His lifelong friend Christiaan T. van Valkenburg reported in his brief but fine book on Huizinga that together they had attended a university course on Shakespeare to satisfy their mutual interest in the subject, but stopped after the third lecture when they found the lecturer too dull.[16] In notes for the article he published on 'Rosenkranz and Guildenstern', arguing that Shakespeare had found these Danish names on a portrait of the Danish

16 Van Valkenburg, *J. Huizinga*, p. 12.

astronomer Tycho Brahe engraved by the Dutch artist Jacques de Gheyn, Huizinga's comments and pieces of evidence are limited to the engraving itself. There is not a single word of enthusiasm for Shakespeare the author.[17] Much the same is true of his passion for the work of Balzac. We would not know from Huizinga's archives that around 1900 he was deeply interested in Balzac; this aspect of his reading is revealed by a passing remark in his correspondence.[18] The only physical evidence of this intellectual interest is a copy of Balzac's *Lettres à l'étrangère*, which was in Huizinga's private library.[19]

5 Huizinga's Library

Despite the many books Huizinga borrowed from libraries and his extensive research notes compiled in the archives, a focus on Huizinga's private book collection has its own value. Extensive annotations in his books are rare and mainly given for practical reasons. In his own copy of the Basel edition of his Erasmus biography, the list of portraits shows many remarks Huizinga made.[20] He knew which books he possessed and did not keep a card system. His only habit was to underline the capital of the author's name, to know where he had to return the book after having used it. Though he once made his own ex libris, so far no books containing this ex libris have been found. Generally he only wrote his name in the upper-right corner of the title page: J. Huizinga. The search continues to track down books Huizinga owned.

One of Huizinga's best friends was the Dutch author and poet, the Marxist-leaning Henriette Roland Holst-van der Schalk. Her works are scarcely read today. Huizinga had supposed that her fame would be such that it would inspire people to learn Dutch. Yet he himself was too modest to think that one day people might want to read his writings in their original Dutch, either published or unpublished, in his archives or in his library. The Special Collections Reading Room of Leiden University Libraries – and soon the Huizinga website – makes this possible.

17 Huizinga, 'Rosenkranz und Güldenstern'. There is no English translation.

18 J. Huizinga to J.A.J. Barge, 29 August 1943: 'Ruim veertig jaar geleden heb ik heel wat Balzac gelezen' (Huizinga, *Briefwisseling*, III, p. 397).

19 The first volume. The shield with the title is written in Huizinga's hand. UBL: HUIZIN 2020.

20 Huizinga, *Erasmus*; UBL: HUIZIN 122 dui 1.

The grand exposition of *Les Primitifs flamands*, mounted in Bruges during the summer of 1902, had a galvanizing impact on the 29-year-old Johan Huizinga.[1] This fact is well known; what has gone unremarked is the significance of its timing. That summer marked the sexcentenary of the Battle of Kortrijk (Courtrai), fought on 11 July 1302, when citizen militias from Bruges, Ghent, and other Flemish towns had vanquished a heavily armed invading French army on the frontier of then-independent Flanders. It would become known as the De Slag der Gulden Sporen (Battle of the Golden Spurs) because of the hundreds of gilded accessories wrested from fallen French *chevaliers* on that muddy field, and later dedicated in the Onze-Lieve-Vrouwekerk nearby. Within just a few years after the uneasy formation of Belgium in 1830, the memory of this victory and the politics of its commemoration were becoming symbolic of larger divisions within a multilingual kingdom whose only official language was French. Although German- and Flemish-speaking citizens were free to use 'the idiom best suited to their interests and habits', it was decreed that the local varieties of these vernaculars were so numerous 'that it would be impossible to publish an official text' in all of them.[2]

Early efforts to make this medieval battle a point of unifying national pride were therefore unsuccessful. When Nicaise de Keyser's heroic painting of it was exhibited at the Brussels Salon in 1836, it inspired Hendrik Conscience (1812-1883) – a devotee of Sir Walter Scott and a pioneer of Flemish literature (despite his Francophone father) – to promote a very different narrative in *De Leeuw van Vlaenderen* (The lion of Flanders).[3] In his foreword, Conscience explicitly characterized his historical novel as a celebration of Flemish '*nationalism*' ('*nationaliteit*', italics original), dedicated to a readership suffering from the 'regret and shame' ('spyt en schaemte') of a lost Fatherland and eager to repel a new force of French invaders. Unlike these bureaucrats, 'We Flemings have a history, a heritage, as *a country and a people*, while the Walloons [...] have a history only as *separate cities*'.[4] While proclaiming his loyalty to the Belgian king, Conscience passionately

All translations are my own, except as otherwise noted.

1 Haskell, 'Huizinga and the "Flemish Renaissance"'.

2 *Bulletin des arrêtés et actes du gouvernement provisoire, 20 November 1830, nr. 33*, reproduced in Coopman and Broeckaert, *Bibliographie*, I, p. 96, no. 238: 'l'idiôme qui convient le mieux à ses intérêts ou à ses habitudes [...] qu'il serait impossible de publier un texte officiel'. For a selection of relevant translated documents, see Hermans et al., *The Flemish Movement*.

3 See Hermans, 'Highs and Lows'.

4 Conscience, *De Leeuw van Vlaenderen*, pp. i, vi. 'Wy Vlamingen hebben eene geschiedenis, eenen voorledenen *als Land en als volk* terwyl de Walen (Luik alleen) slechts eene geschiedenis van *afzonderlyke Steden* hebben.'

denounced the linguistic and cultural tyranny that had been built into the Belgian state from its inception.[5]

In 1847, Conscience coauthored a pamphlet explaining the aims of the Vlaemsche Beweging (Flemish Movement), whose goal was total institutional equality for the Flemish language, its universal instruction in schools, funding for Flemish literature and theater, and a requirement that all government officials and army officers be proficient in 'the Dutch language' ('der nederlandische tael').[6] That very same year, his novel's enormous popularity inspired a play which introduced 'De Vlaamse Leeuw' ('The Flemish lion'), a rousing anthem so evocative of 'medieval' sentiments that it is still widely believed to be a folk song.[7]

He's fought a thousand years by now	*Hij strijdt nu duizend jaren voor*
for freedom, land, and God,	*vrijheid, land en God;*
And still his strength is ever young,	*En nog zijn zijne krachten*
sprung from his native sod.	*in al haar jeugdgenot.*
Should someone think him beaten	*Als zij hem machteloos denken*
or taunt him with a blow,	*en tergen met een schop,*
He'll rise right up again in might	*Dan richt hij zich bedreigend en*
and lay tormentors low.	*vrees'lijk voor hen op.*
Chorus:	
No they will never tame him,	*Zij zullen hem niet temmen,*
not while one Fleming lives	*zolang een Vlaming leeft,*
Not while the Lion can claw,	*Zolang de Leeuw kan klauwen,*
and not while his teeth can grip.	*zolang hij tanden heeft.*[8]

5 In 1823, upper- and middle-class Francophone citizens in the Flemish provinces of the United Kingdom of the Netherlands had opposed a measure that would have mandated Dutch as the official language there: it was one of the factors that led to the Belgian Revolution in 1830, when that same powerful linguistic minority prevailed.

6 Conscience and Snellaert, *Vlaemsche beweging*.

7 *Willem van Dampierre* was written by Hippoliet Jan Van Peene (1811-1864), who collaborated with the composer Karel Miry (1823-1899). 'De Vlaamse Leeuw' was not included in the published script of the play (1850), suggesting that it initially circulated via the quasi-medieval formats of manuscript and oral transmission. It was preserved in the *Volks-Almanak voor 1854, bevattende Verhalen, Liedjes, Anekdoten Enz*, with music inserted on a separate leaf. It is still identified as a "Flemish folksong" in popular media, e.g., http://muzikum.eu/nl/123-90-2413/het-vlaams-volkslied/de-vlaamse-leeuw-songtekst.html (accessed 9 August 2017), and is still the 'national anthem' of Flanders and of the Flemish separatist movement.

8 I have translated only the first of five stanzas to represent the tenor of the whole.

By 1887, when a monumental statue of Kortrijk's working-class heroes – the butcher Jan Breydel and the weaver Pieter de Coninck – was erected in the marketplace of a fossilized medieval Bruges, this song was underscoring a burgeoning Flemish *separatist* movement, led not only by intellectuals but by disenfranchised laborers.[9] In 1895, their campaign for universal male suffrage (which would not be achieved until 1919) inspired a nascent campaign for Flemish national rights. Defying state-sponsored calls for national harmony, the Algemeen Nederlands Verbond (United Dutch Association) adopted placards featuring the grim-faced warriors of Kortrijk, chained to one another in solidarity.[10] In the face of these very real linguistic, political, and socioeconomic ruptures, Henri Pirenne (1862-1935) was striving to give Belgium what every other European nation either had or wanted: a medieval past. The first volume of his attempt 'to trace the history of Belgium to the Middle Ages, thereby recovering, above all, its unified character' appeared just two years before the Bruges exhibition and was rapidly revised and reprinted in 1902, coinciding with the sexcentenial commemoration of Kortrijk.[11]

It was against this embattled medieval backdrop, therefore, that Huizinga inspected the unprecedented display of some 400 Flemish 'primitives', many from private collections, assembled in Bruges. He was probably already familiar with the Flemish Movement, which many Dutch intellectuals had long supported.[12] But the self-conscious medievalism of Flemish nationalism was probably foreign to him. Although Conscience's novel was widely read in the Netherlands, there was no analogous attachment to the Middle Ages as a locus of collective identity. The Dutch war of independence from Spain and the Reformation were the touchstone events, making the sixteenth and seventeenth centuries the era of national becoming. Perhaps as a result, both medieval history and philology – including the study of Old and Middle Dutch – lagged far behind in the Netherlands. As Joep Leerssen has put it, 'the constitutional split between Holland and Flanders entailed a divorce between the stock-in-trade of their historical memories'.[13]

In Bruges, Huizinga thus confronted a culture at once very similar and very different from his own. Meanwhile, his interest in Flemish artworks

9 Leerssen, 'Novels and Their Readers'.

10 The artist was Alfred Ost (1884-1945), a popular Flemish illustrator known for powerful, muscular figures: see Tollebeek, 'Le culte de la bataille', p. 224. *Wij willen* had originally been the name adopted by a Flemish artistic collective in Ghent, founded in 1887.

11 Pirenne, *Histoire de Belgique*, I, p. vii: 'de retracer l'histoire de Belgique au moyen âge, en faisant ressortir surtout son caractère d'unité'.

12 See, eg., De Clerq, *Tegenwoordig België*.

13 Leerssen, 'Novels and Their Readers', p. 245.

had already been piqued by their centrality to a decades-long debate over their 'national' characteristics and place in art history.[14] Were these 'primitives' exemplary of modern progress and a fresh new artistic perspective? Or were they grotesque products of late medieval decline? Alternatively, were they 'primitive' in representing a purer, more pious sensibility than the decadent pagan aesthetics of Italy in the same period?[15] Regardless of the way the question was framed, the answer had political implications. Jacob Burckhardt's famous narrative of Italian Renaissance civilization, published in 1860, had removed the artistic products of Burgundy's 'Belgian' court (topic of his maiden monograph, in 1842) from the narrative of Western artistic development; the Swiss historian had insisted that visual art forms were the ultimate indices of a culture's essence and that Renaissance Italy owed nothing to Transalpine Europe.[16] In France, in the wake of the antimonarchical revolutions of 1848, some critics had rejoined that late medieval Burgundian court arts were accordingly more 'bourgeois' and therefore more truly French than such 'elitist' Italian classicism. Then again, after 1870 and the disastrous loss of Alsace-Lorraine to the new German Empire, Hippolyte Taine's doctrine of *race, milieu, moment* was invoked to argue that all 'Germanic' arts – including English, Flemish, and Dutch forms – were ugly and decadent. *Real* French art, like that of Italy, was derived from classical, Roman models.[17]

The dilemma posed by Burgundian art – Flemish or French? medieval or modern? – was further heightened in 1902 by the fraught politics of the exhibition's organization. It had initially been planned for (modern) Brussels, to commemorate 'a moment of national renewal and glorification'.[18] When it was belatedly moved to (medieval) Bruges, in close proximity to the divisive battlefield of Kortrijk, the crumbling city's own powerful aesthetic became a potent factor in the exhibition's reception.[19] On the one hand, visitors' impressions were primed by the fame of Georges Rodenbach's modern symbolist novel *Bruges-la-morte* (1892), with its black-and-white

14 Jongkees, 'Une génération d'historiens', pp. 79-80.

15 Haskell, 'Huizinga and the "Flemish Renaissance"', p. 447.

16 Burckhardt, *Die Kunstwerke der belgischen Städte* (1842) versus *Die Kultur der Renaissance in Italien*. At the same time, Burckhardt freely claimed a number of non-Italian, medieval artworks for Renaissance Italy: see Symes, 'When We Talk about Modernity'.

17 Krul, 'Realism, Renaissance, and Nationalism', pp. 252-269.

18 Ibid., p. 278. On the circumstances, see Jongkees, 'Une génération d'historiens', p. 83; Haskell, 'Huizinga and the "Flemish Renaissance"'.

19 On the local, national, and international politics behind the exhibition, see Tahon et al., *Impact 1902 Revisited*.

photographs of a weird medieval cityscape dissolving into mist. On the other, they encountered the exhibit after having walked through those same streets, passing the very houses and churches for which many of these artworks had been created, past the modern memorial to Kortrijk's heroes in the vast medieval marketplace. There was no separating the medieval from the modern. Indeed, the Flemish poet Karel van de Woestijne, in a lengthy appreciation of the exhibit and its site, explicitly saw both the medieval city and its medieval artifacts as prefiguring the decay of his own modern age.[20] Other viewers, however, saw in these 'primitives' an antidote for 'le désastre des arts modernes'[21] and called for 'the renewal' and rehabilitation of modern art through the 'mysteries' of the later Middle Ages.[22] To many French critics of modernist art, the exhibition reversed the judgment of the previous generation: clearly, they argued, the art of Burgundy was thoroughly 'French'. (Had not Rogier van der Weyden been born in Wallonia?) They even expressed umbrage at the Flemish appropriation of 'their' French heritage, and arranged for the hastily assembled Parisian exhibition of 'primitifs français' in 1904.[23]

These dueling exhibitions were among many contemporary manifestations of a much more widespread phenomenon. Huizinga had come of age in a Europe where the medieval past was the nostalgic terrain on which battles for national identity and cultural patrimony were perpetually waged. The adjective 'medieval' and the proper noun 'Middle Ages' had emerged into common parlance in the 1830s, marking the need for a vocabulary to describe the era of modern Europeans' emergence into the light of history.[24] In Italy, that era was classical antiquity, reflected in the unifying political propaganda of the Risorgimento.[25] But beyond the Alps, modern European nation-states had either begun as provincial colonies of the Roman Empire or benighted backwaters: tantamount to the peoples of their own 'dark' colonies. In the sixteenth and seventeenth centuries, indeed, the shock of 'discovering' the existence of outlandish peoples had been negotiated by

20 Van de Woestijne, *De Vlaamsche Primitieven*, p. 15.

21 Lafenestre, 'L'exposition des primitifs français', p. 354.

22 Mâle, 'Le renouvelement de l'art'.

23 Jongkees, 'Une génération d'historiens', pp. 80-81; Krul, 'Realism, Renaissance, and Nationalism', p. 279.

24 Symes, 'When We Talk about Modernity'. See also Geary, *Myth of Nations*. This is not to say that there had not been conceptualizations of what we call the 'medieval' past in previous centuries; see, e.g., Damian-Grint, *Medievalism and* manière gothique.

25 That said, medievalism mattered in Italy, too. See, e.g., Di Carpegna Falconieri, 'Il Medievalismo et la Grande Guerra'.

associating them with the primitive 'dark age' that Europeans themselves claimed to have escaped.[26]

Thereafter, in the wake of revolutionary failures, the redrawing of Europe's political map, and a wave of renewed imperial ventures, Europe's post-Roman and premodern past was opened up to new interpretations. Novel political entities had to be filled with venerable – but disputed – cultural capital.[27] Scandinavian, German, and English scholars all tussled for rights to the sole ownership *Beowulf.* French scholars strove to occlude the fact their national language – exemplified by the *Chanson de Roland* – had originated in Anglo-Norman England or independent Picard Flanders. The establishment of history as a professional discipline, subsidized by national libraries and imperial museums as well as universities, sharpened this competition. The *Monumenta Germaniae Historica*, an ongoing publishing enterprise launched in 1819, counted as 'monuments of German history' all historical and literary works produced in the lands of Charlemagne's ninth-century empire – lands that were located in, or allocated to, France, Belgium, Switzerland, or Italy. Rival collecting and publishing projects followed suit in other countries, requiring an army of philologists and curators.[28]

The Franco-Prussian War can even be understood as a more weaponized phase of already-entrenched disputes about the medieval origins of national sovereignty.[29] Combatants on both sides were aware that the war was being fought on a frontier created when the empire of the Frankish king Charles the Great (d. 814) – or Charlemagne or Karl der Große – was divided among his three grandsons in 840. France's 'loss' of Alsace-Lorraine – or, for the Germans, the (re)gaining of Lotharingia – was rendered all the more significant for the former because this had been Joan of Arc's homeland. The popular revival of her cult in France was immediate. In 1874, the French government commissioned a gilded bronze equestrian statue of La Pucelle from the sculptor Emmanuel Frémier (1824-1910). It was meant to be prophetic: 'France would not die because Joan would be reborn'.[30]

Peoples who had lost the contest for statehood in the realignments of the modern era – as the Flemish had – were also turning to medieval

26 The essential study is that of Davis, *Periodization and Sovereignty*. See also Biddick, *Shock of Medievalism*.

27 Geary and Klaniczay, *Manufacturing Middle Ages*.

28 This argument is developed in Symes, 'Manuscript Matrix, Modern Canon'.

29 These examples are discussed in Symes, 'Medieval Battlefields and National Narratives'.

30 De Biez, *E. Frémiet*, p. 140: 'La France n'était morte parceque Jeanne venait de renaître.' Joan was not formally beatified until 1909. Indeed, prior to 1870 and the Catholic revival in France, she had largely been forgotten.

battlefields for meaning and inspiration. Serbs, for whom the Battle of Kosovo (15 June 1389) was the beginning of their subjection to the Ottoman Empire, would transfer that grievance to Austria-Hungary after 1878.[31] A young Serb would later strike a blow for the restoration of medieval rights in Sarajevo, on 28 June 1914, just four days after the Scots celebrated the 600th anniversary of their short-lived triumph over the English at Bannockburn. In partitioned Poland, the Battle of Grunwald (15 July 1410) was celebrated as marking the date when the united forces of Poland and Lithuania had trounced an army of Teutonic Knights. For stateless Poles, verbal and symbolic references to this order had become coded ways of referring to German aggression and imperialism.[32] The monument to the quincentenary of this battle in 1910, erected in Kraków – former capital of the medieval kingdom – was thus a nostalgic reminder of what Poland had once been and a blatant expression of nationalist aspirations for the future. As such, it was destroyed by the German occupying forces in 1939.[33]

In this context, we can better appreciate the fact that Huizinga's first work of explicitly historical scholarship, published in 1912, roundly rejected this dangerous, zero-sum game of nationalistic one-upmanship. As such, it prefigures the critique of medievalism which, as I argue, he advanced in *Herfsttij der Middeleeuwen* (1919) – long before his passionate denunciations of toxic nationalism in the 1930s. In an essay on 'The Early History of Our National Consciousness', derived from a lecture he delivered in the presence of Henri Pirenne, Huizinga debunked the myth that modern nations or national sentiments could be traced back to the Middle Ages, thus countering the whole premise of Pirenne's history, published a decade before.[34] He reminded his audience that Flemish and French artists, among many others, had come together in Burgundy in the service of a cosmopolitan French-speaking court – not a nation-state – and he forthrightly rejected Pirenne's claim that Burgundian dukes were 'Belgian princes'.[35]

In the years that followed, Huizinga would find even more reasons to condemn the recourse to medievalism in the service of modern nationalist

31 Popovich, 'Medievalism in Serbian Painting'; Johnson, *Central Europe*, pp. 24-25, 172-175.

32 Johnson, *Central Europe*, p. 44; Welch, *Germany, Propaganda and Total War*, pp. 210-212; Clark, *Iron Kingdom*, pp. 655-670.

33 On the histories generated by this battle, see Jučas, *Battle of Grünwald*; Gouguenheim, *Tannenberg*; Paravicini et al., *Tannenberg, Grunwald*. On the context of its commemoration, see Stauter-Halsted, 'Rural Myth and the Modern Nation'; Dabrowski, *Commemorations*, pp. 165-183.

34 Huizinga, 'Uit de voorgeschiedenis'. See Jongkees, 'Une génération d'historiens', pp. 86-87.

35 Pirenne, *Histoire de Belgique*, II, e.g., pp. 178, 207, 220, 345, 370.

projects. For even as he worked to compass the rich and overripe culture of medieval Burgundy, the lands of which he wrote became the bloody frontier of the Western Front. If the origins of modernity *were* to be located in an age of political, cultural, and moral decay – as he posited – then his study of that age can also be read as a searing reflection on his own time, whose paradoxes he both *discerned in* and *projected onto* the past. If this was not a conscious process in the early phases of the book's development, it became evident by the time of its publication. In his preface to *Herfsttij*, Huizinga appears to paraphrase Van de Woestijne's evaluation of the Flemish 'primitives' displayed at Bruges, which (according to the poet) reflected the worldview of those who 'looked with awe at the burning gold of that setting sun' ('Zij bewonderen het brandend goud dezer avondzon') and whose art was like a 'fiercely red but already fading rose' ('deze fel-roode, maar reeds welkende roos').[36] Huizinga combines and darkens these two striking images, making himself the viewer of those portents: 'My gaze, during the writing of this book, was ever fixed on the depth of the evening sky – but on a sky of bloody red, heavy with ominous leaden clouds tinged with the false glow of copper' ('De blik is bij het schrijven van dit boek gericht geweest als in de diepten van een avondhemel – maar van een hemel vol bloedig rood, zwaar en woest van dreigend loodgrijs, vol valschen koperen schijn').[37]

Just over this horizon of the neutral Netherlands, Huizinga had been observing the deadly efficacy of his contemporaries' passionate and divisive embrace of nationalist medievalisms. Having played no small part in the bellicose ideologies undergirding the war, they were now furnishing the imagery, vocabulary, and emotional charge of wartime propaganda on all sides. In England, during the first months of the war, references to medieval battles were a leitmotif in newspaper jingoism. On 25 October, the anniversary of Agincourt (1415), a front-page editorial entitled 'Agincourt and the Modern Soldier' mused on 'the difference between battles in the past and battles now', concluding that there was little difference.[38] It was rumored that angelic English bowmen from that nearby iconic battlefield had helped to reverse a desperate situation during the British force's first major engagement, at Mons on 22-23 August. Arthur Machen's story on that theme, published in the London *Evening News* on 29 September, had quickly

36 Krul, 'Realism, Renaissance, and Nationalism', pp. 278, 286; Van de Woestijne, *De Vlaamsche Primitieven*, pp. 17 and 81.

37 Huizinga, *Herfsttij* (2nd ed.), pp. vii-viii.

38 'Agincourt and the Modern Soldier'.

passed into popular mythology.[39] A year later, when the quincentenary of Agincourt arrived, the *Times* acknowledged it by quoting the whole of Shakespeare's 'St. Crispin's Day' speech, from *Henry V*, under the headline '1415. October 25. 1915'.

Across the channel, the French, too, seized on this day as an occasion to revisit the actual site of the battle with their English counterparts. The new French weekly *L'illustration* printed a photograph of a French light infantry battalion commander delivering a lecture to a delegation of English officers, shown studying maps of the medieval battlefield on which they stood.

> Five centuries ago, the French and English armies met on the field of Agincourt. [...] The French nobility, victim once more of their own audacity, was torn in pieces by the soldiers of Henry V. Today, on the battlefields of the Artois, the two armies are brothers in the same fight, inseparably united by the shared memory of past antagonisms. [...] And at the same time, the English can also pay sincere homage to Jeanne d'Arc [...] for on the identical spot of yesteryear's battle, [French infantrymen] invite their Britannic neighbors to join together in calling forth a memory of mutual esteem.[40]

Joan herself came into her sanctity during this war. Officially beatified in 1909, the miracles necessary to her canonization in 1920 were rapidly accruing. When the cathedral of Reims was largely destroyed by German shellfire on 19 September 1914, she appeared on countless postcards and placards to remind the horrified world – unused as yet to the targeted destruction of cultural patrimony – that this had been the place of the first French king's baptism (Clovis, in 496) and the place where she herself had led the Dauphin to be crowned in 1429. In one such image, she confronts a complacent Kaiser Wilhelm, brandishing her white banner and pointing at the burning Gothic edifice with her sword. 'Nothing satisfies you, murderer of babies, king of bandits and vandals [...] you blaspheme and you destroy

39 On this phenomenon, see Clarke, *Angel of Mons*.

40 '1415-1915: Le Cinquième centenaire d'Azincourt': 'Il y a cinq siècles, les armées française et anglaise se recontraient dans la plaine d'Azincourt. [...] La noblesse française, victime une fois de plus de son orgueilleuse témerité, y était taillée en pièces par les soldats d'Henri V. Aujourd'hui, sur les champs de bataille de l'Artois, les deux armées fraternisent dans une même lutte, inséparablement unies par la mémoire même des antagonismes passés, ardents mais loyaux. Et de même que les Anglais, cette année, ont pu rendre à Jeanne d'Arc un hommage sincère [...] sur le lieu même de la bataille de jadis, invitèrent leurs voisins britanniques à évoquer communément un souvenir d'estime mutuelle.'

our beautiful cathedrals'.[41] It was said that she would appear to rally the timid, or that she could be glimpsed at the head of an army of historic heroes, to avenge the loss of her homeland.[42] In October of 1918, the cover of the American *Red Cross Magazine* featured Joan and her medieval ally, St. George, riding with George Washington into the breach of the retreating German army.

In Belgium, German propaganda stressed the importance of the Flemings' shared Germanic ancestry and language: a policy known as *Flamenpolitik*.[43] In 1917, Flemish prisoners of war in the German camp at Göttingen were even encouraged to organize a formal celebration of their national holiday on the anniversary of Kortrijk.[44] A photograph of unknown provenance shows members of the Vlaamse Werkkring (Flemish Working Circle) on that occasion, with a rough placard displaying the Lion of Flanders.[45] The printed program of the day's proceedings announces a special address by one of the camp's prominent prisoners, René Gaspar (1893-1958), a young professor of Germanic philology at Louvain who had been captured after the German occupation of the city and the deliberate destruction of the university's medieval library, town hall, and church.[46] The title of his lecture was 'Het Vlaamse Volkslied' ('The Flemish folksong'). On the same day – as Gaspar probably knew – a fellow philologist, Adiel Debeuckelaere, published an open letter to King Albert I, vehemently protesting the abuse of Flemish soldiers by their French-speaking officers, who prohibited such celebrations in their ranks, along with Flemish literature and all other cultural expressions. As he pointed out, those same officers were perfectly willing to learn various African languages when they served in the Congo, but at home they treated the Flemings like slaves and savages. If the Germans had been successful in establishing a Flemish University in Ghent, Debeuckelaere declared, that was the fault of the government which had ignored calls for linguistic and cultural equality since 1830.[47]

41 Photomontage by Boulanger/Gloria, 1914: see Bihl, 'Le bombardement de la cathédrale de Reims'. For numerous other images, see Bouxin, 'Le martyre de la cathédrale'; Harlaut, 'L'incendie de la cathédrale'.

42 One famous story is retold by Van Dyke, *Broken Soldier*.

43 De Schaepdrijver, 'Violence and Legitimacy'.

44 Tollebeek, 'Le culte de la bataille', p. 226. On the broader context, see De Schaepdrijver, 'Occupation, Propaganda'.

45 This image, labeled 'Flamingantische Soldaten vieren de Vlaamse feestdag', included in the Wikipedia entry for 'Battle of the Golden Spurs', was deleted on 5 February 2017, according to the revision history for this page.

46 Lipkes, *Rehearsals*, pp. 444-452.

47 Debeuckelaere, *Open brieven*.

In 1940, an older Huizinga would decry the fetishization of 'folkish' national anthems that fostered toxic nationalist sentiments.[48] In 1919, a younger Huizinga had presciently noted: 'How eagerly we have examined medieval civilization for the beginnings of modern culture'![49] How eagerly had the French and the Germans vied to establish sole claim to Charlemagne's imperial greatness and their disputed medieval border; how deeply had claims to modern sovereignty been staked in the medieval past; how often had the literary and artistic monuments of the Middle Ages been the site of proxy wars that had finally, in late summer of 1914, broken out in real violence. Nor was this tragic process arrested by the armistice. Even as Huizinga wrote these words, his former colleague at Leiden, the Ghent-born Willem Lodewijk de Vreese (1869-1938), an eminent professor of medieval philology, was helping to write a medievalist manifesto. Addressed to Woodrow Wilson and the delegates to the Paris Peace Conference, it argued that the principles of self-determination should apply to the Flemish people 'living in Belgium', by virtue of their medieval vernacular and culture ('Pro Flandria servanda: Vlaanderen's Recht en Eisch tot Zelfstandigheid gesteld, toegelicht, gestaafd' ['Pro Flandria servanda: Flanders' right and claim for autonomy: Formulated, explained, justified']). René Gaspar, the former Flemish POW, would head the committee charged with translating it.[50]

Although these activists' argument for Flemish national sovereignty was far less specious than the narrative of 'medieval' Belgian unity concocted by Pirenne at the turn of the century, it was being advanced by scholars exiled for their pro-Flemish activities during the war, which made them vulnerable to charges of collaboration and rendered their petition politically impossible. But even had that not been the case, Woodrow Wilson's special intellectual advisor, the American medievalist Charles Homer Haskins, had already been decisively influenced by Pirenne's anachronistic argument. Haskins deplored the Germans' 'deliberate attempt to divide [Belgium's] people into two separate Walloon and Flemish states', despite the 'fact' that 'her [Belgium's] national history goes back into the Middle Ages', when it was the 'middle kingdom' of Charlemagne's partitioned empire.[51] Perhaps

48 Huizinga, *Patriotisme en nationalisme*, trans. as Huizinga, 'Patriotism and Nationalism', p. 153.

49 Huizinga, *Herfsttij*, p. vii: 'Hoe ijverig heeft men in de middeleeuwsche beschaving naar de kiemen der moderne cultuur gespeurd'.

50 De Vreese et al., *Pro Flandria servanda*.

51 Haskins and Lord, *Some Problems*, pp. 48, 50, 53. In 1917, Flemish activists in German-occupied Belgium had been encouraged to form a parliamentary council, which issued a declaration of independence on 22 December of that year.

deliberately, Haskins did not even mention the importance of the Flemish language and medieval heritage, because these were being accepted as decisive to other bids for self-determination, elsewhere in Europe.[52] The Flemish cause was therefore lost. The following year, 1920, Ernest Claes (1885-1968) published his popular novel, *De Witte*, which reduces Flanders' storied medieval past to a young boy's role-playing obsession.[53] In 1924, Huizinga himself delivered one of the *Lectures on Holland* to an audience of American students at the University of Leiden, in which he studiously avoided a nationalistic, teleological, and anachronistic narrative of the Low Countries' collective and separate histories.[54]

Rereading Huizinga's *Herfsttij* while bearing the contemporary weight of medievalism in mind, we can begin to discern the author's own growing consciousness of his argument's contemporary implications. Most of the major sentiments and trends which Huizinga attributes to the 'life- and thought-forms' of late medieval Burgundian culture are also those of his own generation. 'We newspaper readers', he says, cannot appreciate the power of the spoken word or the lure of images; and yet medieval imagery, along with medieval slogans, mobilized whole modern populations.[55] Ostensibly arguing for the radical alterity of the medieval psyche, Huizinga constantly analyzes that of modernity – and often signals that he is doing so, as when he evokes the emotional responses aroused 'even today' by public processions and other patriotic shows.[56] When he describes the 'drive for revenge' ('wraakbehoefte') that characterized medieval Burgundian politics,[57] he is also describing that which motivated the French to recapture Alsace-Lorraine: the drive so vividly captured by Albert Bettanier's famous painting, *La Tache noire* (The black stain) of 1887. When Huizinga laments 'the strongly emotional character of partisanship and princely solidarity' that was advanced through medieval 'party tokens, colors, emblems, devices, and mottoes', he also reveals how national 'medieval' stereotypes were distilled and infused into wartime propaganda.[58] His discussion of mourning and its monuments prefigures and predicts the near-universal medievalism (Gothic, Romanesque, Celtic) of Great War memorials – from those which

52 Haskins and Lord, *Some Problems*, pp. 14-15.
53 Leerssen, 'Novels and Their Readers', pp. 235-237.
54 Huizinga, 'How Holland Became a Nation'.
55 Huizinga, *Herfsttij*, p. 6: 'Wij krantenlezers'.
56 Ibid., p. 12.
57 Ibid., p. 25.
58 Ibid., p. 29: 'Het sterk bewogen karakter van partijgevoel en vorstentrouw, [...] er uitging van al de partijteekens, kleuren, emblemen, deviezen, kreten.'

depict Joan cradling a fallen French soldier to the medieval knight leading a Scottish regiment from Bannockburn to the Somme.[59] Examples like these could be multiplied ad infinitum. 'It is a wicked world. The fires of hatred and violence burn brightly', he observed.[60]

Placing Huizinga's masterwork in the context of belligerent medievalism not only illuminates our reading of that text, it restores Huizinga's later denunciations of patriotism and nationalism – the 'two forces that, for good or evil, are straining and convulsing the world like a fever' – to their key place in his own intellectual genealogy.[61] When his younger contemporary Pieter Geyl (1887-1966), a longtime supporter of Flemish separatism, assailed him as 'the accuser of his age', he was denouncing Huizinga's humane antipolemics of the 1930s as aberrations unworthy of his previous scholarship, especially *Herfsttij*.[62] Noting that Huizinga had been among the many intellectuals galvanized by Oswald Spengler's *The Decline of the West* (*Der Untergang des Abenlandes*, 1918), Geyl alleged that this work – contemporaneous to *Herfsttij* – was the source of Huizinga's later, supposedly derivative, disquiet.[63] A survivor of Buchenwald, Geyl had a vested interest in arguing that only 'countries that had fallen under totalitarian regimes' were responsible for the tragedies of the 1930s and 1940s.[64] He thereby dismissed, or failed to acknowledge, the dangerous medievalism that had inflamed the hatreds of the previous war, informed the Paris Peace Conference, and contributed so much to the violence of his own time.

So even if his vision was partly veiled, even from himself, Huizinga had seen that the roots of World War II were planted in the medieval-manured soil that had produced World War I. In 1932, when his early champion Gabriel Hanotaux finally managed to get *Le déclin du Moyen Age* published for a French audience, Hanotaux's preface looked forward as well as back. 'Let us', he wrote, 'read this book with the profound attention that it merits.'[65] Let us, in our own foreboding moment, do the same.

59 Ibid., p. 91. See Symes, 'Medieval Battlefields and National Narratives'; Goebel, *Great War and Medieval Memory*.

60 Huizinga, *Herfsttij*, p. 44: 'Het is een booze wereld. Het vuur van haat en geweld brandt hoog.'

61 Huizinga, 'Patriotism and Nationalism', p. 97. These lectures were prefigured by *In de schaduwen van morgen*.

62 Geyl, *Huizinga als aanklager van zijn tijd*.

63 Ibid., p. 214.

64 Ibid., p. 193.

65 Hanotaux in Huizinga, *Le déclin du Moyen Age*, p. 7: 'Qu'on lise le livre avec la profonde attention qu'il mérite.'

About the Author

Carol Symes is Associate Professor of History and Medieval Studies at the University of Illinois, Urbana-Champaign. Her first book, *A Common Stage: Theatre and Public Life in Medieval Arras* (Cornell University Press, 2007) was the recipient of numerous prizes. Her current project, "Mediates Texts and Their Makers in Medieval Europe" is under contract with Penn Press. She is also writing a book about medievalism during World War I.
symes@illinois.edu

11 Huizinga, Theorist of Lateness?[1]

Birger Vanwesenbeeck

Abstract

The purpose of this chapter is to position Huizinga's notion of the 'late' Middle Ages with regard to the contemporary debate on late style and lateness, and to evaluate what his insights may have to contribute to this debate.

Keywords: late style, lateness, Theodor Adorno, Edward Said

The past decade has witnessed a return to questions of lateness, endings, and lastness in humanities scholarship. Published in the wake of Edward Said's influential account *On Late Style* (2006) and many of them inflected through the work of the philosopher Theodor Adorno, recent studies by literary critics, art historians and musicologists have given new momentum and relevance to questions that first came to preoccupy (literary) scholars in the 1960s, following the equally momentous publication of Frank Kermode's *The Sense of an Ending* (1967).[2] That the work of Johan Huizinga is yet to be given a place in this debate is surprising since his 1919 study *The Autumn of*

1 I am grateful for a Scaliger fellowship from Leiden University that allowed me to carry out research at the Huizinga archive in the Leiden University Library during the summer of 2015. I am likewise thankful for a Professional Development Grant from my home institution that enabled me to consult the manuscript of Georges Rodenbach's *Bruges-la-Morte*, housed in the Royal Library of Brussels, in the winter of 2013. I also wish to express my gratitude to Anton van der Lem and Wessel Krul for sharing with me their thoughts and ideas about Huizinga's relationship to the literature of the symbolists as I began work on this project. Any inaccuracies in what follows are my own.

2 See, among others, McMullan, *Shakespeare*, as well as McMullan and Smiles, *Late Style*; Hutchinson, *Lateness*; Vendler, *Last Looks*. For an earlier valuable intervention in the discourse on lateness, see Scarry, *Fins de Siècle*. As McMullan reminds us, the contemporary scholarly interest in lateness is by no means limited to the field of literary studies but has experienced a similar revival in the fields of musicology and painting, to name just a few.

Arnade, Peter, Martha Howell, and Anton van der Lem (eds), *Rereading Huizinga: Autumn of the Middle Ages, a Century Later.* Taylor & Francis Group, 2019
DOI: 10.5117/9789462983724_CH11

the Middle Ages constitutes, arguably, one of the first extensive examples of what is now often referred to as 'epochal lateness',[3] i.e., the lateness of artistic movements or eras on their way out. Its central hypothesis – that the works of early-fifteenth-century Netherlandish painters such as Jan van Eyck and Rogier van der Weyden should be seen not as the beginning of a 'Northern Renaissance' (as turn-of-the-century art historians such as Louis Courajod, Hippolyte Fierens-Gevaert, and Karl Voll had argued) but as the 'medieval society in its last stage, like a tree with overripe fruit, fully developed'[4] – not only offers a particularly rich and detailed account of the late period in question but also cuts across disciplinary bounds in the way that contemporary lateness studies do as well. Huizinga's study focuses on music, literature, sculpture, and painting (in addition to considering folkloric elements such as the late medieval relationship to death, religious practice, and the cultural significance of the festival), highlighting how each negotiates the spirit of lateness surrounding them. Like Spengler's *The Decline of the West*, the first volume of which appeared one year earlier, *Autumn* casts a wide net but unlike the latter, whose chosen framework is ultimately too broadly conceived to allow for any methodological applicability outside of its subject – the West – Huizinga's book remains, at its heart, a traditional period study, devoted to art and literary forms of the fourteenth and fifteenth century in the Netherlands and Northern France.[5] As such both its scope and methodology closely mirror that of contemporary lateness studies and should in theory be compatible with them.

My aim in this essay is to explore what Huizinga's insights might contribute to the contemporary debate on lateness. A number of caveats may be in order before pursuing this vision of Huizinga as a theorist of lateness. First, it may seem counterintuitive to ascribe such a generalizing thrust to a thinker who was, after all, a historian, not a philosopher. Although Huizinga is now often seen as a practitioner of cultural studies avant la lettre, it should be noted that this reputation rests primarily on other works (such as *In the Shadow of Tomorrow* and *Homo ludens*) and not on *Autumn*. Notwithstanding the latter's continued popular appeal across the past century, Huizinga's celebrated study remains very much a discipline-specific work, preoccupied with that most defining preoccupation of the historian's historian:

3 McMullan, *Shakespeare*, p. 42.

4 Huizinga, *Herfsttij der Middeleeuwen* (Amsterdam: Olympus, 1997), p. 13. Hereafter referred to as *Herfsttij*. All translations are, unless otherwise noted, my own.

5 As Huizinga puts in the preface to the 1919 edition, 'The starting point of this study has been to understand the art of the brothers Van Eyck and to conceptualize it within the context of their time' (p. 14). I return to his preface later in this chapter.

the beginnings of modernity. More pertinently still, *Autumn* remains, of course, a study of a particular period and not a reflection on the process of periodization as such. Hence any attempt to distill a late style theory from it risks becoming entangled within the specificities of the chosen period. Still the book includes a number of passages that suggestively hint at the beginnings of precisely such a more generalizing approach. Thus, at the outset of the first of two chapters devoted to the word and image relationship, Huizinga ruminates that 'in periods, when the creation of beauty limits itself to mere description and expression of ideas that have already sunk in, the visual arts tend to acquire a higher value than literature'.[6] Do all aesthetic styles – say the Renaissance, the Baroque, or Modernism – follow this transhistorical pattern, whereby the sense of exhaustion first makes itself felt in the written word before affecting the visual imagination? If so, does this late-style superiority of the visual arts only reveal itself in hindsight, as Huizinga also argues, noting the late medieval infatuation with the bombast of its verbal practitioners? It's an enticing and suggestive hypothesis but one that requires more elaboration than the passing remark that Huizinga devotes to it. Similarly, when describing the late medieval artist's preference for excessive detail, Huizinga speculates that the *horror vacui* underwriting such preference 'may perhaps be called a characteristic of any ending period'.[7] Again the reader is left to wonder what – if any – particular periods Huizinga has in mind here. Is he thinking of the Rococo, that outgrowth of the Baroque? What about the 'late realism' of the naturalists? Is their retreat to extensive, scientifically grounded descriptions to be understood as – to employ Huizinga's terminology – 'coloring in and decorating'[8] what Flaubert and Balzac founded?

What these recurring references to lateness do signal, in any case, is a larger preoccupation on the part of their author with the process of periodization as such. Such a preoccupation is also echoed in at least one of the preparatory notes for *Autumn*. In an envelope with loose notes assembled under the headings 'emptiness of thoughts, thought exhausted, emptiness, hollowness', Huizinga asks, 'In what periods is the prose good and the poetry bad? / If poetry remains strongly attached to exhausted forms / This is moreover the first period in which a free prose exists'.[9] As with the two

6 Huizinga, *Herfsttij*, p. 359.

7 Ibid., p. 329.

8 Ibid., p. 347.

9 This envelope, entitled 'Aanteekeningen', has been cataloged as no. 114 in the inventory of the Huizinga Papers at Leiden University. See Van der Lem, *Inventaris*, p. 192.

examples cited above, Huizinga's specific concern with the late Middle Ages here opens up onto the broader playing field of periodization in general. Finally, it is worth pointing out that even when the question of periodization as such is not explicitly raised as a theme, there is in Huizinga's observations throughout a level of abstraction that makes them particularly amenable to such generalizations. A case in point is the discussion of the transition from symbol to allegory that he sees as characteristic of late medieval artistic production. Alluding to Goethe's well-known distinction of the two tropes, Huizinga suggests that 'allegory is what happens to symbolism when it is projected unto the surface of the imagination, when a symbol is fully worked out and therefore also exhausted, when a passionate scream is turned into a grammatically correct sentence'.[10] What follows are ten pages devoted to describing this transition which, although they remain fully grounded in late medieval examples every step of the way, also seem to point beyond themselves. Are these still the historian's reflections on his chosen period? Or are we instead being afforded a glimpse into a more general philosophy of epochal lateness, comparable to the late style ruminations of Adorno and Said? Part of my purpose in the following pages will be to make sense of these scattered hints throughout *Autumn* in order to explore to what extent they amount to something like a 'theory' of lateness as such; and whether Huizinga's observations can be productively compared to the late style insights of Said and Adorno. Before doing so, however, I want to briefly revisit the one event that, in an autobiographical sketch, Huizinga himself credited with having first introduced him to the paintings of the Flemish Primitives; and to consider it in juxtaposition with his early interest in the symbolist literature of the day. This will allow me to set the stage for the particular notion of lateness as Huizinga was to develop it in *Autumn* two decades later.

As is well known, Huizinga's initial interest in the Middle Ages, as well as his interest in the process of ending proper, was shaped by his readings of the francophone and English symbolist writers of the fin de siècle, such as Joris-Karl Huysmans (mentioned in *Autumn*), whose work had brought about a revived interest in this period.[11] Equally well known is the fact that Huizinga's first extensive exposure to the paintings of the Van Eycks and

10 Huizinga, *Herfsttij*, p. 268.

11 Among the scholars who have investigated Huizinga's relationship to symbolist literature, see Krul (*Historicus*, pp. 90-98; 'Teleurstellingen en ontdekkingen', passim), Thys, and Van der Lem. Also Tollebeek refers to *Autumn* as recalling 'the atmosphere of the decadent fin-de-siècle literature' ("Renaissance" and "Fossilization", p. 358). For a more critical assessment of the influence of the Decadentists on *Autumn*, see Van der Lem, *Johan Huizinga*, p. 146.

their contemporaries dates from his visit to the pioneering 1902 exhibit of the Flemish Primitives in Bruges, a trip that he would later refer to as an 'experience of the utmost importance'.[12] Less well known, however, is fact that the very location of this exhibit – Bruges – brought together the Primitives and the idea of decadence or lateness in a very palpable fashion. For by the time of the Primitives exhibit in the summer of 1902, Bruges had acquired something like the status of Europe's unofficial capital of melancholia, following the publication, a decade earlier, of Georges Rodenbach's *Bruges-la-Morte* (1892).[13] In this symbolist novella, which elicited the praise of Stéphane Mallarmé and Huysmans, and which was originally serialized in *Le figaro*, the widower Hugues Viane withdraws to the city of Bruges in order to mourn the loss of his wife. It is only in Bruges, 'from which the sea had withdrawn, as his great happiness had withdrawn from him',[14] that the inconsolable Viane finds 'analogies'[15] for his grief in the solitary daily evening walks that he takes next to the city's canals. In this fashion Viane seeks to put off the 'second death' that occurs when 'the faces of the dead, which are preserved in our memory for a while, gradually deteriorate [...] like a pastel drawing that has not been kept under glass, allowing the chalk to disperse'.[16] Because of the curious fate that history bestowed upon it, Bruges could arguably be called 'a city under glass' in that it 'artificially' preserved its medieval heritage whereas comparable cities lost theirs in subsequent urban development. The private 'museum' where Viane has assembled relics of his wife, including, most importantly, a lock of her hair, functions in this regard as a mise en abyme for the city as a whole. The particular vision of 'lateness' as it emerges from Rodenbach's *Bruges-la-Morte*, then, is one that is steeped in the decadentist logic of its time, exhibiting at once a fascination with artifice – and the 'stilling' of time that it affords – and the Baudelairian aestheticization of everyday life more generally. Although Rodenbach stops short of referring to his protagonist's walking as *flâner* – the term, strikingly, is crossed out in an earlier version of the novella, being replaced by *acheminer* – there is nonetheless something of the artist in Viane, who traverses his work of mourning – as Freud was to call it a decade later – as

12 Huizinga, *Mijn weg*, p. 47. The exhibit was held in the Provinciaal Hof in Bruges from 15 June to 5 October 1902.

13 To my knowledge Haskell is the only Huizinga scholar who alludes, if only briefly, to *Bruges-la-Morte* ('Huizinga and the "Flemish Renaissance"', p. 460) in discussing the significance of the 1902 exhibit.

14 Rodenbach, *Bruges-la-Morte*, trans. by Mike Mitchell, p. 61.

15 Ibid., p. 60.

16 Ibid., p. 35.

if it were in fact a work of art.[17] As does, initially, the picture of Dorian Gray to Oscar Wilde's eponymous protagonist, the medieval surroundings of Bruges appear to Viane as one of those privileged pockets where the past lingers still, where the onslaught of time has temporarily been ground to a halt, thus offering both protagonists (and their creators) something to latch on to in a century on its way out. Ultimately, it's only murder that allows both protagonists to sustain this illusion of stilled time. Much like Dorian puts a definitive end to the growing disparity between himself and the portrait by destroying it (and thereby also himself), so Viane kills Jane, the lookalike that he has come to regard as the reincarnation of his dead wife, thus causing the two women to become 'fused into one. So alike in life, even more alike in death'.[18]

Although no documentary evidence suggests that Huizinga read *Bruges-la-Morte*, it is highly likely that he would at least have been familiar with it given his well-documented interest in the symbolist literature of the day. Is it Rodenbach who Huizinga has in mind when, in another titillating passing reference, he compares the highly stylized, 'elephant-like' bombast of the fourteenth-century Flemish francophone poet Georges Chastellain to that of 'contemporary Belgian writers'?[19] (Mallarmé, noting the elevated stylistic register of *Bruges-la-Morte*, called it a 'poem in prose'.) To be sure, Rodenbach was not the only turn-of-the-century writer to befit such a description but even its two other most likely candidates – the symbolist poets Karel Van de Woestijne and Emile Verhaeren – would have led Huizinga back to Bruges and to Rodenbach; the former wrote an extensive review of the 1902 exhibit, the latter was a close friend of Rodenbach's. As an avid reader of the *Mercure de France*, Huizinga might moreover also have encountered Rodenbach's name among those interviewed for a 1898 survey of the journal about the desirability of including images to accompany text.[20] (Like Huizinga, Rodenbach did not think too highly of such inclusions.[21]) Last but not least, Huizinga would have come across Rodenbach's name as the dedicatee of Hippolyte Fierens-Gevaert's *La Renaissance septentrionale* (1905), which is

17 The crossed-out reference to *flâner* occurs on p. 3 of the original manuscript of *Bruges-la-Morte*, held at the Royal Library in Brussels.

18 Rodenbach, *Bruges-la-Morte*, trans. by Mike Mitchell, p. 131.

19 Huizinga, *Herfsttij*, p. 371.

20 Parts of this survey are included in the 'dossier' appended to Jean-Pierre Bertrand and Daniele Grojnowski's edition of *Bruges-la-Morte*.

21 In the case of Rodenbach, this negative view toward images is somewhat surprising since one of the (posthumous) claims to fame of his novella is that, in hindsight, *Bruges-la-Morte* appears to have been the very first work of fiction to include photographs.

referenced in *Autumn*.[22] Indeed, so vast was the continental influence of Rodenbach's novella around the turn of the century that many of Huizinga's contemporaries, among them Stefan Zweig, Huysmans, and Marcel Proust, flocked to Bruges that particular summer of 1902 with *Bruges-la-Morte* in their back pockets. Reading Zweig's impressions of his visit, one is already in more than one sense reminded of the evocation of medieval town life, with its tolling bells and autumnal feeling, as Huizinga was to describe it a decade later in the opening chapter of *Autumn*. Zweig writes:

> It's hard to wander in the evening through the dark and confined streets of this dreaming town without abandoning oneself to a serene melancholy, that gentle nostalgia aroused by the last days of autumn; no longer the shrill feasts of the fruiting season, but the more restful drama of decay and natural forces in decline. Carried by the uninterrupted wave of the pious carillon of vespers, one gradually sinks into this boundless ocean of enigmatic memories that cling to every door and wall gnawed away by time. [...] No other town possesses a greater power to symbolise the tragedy of death, and perhaps even more terrifying the actual death throes, than does Bruges.[23]

Is this also how the town struck Huizinga upon his arrival there in the summer of 1902? Put more provocatively, is it here, in the mournful footsteps of Viane as it were, that we should locate the origin of *Autumn*'s 'lateness' hypothesis, and not, as Huizinga himself was to reflect in an essay written nearly four decades later, during a 1907 walk next to the Damsterdiep canal in Groningen?[24] To be sure, the future author of *Autumn* would have had little reason to feel melancholic, coming as the visit did at the tail end of his honeymoon. Letters sent from this period likewise attest to the fact that he initially saw the Primitives as the harbingers of all that was modern in painting. This, certainly, was how the exhibit sought to fashion itself, having been designed as an ideological tool on the part of the young Belgian state to bolster its cultural patrimony as a modern state. None other than the king himself, Leopold II, had opened it; its hosting city, if not for Bruges' steadfast refusal to loan out any of its works unless the exhibit was held on

22 Huizinga, *Herfsttij*, p. 358. The fact of this dedication is mentioned in Haskell, 'Huizinga and the "Flemish Renaissance"', p. 463.

23 Zweig, *Journeys*, p. 8.

24 As Anton van der Lem points out, the only source for this anecdote is Huizinga's *Mijn weg* (p. 136).

its premises, would have been Brussels, where the Belgian revolution had taken place a mere 70 years earlier.[25] And yet how could the visitor familiar with Rodenbach's novella (or indeed his poetry about Bruges) not have been struck by the marked contrast, as seems to have been Zweig, between its setting and this purported ideological program?

Because of its close association with the calendrical closure of a century on its way out, it should be fairly obvious that the concept of lateness, as it is employed in a symbolist novella such as *Bruges-la-Morte*, belongs to Said's 'first type' of lateness, i.e., lateness as culmination or crowning, or, in the Decadentists' rather more morbid imagination, as exhaustion and decay. This, it should be noted, is also the logic underscoring Huizinga's notion of 'autumn', as his preference for organic metaphors – the late Middle Ages are referred to, among others, as 'a tree with overripe fruit',[26] 'the drying up and fossilization of society',[27] 'the atrophy of thought'[28] – all too clearly attests. At the same time, Huizinga seldom shows himself to be more critical in *Autumn* than when describing those art historians who wish to view the art of the Van Eycks as somehow detached from the culture and society of their time. Huizinga's discussion of the 'Johannes de Eyck fuit hic, 1434' inscription on Van Eyck's *The Arnolfini Portrait* offers a case in point:

> Jan Van Eyck was here. Just now. In the echoing silence of the interior the sound of his voice can still be heard. The intimacy and peaceful quiet, such as only Rembrandt will revive them, lie enclosed within this artwork, as if it were Jan's very own heart. Here, all of a sudden, is once again that evening of the Middle Ages, so familiar to us, and that we yet so often look for in vain in the literature, history, and religious experience of the time; the happy, noble, serene and simple Middle Ages of the folkloric song and church music. How far have we not drifted from their sharp laughter and boundless passion!
>
> And then no doubt our imagination starts seeing a Jan Van Eyck who stood outside of the frivolous life of his time, an ordinary man, a dreamer, who walked with bent head through life, gazing inward. Careful, or you'll have an art historical novella on your hands: how this 'varlet de chambre' unwillingly served his masters, how he and his artistic comrades

25 On the ideological significance of the exhibition, see Deam, 'Flemish versus Netherlandish', and Haskell, 'Huizinga and the "Flemish Renaissance"', and the contribution by Carol Symes, Chapter 10 in this volume.

26 Huizinga, *Herfsttij*, p. 13.

27 Ibid.

28 Ibid., p. 371.

> saw themselves forced to disavow their artistic inclinations in order to contribute to court parties and the decoration of the fleet.[29]

This is art criticism reimagined as parody – call it the Primitive-as-misfit – with Huizinga's Shakespearian skill for dramatization and psychologization here put to use in order to undermine his predecessors' viewpoints via hyperbole. In all of this, so it would seem, Huizinga's vision of lateness could not be further removed from that of Adorno who precisely shuns the organic metaphor – 'the maturity of late works of significant artists does not resemble the kind one finds in fruit', so the philosopher unequivocally states[30] – and for whom late style is synonymous, if not with serenity, then at least with a mode of letting go, where the artist's relationship to his material assumes a mode of minimal interference:

> Thus in the very late Beethoven the conventions find expressions as the naked representation of themselves. This is the function of the often-remarked upon abbreviation of his style. It seeks not so much to free the musical language from mere phrases, as rather, to free the mere phrase from the appearance of subjective mastery. The mere phrase, unleashed and set free from the dynamics of the piece, speaks for itself.[31]

For Adorno, a late work such as one of Beethoven's final piano sonatas does not simply transcend the particular time period of its composition, but it also moves, in a more important way, beyond its own creator. It's in this fashion that Adorno seeks to avoid what he sees as the all too facile psychologizing reading of Beethoven's late works, whereby the apparent lack of harmony that characterizes his final piano sonatas, is seen as the product of an 'uninhibited subjectivity' that stems from the aging artist's fear of death. Such a mimetic reading misrecognizes the transformation that, so Adorno contends, subjectivity undergoes within late works, where the artist comes to relate to his/her oeuvre as if from the outside in: 'The power of subjectivity in late works of art is the irascible gesture with which it takes leave of the works themselves. It breaks their bonds, not in order to express themselves, but in order, expressionless, to cast off the appearance of art'.[32] It is here, in this insistence on what Said calls the 'untimeliness' that Adorno ascribes to

29 Ibid., pp. 340-341.
30 Adorno, *Essays on Music*, p. 564.
31 Ibid., pp. 566-567.
32 Ibid., p. 566.

late style, that we come upon one of the fundamental contrasts between his and Huizinga's notion of period lateness. For the disinterested vantage point of the 'last look' – to borrow Helen Vendler's term – with which an aging artist is able to survey his/her life and oeuvre in a quasi-detached fashion, remains entirely unavailable for artists who are 'late' in the epochal sense of the term. As vast as the totality of a single oeuvre and/or life may be, it is still circumscribed by the figure of its creator, and it is from that center that a totalizing viewpoint can emerge. Put differently, the move beyond subjectivity that Adorno describes can only really take place because there is a self to begin with. Where else would we locate the 'irascible gesture' with which the subject in late works 'takes leave' of the works?

Matters are quite different, however, for artists who are latecomers to a period or era on its way out, as are the Van Eycks and their contemporaries. For there is no comparable identifiable center within late periods from which such a totalizing vision could emerge, let alone a proverbial oasis of calm from which the period in question could be grasped in the detached, disinterested mode that Adorno attributes to late Beethoven. As Huizinga reminds us in the paragraph immediately following the above-cited parody, 'the art of the Van Eyck brothers that we admire fully originated in the court life that repulses us'.[33] With this insistence on the worldliness of the paintings of the Van Eycks, as opposed to their supposed serenity and transcendental grace, Huizinga may be said to anticipate the contemporary critique of late style by scholars such as McMullan and Smiles. Against the still prevalent view that the late works of great artists exhibit serenity and otherworldly calm, they, like Huizinga, foreground the 'contingencies' of late style, i.e., the way in which it is fully embedded in the sociohistorical context from which it sprang.[34]

Moreover the very plethora of different but by no means exhaustive perspectives on late medieval life that Huizinga offers in subsequent chapters of *Autumn* serves as a reminder of the vastness of the period, one which neither the historian, let alone its contemporaries, is able to survey in full. Such is also the disclaimer that Huizinga offers in the preface to the first edition of *Autumn*:

> The starting point of this work has been the desire to understand the art of the Van Eycks and their followers, and to conceptualize it within the context of their time. The culture of Burgundy was the unity [*een-heid*] that I wanted to capture: it appeared possible to see the latter as a

33 Huizinga, *Herfsttij*, p. 341.

34 McMullan and Smiles, *Late Style*, p. 7.

> distinct society [*afgeronde beschavingskring*] as complete as the Italian quattrocentro, and the book was initially to be called, The Century of Burgundy. However, as its conceptual scope grew, this limitation had to be abandoned; only in a very limited sense could one speak of a unity of Burgundy culture; the non-Burgundy-governed France required as much attention.[35]

If part of this apparent inability to attain a complete, unified perspective stems from its author's universalist bent (i.e., Huizinga's above-discussed penchant for abstraction), then it is further impeded by the Burgundy era's apparent resistance to it, spilling over as its culture does into neighboring linguistic zones as well as later centuries. Hence the need to see the Van Eycks and their contemporaries as the belated exponents of their time, not as the detached appendices to it. For when it comes to period lateness the growth (and decline) metaphor seems as necessary as it is unavoidable. Contrary to Hamletian wisdom, there is no time that is out of joint, no untimeliness when it comes to eras on their way out, only late-coming outliers within the oeuvre of a given writer or artist. If such a historicist perspective will be music to the ears of Marxist scholars, then it should be noted that Huizinga's lateness approach owes part of its rhetorical strength to the fact that its insights do not so much stem from a historical materialist methodology but from a careful reading of the artworks themselves. Indeed, *Autumn* has often been criticized for devoting such scant attention to the economic relations of the time. Not unlike Adorno's 'negative dialectics' then, which seemingly ascribed to Marxist orthodoxy if only to revise it from within, so 'Huizinga's Marxism', too, is one that takes seriously the call to 'always historicize' without, however, succumbing to the closure of totalization. If history is an impersonal force, working on individuals rather than being shaped by them, then such a vision does not preclude the possibility for artists to thrive aesthetically above their historical contexts of societal and – in the case of individual late style – physiological decline. In this Huizinga and Adorno show themselves to be remarkably kindred spirits, as they do in their treatment of late style as at once the subject and the method of their writings. For just as the fragmentariness and sparseness that Adorno ascribes to Beethoven's late style is all too obviously mirrored in his own writings on it, so, Huizinga, too, in describing the all too ornate and pompous style of the late medieval artists and courts, does so in a style that is notoriously florid (if also often vivacious) and at times appears to

35 Ibid., p. 14.

be vying with its subject for domination. 'In the writing of this book', so Huizinga writes dramatically in the preface to the first edition, 'my gaze has been directed as if into the depths of an blood-red evening, wild and heavy with ominous leadlike grey, filled with faux copper appearance'.[36] In the same way as Said speaks of the 'sheer intelligence' of Adorno's sentences, 'their incomparable refinement', so the reader of Autumn, too, cannot help but be struck by its lexical-syntactical prowess. (The standard Dutch dictionary, *Van Dale*, contains no less than 282 Huizinga quotations, the majority of which stem from *Autumn*.[37])

For both Adorno and Huizinga, then, the interest in late style is apparently inseparable from their mode of writing about it. This is, of course, because both Adorno and Huizinga saw themselves as latecomers to the respective cultures in which they lived so that their late-style writings have a comparable performative quality to them, one that compels their authors to 'act out' the very late-style strategies they write about. What is to be gained strategically from such an approach is that, like their subjects, they, too, seek to stall the flow of time, if only temporarily. For what characterizes the latecomer in any given period, whether they be a musician, a painter, a historian, or a philosopher, is the implicit desire to stop or move beyond time. In the case of Adorno this halting of time occurs through a writing style that undoes narrative from within by resorting to a fragmentary (and notoriously difficult) syntax that prevents any totalizing unity from emerging. As such his (late-style) writings can be seen as, as Said argues, an alternative indeed a 'negative', to the grand narratives of dialectical progression of traditional Marxists such as Lukács.[38] In the case of Huizinga, I would argue that it is the very vivacity and visual character of his style – it would not be too much to speak of *Autumn* as a multifloor museum filled with gallery after gallery of late medieval canvasses – that accomplishes a similar effect. In the same way as the trope of ekphrasis, the verbal description of a visual work of art, has afforded the writers of totalizing genres such as epic a momentary standstill at least since Virgil's Aeneas shed his 'tears of things' in front of the mural at Dido's palace,[39]

36 Ibid., p. 13.

37 This fact is mentioned in Van der Lem, *Johan Huizinga*, p. 144, regarding the 11th edition of Van Dale.

38 Said, *On Late Style*, p. 18.

39 Virgil, *Aeneid*, bk I, l. 462. Although this is not the earliest instance of ekphrasis in literature, it's arguably one of the first where the trope (and the mourning that it triggers in Aeneas) explicitly plays the role of 'slowing' down the epic's forward progression – *ad urbem conditam*. I owe the insight about the 'slowing' function of ekphrasis within the epic genre to Wells.

so, too, Huizinga's extensive descriptions of late medieval life bring the period to a temporary (or virtual) standstill. The ultimate effect of *Autumn* on the reader, notwithstanding its author's Shakespearean gift for drama, is therefore, not that of a moving film but rather of a single-stilled image depicting the Middle Ages in its autumnal tide. Here is indeed a 'historian against the time' (as the title of Wessel Krul's biography refers to Huizinga), for what drives the author of *Autumn* is less the historian's traditional desire to preserve the past than that he seeks to bring the latter to a (momentary) standstill. In this sense William Bouwsma quite accurately refers to Huizinga's evocation of late medieval scenes as 'historical still lives' that, ultimately, are 'hardly helpful in accounting for the "autumn of the middle ages"'.[40] Tollebeek similarly has argued that, contrary to other scholars' penchant for locating the dawn of modernity earlier and earlier (hence the appeal of the term 'early modern'), Huizinga's vision offers historians a 'long Middle Ages' instead.[41]

Perhaps the difference between Adorno and Huizinga's respective late-style visions may, ultimately, be described as the attempt to move beyond time vis-à-vis the attempt to bring time to a halt. The former, I would argue, is essentially a Romantic notion, one that not only characterizes the late Beethoven of Adorno – and indeed Adorno himself – but also such different exponents of the era as Faust's desire for immortality, the 'absolute spirit' of Hegel's dialectic (which put an 'end' to history), and the Grecian urn of Keats's famous ode. The slightly more humble notion of halting time, on the other hand, is essentially a heritage of the symbolist era. Coming at the tail end of a century that itself discovered (and cemented) the idea of history as progression (as captured in such different insights as Hegel's dialectic, Darwinian evolution, and the rise of the *Bildungsroman*), the fin de siècle era bestowed on its successors a desire to stop, or at least slow down, time. It's this aesthetic that also the Huizinga of *Autumn* – belatedly – joins. Like the man-made and stagnant canals next to which the Decadentists were prone to walk – whether they be the Damsterdiep in Groningen or the canals of Bruges skirted by Viane and Zweig – Huizinga's descriptions of late medieval life have brought time to a halt. And they move us still.

40 Bouwsma, '*The Waning of the Middle Ages* Revisited', p. 333.

41 Tollebeek, "Renaissance" and "Fossilization", p. 362.

About the Author

Birger Vanwesenbeeck is Associate Professor of English at the State University of New York at Fredonia. He is the coeditor of two books: *William Gaddis, 'The Last of Something': Critical Essays* (McFarland, 2009) and *Stefan Zweig and World Literature* (Camden, 2015). His scholarly essays and book reviews have appeared in various journals, including *Postmodern Culture*, the *Journal of Austrian Studies*, the *Electronic Book Review*, and the *Los Angeles Review of Books*.
Birger.Vanwesenbeeck@fredonia.edu

12 Huizinga: Anthropologist Avant la Lettre?

Peter Arnade

In 1919, books on medieval European history hardly made reference to Vedic writing and Indian mysticism, to the phallic symbolism of late medieval marriage rites, or to American evangelical revivals and the Salvation Army.[1] But then again, there was no book quite like *The Autumn of the Middle Ages* nor a medievalist quite like Johan Huizinga. Even the book's title word, *Herfsttij* (Autumn-Tide,) was novel, a neologism in Dutch settled upon after provisional titles like 'The Century of Burgundy' were discarded.[2] Huizinga was a remarkably different medievalist in part because he was not really a historian.[3] He received his doctorate at Groningen University in classical Sanskrit, and published in this field before turning to medieval European history out of a nagging sense that the ancient South Asian world was too remote, its religion and culture too formalistic.[4] Unusual for his era, Huizinga never fixed upon a single subject or area. The book he published right before *Autumn*, a study of the United States, could hardly have been more different nor more odd a move for a Sanskrit scholar turned European

1 I have used the Payton and Mammitzsch translation of *Herfsttij der Middeleeuwen* throughout this chapter. These references are found in Huizinga, *The Autumn of the Middle Ages* (Chicago: University of Chicago Press, 1996), pp. 6, 129, and 229. The problems with this translation, and the vexing history of the multiple editions and translations of Huizinga's work, is expertly considered in Peters and Simons, 'The New Huizinga'. Huizinga's collected works are *Verzamelde werken* (hereafter *VW*). Where good English translations exist of Huizinga's work, I cite these instead. For Huizinga's correspondence, see Huizinga, *Briefwisseling*.

2 Thys, 'Huizinga en de Beweging van Negentig', p. 35.

3 As Huizinga himself admitted: 'Een pur sang geschiedvorser ben ik nooit geworden' (*Mijn weg*, p. 67).

4 His doctorate on the fool in Sanskrit drama was published as *De vidusaka in het Indisch tooneel*. It, and his other writings on India and Buddhism, are assembled in *VW*, I, 'Oud Indië'. On Huizinga's intellectual autobiography, see Van der Lem's new annotated and illustrated edition of his *Mijn weg tot historie & Gebeden*. For his waning interest in the classical Indian world, see pp. 57-61.

Arnade, Peter, Martha Howell, and Anton van der Lem (eds), *Rereading Huizinga: Autumn of the Middle Ages, a Century Later*. Taylor & Francis Group, 2019
DOI: 10.5117/9789462983724_CH12

medievalist who had no expertise on the subject.[5] It was one of many of Huizinga's quirky professional choices for scholarship that make him nearly unique for his generation of historians.

Yet for all of Huizinga's singularity, he was no outlier but rather an established scholar of abiding curiosities and restless interests.[6] In the institutional arena, he was fairly conventional and had chairs of history at Groningen and Leiden universities, where he eventually served as rector. He was well liked, a traditionalist in cultural tastes, and a moderate politically in an era of extremes.[7] He read ferociously and broadly – Dante, Shakespeare, even American writers like Nathaniel Hawthorne were among his favorites – was a proud aesthete, was impressively skilled in classical and contemporary languages, had rigorous training in philology, and was no stranger to *Quellenforschung*, as was made evident in his work on medieval charters in Haarlem. He was neither a devoted student of historiography nor theory, though he knew both well enough.[8]

Huizinga established no school of history nor did he produce many students, though he was respected beyond the confines of the Dutch academic world. He corresponded widely, including with his famous Belgian contemporary Henri Pirenne, but traveled little.[9] His impact was profound nevertheless, especially to later, more receptive generations who saw his ensemble of work as anticipating new directions the field of history eventually would take, cultural history foremost. His book of greatest consequence was not *Autumn of the Middle Ages* but rather *Homo ludens*, a pioneering study of the rites and meanings of play in human society, published in 1938. Its timing was oddly placed. Huizinga penned this cheerful, original book during a dreadful time of imminent war. Game theorists consider it the foundational text in their field. The 'magic circle', a term Huizinga coined in *Homo ludens* for the boundaries between imagination and reality that the act of play imposes, today thrives as an internet buzzword, seized upon by

5 Best accessible treatments of Huizinga are Van der Lem, *Johan Huizinga*; Hanssen, *Huizinga*; Krul, *Historicus*.

6 The sense that Huizinga was a loner is the premise, for example, of the otherwise excellent Lyon, 'Was Johan Huizinga Interdisciplinary?'

7 This part of Huizinga's whimsical personality is best captured by Otterspeer, *Reading Huizinga*.

8 'Het aesthetische bestanddeel van geschiedkundige voorstellingen', Huizinga, *VW*, VII, for Huizinga's famous essay on aesthetics. His most positivist work, the study of Haarlem's medieval legal charters, is *Rechtsbronnen*.

9 On Bloch's review and the reception of the 1919 study in general, see the overview by one of Huizinga's best known students: Hugenholtz, 'The Fame'. See also Boone, '"L'automne du Moyen Age"'.

gamers and programmers alike. It is richly ironic that a cultural conservative like Huizinga (consider, for example, his worry that cinema was vulgarizing aesthetics and literature) would become tech-savvy millennials' pioneer thinker of digital play.[10]

Autumn of the Middle Ages got mixed reviews when it was published. A few scholars at the time warmed up to it, including Marc Bloch and Henri Pirenne, though both were cautious of Huizinga's scholarship in other ways, as Marc Boone and Myriam Greilsammer make clear in their essays in this volume. But many of Huizinga's closer colleagues found it puzzling and distasteful; one even warily grumbled that it was Huizinga's 'crime novel'. As Willem Otterspeer recently observed, there was an attempt in the Netherlands to deny Huizinga's posthumous importance on the part of historians of more conventional stripes. He attributes such criticism to a combination of jealousy and a curious Dutch tendency to clip the wings of original thinkers. Huizinga's contemporaries bemoaned his lack of empiricism and his penchant for broad-brush essays rather than empirical, archival work.[11] To many, Huizinga was just too much the roving chameleon, the Sanskrit scholar turned student of the late medieval and early modern Netherlands, turned mid-century social critic and ultimately a kind of anthropologist and social psychologist. His one solid empirical study, on the medieval charters of Haarlem, seemed the exception to a career that ranged, in the minds of some, too freely.

The wave of cultural history that crested between the 1970s and 1990s softened and then reversed these perceptions, and the odd man out became the pioneer of a field cut loose from positivist, structuralist, and Marxist currents of thought. It was Jacques Le Goff and Peter Burke, among others, who hailed Huizinga as a father of cultural history, a scholar open in an era, slightly before Marc Bloch and Lucien Febvre, to literary history, psychology, anthropology, sociology, and philosophy.[12] Others agreed, and after the first interactions between anthropology and history in the 1970s turned more solid, a few like Mayke de Jong and Ilse Bulhof, and later Wiebe Bergsma, touted Huizinga's anthropological temperament as especially

10 Standard English translation is Huizinga, *Homo ludens*. On Huizinga's distaste for cinema, see Huizinga, *America*, pp. 112-113. I will consider Huizinga's writings about the United States more fully later. On Huizinga and game theory, see Rodriguez, 'The Playful and the Serious', and Goggin, 'Legos'.

11 Peters and Simons, 'The New Huizinga', p. 614, esp. n. 89, and its citations. Otterspeer, *Reading Huizinga*, pp. 13-14.

12 Le Goff, 'Huizinga (Johan)', p. 242: 'Sa conception de l'histoire était très large' with the above fields cited. Burke, *What Is Cultural History?* Also see Colie's sharp 'Johan Huizinga'.

praiseworthy.[13] These scholars were on to something. For Huizinga was among the first medieval historians to take seriously ritual, symbol, and the cultural imaginary in a way different from interests in these subjects in earlier centuries.[14]

But Huizinga did not begin *Autumn* with anthropology in mind; his initial inspiration, and in fact a major theme of the book, reflects his youthful interest in art, literature and music. Some of his closest intellectual associates, men like André Jolles – from whom he eventually broke when Jolles fell under the sway of fascism – were students of the primacy of cultural *vormen* – a protostructuralist pursuit of universal linguistic and cultural codes, especially in literature and art.[15] *The Autumn of the Middle Ages* was inspired, as is well known, by an emerging interest in the canonical art of Flemish Primitives, inaugurated by a 1902 exhibition in Bruges on Jan van Eyck and his contemporaries.[16] Much of the book grapples with the gap between artistic currents, painting in particular, and cultural practices on the ground. Van Eyck himself was even considered as part of *Autumn*'s possible book title. Curiously, however, art historians of the era for the most part did not return Huizinga's interest, though as Diane Wolfthal argues in her essay, Huizinga's reputation would later grow among art historians even as his various readings of late medieval Franco-Burgundian art were rejected. Erwin Panofsky, the father of iconography, acknowledged *Autumn of the Middle Ages* but essentially ignored it. Millard Meiss, whose work on painting and the Black Death in Siena and Florence a reader would suppose owed debts to Huizinga's art and cultural model of analysis, instead dismissed it as 'nonsense', though there is evidence, including his misspelling of Huizinga's name and his characterization of him as a 'Dutch republican', that he had barely confronted the work.[17]

13 Apart from Le Goff, see De Jong, 'Foreign Past', and Bulhof, 'Huizinga'. A fuller consideration is Bergsma, *Huizinga*.

14 On the post-Reformation engagement between what became the social sciences and the study of ceremony and ritual, see Buc, *The Danger of Ritual*. Buc's criticism of the facile acceptance by contemporary historians of the functionalist school of ritual studies inspired a lively rejoinder by Koziol, 'Danger of Polemic'. Huizinga's closest contemporaries with anthropological interests were Marc Bloch and his *Les rois thaumaturges*, published in 1925, followed by Ernst Kantorowicz, especially his *Laudes Regiae*. While Bloch and Kantorowicz shared with Huizinga a fascination with the role of symbol and ritual in political and cultural ideology and practice, both had other intellectual commitments, in political, institutional, and economic history, that Huizinga did not fully share.

15 Thys, 'Uit het leven en werk van André Jolles'.

16 Peters and Simons, 'The New Huizinga', pp. 598-599 especially.

17 Ibid., p. 615. For Meiss's quote, see Meiss, *French Painting in the Time of Jean de Berry: The Limbourgs*, I, p. 433, n. 16.

While Huizinga's affection for art and literature is clear, his affinity for anthropology and ethnography avant la lettre is trickier terrain. His silence, in his earlier work, regarding any debts to theory, his sprawl of interest, and his habit of citing original sources over secondary literature do not cast obvious light on his intellectual engagement with the era's emerging social sciences. *Autumn of the Middle Ages* charts the power and practice of ritual without being a book about either, though it plants the seeds for a fuller interest in the subject that culminated in *Homo ludens*. Never a strict theorist, Huizinga's interest in ritual and symbol had less to do with their primacy as heuristic categories than with their usefulness as general descriptors of what the late medieval condition meant for northwest Europe. Huizinga thus deploys both ritual and symbol more like a painter's brush on a broad canvas than as precision tools of analysis. Ritual and symbol were not the signposts toward a grand theory in *Autumn*. Rather, they were symptoms of a broader cultural mood and style that reached maturity in the Burgundian Netherlands and northern France.

This Franco-Burgundian late medieval condition had for Huizinga a whiff of the anthropologist's 'primitivism' about it, though Huizinga did not consider this era in European history as primitive *tout court*.[18] To Huizinga, the late medieval condition in the Franco-Burgundian north turned around the bright contrasts that serve as set pieces in *Autumn* – between social practice and thought, between life and death, between reality and dreams of better worlds, between the brutal reckonings of violence and the aristocratic sheen of chivalry, between excessive religiosity and the fetishization of images and pietistic movements such as the *Devotio Moderna*, between life and art more generally, as captured in the great Flemish masters like Van der Weyden and Van Eyck. Northern France and the Burgundian Netherlands were mired in such opposites, swinging in mood and tenor between artistic and religious idealism – the brilliant colors and microscopic, burnished detail of the art's brushwork – and a pessimistic strain he found in poets like Eustache Deschamps, who bemoaned the 'age of tears, envy and torment' in which he lived.[19] Huizinga interpreted this surfeit of feeling and overwroughtness of temperament as an end point, famously setting his study against the new dawn of individualism and cultural flourishing that Burckhardt, a scholar whom he admired, had celebrated in the Italian south.[20]

18 Huizinga, *Homo ludens*, p. 179: 'Mediaeval culture was crude and poor in many respects, but we cannot call it primitive.'

19 Huizinga, *Autumn*, p. 32.

20 In a letter of 9 November 1919 to Henri Pirenne, Huizinga expresses his admiration for Burckhardt, and his effort to showcase the Burgundian north as the opposite of Burckhardt's

Huizinga only used the word 'ritual' twice in *Autumn*, but if ritual is understood as formal behavior of scripted gestures, acts, and movements, then its practice pervaded the Franco-Burgundian north.[21] *Autumn*'s first chapter – ''s Levens felheid' – sketches the cultural terrain upon which Huizinga constructed his subsequent chapters as the play of binaries: between reality and aspiration, between the extremes in blood and violence of ordinary life and the ideals in art, cultural practice and religious feeling which issued forth from this turmoil. Life was volatile, and proceeded apace in ritual practice that at once routinized and numbed its harshness. 'Every event, every action' Huizinga begins, 'was defined in given and expressive forms and was in accord with the solemnity of a tight, invariable life style [*vasten levensstijl*]'.[22] Grand processions marked all solemn and festive occasions, but also 'lesser events', even seemingly trivial ones, prompted 'a multitude of blessings, ceremonies, sayings and conventions'.[23]

Late medieval life in the Franco-Burgundian realm was, to Huizinga, a surfeit of ritual practices and symbols, all described in evocative tones and hues – the clinging of bells, the death rattles of lepers, the trumpet blasts of town criers, the dazzle of court ritual, the wafting smells of blood, smoke, and dirt, of incense, candles, and Gothic interiors. Grand processions were exercises in color, formation, rank, and gesture; people marked themselves almost tribally by dress, escutcheon, motto, faction, city, kin, and alliance. Catholic religious practice succumbed to externalities – gestures, images, numbing rites of devotion. Huizinga's favorite religious thinker in *Autumn*, Jean Gerson, chancellor of the University of Paris, keenly observed and famously bemoaned the yawning chasm between religious behavior and thought. Popular rituals – processions, jousts, carnival, executions, funerals, among others – were expressions of the 'forms of thought and life' – and palliative exercises to give meaning to life's threats. Aristocratic and princely ritual functioned as the European version of a North American potlatch, theaters of wasteful excess to tout superiority, wealth, power, and social place. Huizinga's favorite example of Burgundian court ceremony is the 1454 Feast of the Pheasant at Lille, with its extravagant *entremets* – live musicians in a giant pie for example. The banquet was in the service of a fantasy crusade that never got off the ground because, after all, the era of the crusades was

Italy. See Huizinga, *Briefwisseling*, I, pp. 271-272, no. 269. Huizinga wrote much the same in another letter to Gerard Brom (Huizinga, *Briefwisseling*, I, pp. 256-258, no. 256).

21 For these citations, I consulted the 1949 edition of *Herfsttij* in *VW*, III, pp. 3-345. For citations to ritual, see ibid., pp. 99, 132.

22 Huizinga, *Autumn*, p. 1.

23 Ibid., p. 1.

long past, though the memory of their noble virtue haunted late medieval aristocrats whose cultural appetites were shorn of larger purpose.[24]

Such was the late medieval condition of the Franco-Burgundian north, a world far different from the twelfth-century Renaissance about which Huizinga wrote approvingly in his essays on John of Salisbury, Alain de Lille, and Peter Abelard. Contrasted against this spring of the Middle Ages, full of Gothic vitality and intellectual and artistic originality, the fifteenth-century Low Countries sat mired in its exterior excesses, cultural malaise, and intellectual slippages.[25] To Huizinga, an anthropological condition explained what ailed this region and era. While Huizinga did not consider the Burgundian north as primitive, traces of these impulses pressed up against the surfaces, awakened from its subterranean slumbers by the pressure of the extremities of the age.

Like early anthropologists from whom Huizinga borrowed the term, primitivism to Huizinga denoted a society and peoples in the early evolutionary stages of development, when magic – defined as the crude use of cause and effect incantations – preceded religion, and when 'la pensée sauvage' – which Lucien Lévy-Brühl invoked in 1910 to describe a mythopoeic worldview – had currency still in structures of belief.[26] Primitivism as a term and phase of social development was instrumental to the development of anthropology as a field. In 1871, Edward Burnett Tylor's *Primitive Culture: Researches into the Development of Mythology* argued that history is cultural evolution, and cultural evolution is a feature therefore of all world societies.[27]

Huizinga cited neither Tylor nor other early anthropologists in *Autumn*, though he noted elsewhere that he had read Tylor's book.[28] In fact, he cited almost no secondary sources at all, and his one nod to studies beyond the classical or medieval world of Europe or India was to a handbook on US History which touches upon indigenous peoples.[29] Yet 'primitive' as adjective and 'primitivism' as a noun occur 31 times in *Autumn*, invoked uniformly to offer reasons for the crude underbelly of late medieval cultural practices in what otherwise was a prosperous urban society. Huizinga referenced the primitive to explain the essence of late medieval festivity. Festivity 'had the purpose that it had among primitive peoples: that is, the

24 Ibid., pp. 302-303. Late medieval banquets have received consideration for the cultural work they achieve in Normore, *Feast for the Eyes*.

25 A study of Huizinga's celebration of the 'spring' of the Middle Ages: Nauta, 'Huizinga's Lente'.

26 Translated into English: Lévy-Bruhl, *Natives*.

27 Tylor, *Primitive Culture*.

28 Bergsma, *Huizinga*, p. 41.

29 Huizinga, *Autumn*, p. 430, n. 33, citation to Farrand, *Basis of American History*.

sovereign expression of the culture, to be the form in which the highest joy of life was expressed by the community, and to express the sense of that community'.[30] More generally, Huizinga detected motifs of primitivism in most Franco-Burgundian religious and cultural practices – from the habit of giving inanimate objects names to the very essence of why cultural and religious *vormen* mattered for their very concreteness. 'Primitivism of thought', observed Huizinga, suffered from a 'weak ability to perceive the boundaries between things', so that, in the case of religious devotion or symbolic invocations more broadly, the signifier became the signified, the statue the god, the object the idea. Although Huizinga was no formal student of semiotics or De Saussure, he seems to have waded into this field, too.[31]

Whence this primitive impulse in the late medieval Low Countries with its high literacy rates, commercial sophistication, and wealthy court? The answer lies in Huizinga's unacknowledged indebtedness to early anthropologists like Tylor, William Robinson Smith, and James Frazer, among others, and their teleology of the cultural passage of all human societies from the primitive to the civilized, from magic to religion, to science.[32] Huizinga's celebrated opening of *Autumn* was an embrace of this theoretical position:

> When the world was half a thousand years younger all events had much sharper outlines than now. The distance between sadness and joy, between good and bad fortune, seemed to be greater then for us; every experience had that degree of directness and absoluteness that joy and sadness still have in the mind of a child.[33]

Childlike: Huizinga evokes youth in the opening sentences of *Autumn* as a lens by which the contemporary reader can grasp the gravitational pull of primitivism and the sharp contrasts in emotion that are so jarring to contemporaries trying to make sense of late medieval sensibilities. In *Autumn*, Huizinga occasionally revisits *kindergeest* as a key to unlock the curious strains of primitive thought and action in the Burgundian north – in religious practice, in ideas, in symbolic thought, and in cultural practice.[34]

Primitivism, to Huizinga, was a cultural constant, nagging even at his own troubled, contemporary world. Huizinga's interpretation of what he

30 Ibid., p. 303.

31 Ibid., p. 236.

32 An excellent overview of this school of thought in Bell, *Ritual*, pp. 3-20.

33 Huizinga, *Autumn*, p. 1.

34 See, for example, ibid., p. 268.

once titled 'the century of Burgundy' stands almost as a counterpoint to his study of the modern United States, *Man and Masses in America*, a small book he wrote during the same years he was preparing *Autumn*. Appearing in a collection of four essays assembled after having taught a course on American history at Leiden University during the 1917 academic year, the book puzzles Huizinga scholars, so much so that it has often been either ignored or bracketed as one of Huizinga's intellectual peculiarities. It puzzled Huizinga himself, who admitted he had no previous interest in or affection for the United States, though he was eventually drawn enough to the topic that he visited the country in 1926. He admitted that the United States attracted him less than it commanded his and other Europeans' attention in part because it had entered World War I in 1917, a battle fought on the very terrain at the heart of Huizinga's Burgundian work.[35]

In a way not fully appreciated, the United States served Huizinga as the surest example of contemporaneity and of the modern condition, just as *Autumn* served to reveal the character of late medieval civilization. Tension between the two is evident in both his thinking and his writing, and the anthropological feeling – imprecise yet evident – that colored both sets of interests, shows the one, so wholly different, in conversation with the other. The problematic cultural ripeness of the late medieval north was made all the more evident to Huizinga by the youthful modernity confronting the world through the United States' ascendant power. The late medieval condition of the Burgundian north was in turn thrown most sharply into relief by the mechanization and somewhat crude democratization of life and society Huizinga understood as a leitmotif of American culture. Willem Otterspeer got it right when he observed that *Man and Masses in America* became the counterpart to *Autumn of the Middle Ages*.[36]

It's instructive that in Huizinga's 1918 study of the United States, he also found the residue of primitivism in the society he considered the exemplar of modernity. He saw it in the American frontier spirit and behind the forms of association and sociability he read as so important to American public life – the rites of political parties, the love of civic clubs, and so forth.[37] Huizinga's study of the United States, though ignored, is consequential

35 Huizinga published two works on the United States, the first in 1918 under the title *Mensch en menigte in Amerika* and the second in 1927, essentially a diary, *Amerika levend en denkend*, following his visit to the country. Both were translated and published together in Huizinga, *America*. A very good grasp of these works' importance is Van der Lem, *Johan Huizinga*, pp. 213-219.

36 Otterspeer, *Reading Huizinga*, p. 46.

37 Huizinga, *America*, pp. 31, 33. A rare and smart consideration of Huizinga's writings on the United States is Kammen, '"This, Here, and Soon"'.

for his framing of *Autumn*, even if scholars like Michael Kammen see no relationship between the two works, and consider their twinning – the study of the United States published in 1918 and *Autumn* in 1919 – as a genuine puzzle. The link, as Kammen notes, is not obvious, and the works are utterly different. As an amateur student of the United States, Huizinga is the outsider peering in, the medievalist working with printed sources available at Leiden University, grappling with a country and cultural phenomenon toward which he felt both caution and attraction. As the author of *Herfsttij*, Huizinga is a master of the primary source, a scholar with both intense familiarity with the Burgundian Low Countries and a deep affinity for it.

In his book on the United States, Huizinga confronts modernity, its primitive traces, and its historical consequences. The United States to him was what the Middle Ages were not, even if it exhibited faint traces of primitivism and medievalism. His study of America, therefore, was a history unburdened by the past he knew and the past that most of the world experienced. The Burgundian Low Countries and the United States as opposites explains, too, the strikingly different orientation toward sources Huizinga employs in two studies. For the United States, Huizinga relies on a grab bag of printed primary and secondary sources, from *The Federalist Papers* to early-twentieth-century economic data. He relies heavily on the work of two American historians: Frederick Jackson Turner and Charles Beard, the dean of populism as a scholarly field, and perhaps the most famous Americanist of his era. The result is that Huizinga's study takes a decidedly economic, materialist turn in utter contrast to the visual and literary elements of *Autumn*. Huizinga even corresponded with Turner, engaging him in a conversation about his frontier thesis.[38] It is ironic that as a cultural historian, Huizinga would turn to men like Turner and Beard for the role of the frontier in American expansionism and the driving force of materialist interests in shaping the American constitution and the emergence of American global hegemony in the early twentieth century.[39] Instead of Chastellain, Froissart, Van Eyck, or Deschamps, Huizinga explores sources like the US Federal Trade Commission's report on the meat packing industry from 1918![40]

Part of what attracted Huizinga to the United States were strands in American history with resonance for a Dutch historian. What Huizinga

38 For example, Huizinga, *Briefwisseling*, I, pp. 246-247, no. 242.

39 An excellent overview of Turner and Beard and their contributions to the historiography of American history is found in Novick, *Noble Dream*, pp. 87, 92-96.

40 Huizinga, *America*, pp. 81, n. 15. US Federal Trade Commission, *Summary of the Report of the Federal Trade Commission on the Meat-Packing Industry* (Washington, DC: GPO, 1919).

deemed as 'forms of association', what he saw as an untamed individualism, and even the American Revolution itself, recalled the individualism and corporatism of the Middle Ages, and the federalist, republican commitments of the Revolt of the Netherlands, even if he considered the American Revolution more conservative.[41] Yet such traces of a familiar European past faded in the blaze of industrial capitalism, the 'mechanization' of the early-twentieth-century United States, and the mass, popular consumerism which it birthed. Here Huizinga plants the seeds of the cultural critic of modernity he would become in his later life, when he despaired over the devastation of World War II, and railed against the 'demented world' which had swallowed Europe. And here, too, Huizinga becomes less the De Tocqueville-esque European learned student of the United States than the elitist critic of American life and society. In his 1918 study, the United States is the incubator of mechanization, consumerism and popular media and Huizinga is the charmed, curious student of these hallmarks. By the time of the publication of his reflections on his 1926 visit to the US, Huizinga has become shriller about the country – and the contemporary world more generally. He faults the United States for cultural shallowness and the unassailable grip of economic and market imperatives. The enthusiastic pupil of the United States has become the eulogist of its perils – planting the seeds of the deep cultural pessimism which, apart from his spry *Homo ludens*, would characterize the final writings in Huizinga's corpus. Huizinga's conviction that the United States was the modern condition at its rawest and fullest brightened the alterity of the late medieval Burgundian world. Hence the anthropological feeling of Huizinga's writing and the nod to ritual, symbol, ceremony, and the lure of the primitive.

When Huizinga published *Autumn*, however, anthropology as a field was in its infancy, more the brainchild of libraries and grand theories than empirical research and field work. The full blossoming of the ethnographic movement with studies of Pacific Islanders and African rural communities would come two decades later, and with it, theories of ritual grounded in research. The first ethnographers, scholars like Bronislaw Malinowski and Alfred Radcliffe-Brown, ushered in the theoretical primacy of functionalism. Functionalists were exemplars of the mid-twentieth-century confidence in the social sciences – that data collection would result in the ability to know – in this instance, Europeans' ability to know others, often their former colonial subjects. They offered rich descriptions of the categories of a given society – religion, belief, kinship, social and political organization,

41 Huizinga, *America*, pp. 18-20, 33-35.

land tenureship, economic practices, farming and fishing practices, and other societal components – in an effort to interpret how they worked in tandem to order a society.[42] Functionalists aimed to comprehend a society and its peoples, more interested in the here and now than history, change, and conflict.

Through academic circles in England and the Netherlands, Huizinga befriended Bronislaw Malinowski, the Polish-born scholar who made his career in England and the United States. The two men started a correspondence in 1926, seven years after Huizinga published *Autumn* and four years after Malinowski published one of anthropology's canonical masterworks, *Argonauts of the Western Pacific*, a study of the Trobriand islanders of Melanesia, the first of a trio of books by Malinowski on these Pacific islanders.[43] In a letter dated 30 July 1931, Malinowski wrote to Huizinga: 'Your method in history strikes me as being the right sort of really anthropological approach'.[44] As vastly apart in fields as the two men were, they saw intellectual affinities. In the decade of the troubled 1930s and because of his friendship with Malinowski, Huizinga deepened his attraction to anthropology and non-European history, and began to read more broadly, if unevenly, in these fields.

Huizinga wrote *Autumn* before he met Malinowski, before he read much anthropological literature, and before the advent of ethnography and the subsequent theoretical turns in anthropology that culminated in the fields of functionalism, structuralism, and eventually, fully realized studies of ritual by scholars like Arnold van Gennep, Max Gluckman, and Victor Turner, who advanced in turn new interpretive interests in the impact of social conflict and change upon cultural practices.[45] Yet Malinowski sensed Huizinga's anthropological temperament, if not his intellectual restlessness and scholarly range. No surprise, since any astute reader of *Autumn* not only could grasp Huizinga's desire to paint the mental landscape of the late medieval north, but also employ the terminology of early anthropology in interpreting its cultural component. What other medievalist in 1919, for example, would write that knighthood ceremonies were 'a socially elaborate puberty ritual'?[46]

42 Jarvie, *Functionalism*; Harris *The Rise of Anthropological Theory*. A foundational text is Malinowski, *Argonauts*. Less than two decades later: Evans-Pritchard, *The Nuer*.

43 For Huizinga and Malinowski's correspondence, see Huizinga, *Briefwisseling*, II, starting p. 132. In the first letter, dated 12 December 1926, Huizinga thanks Malinowski for sending him three of his books.

44 Huizinga, *Briefwisseling*, II, p. 344.

45 For a fine overview of these developments, Bell, *Ritual*, pp. 35-42.

46 Huizinga, *Autumn*, p. 91.

Apart from the late-nineteenth-century pioneers of anthropology like Tylor or early ethnographers like Malinowski, Huizinga's anthropological leanings seem to anticipate the emergence of symbolic anthropology, especially the work of Clifford Geertz. In this sense, Huizinga's *Autumn of the Middle Ages*, and his landmark *Homo ludens*, have a more contemporary aspect to them, even if their language and intellectual shape bear the markings of the years during which they were written. Geertz, a scholar whose career from the 1960s to 1990s zig-zagged back and forth between Indonesia and Morocco as field sites, strove to move anthropology past the obligations of social scientific heuristics and taxonomies to break the field free of the burdens of linear 'schools of thought'.[47] He advanced a literary style in his writing and commitment to the primacy of signs, symbols, and their meanings over the assemblage of social and institutional categories. Instead of tables, charts, timelines, lists of the organizing principles of a society, he foregrounded narration and how language and cultural practices spin webs of signification by which meaning is produced in human societies.

Geertz's culturalism was a full-blown theory of signification. Huizinga's was hardly that, though affinities between the two exist, even if they are scholars of different generations and entirely different fields. Some historians have noted the Geertzian element in Huizinga's Burgundian world. In 1985, Wim Blockmans and Walter Prevenier drew on one of Geertz's most celebrated books to describe late medieval Burgundy as a 'theater state', a development other historians amplified.[48] Geertz meant something very specific when he invoked the dramaturgy of the state to describe the nineteenth-century Balinese *Negara*: the court as ritual itself, but ritual determined by a very specific political economy and ecology.[49] *Negara* was not the Burgundian court. The only element the two shared in any concrete way was their status as traditional courts. But of all European medievalists of his era, it was Huizinga who advanced the notion of a court as a performative act, as the charismatic center that models power and comportment to its clients and subjects. Huizinga was enough of a scholar of his era to believe that such figurations of power were acts of propaganda – means to an end. Geertz saw them instead as the very essence of the state itself – means and end collapsed into ritual as the very thing itself. That said, Huizinga's freshness as an early theorist of court ceremony is remarkable.

47 Geertz, *After the Fact*.

48 Blockmans and Prevenier, *Burgundian Netherlands*; Arnade, *Realms of Ritual*.

49 Geertz, *Negara*.

Huizinga's anthropological temperament eventually brought him not to a general theory of ritual or symbol but rather play. But here too, Huizinga and Geertz seem to bump up against each other's interests. Geertz's most celebrated essay, on the significance of cock fighting among Balinese men, advanced the term 'deep play' in its title and its argument.[50] Deep play was a reference Geertz borrowed, however, not from Huizinga, but from Jeremy Bentham, to signify play that is paradoxical because, from the perspective of utilitarianism, it is of such consequence that it threatens self-interest. Geertz was after why cock fighting in Bali, at the time illegal but widely practiced, mattered so much to Balinese men. He did not reference Huizinga's *Homo ludens*, but he easily could have, and from it drawn lessons about the human zeal for play that is so firmly fixed, historically and psychologically, that it oversteps caution.

Homo ludens was Huizinga's theoretical valedictory, a bravura intellectual feat in which he drew upon his deep reservoir of skills in languages, philology, literature, history, and a more mature familiarity with anthropology as it emerged as a discipline. His query was the human propensity toward play in all forms of activity, from intellectual to physical, and how games and their rules shaped everything from oratory to military formations, from the world of work to the world of recreation. The book was a primer of play forms, a capacious definition of what ludic behavior encompassed – ritual and festivity included – and an intellectual defense of taking play seriously. It did not, however, propose a grand theory of play so much as it insisted that play was essential to society, culture, and institutional life, and that it colored how humans frame much of their drive for competition and social display.

Historians essentially ignored *Homo ludens*, but social scientists did not; the text is now a landmark in game theory especially and remains referenced and debated today. The late medieval Burgundian north made its appearance in *Homo ludens* but was given no more prominence than the many other places, times, and peoples Huizinga drew upon, including the Trobriand Islanders about whom he had learned much from Malinowski, the ancient South Asian world of his intellectual youth, and the Pacific Northwestern indigenous peoples whose potlatch practice had already made its debut in *Autumn*. Yet *Autumn of the Middle Ages* remains Huizinga's must enduring work other than *Homo ludens*. The interdisciplinary spirit that gave *Autumn* its unique quality was the obvious prelude to the full-blown theory of cultural practice advanced in *Homo ludens*. The relationship between the two books is obvious. Less clear but no less important is Huizinga's fascination with

50 Geertz, 'Deep Play'.

primitivism and its rites, gleaned from early anthropological theory, and reinforced by the professionalization of the discipline and anthropology's emergence as an academic discipline. Primitivism provided Huizinga with a piece of his theoretical perch on which to construct his portrait of the late medieval condition of the Burgundian north. Both its residue in modern American culture, and mass society more generally, and all the ills of his contemporary world, gave Huizinga the means to define modernity to better comprehend medievalism's northern autumn.

About the Author

Peter Arnade is Professor of History and Dean of the College of Arts and Humanities at the University of Hawai'i. His most recent book is *Honor, Vengeance and Social Trouble: Pardon Letters in the Burgundian Low Countries* (Cornell University Press, 2015), co-authored with Walter Prevenier.
parnade@hawaii.edu

13 A Late and Ambivalent Recognition

(The *Autumn* of) Johan Huizinga and the French Historians of the *nouvelle histoire*

Myriam Greilsammer

Abstract

The ascendency of Huizinga's *Herfsttij* in French historiography today is an astonishing but established fact. This chapter tries to answer two basic questions. First, has the reception of Huizinga's seminal book by Marc Bloch and Lucien Febvre and the successive generations of the Annales school and of the EHESS always been positive? Secondly, could *Herfsttij* be considered a pioneer work of the *histoire des mentalités*? My analysis demonstrates that Huizinga's recognition in France was very ambivalent from the beginning. Despite many common elements between the two founders of the Annales school and the Dutch scholar, there were from the beginning serious dissonances between them. Bloch's and Febvre's reception of Huizinga's work was quite different. Bloch had strong reservations about Huizinga's vision, partly for personal reasons: Huizinga's negative review of the *Rois thaumaturges* and of *Feudal Society* and some real rivalry because of Huizinga's encroachment upon his own territory. But there were also theoretical reasons: Huizinga's mistrust of psychological interpretations, his rejection of socioeconomic factors and his focus on the aristocracy and its court culture. Febvre had a more positive attitude toward Huizinga, since he did not feel as 'threatened' as his younger colleague, not being himself a medievalist.

Keywords: Annales, Johan Huizinga, Marc Bloch, Lucien Febvre, *histoire des mentalités*, *nouvelle histoire*, EHESS

Arnade, Peter, Martha Howell, and Anton van der Lem (eds), *Rereading Huizinga: Autumn of the Middle Ages, a Century Later.* Taylor & Francis Group, 2019
DOI: 10.5117/9789462983724_CH13

History books still read at university and regularly reedited a century after their publication are quite rare. Johan Huizinga's Autumn of the Middle Ages *is one of those.*[1]

Introduction[2]

This is how, in April 2106, Benoît Bréville begins his review of *Sensible Moyen Âge: une histoire des émotions dans l'Occident médiéval* by Piroska Nagy and Damien Boquet, acknowledging the influence of Johan Huizinga's pioneering work on the study of medieval emotions.[3] Étienne Anheim, in another review of the same book, quotes the Dutch historian's masterpiece as well, underlining the pertinence of some of his intuitions and his important legacy.[4] It is indeed astonishing to see the ascendency of Huizinga's book in French historiography today, almost one hundred years after its first publication (1919), inasmuch as the relationship between the famous Dutch historian and France was, from the outset, far from idyllic. As Christophe de Voogd underlines in his doctoral dissertation, *Le miroir de la France: Johan Huizinga et les historiens français*, the initial reception of Huizinga's writings, in spite of the 'early and continuous attention paid in France to his work', was both 'discreet and ambivalent', and characterized by 'missed opportunities'.[5]

1 'Rares sont les livres d'histoire qui, un siècle après leur parution, continuent d'être lus sur les bancs des universités et font l'objet de rééditions régulières. *L'automne du Moyen Age*, de Johan Huizinga est de ceux-là' (Bréville, 'Émotions médiévales', p. 25). Nagy and Boquet, *Sensible Moyen Âge*.

2 I wish to warmly thank Martha Howell and Peter Arnade who read and corrected this chapter. Their judicious commentaries and insights have enabled me to considerably improve it. I dedicate this chapter to the memory of my mentor and close friend Jacques Le Goff (1924-2014).

3 Nagy and Boquet, *Sensible Moyen Âge*. Huizinga's writings should be analyzed in their totality. This chapter is only focused on *Herfsttij*.

4 'In 1919, in *The Autumn of the Middle Ages*, the Dutch historian Johan Huizinga (1872-1945), underlined the 'easiness of emotions of medieval men and women' ('En 1919, dans l'*Automne du Moyen-Age* (Payot, 2002), l'historien néerlandais Johan Huizinga (1872-1945), soulignait "la facilité d'émotions" des médiévaux, hommes et femmes') (Anheim, 'Le Moyen-Age').

5 I am indebted to the historian Christophe Nicolaas de Voogd, whose Leiden University dissertation, *Le miroir de la France: Johan Huizinga et les historiens français*, analyzes the attitude of Huizinga's French contemporaries toward him. Although I do not fully agree with some of his insights, my analysis of Huizinga's relationship with France, French historians, and in particular with the founders of the *Annales*, Marc Bloch and Lucien Febvre, is based on De Voogd's fundamental archival and bibliographical research and its publication. I will further refer to this study when necessary, since I am in fact conducting a virtual 'dialogue' with him. Moreover, De Voogd published in his dissertation some important texts which he translated into French and which I quote in this short article. See Annexe 2: 'Avertissement à la première

Most puzzling is certainly the fact that Huizinga neither collaborated with the newly founded group of the Annales, nor published any article in its journal, despite what Walter Simons has described as 'the apparent affinity between some work of the *Annales* and that of Johan Huizinga'.[6]

Many misunderstandings and awkward exchanges took place between Huizinga and his French colleagues, as each side failed to grasp the essence of the other's cultural singularity. One of these painful experiences was the considerable effort Huizinga made to publish a translation of *Herfsttij* with the help of the French historian and statesman Gabriel Hanotaux. F.W.N. Hugenholtz wrote rather dramatically that 'the French history of *Herfsttij* contains an element of tragedy'.[7] After the book was rejected by Plon, the press Honoré Champion formally agreed to publish it as soon as 1922. But following eight years of procrastination and excessive financial and editorial demands, Huizinga decided to withdraw from this project.[8] As we all know, the book was eventually published by Payot in 1932, thanks to the initiative of Julia Bastin, a young and determined Belgian medievalist, with a preface by Hanotaux, although the same press strangely declined to publish Huizinga's *Erasmus*.[9]

What, exactly, was the reception of this seminal book in the 1920s by the French establishment, and in particular by the two founders of the Annales, given that it was written by a major Dutch historian whose culture and interests were mostly German and who, like his peers, was influenced by Anglo-Saxon historiography? Did *Herfsttij* and Huizinga's historiographical

edition de *Herfsttij der Middeleeuwen*' (1919); Annexe 3: 'Compte-rendu de Johan Huizinga du livre de Marc Bloch', 1925 (Huizinga, *Verzamelde werken* (hereafter *VW*), IV, pp. 127-129); Annexe 4: 'L'historiographie dans la France contemporaine' (1931) = 'De geschiedschrijving in het hedendaagsche Frankrijk' (*VW*, VII, pp. 249-253); Annexe 5: 'Mon cheminement vers l'histoire' (1943) = 'Mijn weg tot de historie' (*VW*, I, pp. 11-42): in De Voogd, *Le miroir de la France*, pp. 300-325. 'Discreet and ambivalent' ('Discrète et ambivalente'), De Voogd, *Le miroir de la France*, pp. 7 and 43. I also owe a great debt to all those who have previously analyzed Huizinga's work. See inter alia, Koops et al., *Johan Huizinga 1872-1972*. I read carefully most of the numerous writings of the specialists studying the Dutch historian and *Herfsttij*, including Anton van der Lem, coeditor of his *Briefwisseling*, and author of his magnificently documented biography.

6 These details are in Peters and Simons, 'The New Huizinga'. See there one of the bibliographies of Huizinga's works. Also see Huizinga, *Briefwisseling*; Van der Lem, *Johan Huizinga*; Simons, 'The *Annales* and Medieval Studies in the Low Countries', p. 322).

7 Hugenholtz, 'The Fame', p. 243.

8 The problem was the inability of Gabriel Hanotaux to find a French editor. Van der Lem speaks of an ordeal (*un calvaire*) and Wesseling of a 'via dolorosa', in De Voogd, *Le miroir de la France*, p. 45. On this question, see pp. 45-47.

9 Thanks to the help of its translator, Julia Bastin, the book was finally published thirteen years after it first appeared in Dutch.

approach influence the Annales school and its later evolution in France? Could *Herfsttij* be considered a pioneering work of the *histoire des mentalités* in its broad significance?[10] In other words, as Willem Otterspeer might have put it, is there any equivalence between the 'DNA of Huizinga's thinking' and that of the *histoire des mentalités*?[11] This chapter pursues these questions.

1 The Burguière-Evans Controversy

Although these issues have a history that dates back to the 1920s and 1930s, they persist today, as is illustrated by the testy exchange in 2010 between André Burguière, director of studies at the École des Hautes Études en Sciences Sociales (EHESS) and senior member of the editorial board of the *Annales* since 1981,[12] and Richard Evans, professor of history at Cambridge University. In the *London Review of Books*,[13] Evans had penned a polemical review of André Burguière's 2006 book, *L'école des Annales, une histoire*

10 For the meaning of *histoire des mentalités* I refer to André Burguière's simple definition: 'Mentalities, both a cognitive and an emotional structure, a system of representations but also a receptacle for unconscious images that overwhelm the social actor more than they inform him, were for him what makes it possible to recover the color specific to the past, to apprehend a vanished society, in the categories by means of which it conceived of itself'. Burguière adds: 'Mentalities (are) not the servants of economic fluctuations or of the social system but rather the masters of the game, which can elicit adherence as well as panic and the breaking of the social bond' (Burguière, *The Annales School*, pp. 30-32).

11 [1] See Willem Otterspeer's introduction to an edition of Huizinga's texts, Otterspeer, *De hand van Huizinga*, p. 15. See also Otterspeer, *Reading Huizinga*. About the difference between Bloch's and Febvre's definition of the term *mentalités* and their semantic choice: 'The directors of the *Annales* preferred the term "mentalities", more vague but more encompassing than the Durkheimian concept of collective representations, because it retained the socialized character of mental life without reducing it – as did the concept of representations – to intellectualized forms and without neglecting the place occupied in it by individual experience. [...] Bloch always privileged the study of unconscious or routine forms of mental life, that is, those forms most thoroughly incorporated into the organization and institutionalization of social life, whereas Febvre sought to discover the connection between spontaneous forms (such as sensibility, the expression of emotions) and the most relative forms of mental activity, a connection that constitutes the unity of an age and of a person' (Burguière, *The Annales School*, p. 59). Their legacy is different. Marc Bloch is the spiritual father of historical anthropology, whereas Febvre inspired the development of psychological history (ibid., pp. 59-60). For Ariès's definition of the *histoire des mentalités*, see Ariès, 'Naissance et développement'.

12 In fact, André Burguière was *secrétaire de redaction* from 1969, but became a senior member of the editorial board of the journal in 1981. Tackett, 'Foreword', p. x.

13 Evans, 'Cite Ourselves!', pp. 12-14. De Voogd, *Le miroir de la France*, p. 9, analyzes this controversy.

intellectuelle.[14] The title of the review, 'Cite Ourselves!', reveals Evans's caustic attitude not only toward André Burguière himself but toward Lucien Febvre and the Annales's intellectual movement as well.[15]

Evans's main point, which is relevant to my subject, since it is emblematic of a certain fashionable anti-Annales attitude, is that Burguière (dismissively described as 'the long-serving administrative secretary of the journal'),[16] aimed, as had previous *Annales* editors and other members of the EHESS, to falsely convince their public that the *Annales*, founded by Marc Bloch and Lucien Febvre, was a purely French creation. In other words, Burguière's book was another example of a characteristically pretentious French fabrication according to which every major intellectual trend in history occurs somewhere between the Sorbonne and the rue d'Ulm. On the contrary, Evans emphasized that Marc Bloch and Lucien Febvre, both teaching in 1929 at the University of Strasbourg, had strong German cultural backgrounds and were deeply influenced by foreign contemporary trends. As such, they did their utmost to place the *Annales* in an international network of researchers and to embrace comparative perspectives. Evans further criticized Burguière for ignoring the fact that the foundation of a journal of economic and social history was actually the continuation of previous German, Dutch and English initiatives. 'The founding of the *Annales* was not in any case the product of exclusively French influences and circumstances. Far from it.' According to him, 'a similar longing for another kind of historical research appeared in many countries other than France'.[17]

Furthermore, Evans advises that Burguière's is not an impartial history of the *Annales*, since 'Burguière is unable to stand outside the history he is analyzing and break free from the many myths with which it has become entangled'.[18] Evans goes so far as to charge Burguière with intellectual

14 English translation: Burguière, *The Annales School*.

15 Evans writes that Lucien Febvre's goal after the war was 'the conquest of the commanding heights of academia'. According to him, 'self-publicizing was part of the plan'. He adds quite bluntly at the end of his remarks: 'Clearly, Febvre had a higher opinion of his own work than he did of his colleagues'. Evans, 'Cite Ourselves!', p. 13.

16 Ibid., p. 12. Also see note 13.

17 Evans writes: 'The *Economic History Review* was founded in Britain at around the same time as was the *Journal of Economic and Business History* in the U.S.A.' The model for the *Annales* was the *Vierteljahrschrift für Sozial-und Wirtschaftsgeschichte*; moreover 'in Germany during the 1920s, for example, the social sciences were coming together in the manner envisaged by Bloch and Febvre, as sociologists such as Weber and Karl Mannheim began to exert an influence on historical studies, and students of Friedrich Meinecke started to pursue the history of ideas' (ibid., p. 13).

18 Ibid., p. 12.

dishonesty and distortion of the *Annales*'s history: 'he seems to regard his mission as proving its continuing allegiance to the basic principles established by the founding fathers. This is another myth.' Evans concludes with a brutal comment: Burguière's book 'is written seemingly without any knowledge of the wider historiography. [...] [I]t is 'self-important, pompous, pretentious, solipsistic, often obscure, sometimes barely coherent. The translation by Jane Marie Todd renders all these faults with exemplary accuracy'.[19]

Rightly considering himself insulted, Burguière sent a short letter to the *London Review of Books*, arguing that he was 'not sure that Professor Evans read my book properly', and that 'his approach to the *Annales* school's evolution [...] did not fit the analysis I was making in my book'.[20] Moreover, Burguière published a 'droit de réponse' entitled, with a touch of humor, 'Déconstruction d'une démolition' ('Deconstruction of a demolition'), not only blaming Evans for not having read 'seriously and completely my book', but stating that he was certain that Evans had not at all understood his position.[21] Since the essential historical debate concerning the *Annales* not only had developed in France but was still ongoing there, Burguière's decision to focus on France was an obvious one, even if he was fully aware that similar controversies had appeared elsewhere.[22] Burguière thus choose to chronicle the rise of the history of mentalities in an entirely French academic context.[23] Yet, in doing so, he made mention only once of Huizinga,

19 He even dares to accuse Burguière of not being able to read German. Ibid., p. 14.

20 Burguière, Letter.

21 Burguière, 'Déconstruction d'une démolition'.

22 He says very clearly in his short note, as he had already done in his book (see below), that 'I mentioned the fact that their project of a journal of economical and social history was similar to those foreign ventures, such as older German language or English language, as those he cites: 'J'ai évoqué le fait que leur projet de revue d'histoire économique et sociale rejoignait des entreprises étrangères, germanophones plus anciennes ou anglophones comme celles qu'il cite' (Burguière, 'Déconstruction d'une démolition').

23 'I may be criticized for limiting my reflection primarily to the case of French historians. The flaw is all the more inexcusable in that the founders of the *Annales* denounced the Gallocentrism of French historians and sought to form a truly international network around their ideas. My choice was dictated by my greater familiarity with French studies. But there are other reasons for it. [...] It is troubling to observe that most historical debate continues to unfold within a national framework. [...] That compartmentalization is only apparent, however. A concern for coherence impels me to follow the trajectory of the history of mentalities, and of what can be called the anthropological turn, primarily through the studies of French historians. But similar developments could be found elsewhere.' After writing about the 'anthropological turn' in Germany and in Italy (*microstoria*), Burguière concludes: 'The analysis could be extended to many other national cases. In their historiographical development as well, we would find,

an omission Evans found problematic, as Huizinga's *Autumn* was published before the Annales school got off the ground.[24]

2 The Founders of the *Annales* and Huizinga's *Herfsttij*

The historian Walter Prevenier was right to point out that there were 'resemblances' and 'analogies' between Huizinga and the first *Annalistes*, rather than a convergence of their goals and methods.[25] In fact, as Prevenier reminds us, actual contact between Bloch, Febvre and Huizinga began quite late, only after the publication of *Herfsttij* in French (1932). Even if Bloch and Febvre acknowledged Huizinga's book before its French publication, in 1932, they had already staked out their epistemological inspiration, their goals and predominant fields of interest by 1928, when they first read *Herfsttij* in its German translation.[26]

The two French historians and the Dutch scholar, however, had important traits in common. Among them was their shared fierce opposition to

with greater or lesser time lags, a theoretical displacement similar to the anthropological turn I propose to analyze among French historians. [...] Every selection entails a certain arbitrariness. The one required here corresponds neither to a personal honors list nor to a network of friends. Of the works encountered on the historiographical itinerary I decided to follow, I have chosen those that allowed me to reconstitute the continuity and coherence of a sustained argument.' Burguière, *The Annales School*, quotations pp. 5-7 and 10.

24 Evans, 'Cite Ourselves!', p. 13.

25 Walter Prevenier wrote, with good reason, '[W]e must [...] guard against considering as a borrowing from the *Annales* everything that, in Dutch historiography, bears a close resemblance or presents analogies to its philosophy. [...] When *Herfsttij* was published in 1919, [...] the *Annales* did not exist yet. [...] It took a long time for the French to discover Huizinga' ('il faut [...] se garder de considérer comme un emprunt aux *Annales* tout ce qui, dans l'historiographie néerlandaise présente des ressemblances, des analogies avec la philosophie de celle-ci. [...] Lorsque paru en 1919 *Herfsttij*, [...] les *Annales* n'existaient pas encore. [...] Les Français ont mis du temps à découvrir Huizinga') (Prevenier, 'L'école des Annales', p. 48). See also Prevenier, 'Johan Huizinga'.

26 See Marc Bloch's appreciative 1928 review of the German translation of the book. On the other hand, De Voogd underlines Huizinga's various links with Dutch colleagues who introduced him to the French scene and to important French intellectuals, diplomats, and university professors. He was also in contact with the *Centre de synthèse*, directed by Henri Berr, who elected him to be one of the foreign professors on the board of the *section de synthèse historique*, and later of its *Conseil d'administration*. He benefited from early intellectual links with Strasbourg University, the birthplace of the *Annales* movement (with Gustave Cohen, François Schneegans and others). One can add his admiration and lifelong friendship with the Belgian historian Henri Pirenne, befriended as well by Bloch and Febvre, whom he contacted as early as 1908. Huizinga sent letters and food packages to his friend during his internment in Germany during World War I. See De Voogd, *Le miroir de la France*, pp. 40-42.

nationalist historiography. Just as Bloch advocated for the development of comparative history in a broad European perspective, the geographical area covered in the *Herfsttij* was not confined to some narrow national geographical boundaries, unlike most German and French positivist history of the era.[27] As Bloch dared to compare European and Japanese feudalism, Huizinga used his knowledge of Indo-European culture to shed light on European history. He can certainly be considered as the pioneer of the introduction of European culture into its general Indo-European framework, which will become an undeniable focus of the *Annalistes* analysis of medieval social structure and mentalities around 1980.[28]

Both Bloch and Huizinga also rejected traditional 'scientific', positivist, and highly specialized historiography that tended to focus on political and diplomatic sources and the history of events (as in the work of Charles Seignobos in France and Otto Oppermann in the Netherlands), and shared the same enthusiasm about new approaches and subjects.[29] Huizinga also gravitated to topics similar to those of his *Annales* colleagues – medieval capitalism like Bloch and Renaissance and Reformation like Febvre – and shared their interest in the historian's craft and historiography more generally. Another important aspect of Huizinga's intellectual work that aligns him with Bloch, and later with Braudel and Le Goff, is that *Herfsttij* uses the chronological notion of the *longue durée*, fundamental to the *Annalistes*. *Herfsttij* implicitly rejected Burckhardt's chronological bracketing and narrow definition of the Renaissance.[30] Huizinga discussed the matter in a letter to Henri Pirenne, dated 9 November 1919:

27 Schmitt, 'Bloch, Marc', pp. 81-82.

28 The fact that Huizinga was an Orientalist who converted to European history certainly widened his historical insights and his comparative point of view. See, for instance, how in *Herfsttij*, anticipating the historical anthropology of the *Annales*, he makes a comparison between the erotic character of a knightly tournament and the Indian Mahâbhârata: 'In its motives the tournament is closest to the contest of the Indian epics; in the Mahâbhârata, too, fighting over a woman is the central idea' (Huizinga, *Autumn*, p. 89). According to Bloch, 'clearly, the history of societies [...] must be analyzed at the European level [...] and must be comparative' ('de toute évidence, l'histoire des sociétés [...] doive être envisagée sur le plan européen [...] ne puisse être qu'une histoire comparée', Bloch, in his application for his candidature to the Collège de France, 'Projet d'enseignement au Collège de France'. See, for example, Bloch, 'Féodalité et vassalité japonaise', p. 598, and 'Les féodalités, une enquête comparative', p. 591. We find a close stand in Jacques Le Goff's and Georges Duby's analysis of Europe's Indo-European tripartite social construct of medieval society. For instance: Le Goff, 'Les trois fonctions indo-européennes', and Duby, *Les trois ordres*.

29 Peters and Simons, 'The New Huizinga', p. 601.

30 Burckhardt, *Die Kultur der Renaissance*.

> It is now more than thirteen years that I have had to demonstrate to my students the serious faults in Burckhardt's perspective, especially concerning the deep roots in the Middle Ages of the ideas that he identifies with the Renaissance. I don't quite see, then, how my book could give you the impression of my dependence on B., I had rather thought that I had reacted against him.[31]

Also like Bloch and other *Annalistes*, Huizinga did not separate his scholarship from his politics. Huizinga was a humanist who believed in the progress of mankind and in the possibility of improving society with the help of moral and aesthetic values.[32] Similarly to Marc Bloch, Huizinga saw the study of the past not only as an end in itself, but as a tool to better comprehend the present and vice versa.[33] I cannot agree with Bryce Lyon's judgment that the present neither mattered to Huizinga nor interested him, leading him to withdraw from it, 'an act', Lyon wrote, 'that may account for his deep pessimism about the Western World in the 1920's and 1930's'.[34] To the contrary, it seems to me that it was Huizinga's acute understanding of the contemporary political situation that led him, unlike many of his fellow contemporaries, to a realistic understanding of the collapse of the European political system. In his *In the Shadow of Tomorrow* (1935) dedicated to his children, Huizinga wrote in the first chapter, 'Apprehensions of Doom':

> We are living in a demented world. And we know it. It would not come as a surprise to anyone if tomorrow the madness gave way to a frenzy which would leave our poor Europe in a state of distracted stupor, with engines still turning and flags streaming in the breeze, but with the spirit gone.[35]

One can hardly speak here of disinterest or indifference, as Bryce Lyon has alleged. Whatever the reason, Huizinga decided, as did Marc Bloch, to become engaged politically. This led him to very courageous decisions and acts against the ascendant political Nazi ideology that he judged both immoral and irrational. In 1933, as Rector Magnificus of Leiden University (1932-1933), he forbade Johann von Leers, a Nazi official of the German Ministry of Foreign Affairs and leader of the German students' delegation,

31 Cited by Peters and Simons, 'The New Huizinga', p. 603.

32 See Prevenier, 'Johan Huizinga', p. 79.

33 See his engaged texts such as *In de schaduwen van morgen*, whose German translation was very quickly forbidden and put on Goebbels' index list.

34 Lyon, 'Was Johan Huizinga Interdisciplinary?', p. 186.

35 Cited in ibid., p. 186.

to keep attending the conference organized on campus by the International Student Service (originally scheduled from 7 to 12 April 1933). Huizinga's decision was based on the fact that Von Leers[36] had previously published an anti-Semitic pamphlet entitled *Forderung der Stunde, 'Juden Raus'* (The call of the hour: 'Out with the Jews') that treated the ritual murder of Christian children by Jews as a historical truth.[37] Huizinga stood alone, as the Dutch minister of foreign affairs and his university's board of governors expressed their disapproval of his decision of concluding the conference a day earlier than had been intended originally.

Huizinga was not ready to yield, and thus did not hesitate to act, unlike Lucien Febvre who, under the Vichy regime, after the Nazi invasion of France, rather shamefully decided to ask his Jewish coeditor to resign from the direction of the *Annales*, because of his determination to continue publishing the journal in an 'Aryanized form'. Finally, Bloch yielded to Febvre's demand and contributed to the newly founded *Mélanges d'histoire sociale* under the pseudonym 'Fougères', the village where he lived in southern France.[38]

Huizinga paid a very high price for his courage, as did Bloch. Not only had he to endure the open displeasure of his governing board and of the Dutch Foreign Ministry in 1933, he also encountered opprobrium in his country and difficulties in publishing his books in Germany, where his articles were totally banned. Finally, he was dismissed on his own request as a professor

36 Huizinga's decision was clear-sighted: Von Leers served Goebbels as an important ideologue, specializing in anti-Semitic indoctrination, and was a high-ranking propaganda ministry official of Nazi Germany. He became *Sturmbannführer* in the *Waffen SS*. After the war he was an advisor to Perón in Argentina and to Gamal Abdel Nasser in the Egyptian Information Department. He died in 1965. See Wistrich, *Who's Who in Nazi Germany*, pp. 151-153.

37 Otterspeer, *Huizinga voor de afgrond*, English translation, *Huizinga before the Abyss*, title cited p. 396. Otterspeer cites this passage: 'The subject of Jewish ritual murder of innocent non-Jewish children is especially troubling. Among the people, we find it constantly asserted that children are secretly abducted by Jews, that their veins are opened with the same kind of incision used in the slaughter of cattle according to Jewish religious custom, and that the blood of the wretched bleeding body is used for dark purposes' (p. 402). Von Leers adds: 'Mütter, sorgt dafür dass die jüdische Gefahr für Euere arme Kinder aus dem Lande kommt' ('Mothers, see to it that the Jewish menace to your poor children is removed from our land'). As a result of his stand, the editors of the *Historische Zeitschrift* added a text apologizing for publishing Huizinga's last article in their review: 'The article of Professor Huizinga had already been typeset when the editors were notified of his action as rector of Leiden University. If the editors had known of it earlier, they assure their readers, they would not have accepted this article' (p. 407).

38 See on this matter the section entitled 'The Ordeal of the Occupation', in Burguière, *The Annales School*, pp. 43-46.

by the Nazis on 1 June 1942.[39] Having been taken hostage on 7 August in Sint-Michielsgestel, after some intervention on his behalf, he was allowed to live in confinement at a colleague's home in De Steeg in Gelderland, near the town of Arnhem, where he died on 1 February 1945 as a result of poor health and the effects of his ill treatment.[40]

Huizinga was also ahead of his time in his willingness to expand the variety of sources used by historians (such as literary and narrative texts and visual art), and to incorporate developing disciplines such as sociology and anthropology into the 'historian's craft'.[41] It must, however, be acknowledged that this was only part of the program advocated by Bloch and Febvre; they wanted to foster a total history (including collective mentalities)[42] and the interaction between economics and social reality), a project that was not Huizinga's.[43]

Indeed, as Walter Simons argued in his superb 'The *Annales* and Medieval Studies in the Low Countries', the first reaction of Bloch and Febvre to the *Herfsttij* seemed quite warm, as they accepted Huizinga as an ally of their *Annales* project.[44] In his review of *Herfsttij*, Bloch described it as 'a capital book' ('un livre capital'), calling it 'one of the most original and thought-provoking historical works published for quite some time'.[45] Lucien Febvre likewise showed admiration in his review in the *Revue de Synthèse Historique*, deeming 'Huizinga's masterpiece, his *Waning of the Middle Ages*, this admirable monograph'.[46] Yet, these two reviews do not tell the full story. I agree with the judgment De Voogd made in his doctoral dissertation that Bloch's and Febvre's initial positive reaction to the book was the consequence of a real

39 He did not hesitate to harshly criticise the German occupier, defending academic freedom and his countrymen's rights (Hoselitz, 'Introduction', p. 9).

40 Boone, '"L'automne du Moyen Age"', p. 25.

41 Bloch, 'Compte-rendu de "J. Huizinga, Herbst des Mittelalters"', pp. 33-35.

42 See the various publications by Bloch and Febvre in the bibliography.

43 He was very eclectic in his interpretation of artistic sources.

44 Among many others, Barbara H. Rosenwein writes, 'Lucien Febvre, co-founder with Marc Bloch of the *Annales* School of history, much appreciated Huizinga's work. [...] For his own part, Marc Bloch [...] had no qualms about adopting Huizinga's generalizations about medieval emotions' (Rosenwein, 'Even the Devil (Sometimes) Has Feelings', p. 2).

45 'Une des oeuvres historiques les plus originales et suggestives qui aient paru depuis longtemps' (Bloch, 'Compte-rendu de "J. Huizinga, Herbst des Mittelalters"').

46 Febvre, 'Histoire de l'art': 'Le chef d'oeuvre d'Huizinga, son *Déclin du Moyen-Age*, cette admirable monographie.' Walter Simons writes that Lucien Febvre and Marc Bloch 'greatly admire[d] the work of [...] Johan Huizinga' (Simons, 'The *Annales* and Medieval Studies in the Low Countries', p. 99).

misunderstanding ('un malentendu').[47] In the first place, neither Bloch nor Febvre understood how far Huizinga's theoretical thinking was from their own. On the contrary, they assumed that Huizinga's epistemological views corresponded to theirs. In fact De Voogd has remarkably demonstrated that Bloch's and Febvre's major misinterpretation was linked to the fact that the second German translation of the *Herfsttij*, which was the version they first read, was missing an important part of Huizinga's original 1919 introduction. Since the omitted part explaining the subtitle of the book, *Studie over levens- en gedachtenvormen der veertiende en vijftiende eeuw in Frankrijk en de Nederlanden* (A Study of the Forms of Life, Thought and Art in France and the Netherlands in the Fourteenth and Fifteenth Centuries), was not reproduced, they missed Huizinga's rejection of the use of psychological methods in historical research. Huizinga pointed out that he intended only to describe past forms of life and thought, and did not think it at all possible to acquire psychological insights into the past. Rather, the historian's task is to understand peoples' *mentalités*, not to explain them.[48] He wrote that 'history is the explanation of the meaning [het duiden van zin] we have of the past', adding 'history is an hermeneutic'.[49] He refused to decipher medieval mentalities with the help of the new psychology: 'We try here to describe these forms of life and thinking. Will it ever be the goal of historical research to get closer to the content of these forms?'[50]

Neither Bloch nor Febvre understood that Huizinga refused a psychological analysis of past representations.[51] This is why Bloch wrote mistakenly in his first review: 'This is a study of historical psychology, collective psychology of course' ('C'est une étude de psychologie historique, psychologie collective bien entendu'). A further difference is that while Bloch was thinking as a

47 See his Chapter 7.5: 'Le grand malentendu' (De Voogd, *Le miroir de la France*, p. 229). Moreover, it must be underlined that Le Goff's commentary is quite inaccurate. Not only does he miss the early critics of the two *Annalistes*, but he does not see Bloch's early negative view of Huizinga, nor his growing antagonism toward him: 'Welcomed as a masterpiece, in its German translation and then in its French translation by Marc Bloch and Lucien Febvre, the French masters of the *nouvelle histoire*, this work was increasingly criticized by them, in particular by Lucien Febvre' ('Accueilli dans sa traduction allemande, puis dans sa traduction française par les maîtres français de l'histoire nouvelle, Marc Bloch et Lucien Febvre, comme un chef-d'oeuvre, cet ouvrage fut ensuite de plus en plus critiqué par eux, notamment par Lucien Febvre') (Le Goff, 'Huizinga (Johan)', p. 242).

48 As De Voogd (*Le miroir de la France*, p. 239), rightly concludes, 'in one word, he must interpret' ('en un mot, il doit interpréter').

49 'L'histoire est une herméneutique', *VW*, VII, 75, cited in De Voogd, *Le miroir de la France*, p. 239.

50 *VW*, IV, 3. Quoted in De Voogd, *Le miroir de la France*, p. 56.

51 See De Voogd, *Le miroir de la France*, p. 237.

French historian interested in reconstructing the social structure of medieval society, Huizinga aimed to comprehend the medieval *mentalité* with the help of his historical sensibility alone.[52] As he wrote, 'any historian who despises the evocative powers of intuition as scientifically respectable, will lose in depth and scope of vision'.[53] Febvre made the same mistake as Bloch, also describing Huizinga's book as an 'admirable psychological monograph' ('admirable monographie psychologique').[54]

3 Bloch's and Febvre's Conflicted and Conflicting Assessments of Huizinga

It is important, however, to recognize that, despite their common commitment to the methodological and historiographical project of the *Annales*, Bloch and Febvre had somewhat different reactions to Huizinga's work. Bloch's appreciation was not really 'glowing', despite the generous remarks he made in his review first published in 1928 in the *Bulletin de la Faculté des Lettres de Strasbourg*.[55] In fact, even from the beginning, he had strong reservations. For instance, he harshly criticized the absence of research concerning everyday life, as well as Huizinga's omission of significant ecological disasters such as epidemics, an essential element in his eyes, of the late medieval perception of death:

> There is almost no mention of the epidemics that were a constant dread for medieval people: and yet, this perpetual fear of the 'great mortalities' seems to clarify the obsession with death, so significant then in literature and art.

Bloch's other major criticism concerns Huizinga's lack of any social analysis of medieval society:

> Above all, the method seems to have a very serious shortcoming: it deals again and again with society as if it was one […]: however, can we configure

52 Ibid., p. 239.
53 Cited in Lyon, 'Was Johan Huizinga Interdisciplinary?', p. 187.
54 'Admirable monographie psychologique'. Febvre, 'Histoire de l'art', p. 300, cited in De Voogd, *Le miroir de la France*, p. 237.
55 As Walter Simons writes on Bloch's review of the second German edition of 1928. Simons, 'The *Annales* and Medieval Studies in the Low Countries', p. 109.

> a collective psychology that does not tell the difference between the social classes?[56]

Bloch's objections to Huizinga's methodology only increased over time.[57] In 1929, one year after his first review, he criticized *Herfsttij* more fiercely, objecting not only to its title, but also to what he considered its blanket 'psychological analysis' which he thought produced a one-dimensional social analysis:

> The volume that M. Huizinga has devoted to the XIVth and XVth centuries under the somewhat inappropriate title *Herbst des Mittelalters* (German translation, 2nd edition, 1928) [...] [is] regrettably, a psychological overview of an époque, and not a psychological study of the various social milieux at a particular time, that could have enabled us to apprehend reality. In his *Luther*, M. Lucien Febvre has attempted with great success, to highlight the influence of the social milieu on a strong individual personality.[58]

Bloch was not entirely fair to Huizinga; having read the first part of the author's introduction that was translated into German, he was perfectly aware of Huizinga's concerns about the original title of his book.[59] Bloch assumed a more distant tone when direct relations were established with

56 'Il est à peine question des épidémies qui furent pour les hommes du Moyen Âge finissant une terreur constante: pourtant l'angoisse perpétuelle des "grandes mortalités" parait de nature à expliquer cette hantise de la mort, si sensible alors dans la littérature et l'art. [...] Surtout la méthode me parait présenter une lacune vraiment grave: il est sans cesse question de la société du temps comme si elle était une, ou peu s'en faut: peut-on cependant concevoir une psychologie collective qui ne fasse aucune différence entre les classes sociales? [...] Malgré tous ses défauts, l'ouvrage demeure un trésor de particularités [sic] sur un phénomène remarquable de l'histoire de la royauté.' The two citations: Bloch, 'Compte-rendu de "J. Huizinga, Herbst des Mittelalters"', p. 35, and Huizinga's review of *Les rois thaumaturges*, quoted in De Voogd, *Le miroir de la France*, p. 230.

57 See Hugenholtz, 'The Fame', p. 244.

58 'Le volume que M. Huizinga a, sous le titre assez fâcheux de *Herbst des Mittelalters* (traduction allemande, 2ième édition, 1928) consacré aux XIVe et XVe siècles [...] malheureusement, psychologie de toute une époque vue d'ensemble, et non, ce qui permettrait d'observer la réalité, psychologie des divers milieux sociaux à une époque donnée. M. Lucien Febvre, dans son *Luther*, s'est efforcé, avec beaucoup de bonheur, de mettre en lumière la pression du milieu social sur une puissante âme individuelle.' Bloch, 1929, p. 160, n. 399, quoted in De Voogd, *Le miroir de la France*, pp. 230-231.

59 He states it clearly: 'I must confess that I do not appreciate this seasonal comparison, and that I am at ease to confess my displeasure, since afterward M. Huizinga himself seems to have had similar doubts' ('Je dois avouer que je goûte assez peu cette comparaison saisonière et je suis d'autant plus à l'aise pour confesser mes répugnances que des doutes analogues paraissent

Huizinga, four years after the foundation of the *Annales*, when he and Febvre inquired whether he might consider submitting essays for publication to them. As De Voogd has made clear, there were several reasons for Bloch's caution with Huizinga. The first had to do with Huizinga's ambivalent review of Bloch's own *Les rois thaumaturges* in 1925, which failed to appreciate the book's originality.[60] After having underlined that Bloch's subject matter 'requires a remarkable methodological expertise' ('exige des talents remarquables de nature méthodologique'), Huizinga observed that Bloch did not possess the required qualities, and offered this harsh assessment of his competence:

> I am not sure we can witness this (skill) in Bloch's work. A certain verbosity is not unfamiliar to him. He could have avoided many redundancies by adopting a better framework for his subject.

Huizinga's ultimate judgment, while aiming to be positive, was certainly perceived as an insult by Bloch, since the Dutch historian finally judged positively some aspects of his study by linking it to the *histoire événementielle* that he despised so much: 'In spite of its imperfections, the book remains a treasure of peculiarities concerning a remarkable aspect of the history of kingship.' Huizinga then listed some of these 'peculiarities' ('particularités') – a few anecdotes that, rather oddly, interested him – with the following final assertion: 'These remarks should be sufficient to illustrate what this book has to offer to us.' Bloch certainly seems to have resented these comments, for while he kept a file containing most reviews of his work, the file did not include Huizinga's.[61]

In another article devoted to 'L'historiographie dans la France contemporaine',[62] written in 1931, Huizinga seemed completely unaware of the ideological battle raging in France between the positivist establishment and the radical *Annales* historians. He began by praising the historical writings of Gabriel Hanotaux, the second-rate French historian who tried

être venus, après coup, à Monsieur Huizinga lui-même'). Bloch, 'Compte-rendu de "J. Huizinga, Herbst des Mittelalters"', p. 33. Quoted in De Voogd, *Le miroir de la France*, p. 56.

60 In his dissertation, De Voogd translated Huizinga's 1925 review of *Les rois thaumaturges*. See De Voogd, *Le miroir de la France*, pp. 302-303.

61 De Voogd inspected the files containing Huizinga's reviews of his own publications, and did not find in them Huizinga's review of the *Les rois thaumaturges*.

62 Huizinga, 'De geschiedschrijving in het hedendaagsche Frankrijk'. See De Voogd's translation in his *Le miroir de la France*, pp. 304-309.

to help him publish *Herfsttij*, and some of Hanotaux's colleagues.[63] The list of the French medievalists he quoted thereafter, includes the 'mandarins' of the *histoire événementielle*, such as Seignobos, Lavisse, Luchaire, Langlois, Petit-Dutaillis, etc. Then, in a very short paragraph, he praised the *Revue historique* and in particular its reviews. In this context, there is a minor reference to Bloch, along with some other reviewers: 'The work of reviewing, time consuming and sometimes tiresome, is of high quality in the hands of historians such as Bémont, Pfister, Hauser, M. Bloch.' After having added some neutral words about Henri Berr and his collection *L'évolution de l'humanité*, he made a laconic reference to the *Annales d'histoire économique et sociale* that had been founded two years earlier, but under an incorrect title, and even more astonishingly, he reduced it to a mere journal of economic history: 'L'histoire économique [...] dispose depuis peu d'un journal, la *Revue d'histoire économique et sociale* [sic]' ('Economic history recently found itself a journal, the *Revue d'histoire économique et sociale* [sic]'). It is strange that Huizinga failed to mention its two founders and directors, Febvre and Bloch, in his article. Indeed, he seemed unaware of the journal's originality, importance, potential impact, or of the intellectual goals of the *Annales*'s founders, and the breakthrough brought about by their definition of historical research. It may be that Huizinga had not had a chance to read one of the *Annales*'s early articles, or because there was not yet any direct connection between Febvre and Bloch on one hand, and Huizinga on the other. Moreover, while De Voogd characterizes Huizinga's review of Bloch's *Feudal Society* in 1934 as 'ambivalent', Huizinga's judgment of Bloch's magnum opus was, in reality much more negative – cynical, and even antagonistic and scornful:

> Let us read now the exhaustive study on liberty and serfdom recently published by the French historian Marc Bloch. [...] A confused sequence of details instead of a simple framework.[64]

How can we then explain that Bloch nevertheless urged Febvre to try to bring Huizinga to cooperate in their new journal? Once again, this effort resulted from incorrect assumptions, as it seems that the Von Leers incident

63 As is known, Hanotaux discovered Huizinga's *Herfsttij* very early on, and tried for some ten years to have it published in France, without any success.

64 'Qu'on lise maintenant l'étude exhaustive sur la liberté et la servitude que l'historien français Marc Bloch a récemment publiée. [...] Une série embrouillée de nuances remplace le schéma simple.' Cited in De Voogd, *Le miroir de la France*, p. 234.

at Leiden University led Bloch to ask Febvre to try to get in touch with Huizinga. Thus Bloch wrote on 16 November 1933: 'And could we not write to Huizinga, as the German journals are henceforth closed to him since the incident of the ritual murder?'[65] Although Bloch was not thrilled about asking for Huizinga's cooperation, it seems that the two editors were quite desperate to find additional collaborators in their recently created journal. 'But I am in fact looking for young people. [...] And could we not write to Huizinga [...] (indeed odd "youngster").'[66] Febvre then wrote a few days later to Huizinga, on 2 December 1933[67]:

> You certainly know the *Annales* that I founded five years ago and that I manage with Marc Bloch since then. [...] As we draw up the program for next year, it would be most pleasant for us to be able to publish a large and precise study such as those that you are accustomed to write. Would you have anything to offer on the end of the Middle Ages, on Erasmus's society, on the ancient Dutch society or on any other subject? We would be thrilled to publish in France an historian for whose originality and talent we have infinite admiration. It would be most kind of you to give us a short answer without delay. I very much hope it will be positive and I beg you to accept, dear sir and colleague, my highest regards and admiration.[68]

65 'Et ne pourrait-on écrire à Huizinga, auquel les revues allemandes depuis l'incident du crime rituel, sont dorénavant fermées?' *Marc Bloch, Lucien Febvre* [...] *Correspondance* , I, Lettre CLXXI, p. 442, quoted in De Voogd, *Le miroir de la France*, p. 49.

66 'Mais ce sont des jeunes que je voudrais. [...] Et ne pourrait-on écrire à Huizinga [...] (drôle de "jeune" d'ailleurs).' In 1933, Huizinga is 61 years old, Bloch 47 and Febvre 55: none of them is young anymore. *Marc Bloch, Lucien Febvre* [...] *Correspondance* I, Lettre CLXXI, p. 442, quoted in De Voogd, *Le miroir de la France*, p. 49.

67 Huizinga, *Briefwisseling*, II, p. 1055, quoted in De Voogd, *Le miroir de la France*, p. 49.

68 'Vous connaissez certainement les *Annales* que j'ai fondées il y a 5 ans et que je dirige avec Marc Bloch depuis ce temps là. [...] Au moment où nous établissons le programme de la nouvelle année, il nous serait très agréable de pouvoir donner de vous une étude large et précise comme celles que vous avez l'habitude d'écrire. Sur la fin du Moyen Âge; sur la société d'Erasme; sur l'ancienne société hollandaise – ou sur tout autre sujet qu'il vous plairait, n'auriez vous rien à nous offrir? Nous serions heureux de publier en France quelque chose d'un historien dont nous estimons infiniment l'originalité et le talent. Vous serez bien aimable de nous donner un petit mot de réponse sans trop tarder; je souhaite très vivement qu'il soit favorable et je vous prie de croire, Monsieur et cher collègue, à mes sentiments de haute estime et de bien vif dévouement.' *Marc Bloch, Lucien Febvre* [...] *Correspondance*, I, p. 446, Lettre CLXXII, p. 446, cited in De Voogd, *Le miroir de la France*, p. 50.

After Huizinga responded with two proposals for future articles ('The Medieval Origins of Capitalism' and 'The Play Element in History'), Febvre replied with a response that appears to have been influenced by Bloch's skepticism about Huizinga. As De Voogd has argued, they declined Huizinga's proposals for two reasons: Bloch's caution about Huizinga and a nagging sense of rivalry between the two.[69] As De Voogd explains, certain incidents caused these tensions. When Ferdinand Lot, whose student Bloch had been, declined to write the medieval volume in *L'évolution de l'humanité*, he recommended that the editor Henri Berr invite Huizinga to do so.[70] Bloch must have been disappointed, if not enraged, by his mentor's betrayal. As we can see in his 5 February 1933 letter to Febvre, Bloch attempted to discredit Huizinga's qualifications for this task[71]:

> Huizinga, I gather he knows a lot, but in a very restrained topographical frame (you know, as I do, how much his *Autumn* is confined); moreover, I ask myself if he would agree. It appears to me that he turned to quite different problems (the 'origins' of the Renaissance, the Erasmian movement, etc.). [...] The high Middle Ages must be quite unfamiliar to him.[72]

As De Voogd also notes, Bloch was unfair, as Huizinga at this time was mostly engaged in medieval history. He had research underway about the high Middle Ages, while teaching at Leiden University about the feudal system (*leenstelsel*), and in 1930 at the Sorbonne about Alain de Lille, John of Salisbury, and Pierre Abélard.[73] It seems that the French historian wanted to

69 De Voogd (*Le miroir de la France*, p. 53) suggests 'a certain professional rivalry with Huizinga on the part of Bloch himself?' ('une certaine rivalité de métier avec Huizinga de la part de Bloch lui-même?').

70 In De Voogd, *Le miroir de la France*, p. 53; Bloch, *Écrire* La société féodale, p. 68 (letters of 9 and 24 January 1933).

71 As De Voogd (*Le miroir de la France*, p. 54) reveals, we can find further proof of Bloch's resentment of Huizinga in the fact that he did not add Huizinga's review in the *Tijdschrift voor Geschiedenis* of his *Les rois thaumaturges* to his private archive, nor did he cite him in the bibliography of *La société féodale*.

72 'Huizinga: Il sait beaucoup, je crois, mais dans un cadre assez restreint, topographiquement (vous savez comme moi, combien son *Automne* est à ce point de vue limité); en outre je me demande s'il accepterait. Il me paraît tout à fait tourné vers de tout autres problèmes ("origines" de la Renaissance, mouvement érasmien, etc.). La partie haut Moyen-Âge doit lui être très étrangère.' *Marc Bloch, Lucien Febvre* [...] *Correspondance*, letter of 5 February 1933, p. 328. Quoted in De Voogd, *Le miroir de la France*, p. 53; Bloch, *Écrire* La société féodale, p. 70.

73 See Huizinga's writings about 'das Spätmittelalter' (which were ultimately rejected by the German *Weltgeschichte* because of his attitude in the Von Leers affair), John of Salisbury, Alain

keep this editorial project for himself. Although he wrote at first to Febvre that the two most fitting historians for it would be either François Louis Ganshof or himself, he very soon acknowledged that he wanted to undertake this project.[74] Febvre immediately backed his candidacy, writing on the same day, 5 February, to Henri Berr to propose it, not without contradicting his initial appreciation about Huizinga:

> Concerning the *Feudal Society*, [...] in fact, I can take only him into account. From the beginning, I had *in petto* the same objections to Huizinga's candidacy as those clearly expressed by Bloch.[75]

Bloch apparently further convinced his coeditor, as on 8 February, Febvre sent Berr a very critical comment about Huizinga:

> He suggests giving us (and he is the only one able to do so) a study of the social structure that we are still lacking. Thus something very original; nothing to compare to what Calmette or Huizinga would have given us.[76]

In his effort to get the commission for this volume, Bloch failed to grasp the originality of Huizinga's second proposed article, which ultimately turned into his famed book *Homo ludens*.[77] In his letter deprecating Huizinga's proposals, Bloch has this to say about the proposed article on play:

> In his answer to an off-print I sent him, Huizinga wrote to me in such sibylline terms that I am wondering if he received the letter that you probably sent him concerning the subjects proposed by him. This could

de Lille, the Burgundian State, Philip the Good, etc., as well as his numerous reviews of works on medieval studies.

74 As we know now, he was to publish his capital study *La société féodale*.

75 'La société féodale [...] je ne vois en vérité que lui. Dès la première minute, j'ai fait *in petto* à la candidature Huizinga les objections mêmes que Bloch formule en clair.' In this case, although his judgment is accurate concerning Bloch's talent, as nobody can deny the importance of his *Feudal Society*, it is quite insulting to compare Huizinga to Joseph Calmette, a medievalist belonging to the school of the *histoire événementielle*, hated by Febvre. Febvre to Berr, 5-8 February 1933, Bloch, *Écrire* La société féodale, quoted in De Voogd, *Le miroir de la France*, p. 53.

76 'Il (Bloch) s'offre à donner (et il est le seul capable de donner) une étude de structure sociale dont nous manquons. Donc quelque chose de très original; rien de ce que vous donnerait un Calmette ou un Huizinga'. Ibid.

77 Huizinga, *Homo ludens* (1938), French translation in 1951; Febvre, 'Un moment avec Huizinga'.

in fact be the consequence of his lack of experience in using French. Undoubtedly, I am suspicious of the playful [*ludique*].[78]

Bloch's skepticism about Huizinga's proposals for future essays reflected his clear epistemological preferences. He considered the study of *mentalités* the basis of social history (see the chapter on 'the mental atmosphere' in his *Feudal Society*), a view which is the opposite of Huizinga's, who focused on the dreams and illusions of medieval men and their influence on political history. Although Huizinga referenced the French (and American) psychological school and the ethnological works of Marcel Mauss and Marcel Granet, he underlined more than once his reservations about leaning on psychological interpretations and using ethnological concepts and explanations.[79] He did not believe in interdisciplinarity in the manner the *Annalistes* recommended. This is partly because of Huizinga's character: according to his biographers, he was a loner all his life.[80] As Febvre observed, interdisciplinarity asks a lot of historians: 'The task is enormous for the historians. [...] It implies, in order to be carried out properly, [...] the existence of a whole network of alliances.'[81] Le Goff

78 'Huizinga en réponse à un envoi de tirage à part, m'a écrit en des termes si sibyllins que je me demande s'il a reçu la lettre que vous lui avez sans doute adressée à propos des sujets indiqués par lui. Peut-être est-ce simple inexpérience dans le maniement du français. Décidément, je me méfie du ludique.' *Marc Bloch, Lucien Febvre* [...] *Correspondance*, I, letter CLXXXII, p. 462, 24 December 1933. Quoted in De Voogd, *Le miroir de la France*, p. 50.

79 He writes in his foreword to the English translation of *Homo ludens*: 'The reader will find that I have made next to no use of any psychological interpretation of play however important these may be, and that I have used anthropological terms and explanations but sparingly, even where I have had to quote ethnological facts.' Quoted in De Voogd, *Le miroir de la France*, p. 228.

80 For a superficial judgment, see Midgley, 'Cultural History and the World of Johan Huizinga'. In her odd attempt to prove that Huizinga was not at all isolated but did indeed 'benefit from the influences of some of the great historical masters of the late nineteenth century and early twentieth century', Midgley writes that 'Huizinga became friends with Marc Bloch' (sic!). One has to add that not only 'the Dutch historians totally failed to understand the greatness of *Herfsttij*' but that 'the Belgian historians [...] paid very little attention to it'.

81 'La tâche est énorme pour les historiens. [...] Elle suppose pour être menée à bien, la négociation de tout un réseau d'alliances.' Febvre, 'Une vue d'ensemble: Histoire et psychologie', p. 219, quoted in De Voogd, *Le miroir de la France*, p. 229. It must be added that Henri Berr deplored Huizinga's closeness to the German *Kulturgeschichte*: 'At the confluence of historical synthesis and of history-science-of-the-mind, Huizinga's thinking retains some kind of neutrality' ('Huizinga [...] au confluent de la synthèse historique et de l'histoire-science-de-l'esprit, sa pensée garde une sorte de neutralité') (Berr, 'Au bout de trente ans', p. 25, cited by De Voogd, *Le miroir de la France*, p. 229).

later criticized Huizinga similarly, writing that he never achieved any real level of interdisciplinarity.[82]

On the other hand, because Huizinga almost entirely excluded the use of diplomatic and quantitative sources, he ignored the relevance of the socioeconomic factors in historical development. As a consequence, this led him to analyze only a limited part of the late medieval and early modern society: mostly the aristocracy and its court culture (as he did later in *Homo ludens* as well). His stand was also a typical liberal one, in that ethics and moral values were thought to effect change and reshape contemporary society.[83] These views, including Huizinga's stern rejection of Marxist theory,[84] Durkheim's sociological concepts, and the Freudian psychoanalytical school (which he qualified as the 'decadence of culture' ('verval van de cultuur'),[85] surely contributed to Bloch's and Febvre's distance from him as a historian.

It is thus fair to speak of a strong and real (but not openly expressed) antagonism between Bloch and Huizinga. One of De Voogd's most interesting points is how Bloch grew increasingly critical of *Herfsttij* over time. He demonstrates that Bloch intended his *Feudal Society*[86] to be the exact opposite of Huizinga's book.[87] To cite one of his examples: in the section entitled 'Conditions of Life and Mental Climate', Bloch emphasized material culture in its first chapter, entitled 'Material Conditions of Life and Economic Tone', while the chapter on 'Modes of Feeling and Thought' was the second. In contrast, the subtitle of Huizinga's book is *Studie over levens- en gedachtenvormen der veertiende en vijftiende eeuw in Frankrijk en de Nederlanden* (Study of the life and forms of thought in fourteenth- and fifteenth-century France and the Netherlands).[88] What is more, Bloch did not quote Huizinga or cite

82 Le Goff, 'Huizinga (Johan)', p. 244.

83 In a letter to Julien Benda he writes in 1934: 'It is about restoring a moral conviction […] the unchanging and uncompromising ethical principles' ('il s'agit de rétablir une conviction morale […] les principes éthiques inaltérables et absolus'). Cited in Prevenier, 'Johan Huizinga', p. 79.

84 Whereas the influence of Marx's theories on Bloch's analyses of medieval rural society is obvious, Huizinga rejected them vehemently.

85 Huizinga, *VW*, VII, pp. 374-375. Cited by De Voogd, *Le miroir de la France*, p. 238.

86 Bloch, *La société féodale*.

87 'In other words, to conceive this last work as a retort to the first one' ('Autrement dit, concevoir ce dernier ouvrage en partie comme une réplique au premier') (De Voogd, *Le miroir de la France*, p. 231).

88 In 1922 Huizinga answered the painter Antoon Derkinderen who was puzzled by the absence of any social reflexion: 'Yes, because in the limited inquiry I undertook, these questions did not appear. A great deficiency, you might say. I could have acknowledged it if I ever wanted my book to be considered as a complete cultural history of this era. But I named it on purpose: study of the forms of life and thinking, nothing else' ('Oui, parce que dans le questionnement

Febvre found fault with Huizinga's tendency toward anachronism, inasmuch as he tackled the originality of the Middle Ages as a 'clash of contrasts' ('heurt des contrastes') infused with 'the odor of blood and roses' ('l'odeur du sang et des roses'). For Febvre, such a phenomenon certainly did not describe any particular period. Moreover, he found Huizinga too drawn to narrative, whereas, in his view, the chief task of the historian should be to analyze and explain the past. He also grasped how central the notion of decadence was in Huizinga's *Herfsttij*, and even more so in his later moral writings such as *In de schaduwen van morgen*.[96] While more positive than Bloch about Huizinga, Febvre remained critical, even after Huizinga's untimely death. His review of *Homo ludens* was typical of his ambivalence. He expressed his appreciation 'of this clever little book' that 'he read once again with pleasure' but he found it lacking in rigor and structure.[97] For his part, Huizinga seemed to have been hurt by Febvre's cold reception of his two proposed essays on 'capitalism' and on 'the play element of culture', and by the editor's plea for other subjects 'more fitted' to the *Annales*. After the French had treated him quite badly by delaying the translation of *Herfsttij*, Huizinga was not eager to be subjected to any more bad experiences. Having grasped Bloch's negative feelings and Febvre reservations, Huizinga never again suggested contributions he might make to the *Annales*.[98]

In the end, Febvre decided to pay a final homage to Huizinga – 'this sage' ('ce sage') – in his foreword to *Erasmus*, entitled 'l'Érasme d'Huizinga'. Febvre's tone was more supportive, perhaps because of Huizinga's courageous stance during World War II:

> A scholar such as Huizinga is dead, proclaiming with his attitude his faith, his invincible faith, in the spiritual values that the Beast, stronger than ever, strongly strove to wipe out this time.[99]

Voogd concludes by pointing out that 'this book is not only the work of a historian, but that of a philosopher of culture' ('ce livre n'est justement pas celui d'un historien mais celui d'un philosophe de la culture').

96 Huizinga, *In de schaduwen van morgen* (1935). It was translated by his son Jacob Herman Huizinga, with the title *In the Shadow of Tomorrow*.

97 'This very clever little book. I read it again with great pleasure. [...] A tendency to put everything in everything [...] we swim with awe in this ocean. [...] We lose our footing, but how could we find it again in an ocean? ('Ce petit livre ingénieux. Je l'ai relu avec plaisir. [...] Une tendance à mettre tout dans tout' [...] nous nageons avec effroi dans cet ocean. [...] Nous perdons pied, – et comment le reprendre dans un ocean?') (Febvre, 'Un moment avec Huizinga', p. 493).

98 As De Voogd, *Le miroir de la France*, points out, we also perceive in Huizinga's response a real ambivalence, as he is not willing to take the chance that Febvre handed to him.

99 Febvre, 'L'Érasme d'Huizinga', pp. 7-16; Braudel, *On History*, pp. 207-208.

Febvre's quite enthusiastic introduction to the French translation of Huizinga's *Erasmus* can be explained, however, not so much by his respect for Huizinga's politics but by the work's status as a *total history project*: 'However, the originality, the worth, the merit of Huizinga's Erasmus is to be, to wish to be, a total Erasmus. […] Huge innovation, although it hardly appears so.'[100]

The review was a way for Febvre to revise his appreciation of Huizinga's corpus, including *Herfsttij* about which he had once been much more skeptical:

> An outstanding power of evocation and of a singular intelligence. The strength of this historian, which has endowed the historical literature with an original and innovative book, when he wrote his *Autumn of the Middle Ages*. And he did it again, before dying, when he wrote his *Erasmus*.[101]

4 Huizinga's Late and Ambivalent Recognition as One of the Pioneers of the *nouvelle histoire*

After the deaths of Febvre and Bloch, the controversy about Huizinga continued among the next generation of the histoire des *Annales*, some (such as Fernand Braudel), repeating many of the earlier reservations, and others (such as Philippe Ariès), expressing more support for Huizinga. In 1978, however, the *nouvelle histoire* establishment finally hailed him as one of the field's pioneers.[102] In *On History*, Braudel's judgment about *Herfsttij* is fundamentally critical. He begins by commenting approvingly on Henri Brunschwig's argument concerning the origins of German romanticism, that 'social structures and economic relations' were fundamental to the 'reversal of values', of the German *Aufklärung*.[103] Then Braudel, comparing

100 Febvre, 'L'Érasme d'Huizinga', pp. 14, resp. 8, 9: 'Un savant comme Huizinga est mort, en proclamant par toute son attitude sa foi, son invincible foi dans les valeurs spirituelles que la Bête, plus forte que jamais, entendait bien cette fois anéantir'; 'Or l'originalité, la valeur, le mérite de l'Érasme d'Huizinga, c'est d'être, de vouloir être un Érasme total […]. Grande nouveauté, bien qu'il n'y semble guère.'

101 Febvre, 'L'Érasme d'Huizinga', p. 8: 'Une force d'évocation et d'intelligence singulière. La force même de cet historien qui a doté la literature historique universelle d'un grand livre original et neuf, le jour où il écrivit son *Automne du Moyen Age*. Et qui a récidivé, avant de mourir, le jour où il écrivit son *Érasme*.'

102 Although, as Walter Simons writes, 'Braudel […] acknowledged Huizinga's masterpiece as one that in many ways anticipated the goals of the *Annales*' ('The *Annales* and Medieval Studies in the Low Countries', p. 109).

103 'The crucial thing is to try and discern, through all the social structures and economic relations, just what is fundamentally associated with this reversal of values' (of German society

Brunschwig's study to Huizinga's, immediately criticizes *Herfsttij* (in the manner of Marc Bloch), for its own lack of social and economic analysis:

> This is not precisely what was done, in a famous and assuredly fine book by Huizinga, in his study of the 'autumn' of the western Middle Ages, an 'agony of civilisation', as he was to call it.[104]

Of course, Braudel not only totally rejects this notion of agony but also details his criticism:

> But what I would most reproach Huizinga with is having kept his gaze fixed so obstinately high that he considered only the very top of the pyre. What a pity it is that he did not have at his disposal those classic demographic and economic studies today on the major decline in the West in the fifteenth century: it would have given his book the solid foundation it needed. For there is hardly need to repeat that great sentiments, whether the highest or the lowest, do not live their lives independently.[105]

The third generation of the *Annales* at the end of the 1970s marked a turning point in attitudes toward Huizinga. Jacques Le Goff, in particular, thought highly of Huizinga's *Herfsttij*. In an interview with Claude Mettra for the foreword to the 1977 edition of *Herfsttij*, published with the revised title *L'automne du Moyen Âge*, Le Goff singled out Huizinga as the pioneer of his own periodization of 'the long Middle Ages' that deemed the end of the Ancien Régime as the real break with the past and not the Renaissance.[106] For Le Goff, this insight was *Herfsttij*'s key contribution:

> I gather that if we had asked Huizinga what the fundamental topic of his book was, he would have spoken first of the intimate imbrication of the Middle Ages with what we call the Renaissance.[107]

that preferred intuition and romanticism to the *Aufklärung*).

104 Braudel, *On History*, pp. 207-208.

105 Ibid.

106 'Je crois que si l'on avait demandé à Huizinga quel était le sujet fondamental de son livre, il aurait parlé d'abord de l'imbrication intime du Moyen-Age et de ce que nous appelons la Renaissance' (Mettra, 'Entretien de Claude Mettra avec Jacques Le Goff', p. vii). See also Peters and Simon, 'The New Huizinga', p. 604.

107 Ibid.

In this 1977 interview, Jacques Le Goff also underscored Huizinga's fundamental contribution to the *nouvelle histoire*. According to him, by choosing expression of sensibilities as an object of research, and subjects such as dreams and images, Huizinga anticipated several new 'territories of the historian'.[108]

Almost simultaneously, in 1978, Philippe Ariès revealed his debt to the Dutch historian:

> My ongoing research [...] led me to read [...] *The Waning of the Middle Ages* again, and I was surprised by its wonderful freshness.[109]

He recognized that his work on death owed much to Huizinga: 'It is one of these illusions that I wish to study here, by remaining faithful to Huizinga's spirit, even if I deviate a little from his intention, and in homage to his memory'.[110] And he declared emphatically that Huizinga must be considered a founder of the *histoire des mentalités*, since his *Herfsttij* was driven by attention to culture as a historical force. For Huizinga, the history of culture has just as much to do with dreams of beauty and illusions of a noble life, as with population figures and statistics.

Ariès quoted Huizinga's declaration that 'if the history of the Middle Ages is based on political and economic documents only, it will reach erroneous conclusions'.[111] When the Dutch historian discussed how ideals can endure, he actually came close to the position Braudel would adopt, that mentalities are prisoners of the *longue durée*:

108 Le Goff declares that: 'It is a well known fact that we must seek the significance of a society in its system of representation and in the role played by this system in the social structures and in "reality"'. 'Le fait est qu'il faut aller chercher le sens d'une société dans son système de représentation et dans la place qu'occupe ce système dans les structures sociales et dans "la réalité"' (Mettra, 'Entretien de Claude Mettra avec Jacques Le Goff', p. xi). See also Berlioz, 'L'automne du Moyen Age de Johan Huizinga', p. 92.

109 Ariès, 'Huizinga et les thèmes macabres', p. 104: 'Des recherches en cours [...] m'ont amené à relire [...] le *Déclin du Moyen Age*, et j'ai été surpris par sa merveilleuse fraîcheur.'

110 Ibid., p. 104-105: 'Phrase qu'on dirait d'aujourd'hui, qui revendique le droit d'écrire l'histoire des illusions, des choses inaperçues, imaginaires: l'histoire dite aujourd'hui des mentalités. C'est l'une de ces 'illusions' que je voudrais étudier ici, en restant fidèle à l'esprit d'Huizinga, même quand je m'écarte un peu de sa lettre, et en hommage à sa mémoire.'

111 Ibid., p. 104.

> But it could well be that the knightly ideal, artificial and worn-out as it might have been, still continued to exert a stronger influence on the political history of the late Middle Ages than is usually imagined.[112]

Ariès commented enthusiastically:

> A sentence that could have been written today, one that claims the right to write the history of illusions, of things unremarked upon and imaginary: the history called today of the *mentalités*.[113]

In his chapter on the birth and evolution of the *histoire des mentalités*, Ariès cited two kinds of pioneers of 'this other kind of history'[114]: a group of interdisciplinary researchers constituted by historians like Marc Bloch, Lucien Febvre, and Henry Pirenne; geographers like Albert Demangeon, and sociologists such as Lucien Lévy-Brühl and Maurice Halbwachs. But Ariès also acknowledged the impact of some independent personalities: Johan Huizinga, but also Norbert Elias and Mario Praz.[115] Although Ariès' definition of the legacy of these scholars is minimalist, he quotes them in his historiographic study because, according to him, they added new fields of investigation to those belonging to the traditional territory of the historian.[116] Moreover, Ariès stressed as well the continuity of Huizinga's influence on the *histoire des mentalités*, finding a strong parallel between Jacques Le Goff and his plea to study 'the medieval imagination',[117] and Huizinga, for whom 'the field of the imaginary, of feeling, of play, of gift, is as important as the economic terrain'.[118] The fact that Ariès himself was a

112 Ibid., p. 104

113 Ibid., pp. 104-105.

114 Ariès, 'Naissance et développement', p. 403.

115 Ariès, 'Huizinga et les thèmes macabres', p. 104: 'History of mentalities founded by Huizinga, Febvre, Bloch to which I will add M. Praz' ('L'histoire des mentalités fondée justement par Huizinga, Febvre, Bloch, auquel j'ajouterai M. Praz).

116 Ariès, 'Naissance et développement', p. 404: 'That of conscious and voluntary activities, directed toward political decisions, the evolution of ideas, the behavior of men and the course of events' ('Celui des activités conscientes, volontaires, orientées vers la décision politique, la propagation des idées, la conduite des hommes et des événements').

117 Le Goff, *The Medieval Imagination*.

118 'Le domaine de l'imaginaire, du sentiment, du jeu, de la gratuité est aussi important que celui de l'économie.' Ariès quotes the two key sentences of *Herfsttij* (still entitled '*Déclin*'): 'History must deal with dreams of beauty and with literary illusions as well as with demographic figures and taxes' ('L'histoire de la civilisation doit s'occuper aussi bien des rêves de beauté et de l'illusion romanesque que des chiffres de la population et des impôts'); and: 'The very illusion that contemporaries lived in has the value of truth' ('L'illusion même dans laquelle ont vécu les

loner and quite marginal in the Annales school, certainly influenced his warm appraisal of Huizinga, whom he cheerfully labeled the 'illustrious Huizinga'.

Huizinga's recognition as a forerunner of the Annales school was at last 'officially' acknowledged by the chief editors of *La nouvelle histoire*, Jacques Le Goff, Roger Chartier, and Jacques Revel, who decided to include Johan Huizinga in the few biographical citations contained in this work, acknowledging his link with the Annales. As Le Goff wrote, '[t]here are few biographical articles and they concern only the historians or scholars particularly significant for the *nouvelle histoire*'.[119] In fact, Huizinga appears on a shortlist of only four founding fathers of the *nouvelle histoire*, along with Bloch, Febvre, and Pirenne, a significant honor and a final and official consecration.

In France, the role of Johan Huizinga as a pioneer of the *nouvelle histoire* was finally confirmed, even if there lingered mixed assessments of his scholarly legacy. In this chapter, I have already pointed out that Burguière paid scant attention to Huizinga in his study of the Annales school. Here I want to add that he also did not seem to be very appreciative of Huizinga's work. However, he pointed out that Huizinga *could* have had some influence on Febvre:

> But we also discern in Febvre's thinking a *fin de siècle* view of the rise of rational behaviours, a view that is clearly less optimistic and that he may have owed to his familiarity with the work of Johan Huizinga. That view conveyed by Freudianism and by German critical sociology, the latter of which inspired Huizinga, considered the rise of rationality within the psychic economy of the individual as a process at once constructive and repressive.[120]

Burguière's judgment of Huizinga's legacy seems quite negative, given that when he studied the subject of death in the *Annales*'s historiography and considered the works of scholars like Alberto Tenenti and Elisabeth

contemporains a la valeur d'une vérité'). For Ariès the difference lies in the fact that the two founders of the *Annales* succeeded in founding a new historical school, whereas the others failed. Ariès, 'Naissance et développement', p. 403.

119 'Les articles biographiques sont peu nombreux et n'ont retenu que les historiens ou savants particulièrement significatifs pour l'histoire nouvelle.' 'The fathers of the *histoire nouvelle*: the historians Marc Bloch, Lucien Febvre, Henri Pirenne, Johan Huizinga' ('Les pères de l'histoire nouvelle: les historiens Marc Bloch, Lucien Febvre, Henri Pirenne, Johan Huizinga'). Le Goff, 'Une science en marche, une science dans l'enfance', p. 32.

120 Burguière, *The Annales School*, p. 60.

Carpentier, he touted the superiority of their approach by virtue of their divergence from Huizinga's pessimistic vision in *Herfsttij*:

> These studies found in the terrible outbreak of epidemics the material roots for the death torments that inspired the macabre iconography of what Huizinga called – in an expression tinged by a rather too *fin de siècle* pathos – the autumn of the Middle Ages.[121]

Even Le Goff's judgments of Huizinga were still very much entangled with some of the prejudices and misunderstanding of his predecessors. We see this, for example, when Le Goff wrongly states that the book's new title better captured Huizinga's intentions:

> *Herfsttij* [...] translated into French in 1932 under the inaccurate title *The Waning of the Middle Ages*, and republished in 1977 under the correct title *The Autumn of the Middle Ages*. [...]

Or when he emphasized that 'the French translation of the book is a betrayal. [...] Huizinga's comprehensive conception of history is expressed through the word 'autumn'.'[122]

In reality we now know perfectly well that Huizinga preferred the title *The Waning of the Middle Ages* and thought that it was more true to the subject of his book. Since Huizinga followed closely the French translation of *Herfsttij*, he approved of the choice of 'waning' ('déclin'). He wrote to Gabriel Hanotaux about this matter:

> I entitled it *Autumn of the Middle Ages* but I quite regret this. This title seems too precious and too heavy to me. It could perhaps be named 'The

121 Ibid., p. 165. Burguière's French perspective, and his dismissal of Huizinga's influence is confirmed by De Voogd, *Le miroir de la France*, p. 10: 'He never assimilates the central concern of Huizinga's work, otherwise very pertinent and enlightening: the central character of the *mentalité* concept in the *histoire longue* of the *Annales*' ('Il n'intègre jamais l'oeuvre de Huizinga dans sa problématique centrale, d'ailleurs fort pertinente et éclairante: le caractère central du concept de mentalité dans l'histoire longue des *Annales*').

122 '*Herfsttij* [...] traduit en français en 1932 sous le titre infidèle de "*Le déclin du Moyen-Age*" republié en 1977 sous le titre exact de *l'Automne du Moyen Age*. [...] La traduction française du livre est une trahison. [...] Toute la conception que J. Huizinga a de l'histoire s'exprime à travers le mot automne' (Mettra, 'Entretien de Claude Mettra avec Jacques Le Goff', p. i). Of course, Le Goff points out the many elements that link *Herfsttij* to the *histoire des mentalités*, not without reason. But as we saw already, these common elements do not erase the many differences between Huizinga's understanding of historical research and that of the *histoire des mentalités*.

> French Middle Ages at its Waning' or 'The Ending of the Middle Ages' with a subtitle.[123]

In the final analysis, Le Goff ultimately adopted the same French scholarly caution about Huizinga, as made clear in his 1977 interview:

> Thus let us read Huizinga again in a contemporary perspective. By remembering that yesterday, he tore apart the veil of an arrogantly awkward history, and that for us, if he can sometimes be a master of error because of his inaccuracy, his aesthetism and his dilettantism, he is nevertheless unlocking access to the unchartered waters of History.[124]

In spite of these harsh criticisms, Le Goff proclaimed Huizinga as a pioneer of the history of the body, and of all its physiological aspects – from the study of illnesses to the different aspects of the senses.[125]

Jacques Berlioz, a close collaborator of Jacques le Goff and Jean-Claude Schmitt in the Groupe d'Anthropologie Historique de l'Occident médiéval (GAHOM), also wrote clearly and forcefully that *Herfsttij is* 'a visionary book, still essential [...] a brilliant work'. He adds:

> What a magnitude in his approach! What brilliant intuitions! Huizinga opens the world of princely courts, as well as daily life, the environment of medieval men, the history of sensibility, of taste, colors, senses, and sexuality.[126]

123 'Je l'ai nommé *Automne du Moyen Age* mais je m'en repens un peu. Ce titre me semble trop précieux et trop lourd. Peut-être qu'il vaudrait mieux le nommer simplement *Le Moyen Age français à son déclin* ou bien *Moyen Âge finissant* avec un sous-titre.' Cited by De Voogd, *Le miroir de la France*: read about that issue in his chapter entitled 'Tradutore, traditore', in particular pp. 55-57.

124 'Relisons donc Huizinga dans une perspective d'aujourd'hui. En nous rappelant que hier, il déchire le voile d'une histoire orgueilleusement impossible, et que pour nous, s'il peut être par ses à peu-près, son esthétisme, son dilettantisme un maître d'erreur, il est encore un ouvreur des portes qui mènent à l'histoire à faire' (Mettra, 'Entretien de Claude Mettra avec Jacques Le Goff', p. xvi).

125 His own research, with Jean-Louis Biraben, on the first Justinian plague is a good example of this trend, as well as Jean-Claude Schmitt's seminal research on gestures, and his recent study of medieval rhythms. Le Goff and Biraben, 'La peste dans le Haut Moyen Age'.

126 'Un livre visionnaire, aujourd'hui encore indispensable [...] un brillant ouvrage. [...] Que d'ampleur dans la démarche! Que d'intuitions géniales! Huizinga ouvre au monde des cours princières, comme au quotidien et à l'environnement des hommes du Moyen-Age, à l'histoire des sensibilités, des goûts, des couleurs, des sens et de la sexualité' (Berlioz, 'L'automne du Moyen Age de Johan Huizinga').

True enough, Huizinga did, to paraphrase Le Goff, open many doors, including the analysis of the systems of representations and their place in reality,[127] and the centrality of art in society. He further inspired many *Annalistes*, such as Christiane Klapisch-Zuber,[128] with her repeated capital use of iconographic sources, Michel Pastoureau, who analyzes colors and heraldry with anthropological tools,[129] Jérôme Baschet and Jean-Claude Bonne, who emphasize the relevance of artistic sources in historical scholarship,[130] and Jean-Claude Schmitt with his breakthrough analysis of 'images' and unparalleled investigations of avant-garde topics such as gestures and rhythms in the Middle Ages, to cite only a very few.[131]

The younger generation of French medievalists still openly recognizes the intellectual debt to *Herfsttij*. For instance, the history of emotions, of which Huizinga was a forerunner,[132] is led today by scholars linked to the EHESS, such as Elisa Brilli, Pierre-Olivier Dietmar, Piroska Nagy,[133] Damien Boquet, and many others.[134]

In conclusion, while there have been divergent viewpoints about the relation between Huizinga's *Herfsttij* and the *nouvelle histoire*, the Dutch historian has attained, in a little less than 60 years, his rightful place in the pantheon of the pioneers of the Annales school.

127 See Mettra, 'Entretien de Claude Mettra avec Jacques Le Goff', p. xi, n. 117.

128 As A.G. Jongkees writes dans 'Une génération d'historiens devant le phénomène bourguignon', p. 220 for Huizinga: 'historical perception is essentially an evocation of images' ('La perception historique est essentiellement une évocation d'images'). Klapisch-Zuber, *Le voleur de paradis*, was brought to the school by Fernand Braudel.

129 Jongkees, 'Une génération d'historiens', p. 220: 'Forms, images, colors: these words come back constantly under Huizinga's pen. He sees the past in forms, and maybe even more in colors. [...] Not only does Huizinga visualize the colors, but he even conceives them' ('Formes, images, couleurs: sous la plume de Huizinga, ces mots reviennent continuellement. Il voit le passé en formes, mais encore plus peut-être, en couleur. [...] Non seulement Huizinga voit les couleurs, mais il les pense aussi'). See inter alia the various works of Pastoureau, mentioned in the bibliography.

130 A good example of their work is Baschet et al., *Les images*.

131 See his most recent book: Schmitt, *Les rythmes au Moyen Age*.

132 Huizinga's contribution to the study of emotions, a hitherto neglected subject, inspired Lucien Febvre in 1941 to call for 'a huge collective survey on the fundamental sentiments of men and of their modalities' ('une vaste enquête collective sur les sentiments fondamentaux des hommes et leurs modalités'). But it took time for this field to take off. See Berlioz, 'L'automne du Moyen Age de Johan Huizinga'.

133 Nagy, *Le don des larmes au Moyen Age*; Nagy and Boquet, *Sensible Moyen Âge*.

134 See note 122 and 124, and, for instance, the articles of J.-Cl. Bonne, E. Brilli and P.-O. Dietmar in *La performance des images*.

About the Author

Myriam Greilsammer is professor at Bar-Ilan University (Israel) and specializes in the anthropological history of the Low Countries (12th-17th c.). Among her books are *Een pand voor het paradijs. Leven en zelfbeeld van Lowijs Porquin, piemontees zakenman in de zestiende-eeuwse Nederlanden* (Lannoo, 1989); *L'envers du tableau. Mariage et maternité en Flandre mediévale* (Armand Colin, 1990); *Le Livre au Roi* (Académie des Inscriptions et Belles-Lettres Institut de France, 1995); *La roue de la fortune. Le destin d'une famille d'usuriers lombards dans les Pays-Bas à l'aube des Temps Modernes* (Presses de l'EHESS, 2009); *L'usurier chrétien, un Juif métaphorique? Histoire de l'exclusion des prêteurs lombards (XIIIe-XVIIe siècle)* (PUR, 2012), and the forthcoming *Compter l'argent conter la vie. Témoignages inédits concernant les ultimes activités des prêteurs lombards dans les Pays-Bas au seizième siècle* (Droz, Travaux d'Humanisme et Renaissance).
myriam.greilsammer@biu.ac.il

Epilogue

Reading Together

Willem Otterspeer

Why would someone want to read *Pride and Prejudice* 40 times? Why are there people who cannot imagine a year well spent without having reread *Effi Briest*, *Die Verwandlung* or *Tonio Kröger*, *Le rideau cramoisi*, *Un coeur simple*, or *La parure?* Or all those thousands of other jewels from the treasure trove called World Literature? Answering this question in her wonderful book *On Rereading*, Patricia Meyer Spacks writes: 'The dynamic tension between stability and change lies at the heart of rereading.' The book we reread is the same yet different from the book we read, the reader, too, is the same yet changed.

In this sense there is hardly a more profitable author and object for this concentrated act of attention than Huizinga. His work not only invites revisiting again and again, recreating the Manderley of our dream, but the core of it is ritual, the idea that repetition is the law of culture, and renewal the task of man. Rereading Huizinga is to take part in that central activity of culture, emulation, imitation, finding oneself by losing oneself, changing while remaining essentially the same.

'In reading a book which is an old favourite of mine', says Spacks, quoting the nineteenth-century essayist William Hazlitt, 'I have not only the pleasure of imagination and of a critical relish of the work, but the pleasures of memory added to it.' Rereading is reading and remembering at the same time, and the two activities 'bind together the different scattered divisions of our personal identity'. The different scattered divisions of our culture as well, Huizinga might have added.

I haven't read *The Waning of the Middle Ages* (I prefer 'waning' over 'autumn' because 'waning' created my first memory) 40 times, but one of the copies I own is a mess of notes, associations, quotations, ideas, hunches. And my copy of the *Verzamelde werken* (the one that will not be bequeathed) has crossed seas and oceans, is tattered and irreparably mine.

Arnade, Peter, Martha Howell, and Anton van der Lem (eds), *Rereading Huizinga: Autumn of the Middle Ages, a Century Later.* Taylor & Francis Group, 2019
DOI: 10.5117/9789462983724_EPILO

I'm not a real 'Huizinga scholar.' That term applies much better to the authors of this magnificent volume. The new perspectives it brings to the subject, the new insights it provides and new incentives it suggests warrant the expectation that it will be a milestone in Huizinga-studies for years to come.

Two earlier publications come to mind in the history of Huizinga's steady growth to world fame. The first was the result from the Huizinga conference Groningen University organized in December 1972, to celebrate his hundredth birthday. With contributions of, among others, Gerhard Oestreich and Philippe Ariès, J.C. Margolin and E.H. Gombrich, H.R. Guggisberg and Ernst Robert Curtius, the main themes of Huizinga's work were firmly set in their European context. Frits Hugenholtz (his student and coeditor of the *Verzamelde werken*) contributed an essay on *The Waning of the Middle Ages*, 'The Fame of a Masterwork'. How much more do we now know about that fame!

The publication of these papers proved an inspiration to Huizinga studies. An even greater inspiration came from the publication, between 1989 and 1991, of Huizinga's letters, in three volumes, and from the dissertations published by their editors, Léon Hanssen, Wessel Krul and Anton van der Lem. These studies have given a real impetus to a modern approach to Huizinga's work. Van der Lem moreover is the doyen of these studies. He not only published the inventory of Huizinga's archive, thereby making it accessible for international research, but he also created at Leiden University's library a veritable Huizinga research center, a one-man enterprise run with proverbial hospitality.

And now we have this volume, which, I hope, will play a comparable role in a more international environment in the future. It approaches both Huizinga's life and his seminal work from many different angles and, in the combination of biography and history, context and analysis, and in the great variety of topics examined, it is, I believe, a veritable Huizinga primer, for those who come to him for the first time and the veteran scholar alike (and aficionados like me in between).

The concentration on *The Waning of the Middle Ages*, published a hundred years ago, is a happy one, because it is not only Huizinga's most important work, but also, because of its literary style and idiosyncratic method, its politically charged topic and its slow reception, the best entry to this most enigmatic of scholars. If I should select one quality that is characteristic of Huizinga's life and work, one that both delayed his reception and captivated his readership, it would be his inscrutability.

Every life and every work of art that emanates from it, is, certainly if seen through romantic eyes, unfathomable, *ineffable* indeed. By his own definition, 'to be classic means still to be read', Huizinga is a classical author and *The Waning of the Middle Ages* is a classical book. But the surprising thing is not that Huizinga is still read, but that he is being read more widely now than ever before (not only the *Waning* but *Homo ludens* as well) and that the Nobel Prize he was denied is compensated amply by the constant attention to and interpretation of his work that many a Nobel laureate lacks.

If Spacks is right, if the dialectic between permanence and change is the gist of rereading, if rereading is a process of heightened attention that 'can intensify and focus questions of value', then *Rereading Huizinga* fulfills its mission brilliantly. As I see it, 'dialectic' is its main occupation, the dialogue within the reader (between her former and actual self), between readers (then and now) and between different interpretations and the limits of interpretation. It is in this collective reengagement that the core business of critique and of culture is performed, that of attaching value.

This volume performs this activity by its wonderful breadth. From the central topic, Burgundian court culture, *Rereading Huizinga* gives a veritable panopticon of the new political, economic and cultural history of the late medieval north, to continue with a range of methodological implications and possibilities, and ending with new views on Huizinga's historiographical legacy. In each contribution the broad view is combined with sense of detail, with a fine attention to the minutiae of historical life.

Every author in this volume seems to write not only about Huizinga, but also in the spirit of Huizinga. The dialectic between large and small (thing and symbol), time and place (reality and dream), description and norm, said and suppressed, the resonance of other books and other writers, elective affinities and concealed aversions, this all makes this volume not only an important contribution to scholarship, but part of a process Huizinga himself could see as a ritual.

Huizinga viewed the discipline of historiography as a veritable form of association. Historical imagination was not the activity of the individual historian; the historical image consisted of 'a certain catholicity of knowledge, a *consensus omnium*'. This consensus embraced the most local researcher to the most general of world historians; it ranged from *microstorie* to global history, from *The Cheese and the Worms* to *Keeping Together in Time*.

The value of an individual's work does not originate from the fact that he or she is gathering material to be used later in more advanced syntheses. In Huizinga's view even the small town erudite, 'by polishing one of thousands of millions of facets', produces 'the historiography of his age.' The researcher of even the most local form of history constitutes with the small group for whom his theme constitutes a living field of inquiry. They form a full-fledged association of scholarship with its own rituals.

That is why the 'mosaic method', which is discussed in this volume, is at the same time a 'mythical method', reminiscent of what Walter Benjamin practiced in his Arcades Project. For Benjamin the historian is first of all a collector, his heart the battleground of two very strong emotions. On the one hand there is the loyalty to the object, the single thing entrusted to his care. On the other hand he cherishes a stubborn (Benjamin even called it subversive) aversion to the typical, the classifiable. The collector destroys the context of the thing to possess it in its individuality, its incomparability.

Likewise, according to Huizinga, the historian is a collector. The historian also lets destruction precede construction. Every person, every event in the historian's story is first taken out of the continuum of history, before being put back in its proper place. Every fact has its own importance, every person his or hers irreducible individuality, every institution its unique identity.

Next comes the 'montage', the construction of the smallest, most finely polished parts into the mosaic. The analysis of the individual moment, according to Benjamin, is the ability to see the crystalline structure of matter. The historian's tools in this analysis are ideas. The more general, the more radical the idea, the better. Ideas are to things what the constellations are to the stars.

Ideas also transform the historical into the present. History is only 'real' when it gains actuality in the present. Certain aspects of an historical phenomenon can only be seen in a certain time. For Robespierre the antiquity of Rome was a past charged with the present. The French Revolution saw itself as a revived Rome. It 'quoted' Rome so to speak. 'Writing history', according to Benjamin, was 'quoting history'.

To illustrate this activity Benjamin gives a fascinating example. He points to actors entering the stage as if in flight. The moment they become visible for the audience they stand still, as if they feel protected by the gaze of the onlooker. It is this safety, this security, this 'arrest' the historian has to give to the events of the past.

Configurations like these are 'dialectical images', according to Benjamin, their content is 'dialectic in standstill' ('Dialektik im Stillstand'). The image is like a flash of lightning, the text we write nothing but the rumbling of the thunder. Historical thinking is like rereading, it is movement and rest at once. It is about a constellation saturated with tension, a process that comes to a standstill with a shock: the crystallization.

And then there is this other 'elective affinity'. Reading the fine essays in this volume I was reminded of the remark made by Edward Said that philology was a question of 'not jumping to conclusions'. Rereading as practiced here is a form of 'Aufmerksamkeit' (Jakobson), concentrated attention indeed in the definition of Spacks, 'slow scholarship' so difficult to pursue in our hurried academy. This reminded me of Milan Kundera's romanesque plea for slowness in *La lenteur* (Slowness). In this wonderful divertimento slowness is transformed from a deadly sin into a real virtue. 'He who watches the windows of the benevolent God does not get bored; he is happy. In our world slowness is changed into doing nothing, which is something completely different: the idler is frustrated, is bored, is constantly looking for the movement he lacks.'

In this novel Kundera answers the question why idleness leads to frustration. It shows that idlers are not satisfied with looking at God's windows, because they want to get into the house. Their senseless activity is the attempt to find the meaning of life, in this case a door that isn't there. How very Huizinga, who sighed, with Dante's 'mild exhortation', 'State contenti umana gente al quia.' Mortals should content themselves with the *that*; the *how* and certainly the *why* were God's business.

In Kundera's novel idleness is a dangerous sin. It is laziness in its most dangerous form, honored by church and society (and university) alike. It is the only deadly sin that is still practiced, adequately disguised as diligence, successfully dressed up as zeal. Idleness in Kundera's version is sin itself.

If we ask ourselves why we are cruel to animals, disloyal to friends, why we betray ourselves, bow to authority, pursue all kinds of fads, the answer is: because we don't pay attention, because we do not take enough time. Now that politics is reduced to economy and economy to shareholder value, technology is mainly efficiency and speed, art reduced to a question of novelty and the university to a business model, now that culture in brief is a short-term thing; we are reigned by the new idleness.

Kundera's *La lenteur* however is not really about sin, it is about happiness. Its action alternates between the present and the eighteenth century. Its frame is the present, incidental occurrences between politicians, intellectuals, academics, a kaleidoscope of sins without punishment: politics as twitter, engagement as flight, love as a form of wrestling.

This unlucky present is the frame of an eighteenth-century tale, called 'Point de lendemain', which means so much as 'not to be continued.' It is the love story of one night, in which a certain Madame de T. succeeds in giving pleasure to her husband, her lover and her false lover, using all the conventionality and ceremoniousness she has in her, including wire-pulling and a little lie now and then.

In it, the past and the present are bound together with the help of tradition, formality and skepsis, by the conviction that life does not have a meaning and doesn't need to have one. It is the quest for meaning that engenders the restlessness that is the root evil of our times, the seriousness that prevents us from playing. That is why, instead of idleness, Kundera advocates slowness. He detects a secret connection between speed and forgetting on the one hand and slowness and remembering on the other.

It is the connection between beauty and form, between art and exercise, happiness and restriction. It causes us to slow down in museums, it gives us pause to reflect, makes us precise readers, even rereaders. It is not a paradise Kundera defines, no timeless salvation. But neither is it sin or guilt. It is happiness 'with a certain melancholy', and I quote the novel again: 'Man, finding himself surrounded by world's miseries, finds out that the only self-evident and true value of pleasure is, however small, what he himself can enjoy: a draught of fresh water, a glance at the sky (at the windows of the benevolent God), a caress.'

Bibliography

'1415-1915: Le Cinquieme centenaire d'Azincourt', *L'illustration*, 27 November 1915, p. 1.

Adorno, Theodor. *Essays on Music*, ed. Richard Leppert, trans. Susan H. Gillespie. (Berkeley: University of California Press), 2002.

Aertsen, Jan A., and Martin Pickavé, eds., *'Herbst des Mittelalters?': Fragen zur Bewertung des 14. und 15. Jahrhunderts* (Berlin: De Gruyter, 2004).

'Agincourt and the Modern Soldier', *London Times*, 25 October 1914, p. 3.

Altdorfer, Albrecht, *Der Triumphzug Kaiser Maximilians I 1516-1518*, ed. by Horst Appuhn (Dortmund: Bibliophilen Taschenbücher, 1979).

Anchor, Robert, 'History and Play: Johan Huizinga and His Critics', *History and Theory* 17:1 (1978), pp. 63-93.

Angenendt, Arnold, *Geschichte der Religiosität im Mittelalter* (Darmstadt: Wissenschaftliche Buchgesellschaft, 1997).

Anglo, Sydney, *The Great Tournament Roll of Westminster* (Oxford: Clarendon, 1968).

Anglo, Sydney, *Spectacle, Pageantry and Early Tudor Politics* (Oxford: Clarendon, 1969).

Anheim, Étienne, 'Le Moyen-Age, que d'émotions', *Le monde des livres*, 25 December 2015.

Annales Egmundani, ed. by B.J.L. de Geer van Jutfaas (Utrecht: Werken uitgegeven door het Historisch Genootschap, 1863).

Aquinas, Thomas, *Summa Theologica*, trans. by Fathers of the English Dominican Province (New York: Benziger Brothers, 1947).

Ariès, Philippe, *Essais sur l'histoire de la mort en Occident du Moyen Age à nos jours* (Paris: Seuil, 1975).

Ariès, Philippe, 'Huizinga et les thèmes macabres', in *Bijdragen en Mededelingen betreffende de Geschiedenis der Nederlanden* 99 (1973), pp. 104-115; also published, with the same pagination, in *Johan Huizinga 1872-1972*, ed. by W.R.H. Koops et al.

Ariès, Philippe, *Images de l'homme devant la mort* (Paris: Seuil, 1983), trans. by Janet Lloyd as *Images of Man and Death* (Cambridge, MA: Harvard University Press, 1985).

Ariès, Philippe, *L'enfant et la vie familiale sous l'Ancien Régime* (Paris: Plon, 1960; Paris: Le Seuil, 1973), trans. by Robert Baldick as *Centuries of Childhood: A Social History of Family Life* (New York: Knopf, 1962).

Ariès, Philippe, *L'homme devant la mort* (Paris: Seuil, 1977), trans. by Helen Weaver as *The Hour of Our Death* (New York: Knopf, 1981).

Ariès, Philippe, 'Naissance et développement de l'histoire des mentalités. Les pionniers d'une autre histoire', in *La nouvelle histoire*, ed. by Jacques Le Goff et al., pp. 402-423.

Aristotle, *Nichomachean Ethics*, trans. by H. Rackham (Cambridge, MA: Harvard University Press, 1934).

Arnade, Peter, 'Crowds, Banners and the Marketplace: Symbols of Defiance and Defeat during the Ghent War of 1452-1453', *Journal of Medieval and Renaissance Studies* 24 (1994), pp. 471-497.

Arnade, Peter, *Realms of Ritual: Burgundian Ceremony and Civic Life in Late Medieval Ghent* (Ithaca: Cornell University Press, 1996).

Arnade, Peter, 'Secular Charisma, Sacred Power: Rites of Rebellion in the Ghent Entry of 1467', *Handelingen der Maatschappij voor Geschiedenis en Oudheidkunde te Gent* 45 (1991), pp. 69-94.

Arnold, John H., *Belief and Unbelief in Medieval Europe* (London: Hodder Arnold, 2005).

Aston, Margaret, 'Huizinga's Harvest: England and *The Waning of the Middle Ages*', *Medievalia et Humanistica*, n.s. 9 (1979), pp. 1-24.

Aubert, Eduardo Henrik, 'A historia em trajes de brocade: forma, tempo e processo em Johan Huizinga e Herbert Grundmann', *Revista Signum* 12 (2012), pp. 1-37.

Aurell, Jaume, 'Introduction: Medievalism and Medievalists in the Twentieth Century', in *Rewriting the Middle Ages in the Twentieth Century*, ed. by Jaume Aurell and Francisco Crosas (Turnhout: Brepols, 2005), pp. 9-23.

Avril, François, *Jean Fouquet: Peintre et enlumineur du XVe siècle* (Paris: Bibliothèque nationale de France, 2003).

Bailey, Michael D., 'A Late-Medieval Crisis of Superstition?' *Speculum: A Journal of Medieval Studies* 84 (2009), pp. 633-661.

Bakker, Boudewijn, 'Conquering the Horizon: The Limbourg Brothers and the Painting Landscape', in *The Limbourg Brothers: Nijmegen Masters at the French Court*, ed. by Rob Dückers and Pieter Roelofs, trans. by Ted Alkins, Peter Mason, and Yvette Rosenberg (Nijmegen: Ludion, 2005), pp. 190-207.

Balzac, Honoré de, *Lettres à l'étrangère*, 2 vols. (Paris: Calmann-Lévy, 1899).

Baschet, Jérôme, Jean-Claude Bonne, and Pierre-Olivier Dittmar, *Le monde roman: par delà le bien et le mal: pour une iconographie du lieu sacré* (Paris: Arkhé, 2012).

Baschet, Jérôme, Pierre-Olivier Dittmar, and Jean-Claude Schmitt, eds., *Les images dans l'Occident médiéval* (Turnhout: Brepols, 2015).

Bateman, Chris, 'Implicit Game Aesthetics', *Games and Culture* 20 (2014), pp. 1-23.

Baumstark, Reinhold, ed., *Das Goldene Rössl: ein Meisterwerk der Pariser Hofkunst um 1400* (Munich: Hirmer, 1995).

Beaufort-Spontin, Christian, and Matthias Pfaffenbichler, *Meisterwerke der Hof-, Jagd- und Rüstkammer* (Vienna: Kunsthistorisches Museum, 2005).

Beenken, Hermann, *Hubert und Jan van Eyck* (Munich: F. Bruckmann, 1941).

Beiser, Frederick C. *The German Historicist Tradition* (Oxford: Oxford University Press, 2011).

Bell, Catherine M., *Ritual: Perspectives and Dimensions* (Oxford: Oxford University Press, 1997).

Belozerskaya, Marina, *Luxury Arts of the Renaissance* (London: Thames and Hudson, 2005).

Belozerskaya, Marina, *Rethinking the Renaissance: Burgundian Arts across Europe* (Cambridge: Cambridge University Press, 2002).

Belting, Hans, *Likeness and Presence: A History of the Image before the Era of Art* (Chicago: University of Chicago Press, 1994).

Bergsma, Wiebe, *Johan Huizinga en de culturele antropologie: vagabonderende beschouwingen naar aanleiding van het werk van Johan Huizinga* (Rijksuniversiteit Groningen: Instituut voor Culturele Antropologie, 1981).

Berlioz, Jacques, 'L'automne du Moyen Age de Johan Huizinga', *L'histoire* 251 (February 2001), pp. 92-93.

Bernard, G.W., *The Late Medieval English Church: Vitality and Vulnerability before the Break with Rome* (New Haven: Yale University Press, 2012).

Berr, Henri, 'Au bout de trente ans. La revue *Organe du Centre*', *Revue de Synthèse Historique* 50 (1930), pp. 5-27.

Biddick, Kathleen, *The Shock of Medievalism* (Durham: Duke University Press, 1998).

Bihl, Laurent, 'Le bombardement de la cathédrale de Reims et son traitement médiatique', *14-18: Mission Centenaire*, 6 May 2014, http://centenaire.org/fr/espace-scientifique/societe/le-bombardement-de-la-cathedrale-de-reims-et-son-traitement-mediatique.

Blair, Ann M., *Too Much to Know: Managing Scholarly Information Before the Modern Age* (New Haven: Yale University Press, 2010).

Blanton, C.D., *Epic Negation: The Dialectical Poetics of Late Modernism* (Oxford: Oxford University Press, 2015).

Bloch, Marc, *Apologie pour l'histoire ou métier d'historien* (Paris: Armand Colin, 1949).

Bloch, Marc, 'Compte-rendu de "J. Huizinga, Herbst des Mittelalters"', *Bulletin de la Faculté des Lettres de Strasbourg* CXXIX (1928), pp. 33-35.

Bloch, Marc, *Écrire* La société féodale. *Lettres de Marc Bloch à Henri Berr, 1924-1943*, ed. by Jacqueline Pluet-Despatin (Paris: Institut mémoires de l'édition contemporaine, 1992).

Bloch, Marc, *Esquisse d'une histoire monétaire de l'Europe* (Paris: A. Colin, 1954).

Bloch, Marc, 'Féodalité et vassalité japonaise', *Annales d'histoire économique et sociale* 5 (1933), pp. 596-598.

Bloch, Marc, *La société féodale. La formation des liens de dépendance* (Paris: A. Michel, 1939), trans. by L.A. Manyon as *Feudal Society* (Chicago: University of Chicago Press, 1961).

Bloch, Marc, 'Les féodalités, une enquête comparative', *Annales d'histoire économique et sociale* 8 (1936), pp. 589-595.

Bloch, Marc, *Les rois thaumaturges. Étude sur le caractère surnaturel attribué à la puissance royale particulièrement en France et en Angleterre* (Paris and Strasbourg: Librairie Ista, 1924).

Bloch, Marc, *L'étrange défaite* (Paris: A. Michel, 1957).

Bloch, Marc, Lucien Febvre et les Annales d'Histoire économique et sociale, Correspondance, édition établie, présentée et annotée par Bertrand Müller, 3 vols. (Paris: Fayard, 1994-2003).

Bloch, Marc, 'Projet d'enseignement au Collège de France, 1929', Archives du Collège de France.

Bloch, Marc, Review of Charles Blondel, *Introduction à la psychologie collective*, *Revue Historique* 54:160 (1929), pp. 398-399.

Bloch, Marc, *Souvenirs de guerre* (Paris: A. Colin, 1969).

Blockmans, Wim, 'Citizens and Their Rulers', in *Empowering Interactions*, ed. by Wim Blockmans, André Holenstein, and Jon Mathieu, pp. 281-291.

Blockmans, Wim, André Holenstein, and Jon Mathieu, eds., *Empowering Interactions: Political Cultures and the Emergence of the State in Europe, 1300-1900* (Farnham: Ashgate, 2009).

Blockmans, Wim, and Walter Prevenier, *The Burgundian Netherlands* (Cambridge: Cambridge University Press, 1986).

Blockmans, Wim, and Walter Prevenier, *The Promised Lands: The Low Countries under Burgundian Rule, 1369-1530* (Philadelphia: University of Pennsylvania Press, 1999).

Blondeau, Chrystèle, 'A Very Burgundian Hero: The Figure of Alexander the Great under the Rule of Philip the Good', in *Flemish Manuscript Painting in Context: Recent Research*, ed. by Elizabeth Morrison, Thomas Kren, and J. Paul (Los Angeles: J. Paul Getty Museum, 2006).

Blum, Shirley Neilsen, *The New Art of the Fifteenth Century: Faith and Art in Florence and the Netherlands* (New York: Abbeville Press, 2015).

Bogaers, Llewellyn, *Aards, betrokken, en zelfbewust: de verwevenheid van cultuur en religie in katholiek Utrecht, 1300-1600* (Utrecht: Levend Verleden, 2008).

Bonomo, Giuseppe, *Caccia alle streghe: La credenza nelle streghe dal secolo XIII al XIX con particolare referimento all'Italia* (Palermo: Palumbo, 1959).

Boone, Marc, '*Armes, coursses, assemblees et commocions*: les gens de métiers et l'usage de la violence dans la société urbaine flamande à la fin du Moyen Âge', *Revue du Nord* 87 (2005), pp. 7-33.

Boone, Marc, 'Centre et périphéries: les facteurs de croissance économique au Moyen Âge', in *La crescita economica dell'Occidente medievale, un tema storico non encora esaurito. Venticinquesimo convegno internazionale di studi, Pistoia 14-17 maggio 2015*, ed. by Paolo Nanni (Rome: Viella, 2017), pp. 363-381.

Boone, Marc, 'Destroying and Reconstructing the City: The Inculcation and Arrogation of Princely Power in the Burgundian-Hapsburg Netherlands (14th-16th Centuries)', in *The Propagation of Power in the Medieval West*, ed. by Martin Gosman, Arie J. Vanderjagt, and Jan R. Veenstra (Groningen: Egbert Forsten, 1997), pp. 1-33.

Boone, Marc, 'The Dukes of Burgundy and the Dream of Sovereignty', in *The Heritage of Charlemagne, 814-2014*, ed. by Dirk Callebaut and Horst van Cuyck (Ghent: Provinciebestuur Oost-Vlaanderen, 2015), pp. 337-351.

Boone, Marc, '"L'automne du Moyen Age": Johan Huizinga et Henri Pirenne ou "plusieurs vérités pour la même chose"', in *Autour du XVe siècle. Journées d'étude en l'honneur d'Alberto Varvaro. Communications présentées au Symposium de clôture de la chaire Francqui au titre étranger* (*Liège, 10-11 mai 2004*), ed. by Paola Moreno and Giovanni Palumbo (Geneva: Droz, 2008), pp. 27-51; reproduced in Marc Boone, *À la recherche d'une modernité civique: la société urbaine des anciens Pays-Bas au bas Moyen Âge* (Brussels: Éditions de l'Université de Bruxelles, 2010), pp. 13-29.

Boone, Marc, 'L'état bourguignon, un état inventeur ou les limites de l'invention', in *La cour de Bourgogne et l'Europe*, ed. by Werner Paravicini et al., pp. 133-156.

Boone, Marc, 'Un grand commis de l'État burgundo-habsbourgeois face à la mort: le testament et la sépulture de Pierre Lanchals', in *Miscellanea in memoriam Pierre Cockshaw (1938-2008). Aspects de la vie culturelle dans les Pays-Bas Méridionaux* (*XIVe-XVIIIe siècle*), ed. by Frank Daelemans and Ann Kelders (Brussels: Archives et Bibliothèques de Belgique, 2009), pp. 63-88.

Boone, Marc, and Sarah Keymeulen, '"Personne ne songe à l'Europe, sauf quelques utopistes sans voix et sans force": Henri Pirenne (1862-1935) et l'histoire de l'Europe', in *Historiens d'Europe, historiens de l'Europe. Actes du colloque de Firenze 2016*, ed. by Denis Crouzet (Seyssel: Champ Vallon, 2017), pp. 209-226.

Boquet, Damien, and Piroska Nagy, *Sensible Moyen Âge: une histoire des émotions dans l'Occident médiéval* (Paris: Seuil, 2015).

Bossy, John, *Christianity in the West, 1400-1700* (Oxford: Oxford University Press, 1985).

Bossy, John, 'The Mass as a Social Institution 1200-1700', *Past and Present* 100 (1983), pp. 29-61.

Bourdieu, Pierre, *Distinction: A Social Critique of the Judgement of Taste*, trans. by R. Nice (Cambridge, MA: Harvard University Press, 1984).

Bouwsma, William J., '*The Waning of the Middle Ages* by Johan Huizinga', *Speculum* 103:1 (Winter 1974), pp. 35-43.

Bouwsma, William J., 'The *Waning of the Middle Ages* Revisited', in *A Usable Past: Essays in European Cultural History*, ed. by William Bouwsma (Berkeley: University of California Press, 1990), pp. 325-335.

Bouxin, Marc, 'Le martyre de la cathédrale: la riposte de la satire', in *Mythes et réalités de la cathédrale de Reims de 1825 à 1975*, ed. by Marc Bouxin and Sylvie Balcon, pp. 70-82.

Bouxin, Marc, and Sylvie Balcon, eds., *Mythes et réalités de la cathédrale de Reims de 1825 à 1975*, ed. by (Paris [Reims]: Ville de Reims, 2001).

Breisach, Ernst, *Historiography: ancient, medieval, & modern* (Chicago: University of Chicago Press, 1983).

Bozzolo, Carla, and Ezio Ornato, 'Les lectures des français aux 14e et 15e siècles: une approche quantitative', in *Ensi firent li ancessor. Mélanges de philologie médiévale offerts à Marc-René Jung*, ed. by Luciano Rossi, 2 vols. (Turin: Orso, 1996), vol. 2, pp. 713-762.

Braet, Herman, and Werner Verbeke, eds., *Death in the Middle Ages* (Louvain: Louvain University Press, 1983).

Brand, Hanno, 'Floris en Jan van Boschhuijsen: Leidse edelen aan het Beierse en Bourgondische hof', *Leidschrift*, 15 (2000), pp. 64-99.

Braudel, Fernand, *On History*, trans. by Sarah Matthews (Chicago: University of Chicago Press, 1982).

Bredero, Adriaan, *De ontkerstening der middeleeuwen. Een terugblik op de geschiedenis van twaalf eeuwen christendom* (Baarn: Agora, 2000).

Bréville, Benoît, 'Émotions médiévales', *Le monde diplomatique*, April 2016, p. 25.

Brine, Douglas, *Pious Memories: The Wall-Mounted Memorial in the Burgundian Netherlands* (Leiden: Brill, 2015).

Brown, Andrew, *Civic Ceremony and Religion in Medieval Bruges c. 1300-1520* (Cambridge: Cambridge University Press, 2011).

Brown, Andrew, and Graeme Small, *Court and Civic Society in the Burgundian Low Countries c. 1420-1530* (Manchester: Manchester University Press, 2007).

Brown, Andrew, and Hendrik Callewier, 'Religious Practice c. 1220-1500', in *Medieval Bruges, c. 850-1550*, ed. by Andrew Brown and Jan Dumolyn (Cambridge: Cambridge University Press, 2018), pp. 329-388.

Brown, D. Catherine, *Pastor and Laity in the Theology of Jean Gerson* (Cambridge: Cambridge University Press, 1987).

Brown, Howard Mayer, *Music in the Renaissance* (Englewood Cliffs: Prentice-Hall, 1976).

Buc, Philippe, *The Danger of Ritual: Between Early Medieval Texts and Social Scientific Theory* (Princeton: Princeton University Press, 2001).

Buettner, Brigitte, 'Past Presents: New Year's Gifts at the Valois Courts', *Art Bulletin* 83 (2001), pp. 598-625.

Bulhof, Ilse N., 'Johan Huizinga, Ethnographer of the Past: An Analysis of Johan Huizinga's Approach to History', *Clio: An Interdisciplinary Journal of Literature, History and the Philosophy of History* 4:2 (1975), pp. 201-224.
Burckhardt, Jacob, *The Civilization of the Renaissance in Italy* (New York: Harper, 1954).
Burckhardt, Jacob, *Die Cultur der Renaissance in Italien: ein Versuch* (Basel: Schweighauser, 1860).
Burckhardt, Jacob, *Die Kunstwerke der belgischen Städte* (Düsseldorf: J. Buddeus, 1842).
Burgkmair, Hans, et al., *The Triumph of Maximilian I: 137 Woodcuts by Hans Burgkmair and Others*, trans. by Stanley Appelbaum (New York: Dover Publications, 1964).
Burguière, André, *The Annales School: An Intellectual History*, trans. by Jane Marie Todd (Ithaca: Cornell University Press, 2009).
Burguière, André, 'Déconstruction d'une démolition', *Books*, 1 May 2010, http://www.books.fr/droit-de-reponse-dandre-burguiere/.
Burguière, André, Letter responding to R.J. Evans, 'Cite Ourselves!', *London Review of Books* 32:8 (22 April 2010).
Burke, Peter, 'Historians, Anthropologists, and Symbols', in *Culture through Time: Anthropological Approaches*, ed. by Emiko Ohnuki-Tierney (Stanford: Stanford University Press, 1990), pp. 268-283.
Burke, Peter, 'Huizinga, Prophet of "Blood and Roses"', *History Today* 36:11 (November 1986), pp. 23-28.
Burke, Peter, *What Is Cultural History?* (Cambridge: Polity, 2004).
Buylaert, Frederik, 'The "Van Boschuysen Affair" in Leyden: Conflicts between Elite Networks in Late Medieval Holland', *Francia* 35 (2008), pp. 95-113.
Buylaert, Frederik, Wim De Clercq, and Jan Dumolyn, 'Sumptuary Legislation, Material Culture and the Semiotics of "Vivre Noblement" in the County of Flanders (14th-16th Centuries)', *Social History* 36 (2011), pp. 393-417.
Bynum, Caroline Walker, *Christian Materiality: An Essay on Religion in Late Medieval Europe* (New York: Zone, 2011).

Caillois, Roger, *Man, Play, and Games*, trans. by M. Barash (London: Thames and Hudson, 1962).
Cameron, Euan, *Enchanted Europe: Superstition, Reason, and Religion, 1250-1750* (Oxford: Oxford University Press, 2010).
Camille, Michael, *The Gothic Idol: Ideology and Image-Making in Medieval Art* (Cambridge: Cambridge University Press, 1989).
Camille, Michael, 'The Lord's Lands: Men, Women and Machines', in *Mirror in Parchment: The Luttrell Psalter and the Making of Medieval England* (Chicago: University of Chicago Press, 1998), pp. 178-231.

Campbell, Thomas P., *Tapestry in the Renaissance: Art and Magnificence* (New York: Metropolitan Museum of Art, 2006).

Cantor, Norman, *Inventing the Middle Ages: The Lives, Works and Ideas of the Great Medievalists of the Twentieth Century* (Cambridge: Lutterworth Press, 1992).

Cardon, Bert, and Bart Stroobants, 'L'iconographie de la bataille des Éperons d'or', in *1302, le désastre de Courtrai: mythe et réalité de la bataille des éperons d'or*, ed. by Raoul C. van Caenegem et al. (Antwerp: Fonds Mercator, 2002), pp. 170-194.

Carlier, Philippe, 'Contribution à l'étude de l'unification bourguignonne dans l'historiographie nationale belge de 1830 à 1914', *Revue belge d'histoire contemporaine* 16 (1985), pp. 1-24.

Caron, Marie-Thérèse, *Les voeux du faisan, noblesse en fête, esprit de croisade. Le manuscrit français 11594 de la Bibliothèque Nationale de France* (Turnhout: Brepols, 2003).

Caseau, Béatrice, 'The Senses in Religion: Liturgy, Devotion, and Deprivation', in *A Cultural History of the Senses in the Middle Ages*, ed. by Richard G. Newhauser (London: Bloomsbury, 2014), pp. 89-109.

Cauchies, Jean-Marie, *Louis XI et Charles le Hardi. De Péronne à Nancy (1468-1477): le conflit* (Brussels: De Boeck, 1996).

Champion, Matthew S., *The Fullness of Time: Temporalities of the Fifteenth-Century Low Countries* (Chicago: University of Chicago Press, 2017).

Champion, Pierre, *Histoire poétique du XVe siècle*, 2 vols. (Paris: Édouard Champion, 1923).

Chapuis, Julian, *Stefan Lochner. Image Making in Fifteenth-Century Cologne* (Turnhout: Brepols, 2004)

Chastellain, Georges, *Oeuvres de Georges Chastellain*, ed. by Joseph Kervyn de Lettenhove, 8 vols. (Brussels: Heussner, 1863-1866).

Châtelet, Albert, *Early Dutch Painting: Painting in the Northern Netherlands in the Fifteenth Century*, trans. by Christopher Brown and Anthony Turner (New York: Rizzoli, 1981).

Chenu, Marie-Dominique, *La théologie au douzième siècle* (Paris: Vrin, 1957), trans. by Jerome Taylor and Lester K. Little as *Nature, Man, and Society in the Twelfth Century: Essays on New Theological Perspectives in the Latin West* (Chicago: University of Chicago Press, 1968).

Chiffoleau, Jacques, *La comptabilité de l'au-delà. Les hommes, la mort et la religion dans la région d'Avignon à la fin du Moyen Âge (vers 1320-vers 1480)* (Rome: École française de Rome, 1980).

Chiffoleau, Jacques, 'La religion flamboyante v. 1320-v. 1520', in *Du christianisme flamboyant à l'aube des Lumières (XIVe-XVIIIe siècles)*, ed. by François Le Brun (Paris: Seuil, 1988), pp. 11-183, reprinted with a new introduction and appendix as *La religion flamboyante. France (1320-1520)* (Paris: Points, 2010).

Clark, Christopher, *Iron Kingdom: The Rise and Downfall of Prussia, 1600-1957* (Cambridge, MA: The Belknap Press of Harvard University Press, 2006).

Clark, Gregory T., *Made in Flanders: The Master of the Ghent Privileges and Manuscript Painting in the Southern Netherlands in the Time of Philip the Good* (Turnhout: Brepols, 2000).

Clark, Stuart, 'French Historians and Early Modern Popular Culture', *Past and Present* 100 (1983), pp. 62-99.

Clarke, David, *The Angel of Mons: Phantom Soldiers and Ghostly Guardians* (Chichester: Wiley, 2004).

Clerq, Gerrit de, *Tegenwoordig België (Liberalen, Katholyken en Vlaemsche-Beweging), door een' Noord-Nederlander beoordeeld* (Gent: Snoeck-Ducaju en Zoon, 1847).

Cockshaw, Pierre, 'Les archives bourguignonnes, les plus riches d'Europe?', in *La cour de Bourgogne et l'Europe*, ed. by Werner Paravicini et al., pp. 43-54.

Cockshaw, Pierre, 'Les manuscripts de Charles de Bourgogne et de ses proches', in *Charles le Téméraire: exposition organisée à l'occasion du cinquième centenaire de sa mort*, ed. by P. Cockshaw, C. Lemaire, and A. Rouzet (Brussels: Bibliothèque Royale Albert Ier, 1977), pp. 3-19.

Cockshaw, Pierre, and Christiane van den Bergen-Pantens, eds., *L'Ordre de la Toison d'Or de Philippe le Bon à Philippe le Beau*, exh. cat. Brussels KBR (Turnhout: Brepols, 1996).

Cohen, A.E., 'Huizinga als Leids hoogleraar', *Bijdragen en Mededelingen betreffende de Geschiedenis der Nederlanden* 99 (1973), pp. 335-347; ; also published, with the same pagination, in *Johan Huizinga 1872-1972*, ed. by W.R.H. Koops et al.

Cohen, Richard I., 'An Introductory Essay: Viewing the Past', in *Art and Its Uses: The Visual Image and Modern Jewish Society: Studies in Contemporary Jewry: An Annual*, ed. by Ezra Mendelsohn, guest editor, Richard I. Cohen, 6 (1990), pp. 3-8.

Colie, Rosalie L., 'Johan Huizinga and the Task of Cultural History', *American Historical Review* 69:3 (1964), pp. 607-630.

Comblen-Sonkes, Micheline, *Guide bibliographique de la peinture flamande du XVe siècle* (Brussels: Centre National de Recherches 'Primitifs flamands', 1984).

Conscience, Hendrik, *De Leeuw van Vlaenderen: Of, De Slag Der Gulden Sporen (1302)* (Antwerp: L.J. de Cort, 1838).

Conscience, Hendrik, and Ferdinand Augustijn Snellaert, *Vlaemsche beweging: Verklaring van grondbeginselen door de verdedigers der nederduitsche Volksregten aen hunne landgenooten gegeven* (Gent: F. & E. Gyselynck, 1847).

Coopman, Theophiel, and Jan Broeckaert, *Bibliographie van den Vlaamschen taalstrijd*, Koninklijke Vlaamsche Academie voor Taal- & Letterkunde, 10 vols. (Ghent: A. Siffer, 1904-1914).

Coreth, Anna, 'Der Orden von der Stola und den Kanndeln und den Greifen', *Mitteilungen des Instituts für Österreichische Geschichtsforschung* 5 (1952), pp. 34-51.

Courtenay, William J., 'Huizinga's Heirs: Interpreting the Late Middle Ages', in *'Herbst des Mittelalters'?*, ed. by Jan A. Aertsen and Martin Pickavé, pp. 25-36.
Coville, Alfred, *Les premiers Valois et la guerre de Cent Ans (1328-1422)*, in *Histoire de France depuis les origines jusqu'à la Révolution*, ed. by Ernest Lavisse, 9 vols. (Paris: Librairie Hachette, 1900-1911), vol. IV.1 (1902).
Cuneo, Pia, 'Images of Warfare as Political Legitimation: Jörg Breu the Elder's Rondels for Maximilian I's Hunting Lodge at Lermos (c. 1516)', in *Artful Armies, Beautiful Battles: Art and Warfare in Early Modern Europe*, ed. by Pia Cuneo (Leiden: Brill, 2002), pp. 87-105.
Cuyler, Louise, *The Emperor Maximilian and Music* (London: Oxford University Press, 1973).

Dabrowski, Patrice M., *Commemorations and the Shaping of Modern Poland* (Bloomington: Indiana University Press, 2004).
Dameron, George, 'Purgatory and Modernity', in *Bridging the Medieval-Modern Divide: Medieval Themes in the World of the Reformation*, ed. by James Muldoon (Farnham: Ashgate, 2013), pp. 87-105.
Damian-Grint, Peter, *Medievalism and* manière gothique *in Enlightenment France* (Oxford: Voltaire Foundation, 2006).
Davis, Kathleen, *Periodization and Sovereignty: How Ideas of Feudalism and Secularization Govern the Politics of Time* (Philadelphia: University of Pennsylvania Press, 2008).
D'Avray, David, 'Symbolism and Medieval Religious Thought', in *The Medieval World*, ed. by Peter Linehan and Janet L. Nelson (London: Routledge, 2001), pp. 267-278.
Deam, Lisa, 'Flemish versus Netherlandish: A Discourse of Nationalism', *Renaissance Quarterly* 51:1 (1998), pp. 1-33.
De Berg, Jaap, 'Geestesmerken gemunt door Kuyper, niet door Huizinga', *Trouw*, 21 November 2013.
Debeuckelaere, Adiel, *Open brieven van de Vlaamsche frontpartij in het jaar 1917 en vertoogschriften van het Vlaamsche frontverbond* (Brussels: 'Ons Vaderland', 1919).
De Biez, Jacques, *E. Frémiet* (Paris: Jouve, 1910).
De Boer, Dick, and Ludo Jongen, eds., *In het water gevonden: Het Amersfoortse Mirakelboek* (Hilversum: Verloren, 2015).
Decker, John R., *The Technology of Salvation and the Art of Geertgen tot Sint Jans* (Burlington: Ashgate, 2009).
De Jong, Mayke, 'The Foreign Past: Medieval Historians and Cultural Anthropology', *Tijdschrift voor Geschiedenis* 109 (1996), pp. 236-242.
Delumeau, Jean, *La peur en Occident, XIVe-XVIIIe siècles. Une cité assiégée* (Paris: Fayard, 1978).

Delumeau, Jean, *Le péché et la peur. La culpabilisation en Occident, XIIIe-XVIIIe siècles* (Paris: Fayard, 1983), trans. by Eric Nicholson as *Sin and Fear: The Emergence of a Western Guilt Culture, 13th-18th Centuries* (New York: St. Martin's Press, 1990).

Delumeau, Jean, *Rassurer et protéger. Le sentiment de sécurité dans l'Occident d'autrefois* (Paris: Fayard, 1989).

Deregnaucourt, Jean-Pierre, *Autour de la mort à Douai. Attitudes, pratiques et croyances, 1250-1500*, PhD diss., Université Charles de Gaulle, Lille, 1993.

De Schaepdrijver, Sophie, 'Occupation, Propaganda, and the Idea of Belgium', in *European Culture in the Great War: The Arts, Entertainment, and Propaganda*, ed. by Aviel Roshwald and Richard Stites (Cambridge: Cambridge University Press, 1998), pp. 266-294.

De Schaepdrijver, Sophie, 'Violence and Legitimacy: Occupied Belgium, 1914-1918', *The Low Countries: Arts and Society in Flanders and the Netherlands* 22 (2014), pp. 46-55.

Despars, Nicolaes, *Cronijcke van den lande ende graefscepe van Vlaenderen: vande jaeren 405 tot 1492*, ed. by J. de Jonghe, 4 vols. (Bruges: s.n., 1837-1840).

Despriet, Philippe, *De iconografie van de Guldensporenslag: een kritisch-vergelijkende studie* (Kortrijk: Archeologische Stichting voor Zuid-West-Vlaanderen, 2002).

De Tolnay, Charles, *Le Maître de Flémalle et les frères Van Eyck* (Brussels: Éditions de la Connaissance, 1939).

De Voogd, Christophe N., *Le miroir de la France: Johan Huizinga et les historiens français*, PhD diss., Leiden University, 2013.

De Vreese, Willem, et al., *Pro Flandria servanda: Vlaanderen's recht en eisch tot zelfstandigheid gesteld, toegelicht, gestaafd* (Den Haag: Het Vlaamsch Comité, 1919); trans. by René Gaspar as *Pro Flandria servanda: Flanders' Right and Claim for Autonomy: Formulated, Explained, Justified* (The Hague: Martinus Nijhoff, 1919).

Dewulf, Jeroen, 'The Flemish Movement: On the Intersection of Language and Politics in the Dutch-Speaking Part of Belgium', *Georgetown Journal of International Affairs* 13 (2012), pp. 23-33.

Dhanens, Elisabeth, *Hubert and Jan van Eyck* (New York: Alpine Fine Art Books, 1980).

Dhanens, Elisabeth, et al., 'Literatuur en stadscultuur tussen middeleeuwen en nieuwe tijd', *Bijdragen en mededelingen betreffende de geschiedenis der Nederlanden* 106 (1996), pp. 421-450.

Di Carpegna Falconieri, Tommaso, 'Il Medievalismo et la Grande Guerra', *Studi storici* 56:2 (2015), pp. 49-77.

Dierkens, Alain, Gil Bartholeyns, and Thomas Golsenne, eds., *La performance des images* (Brussels: Éditions de l'Université de Bruxelles, 2010).

Dits die excellente cronike van Vlaenderen, ed. by W. Vorsterman (Antwerp, 1531).

Doutrepont, Georges, *La littérature française à la cour des ducs de Bourgogne* (Paris: Honoré Champion, 1909).

Driver, Tom F., *The Magic of Ritual: Our Need for Liberating Rites that Transform Our Lives and Our Communities* (San Francisco: Harper, 1991).

Droogers, André, 'Enjoying an Emerging Alternative World: Ritual in Its Own Ludic Right', in *Ritual in Its Own Right*, ed. by Don Handelman and Galina Lindquist, pp. 138-154.

Duby, Georges, *Les trois ordres ou l'imaginaire du féodalisme* (Paris: Gallimard, 1978), trans. by Arthur Goldhammer as *The Three Orders: Feudal Society Imagined* (Chicago: University of Chicago Press, 1980).

Duffy, Eamon, *The Stripping of the Altars: Traditional Religion in England, c. 1400-c. 1580* (New Haven: Yale University Press, 1992).

Dumolyn, Jan, 'The Vengeance of the Commune: Sign Systems of Popular Politics in Medieval Bruges', in *La comunidad medieval como esfera pública*, ed. by Hipólito R. Oliva Herrer, Jan Dumolyn, and M.A. Carmona Ruiz (Seville: Secretariado de Publicaciones de la Universidad de Sevilla, 2014), pp. 251-289.

Dumolyn, Jan, and Jelle Haemers, '"A Bad Chicken Was Brooding": Subversive Speech in Late Medieval Flanders', *Past and Present*, 214 (2012), pp. 45-86.

Dunning, Eric, 'Sociological Reflections on Sport, Violence and Civilization', *International Review for the Society of Sport* 25:1 (1990), pp. 65-81.

Eco, Umberto, *Art and Beauty in the Middle Ages*, trans. by Hugh Bredin (New Haven: Yale University Press, 1986).

Eco, Umberto, *Écrits sur la pensée au Moyen Âge* (Paris: Grasset, 2016).

Egg, Erich, *Die Hofkirche in Innsbruck* (Innsbruck: Tyrolia, 1974).

Eikelmann, Renate, 'Goldemail um 1400', in *Das Goldene Rössl*, ed. by Reinhold Baumstark, pp. 106-130.

Eikelmann, Renate, 'Zur Geschichte des Marienbildes, genannt Goldenes Rößl', in *Das Goldene Rössl*, ed. by Reinhold Baumstark, pp. 52-57.

Eisenstein, Elizabeth, *The Printing Press as an Agent of Change* (Cambridge: Cambridge University Press, 1979).

Elias, Norbert, *The Civilizing Process: Sociogenetic and Psychogenetic Investigations*, trans. by Edmund Jephcott and ed. by Eric Dunning, Johan Goudsblom, and Stephen Mennell, rev. ed. (Malden: Blackwell, 2000).

Elliott, John H., 'A Europe of Composite Monarchies', *Past and Present* 134 (1992), pp. 48-71.

Evans, R.J., 'Cite Ourselves!', *London Review of Books* 31:23 (3 December 2009), pp. 12-14.

Evans-Pritchard, E.E., *The Nuer: A Description of the Modes of Livelihood and Political Institutions of a Nilotic People* (Oxford: Clarendon Press, 1940).

Exposition de la Toison d'Or à Bruges (juin-octobre 1907). Catalogue (édition définitive) (Brussels: G. van Oest, 1907).

Faggin, Giorgio T., *L'opera completa dei Van Eyck*, intro. by Raffaello Brignetti (Milan: Rizzoli, 1968).

Faggin, Giorgio T., *The Complete Paintings of the Van Eycks*, intro. by Robert Hughes (New York: Harry N. Abrams, 1968).

Falk, Tilman, *Hans Burgkmair* (Munich: Bruckmann, 1968).

Falkenburg, Reindert, *The Fruit of Devotion: Mysticism and the Imagery of Love in Flemish Paintings of the Virgin and Child, 1450-1550* (Amsterdam: Benjamins, 1994).

Farmer, Sharon, 'Aristocratic Power and the "Natural" Landscape: The Garden Park at Hesdin, ca. 1291-1302', *Speculum* 88:3 (2013), pp. 644-680.

Farrand, Livingston, *Basis of American History, 1500-1900* (New York: Harper and Brothers, 1904).

Febvre, Lucien, *Combats pour l'histoire* (Paris: Armand Colin, 1953).

Febvre, Lucien, 'Histoire de l'art, Histoire de la civilisation: de Sluter à Sambin', *Revue de Synthèse Historique* 9 (1935), pp. 288-304; reproduced in *Combats pour l'histoire*, pp. 295-301.

Febvre, Lucien, 'L'Érasme d'Huizinga', in Johan Huizinga, *Érasme* (Paris: Gallimard, 1955), pp. 7-16.

Febvre, Lucien, *Le problème de l'incroyance au XVIe siècle. La religion de Rabelais* (Paris: A. Michel, 1942).

Febvre, Lucien, 'La sensibilité et l'histoire: Comment reconstituer la vie affective d'autrefois?', *Annales d'histoire sociale* 3:1/2 (1941), pp. 5-20; reproduced in *Combats pour l'histoire*, pp. 221-238.

Febvre, Lucien, *Un destin: Martin Luther* (Paris: Presses Universitaires de France, 1928).

Febvre, Lucien, 'Une vue d'ensemble: Histoire et psychologie', in *Encyclopédie française*, 21 vols. (Paris: Larousse, 1935-1966), vol. 8, pp. 12(3)-12(7) [sic]; reproduced in *Combats pour l'histoire*, pp. 207-220.

Febvre, Lucien, 'Un moment avec Huizinga (Johan Huizinga, Homo ludens)', *Annales E.S.C.* 6:4 (1951), pp. 493-496.

Febvre, Lucien, *Vivre l'histoire*, ed. Brigitte Mazon (Paris: Robert Laffont, 2009).

Febvre, Lucien, 'Vivre l'histoire', *Mélanges d'histoire sociale* 3:1 (1943), pp. 5-18.

Filedt Kok, Jan Piet, ed., *Livelier Than Life: The Master of the Amsterdam Cabinet or the Housebook Master*, exh. cat. (Amsterdam: Rijksmuseum, 1985).

Fillitz, Hermann, ed., *Trésors de la Toison d'Or*, exh. cat. (Brussels: Gemeentekrediet, 1987).

Flanders in the Fifteenth Century: Art and Civilization: Catalogue of the Exhibition, Masterpieces of Flemish Art: Van Eyck to Bosch, Oct.-Dec. 1960 (Detroit: Detroit Institute of Arts, 1960).

Fredericq, Paul, *Essai sur le rôle politique et social des ducs de Bourgogne dans les Pays-Bas* (Ghent: A. Hoste, 1875).

From Schongauer to Holbein: Master Drawings from Basel and Berlin, exh. cat. (Washington, DC: National Gallery, 1999).

Frugoni, Chiara, 'Female Mystics, Visions, and Iconography', in *Women and Religion in Medieval and Renaissance Italy*, ed. by Daniel Bornstein and Roberto Rusconi (Chicago: University of Chicago Press, 1996), pp. 130-164.

Geary, Patrick J., *The Myth of Nations: The Medieval Origins of Europe* (Princeton: Princeton University Press, 2002).

Geary, Patrick J., and Gábor Klaniczay, eds., *Manufacturing Middle Ages: Entangled History of Medievalism in Nineteenth-Century Europe* (Leiden: Brill, 2013).

Geertz, Clifford, *After the Fact: Two Countries, Four Decades, One Anthropologist* (Cambridge, MA: Harvard University Press, 1995).

Geertz, Clifford, 'Centers, Kings, and Charisma: Reflections on the Symbolics of Power', in *Rites of Power: Symbolism, Ritual and Politics since the Middle Ages*, ed. by Sean Wilentz (Philadelphia: University of Pennsylvania Press, 1985), pp. 13-40.

Geertz, Clifford, 'Deep Play: Notes on the Balinese Cockfight', *Daedalus* 101:1 (1972), pp. 1-37.

Geertz, Clifford, *The Interpretation of Cultures* (New York: Basic Books, 1973).

Geertz, Clifford, *Negara: The Theater State in Nineteenth-Century Bali* (Princeton: Princeton University Press, 1980).

Geertz, Clifford, 'Ritual and Social Change, a Javanese Example', *American Anthropologist* 59:1 (1957), pp. 32-54.

Gerson, Horst, 'Huizinga und die Kunstgeschichte', *Bijdragen en Mededelingen betreffende de Geschiedenis der Nederlanden* 99 (1973), pp. 348-364; also published, with the same pagination, in *Johan Huizinga 1872-1972*, ed. by W.R.H. Koops et al.

Geyl, Pieter, *Huizinga als aanklager van zijn tijd* (Amsterdam: Koninklijke Nederlandse Akademie van Wetenschappen en Noord-Hollandsche Uitgevers Maatschappij, 1961); reproduced in Pieter Geyl, *Van Bilderdijk tot Huizinga* (Utrecht: Het Spectrum, 1964), pp. 210-255; trans. as 'Huizinga as Accuser of His Time', in Pieter Geyl, *Encounters in History* (Cleveland: Meridian Books, 1961), pp. 188-237; also printed in *History and Theory* 2 (1962), pp. 231-262.

Goebel, Stefan, *The Great War and Medieval Memory: War, Remembrance and Medievalism in Britain and Germany, 1914-1940* (Cambridge: Cambridge University Press, 2007).

Goggin, Joyce, 'Legos and Legacies: Johan Huizinga's Gamified Afterlife', keynote delivered at 'Games of Late Modernity: Homo Ludens 75 Years Later', International School for Philosophy (ISVW), Leusden, 15-17 January 2014, https://vimeo.com/84585240.

Goldthwaite, Richard, *Wealth and the Demand for Art in Renaissance Italy, 1300-1600* (Baltimore: Johns Hopkins University Press, 1993).

Gombrich, Ernst, 'The Early Medici as Patrons of Art', in *Italian Renaissance Studies*, ed. by E.F. Jacobs (London: Faber and Faber, 1960), pp. 279-311.

Gombrich, Ernst, 'Huizinga's *Homo ludens*', in *Bijdragen en Mededelingen betreffende de Geschiedenis der Nederlanden* 99 (1973), pp. 133-154; also published, with the same pagination, in *Johan Huizinga 1872-1972*, ed. by W.R.H. Koops et al.; also reproduced as 'The High Seriousness of Play: Reflections on *Homo ludens* by J. Huizinga (1872-1945)', in *Tributes: Interpreters of Our Cultural Tradition* (Oxford: Phaidon, 1984), pp. 139-163.

Gombrich, Ernst, *Ideals and Idols* (Oxford: Phaidon, 1979).

Gouguenheim, Sylvain, *Tannenberg: 15 Juillet 1410* (Paris: Tallandier, 2012).

Grabmann, Martin, 'Die Lehre des hl. Thomas von die *scintilla animae* in ihrer Bedeutung für die deutsche Mystik im Predigerordens', *Jahrbuch für Philosophie und Speculative Theologie* 14 (1900), pp. 413-427.

Grandmontagne, Michael, *Claus Sluter und die Lesbarkeit mittelalterlicher Skulptur: das Portal der Kartause von Champmol* (Worms: Wernersche Verlagsgesellschaft, 2005).

Grasman, Edward, *Gerson in Groningen* (Hilversum: Verloren, 2007).

Greve, Anke, Émilie Lebailly, and Werner Paravicini, eds., *Comptes de l'Argentier de Charles le Téméraire duc de Bourgogne*, 4 vols. (Paris: Boccard, 2008).

Greilsammer, Myriam, *L'envers du tableau. Mariage et maternité en Flandre médiévale* (Paris: Colin, 1990).

Gröber, Gustav, *Grundriss der romanischen Philologie*, 2 vols. (Strasbourg: K.J. Trübner, 1888-1902).

Grundmann, Herbert, *Religiöse Bewegungen im Mittelalter. Untersuchungen über die geschichtlichen Zusammenhänge zwischen der Ketzerei, den Bettelorden und der religiösen Frauenbewegung im 12. und 13. Jahrhundert und über die geschichtlichen Grundlagen der deutschen Mystik*, 2nd ed. (Darmstadt: Wissenschaftliche Buchgesellschaft, 1961), trans. by Steven Rowan as *Religious Movements in the Middle Ages* (Notre Dame: University of Notre Dame Press, 1995).

Guenée, Bernard, *L'occident aux XIVe et XVe siècles. Les États* (Paris: Presses Universitaires de France, 1981).

Guiette, Robert, 'Georges Doutrepont, 1868-1941', *Revue belge de philologie et d'histoire* 20 (1941), pp. 844-849.

Guyot-Bachy, Isabelle, 'Auguste Molinier et *Les Sources de l'Histoire de France*', in *La naissance de la médiévistique: les historiens et leurs sources en Europe (XIXe-début du XXe siècle)*, ed. by Isabelle Guyot-Bachy and Jean-Marie Moeglin (Paris: Droz, 2015), pp. 315-333.

Haemers, Jelle, 'L'anniversaire gantois de Marie, duchesse de Bourgogne (27 mars 1483). Autour de la participation des sujets urbains à un service commémoratif pour une princesse décédée', *Micrologus* 22 (2014), pp. 341-365.

Haemers, Jelle, and Élodie Lecuppre-Desjardin, 'Conquérir et reconquérir l'espace urbain. Le triomphe de la collectivité sur l'individu dans le cadre de la révolte Brugeoise', in *Voisinages, coexistences, appropriations. Groupes sociaux et territoires urbains* (*Moyen Age-16e siècle*), ed. by Chloé Deligne and Claire Billen (Turnhout: Brepols, 2007), pp. 119-143.

Hall, Bert, *Weapons and Warfare in Renaissance Europe* (Baltimore: Johns Hopkins University Press, 1997).

Hamburger, Jeffrey F., *Nuns as Artists: The Visual Culture of a Medieval Convent* (Berkeley: University of California Press, 1997).

Hamburger, Jeffrey F., *The Visual and the Visionary: Art and Female Spirituality in Late Medieval Germany* (New York: Zone Books, 1998).

Hamburger, Jeffrey F., 'The Visual and the Visionary: The Image in Late Medieval Monastic Devotions', *Viator* 20 (1989), pp. 151-182.

Handelman, Don, 'Epilogue: Toing and Froing the Social', in *Ritual in Its Own Right*, ed. by Don Handelman and Galina Lindquist, pp. 213-222.

Handelman, Don, *Models and Mirrors: Towards an Anthropology of Public Events*, 2nd ed. (Cambridge: Cambridge University Press, 1999).

Handelman, Don, and Galina Lindquist, eds., *Ritual in Its Own Right: Exploring the Dynamics of Transformation* (New York: Berghahn Books, 2005).

Hanselaer, An-Katrien, and Jeroen Deploige, '"Van groeter bannicheit hoers herten": de conditionering van de alledaagse gevoelswereld in vrouwelijke gemeenschappen uit de laatmiddeleeuwse Moderne Devotie', *Tijdschrift voor Geschiedenis* 126 (2013), pp. 480-499.

Hanssen, Léon, *Huizinga en de troost van de geschiedenis. Verbeelding en rede* (Amsterdam: Balans, 1996).

Harbison, Craig, *The Mirror of the Artist: Northern Renaissance Art in Its Historical Context* (New York: Harry Abrams, 1995).

Harbison, Craig, 'Iconography and Iconology', in *Early Netherlandish Painting*, ed. by Bernhard Ridderbos, Anne van Buren, and Henk van Veen, pp. 378-406.

Hardwick, Paul, ed., *The Playful Middle Ages: Meanings of Play and Plays of Meaning: Essays in Memory of Elaine C. Block* (Turnhout: Brepols, 2011).

Harlaut, Yann, 'L'incendie de la cathédrale de Reims, 19 septembre 1914: fait imagé... fait imaginé', in *Mythes et réalités de la cathédrale de Reims de 1825 à 1975*, ed. by Marc Bouxin and Sylvie Balcon, pp. 83-95.

Harman, William P., 'Laughing Till It Hurts... Somebody Else', in *Sacred Play*, ed. by Selva J. Raj and Corinne G. Dempsey, pp. 107-122.

Harris, Marvin, *The Rise of Anthropological Theory: A History of Theories of Culture* (New York: Columbia University Press, 1968).
Haskell, Francis, 'Huizinga and the "Flemish Renaissance"', in Francis Haskell, *History and Its Images: Art and the Interpretation of the Past* (New Haven: Yale University Press, 1993), pp. 431-495.
Haskell, Francis, 'Art and History: The Legacy of Johan Huizinga', in *History and Images: Towards a New Iconology*, ed. by Axel Bolvig and Phillip Lindley (Turnhout: Brepols, 2008), pp. 3-17.
Haskins, Charles Homer, and Robert Howard Lord, *Some Problems of the Peace Conference* (Cambridge: Harvard University Press, 1920).
Heering, G.J., *Johan Huizinga's religieuze gedachten als achtergrond van zijn werken* (Lochem: De Tijdstroom, 1948).
Heinrichs, Ulrike, *Martin Schongauer* (Berlin and Munich: Deutscher Kunstverlag, 2007).
Hendry, Joy, and Massimo Raveri, eds., *Japan at Play: The Ludic and the Logic of Power* (London: Routledge, 2002).
Henning, Uta, *Musica Maximiliana* (Neu-Ulm: Stegmiller, 1987).
Henricks, Thomas S., 'Classical Theories of Play', in *The Handbook of the Study of Play*, ed. by James E. Johnson et al., pp. 163-179.
Henricks, Thomas S., 'Modern Theorists of Play: Huizinga, Caillois, Goffman, and Henricks', in *The Handbook of the Study of Play*, ed. by James E. Johnson et al., pp. 181-194.
Henricks, Thomas S., *Play and the Human Condition* (Urbana: University of Illinois Press, 2015).
Henricks, Thomas S., *Play Reconsidered: Sociological Perspectives on Human Expression* (Urbana: University of Illinois Press, 2006).
Henricks, Thomas S., 'Sociological Perspectives on Play', in *The Handbook of the Study of Play*, ed. by James E. Johnson et al., pp. 101-120.
Hermans, Theo, 'The Highs and Lows of Hendrik Conscience', *The Low Countries: Arts and Society in Flanders and the Netherlands* 22 (1914), pp. 162-169.
Hermans, Theo, et al., eds., *The Flemish Movement: A Documentary History, 1780-1990* (London: Athlone Press, 1992).
Hess, Daniel, *Meister um das 'mittelalterliche Hausbuch': Studien zur Hausbuchmeisterfrage* (Mainz: von Zabern, 1994).
Hobbins, Daniel, 'The Schoolman as Public Intellectual: Jean Gerson and the Late Medieval Tract', *American Historical Review* 108 (2003), pp. 1308-1337.
Hodges, Herbert, *The Philosophy of Wilhelm Dilthey* (London: Routledge & Paul, 1952).
Hofstätter, Hans H., *Spätes Mittelalter* (Baden-Baden: Holle, 1967).

Holenstein, André, 'Introduction: Empowering Interactions: Looking at Statebuilding from Below', in *Empowering Interactions*, ed. by Wim Blockmans, André Holenstein, and Jon Mathieu, pp. 1-31.

Hoogewerff, G.J., *De Noord-Nederlandsche Schilderkunst*, vol. 2 (The Hague: Martinus Nijhoff, 1937).

Hoselitz, Bert F., 'Introduction', in Johan Huizinga, *Men and Ideas*, pp. 9-14.

Howard, Peter, 'Preaching Magnificence in Renaissance Florence', *Renaissance Quarterly* 61:2 (2008), pp. 325-369.

Hübener, Wolfgang, 'Der theologisch-philosophische Konservatismus des Jean Gerson', in *Antiqui und moderni. Traditionsbewußtsein und Fortschrittsbewußtsein im späten Mittelalter*, ed. by Albert Zimmermann (Berlin: De Gruyter, 1974), pp. 171-200.

Hugenholtz, F.W.N., 'The Fame of a Masterwork', in *Bijdragen en Mededelingen betreffende de Geschiedenis der Nederlanden* 99 (1973), pp. 91-103; also published, with the same pagination, in *Johan Huizinga 1872-1972*, ed. by W.R.H. Koops et al.

Hugenholtz, F.W.N., 'Le déclin du Moyen Âge, 1919-1969', *Acta Historiae Neerlandica* 5 (1971), pp. 40-51.

The list of works by Huizinga only record the editions quoted by the contributors to this book.

Huizinga, Johan, 'Abelard', in *Men and Ideas: History, the Middle Ages, the Renaissance*, pp. 178-195.

Huizinga, Johan, 'The Aesthetic Element in Historical Thought', in *Dutch Civilisation in the Seventeenth Century and Other Essays*, pp. 219-243.

Huizinga, Johan, *America: A Dutch Historian's Vision, from Afar and Near*, trans. by Herbert Harvey Rowen (New York: Harper & Row, 1972).

Huizinga, Johan, *The Autumn of the Middle Ages*, trans. by Rodney J. Payton and Ulrich Mammitzsch (Chicago: University of Chicago Press, 1996).

Huizinga, Johan, 'Bernard Shaw's Saint', in *Men and Ideas: History, the Middle Ages, the Renaissance*, pp. 207-239.

Huizinga, Johan, *Briefwisseling*, ed. by Léon Hanssen, W.E. Krul, and Anton van der Lem, 3 vols. (Utrecht and Antwerp: Veen & Tjeenk Willink, 1989-1991).

Huizinga, Johan, 'De geschiedschrijving in het hedendaagsche Frankrijk', in *VW*, VII, pp. 249-253.

Huizinga, Johan, *De hand van Huizinga*, ed. by Willem Otterspeer (Amsterdam: Amsterdam University Press, 2009).

Huizinga, Johan, 'De immoralist die God vond', *De Gids* 95:7 (1931), pp. 124-129 (*VW*, VII, pp. 608-612).

Huizinga, Johan, 'De kunst der Van Eycks in het leven van hun tijd', in *De Gids* 80 (1916) II, pp. 440-462, III, pp. 52-82 (*VW*, III, pp. 436-482); reproduced in Johan Huizinga, *De hand van Huizinga*, ed. by Willem Otterspeer, pp. 210-255.

Huizinga, Johan, *De Nederlandse natie: vijf opstellen* (Haarlem: Tjeenk Willink, 1960). Contains: Uit de voorgeschiedenis van ons nationaal besef (pp. 1-80); Uitzichten: 1533, 1584 (pp. 81-99); De betekenis van 1813 voor Nederland's geestelijke beschaving (pp. 100-118); De middelaarsrol der Nederlanden tussen West- en Midden-Europa (pp. 119-143); Nederland's geestesmerk (pp. 144-187).

Huizinga, Johan, 'De opkomst van Haarlem', *Bijdragen voor Vaderlandsche Geschiedenis en Oudheidkunde*, 4th series, 4 (1905), pp. 412-446, and 5 (1906), pp. 16-175 (*VW*, I, pp. 203-364).

Huizinga, Johan, *De taak der cultuurgeschiedenis*, ed. by Wessel E. Krul (Groningen: Historische Uitgeverij, 1995).

Huizinga, Johan, *De wetenschap der geschiedenis* (Haarlem: Tjeenk Willink, 1937) (*VW*, IV, pp. 104-172).

Huizinga, Johan, 'Dutch Civilisation in the Seventeenth Century', in *Dutch Civilisation in the Seventeenth-Century and Other Essays*, pp. 9-104.

Huizinga, Johan, *Dutch Civilisation in the Seventeenth-Century and Other Essays*, ed. by Pieter Geyl and F.W.N. Hugenholtz, trans. by Arnold J. Pomerans (London: Collins, 1968; also edited: New York: Harper & Row, 1969). Contains: Dutch Civilisation in the Seventeenth Century (pp. 9-104); The Spirit of the Netherlands (pp. 105-137); The Netherlands as Mediator between Western and Central Europe (pp. 138-157); Two Wrestlers with the Angel (pp. 158-218); The Aesthetic Element in Historical Thought (pp. 219-243); My Path to History (pp. 244-276).

Huizinga, Johan, *Erasmus* (Basel: Schwabe, 1928).

Huizinga, Johan, *Erasmus* (New York: Scribner, 1924).

Huizinga, Johan, *Erasmus*, 5th ed. (Haarlem: Tjeenk Willink, 1958).

Huizinga, Johan, *Geschonden wereld: een beschouwing over de kansen op herstel van onze beschaving* (Haarlem: Tjeenk Willink, 1945).

Huizinga, Johan, 'Hendrik Kern', in *Mannen en vrouwen van beteekenis in onze dagen* 30 (1899), pp. 297-343 (*VW*, VI, pp. 277-315).

Huizinga, Johan, 'Henri Pirenne', *Handelingen en levensberichten van de Maatschappij der Nederlandsche Letterkunde te Leiden*, 1934-1935, pp. 179-184 (*VW*, VI, pp. 501-507).

Huizinga, Johan, *Herfsttij der Middeleeuwen: Studie over levens- en gedachtenvormen der veertiende en vijftiende eeuw in Frankrijk en de Nederlanden* (Haarlem: Tjeenk Willink, 1919 [2nd ed., 1921; 3rd ed., 1928; 4th ed., 1935; 5th ed., 1941; 6th ed., 1947]).

Huizinga, Johan, *Herfsttij der Middeleeuwen. Studie over levens- en gedachtenvormen der veertiende en vijftiende eeuw in Frankrijk en de Nederlanden*, 13th ed. (Groningen: Wolters, 1975 [17th ed., 1984]).

Huizinga, Johan, *Herfsttij der middeleeuwen. Studie over levens- en gedachtenvormen der veertiende en vijftiende eeuw in Frankrijk en de Nederlanden*, ed. and ill. by Anton van der Lem (Amsterdam: Contact, 1997).

Huizinga, Johan, *Herfsttij der Middeleeuwen. Studie over levens- en gedachtenvormen der veertiende en vijftiende eeuw in Frankrijk en de Nederlanden*, ed. by Anton van der Lem (Amsterdam: Olympus, 1997).

Huizinga, Johan, *Het aesthetische bestanddeel van geschiedkundige voorstellingen* (Haarlem: Tjeenk Willink, 1905) (*VW*, VII, pp. 3-28); reproduced as 'Het esthetische bestanddeel in geschiedkundige voorstellingen', in Johan Huizinga, *De hand van Huizinga*, ed. by Willem Otterspeer, pp. 89-113 and 424-426.

Huizinga, Johan, 'Historical Ideals of Life', in *Men and Ideas: History, the Middle Ages, the Renaissance*, pp. 77-96.

Huizinga, Johan, *Homo ludens: A Study of the Play-Element in Culture* (Boston: Beacon Press, 1955).

Huizinga, Johan, *Homo ludens: A Study of the Play Element in Culture* (London: Paladin, 1970).

Huizinga, Johan, *Homo ludens: A Study of the Play Element in Culture* (New York: Roy Publishers, 1950).

Huizinga, Johan, *Homo ludens: A Study of the Play Element in Culture,* trans. from the German (after the Dutch) by R.F.C. Hull (London: Kegan Paul, Trench, Trubner, 1949).

Huizinga, Johan, *Homo ludens. Proeve eener bepaling van het spel-element der cultuur* (Haarlem: Tjeenk Willink, 1938).

Huizinga, Johan, 'How Holland Became a Nation', in *Lectures on Holland Delivered in the University of Leyden during the First Netherlands Week for American Students, July 7-12, 1924* (Leiden: A.W. Sijthoff, 1924), pp. 1-18 (*VW*, II, pp. 266-283).

Huizinga, Johan, *In de schaduwen van morgen* (Haarlem: Tjeenk Willink, 1935) (*VW*, VII, pp. 313-428).

Huizinga, Johan, *In de schaduwen van morgen*, trans. by J.H. Huizinga as *In the Shadow of To-Morrow: A Diagnosis of the Spiritual Distemper of Our Time* (New York: W.W. Norton & Co., 1936).

Huizinga, Johan, *L'automne du Moyen Âge,* intro. by Jacques Le Goff (Paris: Payot, 1977).

Huizinga, Johan, *Le déclin du Moyen Âge,* trans. by Julia Bastin with a preface by Gabriel Hanotaux (Paris: Payot, 1932).

Huizinga, Johan, 'L'état bourguignon. Ses rapports avec la France et les origines d'une nationalité néerlandaise', *Le Moyen Âge,* 3e série, 1 (1930), pp. 171-193, and 2 (1931), pp. 11-35, 83-96 (*VW*, II, pp. 161-215).

Huizinga, Johan, *Men and Ideas: History, the Middle Ages, the Renaissance: Essays,* trans. by James S. Holmes and Hans van Marle (Princeton: Princeton University Press, 1959) (2nd ed., 1984). Contains: The Task of Cultural History (pp. 17-76); Historical Ideals of Life (pp. 77-96); Patriotism and Nationalism in European History (pp. 97-155); John of Salisbury: A Pre-Gothic Mind (pp. 159-177); Abelard (pp. 178-195); The Political and Military Significance of Chivalric Ideas in the Late Middle Ages (pp. 196-206); Bernard Shaw's Saint (207-239); The Problem of the Renaissance (pp. 243-287); Renaissance and Realism (pp. 287-309); In Commemoration of Erasmus (p. 310-326); Grotius and His Time (pp. 327-341).

Huizinga, Johan, *Mensch en Menigte in Amerika: vier essays over moderne beschavingsgeschiedenis* (Haarlem: Tjeenk Willink, 1918) (*VW*, V, pp. 249-417). English translation by Herbert H. Rowen, in Johan Huizinga, *America: A Dutch Historian's Vision, from Afar and Near* (New York: Harper & Row, 1972).

Huizinga, Johan, *Mijn weg tot de historie* (Haarlem: Tjeenk Willink, 1947) (VW, I, pp. 11-42); reproduced in Johan Huizinga, *De hand van Huizinga*, ed. by Willem Otterspeer, pp. 25-55.

Huizinga, Johan, *Mijn weg tot de historie ॐ Gebeden*, ed. by Anton van der Lem (Nijmegen: Vantilt, 2016). Annotated and illustrated edition, based on both of the manuscripts by Huizinga. With first edition of Huizinga's prayers, pp. 91-105.

Huizinga, Johan, 'My Path to History', in *Dutch Civilisation in the Seventeenth-Century and Other Essays*, pp. 244-276.

Huizinga, Johan, 'Over de oudste geschiedenis van Haarlem', in *VW*, I, pp. 363-388.

Huizinga, Johan, *Over studie en waardeering van het Boeddhisme* (Haarlem: Tjeenk Willink, 1903) (*VW*, I, pp. 148-172); reproduced as 'Over studie en waardering van het Boeddhisme', in Johan Huizinga, *De hand van Huizinga*, ed. by Willem Otterspeer, pp. 67-88 and 421-424.

Huizinga, Johan, 'Patriotism and Nationalism in European History', in *Men and Ideas: History, the Middle Ages, the Renaissance*, pp. 97-155.

Huizinga, Johan, *Patriotisme en nationalisme in de Europeesche geschiedenis tot het einde der 19e eeuw* (Haarlem: Tjeenk Willink, 1940).

Huizinga, Johan, 'Renaissance and Realism', in *Men and Ideas: History, the Middle Ages, the Renaissance*, pp. pp. 287-309.

Huizinga, Johan, '[Review of] *La fin du Moyen Age. I. La désagrégation du monde médiéval, 1285-1453*', *Tijdschrift voor Geschiedenis* 47 (1932), pp. 79-83 (*VW*, III, pp. 563-566).

Huizinga, Johan, Review of *Les rois thaumaturges*, by Marc Bloch, *Tijdschrift voor Rechtsgeschiedenis* 6:3 (1925), pp. 354-356 (*VW*, IV, pp. 124-127).

Huizinga, Johan, 'Rosenkranz und Güldenstern', *Jahrbuch der deutschen Shake-speare-Gesellschaft* 46 (1910), pp. 60-68 (*VW*, VI, pp. 320-331).

Huizinga, Johan, 'The Task of Cultural History', in *Men and Ideas: History, the Middle Ages, the Renaissance*, pp. 17-76.

Huizinga, Johan, 'Twee worstelaars met den Engel', *De Gids* 85:6 (1921), pp. 454-487, and 85:7 (1921), pp. 80-109 (*VW*, IV, pp. 441-497).

Huizinga, Johan, 'Uit de voorgeschiedenis van ons nationaal besef', *De Gids* 76 (1912), pp. 432-487 (*VW*, II, pp. 97-162).

Huizinga, Johan, *Van den vogel Charadrius* (Amsterdam: Johannes Müller, 1903) (*VW*, I, pp. 173-187).

Huizinga, Johan, *Verzamelde werken*, 9 vols. (Haarlem: Tjeenk Willink, 1948-1953).

Huizinga, Johan, *The Waning of the Middle Ages: A Study of the Forms of Life, Thought and Art in France and the Netherlands in the XIVth and XVth Centuries*, trans. by F. Hopman (London: Edward Arnold & Co., 1924).

Huizinga, Johan, *The Waning of the Middle Ages: A Study of the Forms of Life, Thought, and Art in France and the Netherlands in the Fourteenth and Fifteenth Centuries*, trans. by F. Hopman (Harmondsworth: Penguin, 1968).

Huizinga, Johan, *The Waning of the Middle Ages*, trans. by F. Hopman (Harmondsworth: Penguin, 1982).

Huizinga, Johan, ed., *Rechtsbronnen der stad Haarlem*, Werken der Vereeniging tot Uitgave der Bronnen van het Oud-Vaderlandsche Recht, 2nd series, XIII (The Hague: Nijhoff, 1911). Not in *VW*.

Huizinga, Leonhard, *Herinneringen aan mijn vader* (Den Haag: H.P. Leopold, 1963).

Humphrey, Caroline, and J.A. Laidlaw, *The Archetypal Actions of Ritual: A Theory of Ritual Illustrated by the Jain Rite of Worship* (Oxford: Oxford University Press, 1994).

Hunt, Lynn, ed., *The New Cultural History* (Berkeley: University of California Press, 1989).

Hüsken, Ute, *When Rituals Go Wrong: Mistakes, Failure and the Dynamics of Ritual* (Leiden: Brill, 2007).

Hutchinson, Ben, *Lateness and Modern European Literature* (Oxford: Oxford University Press, 2016).

Iggers, Georg G., *The German Conception of History: The National Tradition of Historical Thought from Herder to the Present* (Middletown: Wesleyan University Press, 1968).

Jacobs, Lynn F., *Early Netherlandish Carved Altarpieces, 1380-1550: Medieval Tastes and Mass Marketing* (Cambridge: Cambridge University Press, 1998).

Jardine, Lisa, 'The Afterlife of Homo Ludens: From Johan Huizinga to Natalie Zemon Davis and Beyond', in Lisa Jardine, *Temptation in the Archives: Essays in Golden Age Dutch Culture* (London: UCL Press, 2015), pp. 84-101.

Jarvie, I.C., *Functionalism* (Minneapolis: Burgess Publishing Co., 1973).

Jenkins, A.D. Fraser, 'Cosimo de' Medici's Patronage of Architecture and the Theory of Magnificence', *Journal of the Warburg and Courtauld Institutes* 33 (1970), pp. 162-170.

Johnson, James E., et al., eds., *The Handbook of the Study of Play* (Lanham: Rowman & Littlefield, 2015).

Johnson, Lonnie, *Central Europe: Enemies, Neighbors, Friends* (New York: Oxford University Press, 1996).

Jongkees, A.G., 'Une génération d'historiens devant le phénomène bourguignon', in *Bijdragen en Mededelingen betreffende de Geschiedenis der Nederlanden* 99 (1973), pp. 73-90; also published, with the same pagination, in *Johan Huizinga 1872-1972*, ed. by W.R.H. Koops et al.

Jučas, M., *The Battle of Grünwald* (Vilnius: National Museum, 2009).

Jugie, Sophie, 'The Tomb of Philip the Bold', in *Art from the Court of Burgundy: The Patronage of Philip the Bold and John the Fearless, 1364-1419*, ed. by Stephen N. Fliegel, Sophie Jugie and Virginie Barthélémy, exh. cat. (Dijon and Cleveland: Cleveland Museum of Art, 2004), pp. 223-235.

Kaegi, Werner, 'Das historische Werk Johan Huizingas', *Schweizer Beiträge zur allgemeinen Geschichte* 4 (1946), pp. 5-37.

Kahsnitz, Rainer, 'Kleinod und Andachtsbild. Zum Bildprogramm des Goldenen Rössls', in *Das Goldene Rössl*, ed. by Reinhold Baumstark, pp. 58-89.

Kalff, Gerrit, *Geschiedenis der Nederlandsche letterkunde*, 7 vols. (Groningen: J.B. Wolters, 1906-1912).

Kamerbeek, J., Jr., 'Huizinga en de Beweging van Tachtig', *Tijdschrift voor Geschiedenis* 67 (1954), pp. 145-164.

Kaminsky, Howard, 'From Lateness to Waning to Crisis: The Burden of the Later Middle Ages', *Journal of Early Modern History* 4 (2000), pp. 85-125.

Kammen, Michael, '"This, Here, and Soon": Johan Huizinga's *Esquisse* of American Culture', *Bijdragen en Mededelingen betreffende de Geschiedenis der Nederlanden* 97 (1982), pp. 589-616.

Kantorowicz, Ernst, *Laudes Regiae: A Study in Liturgical Acclamations and Mediaeval Ruler Worship* (Berkeley: University of California Press, 1946).

Kavaler, Ethan Matt, *Renaissance Gothic: Architecture and the Arts in Northern Europe, 1470-1540* (New Haven: Yale University Press, 2012).

Kawano, Satsuki, 'Mortuary Rituals', in *The Ashgate Companion to Anthropology*, ed. by Andrew J. Strathern and Pamela J. Stewart (London: Taylor and Francis, 2016), pp. 52-68.

Keck, Gabriele, Susan Marti, and Till-Holger Borchert, eds., *The Splendours of the Burgundian Court: Charles the Bold (1433-1477)*, exh. cat. Bern, Bruges, Vienna (Antwerp: Mercatorfonds, 2009).

Keen, Maurice, 'Huizinga, Kilgour and the Decline of Chivalry', *Medievalia et Humanistica* 5 (1977), pp. 1-20.

Kempers, Bram, 'De verleiding van het beeld. Het visuele als blijvende bron van inspiratie in het werk van Huizinga', *Tijdschrift voor Geschiedenis* 105 (1992), pp. 30-50.

Lecuppre-Desjardin, Élodie, *La ville des cérémonies. Essai sur la communication politique dans les anciens Pays-Bas bourguignons* (Turnhout: Brepols, 2004).

Lecuppre-Desjardin, Élodie, *Le royaume inachevé des ducs de Bourgogne (XIVe-XVe siècles)* (Paris: Belin, 2016).

Ledwidge, Francis, 'Relations de famille dans la correspondence de Gerson', *Revue Historique* 271 (1984), pp. 3-23.

Leeder, Karen, ed., *Figuring Lateness in Modern German Culture*, special issue of *New German Critique* 42:2 (2015).

Leerssen, Joep, 'Novels and Their Readers, Memories and Their Social Frameworks', in *Performing the Past: Memory, History, and Identity in Modern Europe*, ed. by Karin Tilmans, Frank van Vree, and J.M. van Winter (Amsterdam: Amsterdam University Press, 2010), pp. 235-256.

Le Goff, Jacques, 'Huizinga (Johan)', in *La nouvelle histoire*, ed. by Jacques Le Goff et al., pp. 242-245.

Le Goff, Jacques, 'Later History', *Past and Present* 100 (1983), pp. 14-28.

Le Goff, Jacques, 'Les trois fonctions indo-européennes, l'historien et l'Europe féodale', *Annales Economie, Société, Civilisation* 34 (1979), pp. 1187-1215.

Le Goff, Jacques, *The Medieval Imagination*, trans. by Arthur Goldhammer (Chicago: University of Chicago Press, 1988).

Le Goff, Jacques, 'Une science en marche, une science dans l'enfance', in *La nouvelle histoire*, ed. by Jacques Le Goff et al., pp. 11-36.

Le Goff, Jacques, and Jean-Noël Biraben, 'La peste dans le Haut Moyen Age', *Annales Economie, Société, Civilisation* 24:6 (1969), pp. 1484-1510.

Le Goff, Jacques, Roger Chartier, and Jacques Revel, eds., *La nouvelle histoire* (Paris: Retz-CEPL, 1978).

Lemaître, Jean-Loup, ed., *L'église et la mémoire des morts dans la France médiévale* (Paris: Institut d'Études augustiniennes, 1986).

Lerner, Robert E., *Ernst Kantorowicz: A Life* (Princeton: Princeton University Press, 2017).

Lévy-Bruhl, Lucien, *How Natives Think* (New York: Harper and Row, 1926).

Lhotsky, Alphons, 'AEIOV, Die "Devise" Kaiser Friedrichs III. und sein Notizbuch', *Mitteilungen des Instituts für österreichische Geschichtsforschung* 60 (1952), pp. 155-193.

Lindquist, Sherry C.M., *Agency, Visuality and Society at the Chartreuse de Champmol* (Aldershot: Ashgate, 2008).

Lipkes, Jeff, *Rehearsals: The German Army in Belgium, August 1914* (Louvain: Louvain University Press, 2007).

Littell, Jonathan, *Le sec et l'humide* (Paris: Gallimard, 2008); Dutch edition: *Het droge en het vochtige: een korte verkenning op fascistisch grondgebied* (Amsterdam: Arbeiderspers, 2009).

Little, Lester K., and Barbara Rosenwein, 'Religion and Society', in *Debating the Middle Ages*, ed. by Lester K. Little and Barbara Rosenwein, pp. 301-309.

Little, Lester K., and Barbara Rosenwein, eds., *Debating the Middle Ages: Issues and Readings* (Malden: Blackwell, 1998).

Lloyd, Benjamin, 'Disguised Symbolism Exposed and the History of Early Netherlandish Painting', *Studies in Iconography* 2 (1976), pp. 11-24.

Loise, Ferdinand, 'Ghillebert de Lannoy', in *Biographie Nationale de Belgique*, Académie Royale des Sciences, des Lettres et des Beaux-Arts de Belgique (Bruxelles: Bruylant-Christophe, 1890-1891), vol. 11, cc. 308-322.

Lorcin, Marie-Thérèse, *Vivre et mourir en Lyonnais à la fin du Moyen Âge* (Paris: CNRS, 1981).

Luber, Katherine Crawford, 'Albrecht Dürer's Maximilian Portraits: An Investigation of Versions', *Master Drawings* 29 (1991), pp. 30-47.

Lucas, Edna Louise, *Art Books: A Basic Bibliography on the Fine Arts* (Greenwich: New York Graphic Society, 1968).

Lyon, Bryce, *Henri Pirenne: A Biographical and Intellectual History* (Ghent: Story-Scienta, 1974).

Lyon, Bryce, 'Was Johan Huizinga Interdisciplinary?', *Handelingen van de Maatschappij voor Geschiedenis en Oudheidkunde te Gent* 38 (1984), pp. 181-188.

MacKay, Edwald, 'Johan Huizinga: Christianus Infirmissimus?', *Transparant* 6 (1995), pp. 14-19.

Malaby, Thomas, 'Anthropology and Play: the Contours of Playful Experience', *New Literary History* 40:1 (2010), pp. 205-218.

Malaby, Thomas, 'Beyond Play: A New Approach to Games', *Games and Culture* 2 (2007), pp. 95-113.

Mâle, Émile, 'Le renouvelement de l'art par les "mystères" a la fin du Moyen âge', *Gazette des beaux arts* 31:3 (1904), pp. 89-106, 215-230, 283-301, 379-394.

Malinowski, Bronislaw, *Argonauts of the Western Pacific: An Account of Native Enterprise and Adventure in the Archipelagoes of Melanesian New Guinea* (New York: E.P. Dutton and Co., 1922).

Manselli, Raoul, *La religion populaire au moyen âge. Problèmes de méthode et d'histoire* (Montreal: Institut d'Études Médiévales, 1975).

Mareel, Samuel, 'Urban Literary Patronage in the Early Modern Low Countries: Public Festive Culture and Individual Authorship', *Renaissance Quarterly* 64:1 (2011), pp. 50-78.

Marnef, Guido, and Anne-Laure Van Bruaene, 'Civic religion: gemeenschap, identiteit en religieuze vernieuwing', in *Gouden Eeuwen. Stad en samenleving in de Lage Landen, 1100-1600*, ed. by Anne-Laure Van Bruaene et al. (Ghent: Academia Press, 2016), pp. 165-206.

McGinn, Bernard, *The Harvest of Mysticism in Medieval Germany (1300-1500)* (New York: Crossroad, 2005).
McMullan, Gordon, *Shakespeare and the Idea of Late Writing: Authorship in the Proximity of Death* (Cambridge: Cambridge University Press, 2010).
McMullan, Gordon, and Sam Smiles, *Late Style and Its Discontents: Essays in Art, Literature, and Music* (Oxford: Oxford University Press, 2016).
McNamer, Sarah, *Affective Meditation and the Invention of Medieval Compassion* (Philadelphia: University of Pennsylvania Press, 2010).
Mehl, Jean-Michel, *Des jeux et des hommes dans la société médiévale* (Paris: Champion, 2010).
Meiss, Millard, *French Painting in the Time of Jean de Berry: The Late Fourteenth Century and the Patronage of the Duke*, 2 vols. (London: Phaidon, 1967).
Meiss, Millard, *French Painting in the Time of Jean de Berry: The Limbourgs and Their Contemporaries*, 2 vols. (New York: Braziller, 1974).
Metropolitan Museum of Art, *The Secular Spirit: Life and Art at the End of the Middle Ages* (New York: E.P. Dutton & Co., 1975).
Mettra, Claude, 'Entretien de Claude Mettra avec Jacques Le Goff', in Johan Huizinga, *L'automne du Moyen Âge*, trans. by Julia Bastin (Paris: Payot, 1975), pp. vii-xvi.
Michel, Eva, '"For Praise and Eternal Memory": Albrecht Altdorfer's *Triumphal Procession* for Emperor Maximilian I', in *Emperor Maximilian I*, ed. by Eva Michel, pp. 49-65.
Michel, Eva, ed., *Emperor Maximilian I and the Age of Dürer*, exh. cat. (Vienna: Albertina, 2012).
Michelet, Jules, 'Introduction à l'histoire universelle', in *Oeuvres de M. Michelet*, vol. 1 (Brussels: Meline, Cans et compagnie, 1840), pp. 9-52.
Midgley, Anne, 'Cultural History and the World of Johan Huizinga', *Saber and Scroll* 1:1 (2012), http://digitalcommons.apus.edu/saberandscroll/vol1/iss1/11.
Milis, Ludo, *Religion, Culture, and Mentalities in the Medieval Low Countries: Selected Essays*, ed. by Jeroen Deploige et al. (Turnhout: Brepols, 2005).
Milis, Ludo, ed., *De heidense Middeleeuwen* (Rome: Belgisch Historisch Instituut te Rome, 1991), trans. by Tanis Guest as *The Pagan Middle Ages* (Woodbridge: Boydell Press, 1998).
Molinet, Jean, *Chroniques de Jean Molinet*, ed. by G. Doutrepont and O. Jodogne, 3 vols. (Brussels: Palais des Académies, 1935-1937).
Moodey, Elizabeth, *Illuminated Crusader Histories for Philip the Good of Burgundy* (Turnhout: Brepols, 2012).
Moore, R.I., *The Formation of a Persecuting Society*, 2nd ed. (Oxford: Blackwell, 2007).
Morganstern, Anne, *Gothic Tombs of Kinship in France, the Low Countries, and England* (University Park: Pennsylvania State University Press, 2000).

Morris, Brian, *Anthropological Studies of Religion: An Introductory Text* (Cambridge: Cambridge University Press, 1987).

Müller, F. Max, *Biographies of Words and the Home of the Aryas* (London: Longmans, Green, and Co., 1871)

Müller, Jan-Dirk, *Gedechtnus. Literatur und Hofgesellschaft um Maximilian I* (Munich: Fink, 1982).

Müller, Matthias, Klaus Weschenfelder, Beate Böckem, and Ruth Hansmann, eds., *Apelles am Fürstenhof. Facetten der Hofkunst um 1500 im Alten Reich* (Berlin: Lukas, 2010).

Muller Fzn., S., 'Het boek van professor Huizinga', *Onze Eeuw* 20.1 (1920), pp. 78-104.

Munrow, David, *Instruments of the Middle Ages and Renaissance* (Oxford: Oxford University Press, 1976).

Musper, H.T., *Netherlandish Painting from Van Eyck to Bosch*, trans. by Robert Allen (New York: Harry N. Abrams, 1981).

Nagy, Piroska, *Le don des larmes au Moyen Age: un instrument spirituel en quête d'institution (Ve-XIIIe siècle)* (Paris: A. Michel, 2000).

Nagy, Piroska, see also: Damien Boquet, Piroska Nagy, *Sensible Moyen-Âge. Une histoire des émotions dans l'Occident médiéval* (Paris: Seuil, 2015).

Nash, Susie, *Northern Renaissance Art* (Oxford: Oxford University Press, 2008).

Nauta, Lodi, 'Huizinga's Lente der Middeleeuwen: De plaats van de twaalfde-eeuwse renaissance in zijn werk', *Tijdschrift voor Geschiedenis* 108 (1995), pp. 3-23.

Nichols, Stephen G., 'The New Medievalism: Tradition and Discontinuity in Medieval Culture', in *The New Medievalism*, ed. by Marina S. Brownlee, K. Brownlee, and S.G. Nichols (Baltimore: Johns Hopkins University Press, 1991), pp. 1-26.

Normore, Christina, *A Feast for the Eyes: Art, Performance and the Late Medieval Banquet* (Chicago: University of Chicago Press, 2015).

Novick, Peter, *That Noble Dream: The 'Objectivity Question' and the American Historical Profession* (Cambridge: Cambridge University Press, 1988).

Oberman, Heiko A., *The Harvest of Medieval Theology* (Cambridge, MA: Harvard University Press, 1963).

Oestreich, Gerhard, 'Huizinga, Lamprecht und die deutsche Geschichtsphilosophie: Huizingas Groninger Antrittsvorlesung von 1905', *Bijdragen en Mededelingen betreffende de Geschiedenis der Nederlanden* 99 (1973), pp. 1-28; also published, with the same pagination, in *Johan Huizinga 1872-1972*, ed. by W.R.H. Koops et al.

Otterspeer, Willem, *Huizinga voor de afgrond: Het incident Von Leers aan de Leidse Universiteit in 1933* (Utrecht: HES, 1984), trans. by Lionel Gossman and Reinier Leushuis, 'Huizinga before the Abyss: The Von Leers Incident at the University of Leiden, April 1933', *Journal of Medieval and Early Modern Studies* 27:3 (1997), pp. 386-444.

Otterspeer, Willem, 'Johan Huizinga, leven en werk', in Johan Huizinga, *De hand van Huizinga*, ed. by Willem Otterspeer, pp. 7-22.

Otterspeer, Willem, *Orde en trouw: over Johan Huizinga* (Amsterdam: De Bezige Bij, 2006)

Otterspeer, Willem, *Reading Huizinga*, trans. by Beverly Jackson (Amsterdam: Amsterdam University Press, 2010), trans. of *Orde en trouw*.

Otto, André, 'Vormen van het ondermaanse. De mystiek als uitgangspunt in het werk van Johan Huizinga', *Theoretische Geschiedenis* 22 (1995), pp. 40-54.

Panofsky, Erwin, *Early Netherlandish Painting: Its Origins and Character*, 2 vols. (Cambridge, MA: Harvard University Press, 1966).

Paravicini, Werner, 'Die zwölf "Magnificence" Karls des Kühen', in *Formen und Funktionen öffentlicher Kommunikation*, ed. by Gerd Althoff (Stuttgart: J. Thorbecke, 2001), pp. 319-396.

Paravicini, Werner, Rimvydas Petrauskas, and Grischa Vercamer, eds., *Tannenberg, Grunwald, Žalgiris 1410: Krieg und Frieden im späten Mittelalter* (Wiesbaden: Harrassowitz Verlag, 2012).

Paravicini, Werner, Torsten Hiltmann, and Frank Viltart, eds., *La cour de Bourgogne et l'Europe. Le rayonnement et les limites d'un modèle culturel. Actes du colloque tenu à Paris les 9, 10 et 11 octobre 2007* (Ostfildern: Jan Thorbecke Verlag, 2013).

Pastoureau, Michel, *Black, the History of a Color* (Princeton: Princeton University Press, 2008).

Pastoureau, Michel, *Blue, the History of a Color* (Princeton: Princeton University Press, 2001).

Pastoureau, Michel, *Green, the History of a Color* (Princeton: Princeton University Press, 2013).

Pastoureau, Michel, *Red, the History of a Color* (Princeton: Princeton University Press, 2017).

Patterson, Serina, ed., *Games and Gaming in Medieval Literature* (New York: Palgrave Macmillan, 2015).

Paviot, Jacques, 'Ghillebert de Lannoy', in *Les Chevaliers de l'Ordre de la Toison d'or au XVe siècle: Notices bio-bibliographiques*, ed. by Raphaël de Smedt (Frankfurt am Main: Peter Lang, 1994), pp. 42-45.

Périer-D'Ieteren, Catheline, *Dieric Bouts: The Complete Works* (Brussels: Mercatorfonds, 2006).

Peters, Edward, 'Religion and Culture, Popular and Unpopular, 1500-1800', *Journal of Modern History* 59 (1987), pp. 317-330.

Peters, Edward, and Walter P. Simons, 'The New Huizinga and the Old Middle Ages', *Speculum: A Journal of Medieval Studies* 74:3 (1999), pp. 587-620.

Petit-Dutaillis, Charles, *Charles VII, Louis XI et les premières années de Charles VIII (1422-1492)*, in *Histoire de France depuis les origines jusqu'à la Révolution*, ed. by Ernest Lavisse, 9 vols. (Paris: Librairie Hachette, 1900-1911), vol. IV.2 (1902).

Philip, Lotte Brand, *The Ghent Altarpiece and the Art of Jan van Eyck* (Princeton: Princeton University Press, 1971).

Pirenne, Henri, *Bibliographie de l'histoire de Belgique. Catalogue méthodique et chronologique des sources et des ouvrages principaux relatifs à l'histoire de tous les Pays-Bas jusqu'en 1598, et à l'histoire de Belgique jusqu'en 1830* (Brussels: H. Lamertin/Ghent: C. Vyt, 1902).

Pirenne, Henri, 'Die Entstehung und Verfassung des burgundischen Reichs im XV. und XVI. Jahrhundert', *Jahrbuch für Gesetzgebung, Verwaltung und Volkswirtschaft* 32 (1909), pp. 895-925.

Pirenne, Henri, 'The Formation and Constitution of the Burgundian State', *American Historical Review* 14 (1908-1909), pp. 477-502.

Pirenne, Henri, *Histoire de Belgique*, 7 vols. (Bruxelles: H. Lamertin, 1902-1932).

Pirenne, Henri, 'La formation et la constitution de l'état bourguignon (XVe-XVIe siècle)', in *La fortune historiographique des thèses d'Henri Pirenne. Actes du colloque organisé à l'occasion du cinquantenaire de la mort de l'historien belge par l'Institut des Hautes Études de Belgique (Bruxelles, 10-11 mai 1985)*, ed. by Georges Despy and Adriaan Verhulst (Brussels: Archives et bibliothèques de Belgique, 1986), pp. 155-182.

Pirenne, Henri, *L'histoire de Belgique, vol. 2, du commencement du XIVe siècle à la mort de Charles le Téméraire* (Bruxelles: H. Lamertin, 1902, reprint 1908).

Pirenne, Henri, *Manifestation en l'honneur de M. le professeur Henri Pirenne. Bruxelles, 12 mai 1912* (Mons: Léon Dequesne, 1912).

Plamper, Jan, *The History of Emotions: An Introduction* (Cambridge: Cambridge University Press, 2012).

Pleij, Herman, 'De verguizing van de rederijkerij', *Literatuur* 11 (1994), pp. 225-232.

Pleij, Herman, *Het gevleugelde woord. Geschiedenis van de Nederlandse literatuur, 1400-1560* (Amsterdam: Bert Bakker, 2007).

Pleij, Herman, 'Huizinga's *Herfsttij* en de stedelijke literatuur van de lage landen', *Bulletin: Geschiedenis, Kunst, Cultuur* 1 (1992), pp. 3-19.

Popovich, Ljubica D., 'Medievalism in Serbian Painting of the Nineteenth Century', in *Medievalism in Europe*, ed. by Leslie J. Workman (Cambridge: D.S. Brewer, 1994), pp. 208-224.

Post, Paul, 'Ein verschollenes Jagdbild Jan van Eycks', *Jahrbuch der Preussischen Kunstsammlungen* 52 (1931), pp. 120-132.

Prevenier, Walter, 'Johan Huizinga en de geschiedschrijving der 20e eeuw: Dwarsligger of kind van zijn tijd?' *De Vlaamse Gids* 11 (1973), pp. 74-82.

Prevenier, Walter, 'L'école des Annales et l'historiographie néerlandaise', *Septentrion* 2 (1973), pp. 47-54.

Prietzel, Malte, *Guillaume Fillastre, Ausgewählte Werke* (Ostfildern: Thorbecke, 2003).

Prietzel, Malte, *Guillaume Fillastre der Jüngere (1400/07-1473): Kirchenfürst und herzoglich-burgundischer Rat* (Stuttgart: Thorbecke Verlag, 2001).

Prochno, Renate, *Die Kartause von Champmol. Grablege der burgundischen Herzöge 1384-1477* (Berlin: Akademie-Verlag, 2002).

Puigarnau, Alfons, 'Johan Huizinga (1872-1945)', in *Rewriting the Middle Ages in the Twentieth Century, II: National Traditions*, ed. by Jaume Aurell and Julia Pavón (Turnhout: Brepols, 2009), pp. 419-484.

Purtle, Carol J., *The Marian Paintings of Jan van Eyck* (Princeton: Princeton University Press, 1982).

Pycke, Jacques, ed., *Sons, couleurs, odeurs dans la Cathédrale de Tournai au XVe siècle. I: Édition du Cérémonial et des Ordinaires, suivie du Commentaire (1): Les acteurs, les lieux, le mobilier liturgique* (Louvain-la-Neuve: Collège Érasme, 2004).

Pyhrr, Stuart, Donald LaRocca, and Dirk Breiding, *The Armoured Horse in Europe 1480-1620*, exh. cat. (New York: Metropolitan Museum, 2005).

Raj, Selva J., 'Serious Levity at the Shrine of St. Anne in South India', in *Sacred Play*, ed. by Selva J. Raj and Corinne G. Dempsey, pp. 21-36.

Raj, Selva J., and Corinne G. Dempsey, eds., *Sacred Play: Ritual Levity and Humor in South Asian Religions* (Albany: State University of New York Press, 2010).

Raveri, Massimo, 'Introduction', in *Japan at Play*, ed. by Joy Hendry and Massimo Raveri, pp. 1-21.

Rehm, Ulrich, 'Isabeau de Bavière, Königin Frankreichs', in *Das Goldene Rössl*, ed. by Reinhold Baumstark, pp. 13-35.

Richardson, Carol M., 'Art and Death', in *Viewing Renaissance Art*, ed. by Jim W. Richardson, Woods, Carol M., and Angeliki Lymberopouou (New Haven: Yale University Press, 2007), pp. 209-245.

Richter, Gerhard, *Afterness: Figures of Following in Modern Thought and Aesthetics* (New York: Columbia University Press, 2011).

Ridderbos, Bernhard, 'From Waagen to Friedländer', in *Early Netherlandish Painting*, ed. by Bernhard Ridderbos, Anne van Buren, and Henk van Veen, pp. 218-251.

Ridderbos, Bernhard, *Schilderkunst in de Bourgondische Nederlanden* (Louvain: Davidsfonds Uitgeverij, 2014).

Ridderbos, Bernhard, Anne van Buren, and Henk van Veen, eds., *Early Netherlandish Painting: Rediscovery, Reception and Research* (Los Angeles: J. Paul Getty Museum, 2005).

Rigolot, François, 'Les rhétoriqueurs: automne ou printemps d'une civilisation?' En hommage à Johan Huizinga', in *Rhetoric-rhétoriqueurs-rederijkers*, ed. by Jelle Koopmans, Mark Meadow, Kees Meerhoff, and Marijke Spies (Amsterdam: North-Holland, 1995), pp. 9-25.

Roach, Mary, 'By the Book', *New York Times*, 9 June 2016, https://www.nytimes.com/2016/06/12/books/review/mary-roach-by-the-book.html.

Roberts, Ann, 'The Chronology and Political Significance of the Tomb of Mary of Burgundy', *Art Bulletin* 71 (1989), pp. 376-400.

Rodenbach, Georges, *Bruges-la-Morte*, ed. by Jean-Pierre Bertrand and Daniele Grojnowski (Paris: Flammarion, 1998).

Rodenbach, Georges, *Bruges-la-Morte*, trans. into English by Mike Mitchell (Cambs: Daedalus, 2010).

Rodriguez, Hector, 'The Playful and the Serious: An Approximation to Huizinga's *Homo Ludens*', *Game Studies: The International Journal of Computer Game Research* 6:1 (2006), http://gamestudies.org/0601/articles/rodriges.

Rogers, Clifford, 'Tactics and the Face of Battle', in *European Warfare, 1350-1750*, ed. by Frank Tallett and D.J.B. Trim (Cambridge: Cambridge University Press, 2010), pp. 203-235.

Romein, Jan, 'De crisis van onze beschaving in historisch perspectief', *De Nieuwe Stem* 1 (1946), pp. 119-146, reprinted in Romein, *Historische lijnen en patronen*, pp. 301-326.

Romein, Jan, *Historische lijnen en patronen. Een keuze uit de essays* (Amsterdam: Querido, 1976).

Romein, Jan, 'Huizinga als historicus', *De Nieuwe Stem* 2 (1947), pp. 513-528, 604-618, reproduced in Jan Romein, *Historische lijnen en patronen*, pp. 271-326.

Romein, Jan, *Op het breukvlak van twee eeuwen* (Amsterdam: Querido, 1976).

Roodenburg, Herman, 'Empathy in the Making: Crafting the Believer's Emotions in the Late Medieval Low Countries', *Bijdragen en Mededelingen betreffende de Geschiedenis der Nederlanden* 129 (2014), pp. 42-52.

Rosenwein, Barbara H., *Emotional Communities in the Early Middle Ages* (Ithaca: Cornell University Press, 2006).

Rosenwein, Barbara H., 'Even the Devil (Sometimes) Has Feelings: Emotional Communities in the Early Middle-Ages', *The Haskins Society Journal: Studies in Medieval History* 14 (2003), pp. 1-14.

Rosenwein, Barbara H., *Generations of Feeling: A History of Emotions, 600-1700* (Cambridge: Cambridge University Press, 2016).

Rosenwein, Barbara H., 'Thinking Historically about Medieval Emotions', *History Compass* 8:8 (2010), pp. 828-842.

Rosenwein, Barbara H., 'Worrying about Emotions in History', *American Historical Review* 107:3 (2002), pp. 821-845.

Rothstein, Bert L., *Sight and Spirituality in Early Netherlandish Painting* (New York: Cambridge University Press, 2005).

Rubin, Miri, *Corpus Christi: The Eucharist in Late Medieval Culture* (Cambridge: Cambridge University Press, 1991).

Rubin, Miri, *Mother of God: A History of the Virgin Mary* (New Haven: Yale University Press, 2009).

Rubin, Miri, ed., *The Work of Jacques Le Goff and the Challenges of Medieval History* (Woodbridge: Boydell, 1997).

Rubin, Miri, and Walter Simons, eds., *Christianity in Western Europe c. 1100-c. 1500* (Cambridge: Cambridge University Press, 2009).

Rupprich, Hans, 'Das literarische Werk Kaiser Maximilians', *Ausstellung Maximilian I*, exh. cat. (Innsbruck: Tyrolia, 1969).

Said, Edward, *On Late Style: Music and Literature against the Grain* (New York: Vintage, 2006).

Sandler, Lucy Freeman, Review of Michael Camille, *Master of Death*, *Speculum* 73:2 (1998), pp. 482-485.

Santing, Catrien, 'De middeleeuwen ontsluierd. De beoefening van de middeleeuwse geschiedenis in Nederland', in *De geschiedenis van de middeleeuwen aan de Groningse universiteit 1614-1939*, ed. by Catrien Santing (Hilversum: Verloren, 1997), pp. 159-187.

Sauerländer, Willibald, 'Kinder als Nothelfer: Parergon über das sogenannte Goldene Rössl', in *Das Goldene Rössl*, ed. by Reinhold Baumstark, pp. 90-101.

Scarry, Elaine, ed., *Fins de Siècle: English Poetry in 1590, 1690, 1790, 1890, 1990* (Baltimore: Johns Hopkins University Press, 1995).

Schack, Gerhard, *Der Kreis um Maximilian I. Der Jagd in der Kunst* (Hamburg: Parey, 1963).

Schaefer, Claude, *Jean Fouquet an der Schwelle zur Renaissance* (Dresden: Verlag der Kunst, 1994).

Schauerte, Thomas, *Die Ehrenpforte für Kaiser Maximilian I* (Munich/Berlin: Deutscher Kunstverlag, 2001)

Scheicher, Elisabeth, 'Das Grabmal Kaiser Maximilians I. in der Innsbrucker Hofkirche', in *Die Kunstdenkmäler der Stadt Innsbruck. Die Hofbauten*, ed. by Johanna Felmayer et al. (Vienna: Schroll, 1986), pp. 355-426.

Scheichl, Andrea, 'Who Was (or Were) Jörg Kölderer? Innsbruck Court Painter and Tyrolean Master Builder', in *Emperor Maximilian I*, ed. by Eva Michel, pp. 81-89.

Schmalz, Matthew M., 'A Catholic Charismatic Healer at Play in North India', in *Sacred Play*, ed. by Selva J. Raj and Corinne G. Dempsey, pp. 185-204.

Schmid, Karl, and Joachim Wollasch, eds., *Memoria. Der geschichtliche Zeugniswert des liturgischen Gedenkens im Mittelalter* (Munich: Wilhelm Fink, 1984).

Schmitt, Jean-Claude, 'Bloch, Marc', in *La nouvelle histoire*, ed. by Jacques Le Goff et al., pp. 79-82.

Schmitt, Jean-Claude, *Le corps des images. Essais sur la culture visuelle au Moyen Âge* (Paris: Gallimard, 2002).

Schmitt, Jean-Claude, *La raison des gestes dans l'Occident médiéval* (Paris: Gallimard, 1990).

Schmitt, Jean-Claude, *Les rythmes au Moyen Age* (Paris: Gallimard, 2016).

Schmitt, Jean-Claude, 'Introduzione', in: *Religione, folklore e società nell'Occidente medievale* (Bari: Laterza, 1988), pp. 1-20, trans. as 'Religion, Folklore, and Society in the Medieval West', in *Debating the Middle Ages*, ed. by Lester K. Little and Barbara Rosenwein, pp. 376-387.

Schnerb, Bertrand, *L'état bourguignon, 1363-1477* (Paris: Perrin, 1999).

Schoch, Rainer, Matthias Mende, and Anna Scherbaum, *Albrecht Dürer – Das druckgraphische Werk. III. Buchillustrationen* (Munich: Prestel, 2004).

Scholten, Frits, *Isabella's Weepers* (Amsterdam: Rijksmuseum, 2007).

Schrader, J.L., *The Waning Middle Ages: An Exhibition of French and Netherlandish Art from 1350 to 1500 commemorating the fiftieth anniversary of the publication of 'The Waning of the Middle Ages' by Johan Huizinga*, exh. cat. (Lawrence: University of Kansas Museum of Art, 1969).

Schreckenberg, Hella, *Claus Sluter* (Bochum: Brockmeyer, 1987).

Šebková-Thaller, Zuzana, *Sünde und Versöhnung in Jan van Eycks Hochzeitsbild* (Markt Berolzheim: Hernoul-le-Fin Verlag, 1992).

Seipel, Wilfried, *Werke für die Ewigkeit. Kaiser Maximilian I. und Erzherzog Ferdinand II.* (Vienna: Kunsthistorisches Museum, 2002).

Senger, Hans Gerhard, 'Eine Schwalbe macht noch keinen Herbst. Zu Huizingas Metapher vom Herbst des Mittelalters', in *'Herbst des Mittelalters'?*, ed. by Jan A. Aertsen and Martin Pickavé, pp. 3-24.

Senn, Walter, 'Maximilian und die Musik', in *Ausstellung Maximilian I*, exh. cat. (Innsbruck: Tyrolia, 1969), pp. 73-85.

Sennholz, Marco, *Johann von Leers. Ein Propagandist des Nationalsozialismus. Biographische Studien zum 20. Jahrhundert*, vol. 3, *Historische Zeitschrift* 299:2 (2014), pp. 542-543.

Shaw, David G., 'Huizinga's Timeliness', *History and Theory* 37:2 (1998), pp. 245-258.

Silver, Larry, '"Die Guten Alten Istory": Emperor Maximilian I., Teuerdank, and the Heldenbuch Tradition', *Jahrbuch des Zentralinstituts für Kunstgeschichte* 2 (1986), pp. 71-106.

Silver, Larry, 'Glass Menageries: Hunts and Battles by Jörg Breu for Emperor Maximilian I', *Acta Historiae Artium* 44 (2004), pp. 121-127.

Silver, Larry, *Marketing Maximilian: The Visual Ideology of a Holy Roman Emperor* (Princeton: Princeton University Press, 2008).

Silver, Larry, 'The "Papier-Kaiser": Burgkmair, Augsburg, and the Image of the Emperor', in *Emperor Maximilian I*, ed. by Eva Michel, pp. 91-99.

Silver, Larry, 'Power of the Press: Dürer's *Arch of Honor*', in *Albrecht Dürer in the Collection of the National Gallery of Victoria*, ed. by Irena Zdanowicz (Melbourne: National Gallery of Victoria, 1994), pp. 45-62.

Silver, Larry, 'Shining Armor: Maximilian I. as Holy Roman Emperor', *Museum Studies* (*Art Institute of Chicago*) 20 (1985), pp. 8-29.

Silver, Larry, 'Ungrateful Dead: Bruegel's *Triumph of Death* Re-examined', in *Excavating the Medieval Image: Manuscripts, Artists, Audiences: Essays in Honor of Sandra Hindman*, ed. by David S. Areford and Nina A. Rowe (Aldershot: Ashgate, 2004), pp. 265-282.

Simons, Walter, 'The *Annales* and Medieval Studies in the Low Countries', in *The Work of Jacques Le Goff and the Challenges of Medieval History*, ed. by Miri Rubin (Woodbridge: The Boydell Press, 1997), pp. 99-122, reproduced in *The Annales School: Critical Assessments*, ed. by Stuart Clark, 4 vols. (London: Routledge, 1999), vol. 2, pp. 309-330.

Simons, Walter, *Cities of Ladies: Beguine Communities in the Medieval Low Countries, 1200-1565* (Philadelphia: University of Pennsylvania Press, 2001).

Simons, Walter, '"Dieu, li premierz, plus anchiiens et souverains bourgois de tous". Sur la place de la religion dans les villes flamandes (XIIIe-XVe siècles)', in *Villes de Flandre et d'Italie (XIIIe-XVIe siècle). Les enseignements d'une comparaison*, ed. by Élisabeth Crouzet-Pavan and Élodie Lecuppre-Desjardin (Turnhout: Brepols, 2008), pp. 77-105.

Simons, Walter, '[Review of] Johan Huizinga, *Autumn of the Middle Ages*, trans. by Rodney J. Payton and Ulrich Mammitzsch (Chicago: University of Chicago Press, 1996)', *Speculum: A Journal of Medieval Studies* 72 (1997), pp. 488-491.

Small, Graeme, *George Chastelain and the Shaping of Valois Burgundy: Political and Historical Culture at Court in the Fifteenth Century* (Woodbridge: Boydell & Brewer, 2011).

Smeyers, Maurits, *Flemish Miniatures* (Turnhout: Brepols, 1999).

Smith, Jeffrey Chipps, *The Artistic Patronage of Philip the Good, Duke of Burgundy*, PhD diss., Columbia University, 1979.

Snyder, James, *Northern Renaissance Art: Painting, Sculpture, the Graphic Arts from 1350 to 1575* (Upper Saddle River: Prentice-Hall/New York: Harry N. Abrams, 1985).

Sorensen, Lee, ed., 'Hamann, Richard', *Dictionary of Art Historians*, http://www.arthistorians.info/hamannr.

Sorensen, Lee, ed., 'Huizinga, Johan', *Dictionary of Art Historians*, http://www.arthistorians.info/huizingaj.

Sorensen, Lee, ed., 'Mâle, Émile', *Dictionary of Art Historians*, http://www.arthistorians.info/malee.

Spariosu, Mihai I., *Dionysius Reborn: Play and the Aesthetic Dimension in Modern Philosophical and Scientific Discourse* (Ithaca: Cornell University Press, 1989).

Speetjens, Annemarie, 'A Quantitative Approach to Late Medieval Transformations of Piety in the Low Countries: Historiography and New Ideas', in *Pieties in Transition: Religious Practices and Experiences, c. 1400-1640*, ed. by Robert Lutton and Elisabeth Salter (Aldershot: Ashgate, 2007), pp. 109-126.

Spengler, Oswald, *Der Untergang des Abenlandes: Umrisse einer Morphologie der Weltgeschichte* (Vienna and Leipzig: Wilhelm Braumüller, 1918).

Splendours of the Burgundian Court: Charles the Bold (1433-1477), The, Gabrieke Keck, Susan Marti, and Till-Holger Borchert, eds., exh. cat. Bern, Bruges, Vienna (Antwerp: Mercatorfonds, 2009).

Spufford, Peter, *Monetary problems and policies in the Burgundian Netherlands, 1433-1496* (Leiden: Brill, 1970)

Stauter-Halsted, Keely, 'Rural Myth and the Modern Nation: Peasant Commemorations of Polish National Holidays, 1879-1910', in *Staging the Past: The Politics of Commemoration in Habsburg Central Europe, 1848 to the Present*, ed. by Maria Burur and Nancy M. Wingfield (West Lafayette: Purdue University Press, 2001), pp. 153-177.

Stearns, Peter N., with Carol Z. Stearns, 'Emotionology: Clarifying the History of Emotions and Emotional Standards', *American Historical Review* 90 (1985), pp. 813-836.

Steel, Carlos, 'From Siger of Brabant to Erasmus: Philosophy and Civilization in the Late Medieval Low Countries', in *Philosophy and Theology in the Long Middle Ages: A Tribute to Stephen F. Brown*, ed. by Kent Emery Jr., Russell L. Friedman, and Andreas Speer (Leiden: Brill, 2011), pp. 953-979.

Stein, Robert, *Magnanimous Dukes and Rising States: The Unification of the Burgundian Netherlands, 1380-1480*, trans. by Marilyn Hedges (Oxford: Oxford University Press, 2017); trans. from the Dutch of *De hertog en zijn staten. De eenwording van de Bourgondische Nederlanden, ca. 1380-ca. 1480* (Hilversum: Verloren, 2014).

Sterchi, Bernhard, 'Hugo de Lannoy, auteur de *l'Enseignement de vraie noblesse*, de *l'instruction d'un jeune prince* et des *Enseignements paternels*', *Le Moyen Age* 60 (2004), pp. 79-117.

Sternelle, Kurt, *Lucas Cranach. Die Jagd in der Kunst* (Hamburg: Parey, 1963).

Strauss, Walter R., ed., *The Book of Hours of the Emperor Maximilian the First, Decorated by Albrecht Dürer* (New York: Abaris Books, 1974).

Strohm, Reinhard, *Music in Late Medieval Bruges*, rev. ed. (Oxford: Clarendon Press, 1990).

Strøm-Olsen, Rolf, 'Political Narrative and Symbolism in the Feast of the Pheasant (1454)', *Viator* 46:3 (2015), pp. 317-342.

Strong, Roy, *Art and Power: Renaissance Festivals, 1450-1650* (Berkeley: University of California Press, 1984).

Strupp, Christoph, 'A Historian's Life in Biographical Perspective: Johan Huizinga', in *Biography between Structure and Agency: Central European Lives in International Historiography*, ed. by Volker Berghahn and Simone Lässig (New York: Berghahn Books, 2008), pp. 103-118.

Strupp, Christoph, *Johan Huizinga. Geschichtswissenschaft als Kulturgeschichte* (Göttingen: Vandenhoeck and Ruprecht, 2000).

Sutton-Smith, Brian, *The Ambiguity of Play* (Cambridge, MA: Harvard University Press, 1998).

Swaan, Wim, *The Late Middle Ages: Art and Architecture from 1350 to the Advent of the Renaissance* (Ithaca: Cornell University Press, 1977).

Symes, Carol, 'Manuscript Matrix, Modern Canon', in *Middle English*, ed. by Paul Strohm (Oxford: Oxford University Press, 2007), pp. 7-22.

Symes, Carol, 'Medieval Battlefields and National Narratives, 1830-1918', in *Myth, Memory, and the First World War in Scotland: The Legacy of Bannockburn*, ed. by Gill Plain (Lewisburg: Bucknell University Press, 2016), pp. 83-100.

Symes, Carol, 'When We Talk about Modernity', *American Historical Review* 116 (2011), pp. 715-726.

Tabbagh, Vincent, 'La pratique sacramentelle des fidèles, d'après les documents épiscopaux de la France du Nord (XIIIe-XIVe siècles)', *Revue Mabillon* 73 (2001), pp. 159-204.

Taberner, Stuart, *Aging and Old-Age Style in Günter Grass, Ruth Klüger, Christa Wolf, and Martin Walser: The Mannerism of a Late Period* (Rochester: Camden, 2013).

Tackett, Timothy, 'Foreword', in André Burguière, *The Annales School*, pp. I-XIV

Tahon, Eva, et al., *Impact 1902 Revisited: Early Flemish and Ancient Art Exhibition: Bruges, 15th June-15th September 1902*, exh. cat. (Bruges: Musea Brugge, 2002).

Tanner, Marie, *The Last Descendants of Aeneas: The Hapsburgs and the Mythic Image of the Emperor* (New Haven: Yale University Press, 1993).

Terjanian, Pierre, *Princely Armour in the Age of Dürer: A Renaissance Masterpiece in the Philadelphia Museum of Art* (New Haven: Philadelphia Museum of Art in association with Yale University Press, 2011).

Te Winkel, Jan, *De ontwikkelingsgang der Nederlandsche letterkunde*, 7 vols. (Haarlem: Bohn, 1908-1927).

Thiebaux, Marcelle, 'The Medieval Chase', *Speculum* 42 (1967), pp. 260-274.

Thiebaux, Marcelle, *The Stag of Love: The Chase in Medieval Literature* (Ithaca: Cornell University Press, 1974).

Thiry, Claude, 'Le printemps des temps nouveaux', in *Autour du XVe siècle. Journées d'études en l'honneur d'Alberto Varvaro*, ed. by Paola Moreno and Giovanni Palumbo (Geneva: Droz, 2008), pp. 219-228.

Thomas a Kempis, *De imitatione Christi*, ed. by Michael Joseph Pohl (= *Thomae a Kempis* [...] *Opera Omnia*, II) (Freiburg: Herder, 1904).

Thomas, Bruno, 'Harnischstudien I: Stilgeschichte des deutschen Harnisches von 1500-1530', *Jahrbuch der kunsthistorischen Sammlungen in Wien*, n.s. 11 (1937), pp. 139-158.

Thomas, Bruno, 'The Hunting Knives of Emperor Maximilian I', *Metropolitan Museum of Art Bulletin* 13 (1955), pp. 201-208.

Thomas, Bruno, and Ortwin Gamber, *Die Innsbrucker Plattnerkunst*, exh. cat. (Innsbruck: Tiroler Landesmuseum Ferninandeum, 1954).

Thoss, Dagmar, *Das Epos des Burgunderreiches Girart de Roussillon* (Graz: Akademische Druck- u. Verlagsanstalt, 1989).

Thys, Walter, 'Huizinga en de Beweging van Negentig', *Bijdragen en Mededelingen betreffende de Geschiedenis der Nederlanden* 99 (1973), pp. 29-52; also published, with the same pagination, in *Johan Huizinga 1872-1972*, ed. by W.R.H. Koops et al.

Thys, Walter, 'Uit het leven en werk van André Jolles (1874-1946)', *De Nieuwe Taalgids* 47 (1954), pp. 129-137, 199-208.

Tilly, Charles, *Coercion, Capital, and European states, AD 99-1990* (Cambridge, MA: Basil Blackwell, 1990).

Tilmans, Karin, 'Chroniqueurs en kroniekschrijvers. Over de waardering van Nederlandse geschiedschrijvers in Huizinga's *Herfsttij*', *Bulletin: Geschiedenis, Kunst, Cultuur* 4 (1995), pp. 50-69.

Tollebeek, Jo, 'At the Crossroads of Nationalism: Huizinga, Pirenne and the Low Countries in Europe', *European Review of History* 17 (2010), pp. 187-215.

Tollebeek, Jo, '"Au point sensible de l'Europe": Huizinga en Pirenne', *Revue Belge de philologie et d'histoire* 74 (1996), pp. 403-443; reproduced in Jo Tollebeek, *De ekster en de kooi. Nieuwe opstellen over geschiedschrijving* (Amsterdam: Bert Bakker, 1996).

Tollebeek, Jo, *De ijkmeesters: opstellen over de geschiedschrijving in Nederland en België* (Amsterdam: Bakker, 1994).

Tollebeek, Jo, 'De middeleeuwen dromen. Huizinga, *Herfsttij* en de esthetiek van de geschiedenis', in Jo Tollebeek, *De ijkmeesters. Opstellen over de geschiedschrijving in Nederland en België* (Amsterdam: Bert Bakker, 1994), pp. 179-202.

Tollebeek, Jo, *De toga van Fruin. Denken over geschiedenis in Nederland en België* (Amsterdam: Wereldbibliotheek, 1990).

Tollebeek, Jo, *Een slapeloos doordenken van alle dingen. Over geschiedenis en historische cultuur* (Amsterdam: Prometheus, 2017).

Tollebeek, Jo, *Fredericq & zonen. Een antropologie van de moderne geschiedwetenschap* (Amsterdam: Bert Bakker, 2008).

Tollebeek, Jo, 'Le culte de la bataille des Éperons d'or', in *1302, le désastre de Courtrai: mythe et réalité de la bataille des éperons d'or*, ed. by Raoul C. van Caenegem et al. (Antwerp: Fonds Mercator, 2002), pp. 194-239.

Tollebeek, Jo, '"Renaissance" and "Fossilization": Michelet, Burckhardt, and Huizinga', *Renaissance Studies* 15:3 (2001), pp. 354-366.

Tollebeek, Jo, *Writing the Inquisition in Europe and America: The Correspondence between Henry Charles Lea and Paul Fredericq* (Brussels: Commission royale d'histoire, 2004).

Trio, Paul, *Volksreligie als spiegel van een stedelijke samenleving. De broederschappen te Gent in de late middeleeuwen* (Louvain: Universitaire Pers, 1993).

Troescher, Georg, *Claus Sluter und die burgundische Plastik um die Wende des XIV. Jahrhunderts* (Freiburg im Breisgau: Urban, 1932).

Trüper, Henning, *Topography of a Method. François Louis Ganshof and the Writing of History* (Tübingen: Mohr Siebeck, 2014).

Turner, Jane, ed., *The Lure of Falconry*, exh. cat. (Amsterdam: Rijksmuseum, 2012).

Turner, Victor, *From Ritual to Theater: The Human Seriousness of Play* (New York: Performing Arts Journal Publications, 1982).

Tylor, Edward B., *Primitive Culture: Researches into the Development of Mythology*, 2 vols. (London: John Murray, 1871).

Uyttebrouck, André, 'Henri Pirenne et les ducs de Bourgogne', in *La fortune historiographique des thèses d'Henri Pirenne. Actes du colloque organisé à l'occasion du cinquantenaire de la mort de l'historien belge par l'Institut des Hautes Études de Belgique (Bruxelles, 10-11 mai 1985)*, ed. by Georges Despy and Adriaan Verhulst (Brussels: Archives et bibliothèques de Belgique, 1986), pp. 87-111.

Vale, Malcolm G.A., *War and Chivalry: Warfare and Aristocratic Culture in England, France, and Burgundy at the End of the Middle Ages* (London: Duckworth Press, 1981).

Van Bremen, Jan, 'Japan in the World of Johan Huizinga', in *Japan at Play*, ed. by Joy Hendry and Massimo Raveri, pp. 214-227.

Van Bruaene, Anne-Laure, *Om beters wille. Rederijkerskamers en de stedelijke cultuur in de Zuidelijke Nederlanden (1400-1650)* (Amsterdam: Amsterdam University Press, 2008).

Van Buren, Anne H., *Illuminating Fashion: Dress in the Art of Medieval France and the Netherlands*, exh. cat. (New York: The Morgan Library & Museum, 2011).

Van Buren, Anne H., 'Reality and Literary Romance in the Park of Hesdin', in *Medieval Gardens*, ed. by Elisabeth B. MacDougall (Washington, DC: Dumbarton Oaks, 1986), pp. 117-134.

Vandenbroeck, Paul, 'The Axiology and Ideology of Jheronymus Bosch', in *Bosch: The 5th Centenary Exhibition*, ed. by Pilar Silva Maroto (Madrid: Museo Nacional del Prado, 2016), pp. 91-103.

Vandenbroeck, Paul, *Jheronymus Bosch. Tussen volksleven en stadscultuur* (Berchem: Epo, 1987).

Vanderjagt, A.J., 'Burgundian Political Ideas between Laurentius Pignon and Guillaume Huguesnet', *Fifteenth Century Studies* 9 (1984), pp. 197-213.

Vanderjagt, A.J., 'Classical Learning and the Building of Power at the Fifteenth-Century Burgundian Court', in *Centres of Learning: Learning and Location in Pre-Modern Europe and the Near East*, ed. by J.W. Drijvers and A.A. MacDonald (Leiden: Brill, 1995), pp. 267-277.

Vanderjagt, A.J., *Qui Sa Vertu Anoblist: The Concepts of Noblesse and Chose Publicque in Burgundian Political Thought* (Groningen: Mielot, 1981).

Van der Lem, Anton, *Een bibliotheek als wederopstanding: de boeken van Johan Huizinga* (Ruurlo: De Ammoniet, 2013).

Van der Lem, Anton, *Het Eeuwige verbeeld in een afgehaald bed. Huizinga en de Nederlandse beschaving* (Amsterdam: Wereldbibliotheek, 1997).

Van der Lem, Anton, *Inventaris van het archief van Johan Huizinga. Bibliografie 1897-1997* (Leiden: Universiteitsbibliotheek Leiden, 1998).

Van der Lem, Anton, *Johan Huizinga. Leven en werk in beelden & documenten* (Amsterdam: Wereldbibliotheek, 1993).

Van der Lem, Anton, 'Lees met beleid. Ex-librissen ontworpen door Johan Huizinga', *Jaarboek van het Nederlands Genootschap van Bibliofielen* 23 (2015), pp. 211-221.

Van der Lem, Anton, 'Nawoord: Over de totstandkoming van *Herfsttij*', in Johan Huizinga, *Herfsttij der Middeleeuwen*, ed. by Anton van der Lem (Amsterdam: Contact, 1997), pp. 483-497.

Van der Velden, Hugo, *The Donor's Image: Gerard Loyet and the Votive Portraits of Charles the Bold* (Turnhout: Brepols, 2000).

Van de Woestijne, Karel, *De Vlaamsche Primitieven: Hoe ze waren te Brugge* (Uitgever: Den Nederlandschen Boekhandel, 1902); repr. in *Verzameld Werk*, 8 vols. (Brussels: A. Manteau, 1947-1950), IV (1949), pp. 7-130.

Van Deyssel, Lodewijk, *Prozastukken* (Amsterdam: Scheltema & Holtema, 1895).

Van Driel, Joost, 'Kalme gemoedsrust. Jan te Winkel (1847-1927)', in *Der Vaderen boek. Beoefenaren van de studie der Middelnederlandse letterkunde. Studies voor Frits van Oostrom ter gelegenheid van diens vijftigste verjaardag*, ed. by Wim van Anrooij, Dini Hogenelst and Geert Warnar (Amsterdam: Amsterdam University Press, 2003), pp. 121-136.

Van Duyse, Prudens, *De rederijkkamers in Nederland, hun invloed op letterkundig, politiek en zedelijk gebied*, ed. by Florens van Duyse and Frans de Potter, 2 vols. (Ghent: A. Siffer, 1900-1902).

Van Dyke, Henry, *The Broken Soldier and the Maid of France* (New York: Harper & Bros., 1919).

Van Engen, John, 'The Christian Middle Ages as an Historiographical Problem', *American Historical Review* 91 (1986), pp. 519-552.

Van Engen, John, 'The Church in the Fifteenth Century', in *Handbook of European History, 1400-1600: Late Middle Ages, Renaissance, and Reformation: Vol. 1, Structures and Assertions*, ed. by Thomas A. Brady Jr., Heiko A. Oberman, and James D. Tracy (Grand Rapids: Eerdmans, 1994), pp. 305-328.

Van Engen, John, *The Sisters and Brothers of the Common Life: The Devotio Moderna and the World of the Later Middle Ages* (Philadelphia: University of Pennsylvania Press, 2008).

Van Essen, Arthur, *E. Kruisinga: A Chapter in the History of Linguistics in the Netherlands* (Leiden: Nijhoff, 1983).

Van Krieken, Robert, *Norbert Elias* (London: Routledge, 1998).

Van Leeuwen, C.G., *Denkbeelden van een vliesridder: de 'instruction d'un jeune prince' van Guillebert van Lannoy* (Amsterdam: Academische Pers, 1975).

Van Oostrom, Frits, 'De oude orde in verval? Hollandse hofliteratuur en Huizinga's *Herfsttij*', *Literatuur* 3 (1986), pp. 202-210.

Van Oostrom, Frits, 'Middle Dutch Literature as a Mirror of European Culture', *The Low Countries* 2 (1994-1995), pp. 70-80.

Van Oostrom, Frits, *Wereld in woorden. Geschiedenis van de Nederlandse literatuur, 1300-1400* (Amsterdam: Bert Bakker, 2013).

Van Os, Henk, *The Art of Devotion, 1300-1500*, trans. by Michael Hoyle (London: Merrell Holberton, 1994).

Van Peene, Hippoliet Jan, and Karel Miry, 'De Vlaamse Leeuw', in *Volks-Almanak voor 1854, bevattende Verhalen, Liedjes, Anekdoten Enz* (Ghent: I.S. van Doossalaere, 1854), pp. 94-95.

Van Puyvelde, Leo, *Van Eyck: The Holy Lamb*, trans. by Doris I. Wilton (Paris and Brussels: The Marian Press, 1947).

Van Steensel, Arie, 'Noblemen in an Urbanised Society: Zeeland and Its Nobility in the Late Middle Ages', *Journal of Medieval History* 38:1 (2012), pp. 76-99.

Van Valkenburg, C.T., *J. Huizinga: zijn leven en zijn persoonlijkheid* (Amsterdam: Uitgeverij Pantheon n.v., 1946).

Varvaro, Alberto, 'Riconsiderando l'*Autunno del Medioevo*', in *Filosofia, storia, letteratura: scritti in onore di Fulvio Tessitore*, ed. by Giuseppe Cacciatore, Maurizio Martirano, and Edoardo Massimilla (Naples: Morano, 1998), pp. 785-797.

Vauchez, André, *La sainteté en Occident aux derniers siècles du Moyen Age* (Rome: École française de Rome, 1981), trans. by Jean Birrell as *Sainthood in the Later Middle Ages* (Cambridge: Cambridge University Press, 1997).

Vauchez, André, 'Les orientations récentes de la recherche française sur l'histoire de la vie religieuse au moyen âge', *Ricerche di storia sociale e religiosa* 40 (1991), pp. 25-44.

Vauchez, André, 'Un réformateur religieux dans la France de Charles VI: Jean de Varennes (m. 1396?)', *Comptes rendus des séances de l'Académie des inscriptions et belles-lettres* 142 (1998), pp. 1111-1130.

Vaughan, Richard, *Charles the Bold: The Last Valois Duke of Burgundy* (Woodbridge: Boydell, 2002).

Vaughan, Richard, 'Hue de Lannoy and the Question of the Burgundian State', in *Das spätmittelalterliche Königtum im europaïschen Vergleich*, ed. by Reinhard Schneider (Sigmaringen: Thorbecke, 1987), pp. 335-346.

Vaughan, Richard, *John the Fearless: The Growth of the Burgundian Power* (Woodbridge: Boydell, 2002).

Vaughan, Richard, *Philip the Bold: The Formation of the Burgundian State* (Woodbridge: Boydell, 2002).

Vaughan, Richard, *Philip the Good: The Apogee of Burgundy* (Woodbridge: Boydell, 2002).

Vaughan, Richard, *Valois Burgundy* (London: Allen Lane, 1975).

Velaers, Jan, and Herman Van Goethem, *Leopold III: de koning, het land, de oorlog* (Tielt: Lannoo, 1994).

Vendler, Helen, *Last Looks, Last Books: Stevens, Plath, Lowell, Bishop, Merrill* (Princeton: Princeton University Press, 2010).

Verhoeven, Gerrit, *Devotie en negotie. Delft als bedevaartplaats in de late middeleeuwen* (Amsterdam: VU Uitgeverij, 1992).

Vermeulen, E.E.G., *Huizinga over de wetenschap der geschiedenis* (Arnhem: G.W. van de Wiel, 1956).

Vetter, Ewald, *Maria im Rosenhag* (Dusseldorf: Schwann, 1956).

Violante, Cinzio, *Studi sulla cristianità medioevale. Società, istituzioni, spiritualità* (Milan: Vita e Pensiero, 1972).

Virgil, *Eclogues, Georgics, Aeneid I-VI*, trans. by H. Rushton Fairclough (Cambridge, MA: Harvard University Press, 1999).

Vovelle, Michel, *La mort et l'Occident de 1300 à nos jours* (Paris: Gallimard, 1983).

Waldburg Wolfegg, Christoph Graf zu, *Venus and Mars: The World of the Medieval Housebook* (Munich: Prestel, 1998).

Wangermée, Robert, *Flemish Music and Society in the Fifteenth and Sixteenth Centuries* (New York: Praeger, 1968).

The Waning of the Middle Ages: Pomona College Gallery, April 14-May 2, 1965, exh. cat. (Claremont: The Art Gallery, Pomona College, 1965).

Warburg, Aby, 'Zwei Szenen aus König Maximilians Brügger Gefangenschaft auf einem Skizzenblatt des sogenannten Hausbuchmeisters', *Jahrbuch der preussischen Kunstsammlungen* 32 (1911), pp. 180-184.

Warnar, Geert, *Ruusbroec. Literatuur en mystiek in de veertiende eeuw* (Amsterdam: Athenaeum-Polak & Van Gennep, 2003), trans. by Diane Webb as *Ruusbroec: Literature and Mysticism in the Fourteenth Century* (Leiden: Brill, 2007).

Wauters, Alphonse, 'Hugues de Lannoy', in *Biographie Nationale de Belgique*, Académie Royale des Sciences, des Lettres et des Beaux-Arts de Belgique (Bruxelles: Bruylant-Christophe, 1890-1891), vol. 11, cc. 322-325.

Weintraub, Karl J., *Visions of Culture: Voltaire, Guizot, Burckhardt, Lamprecht, Huizinga, Ortega y Gasset* (Chicago: University of Chicago Press, 1966).

Welch, David, *Germany, Propaganda and Total War, 1914-1918: The Sins of Omission* (London: Athlone, 2000).

Wells, Marion, '"To Find a Face Where All Distress Is Stell": "Enargeia", "Ekphrasis", and Mourning in "The Rape of Lucrece"', *Comparative Literature* 54:2 (2002), pp. 97-126.

Wesseling, H.L., *Zoekt Prof. Huizinga eigenlijk niet zichzelf? Huizinga en de geest van de jaren dertig* (Amsterdam: Bert Bakker, 1996).

White, Hayden, 'Fictions of Factual Representation', in Hayden White, *Tropics of Discourse: Essays in Cultural Criticism* (Baltimore: Johns Hopkins University Press, 1978), pp. 121-134.

Wiesflecker, Hermann, *Kaiser Maximilian I.: das Reich Österreich und Europa an der Wende zur Neuzeit*, 5 vols. (Munich: Oldenbourg, 1971-1986).

Winkler, Friedrich, *Die altniederländische Malerei: die Malerei in Belgien und Holland von 1400-1600* (Berlin: Propyläen-Verlag, 1924).

Wistrich, R.S., *Who's Who in Nazi Germany* (London: Routledge, 1955), pp. 151-153.

Yates, Frances, 'Elizabethan Chivalry: The Accession Day Tilts', *Journal of the Warburg and Courtauld Institutes* 20 (1957), pp. 4-25.

Yourcenar, Marguerite, 'Carnets de notes des *Mémoires d'Hadrien*', in Marguerite Yourcenar, *Oeuvres Romanesques* (Paris: Gallimard, Bibliothèque de la Pléiade, 1982), pp. 519-542.

Zweig, Stefan, *Journeys*. ed. and trans. by Will Stone (London: Hesperus Press, 2010).

Index of Names

For Product Safety Concerns and Information please contact our EU representative GPSR@taylorandfrancis.com Taylor & Francis Verlag GmbH, Kaufingerstraße 24, 80331 München, Germany

Batch number: 10347037

Printed by Printforce, the Netherlands